Jonathan Worth

A Biography of a Southern Unionist

Jonathan Worth

Jonathan Worth

A Biography
of a Southern Unionist

by

Richard L. Zuber

The University of North Carolina Press · Chapel Hill

142164

Preface

At a time when the tide of Southern sectional consciousness is once again rising, Jonathan Worth seemed to me to deserve historical and biographical consideration because he represents a type which has not yet been adequately examined, the southern unionist. The basic question I had in mind was this: "What sort of man was it who breasted the tide of secession until it became overwhelming?" Worth appeared to be an ideal subject through whom this question could be approached because—although he once remarked with truth that "I am not a politician by trade"—he happened to occupy a political vantage point during the times when the bonds of union came closest to being completely severed. The fact that he was not primarily a politician was in itself a challenge, for the variety of his activities as businessman, lawyer, educational promoter, and public financier promised to lead, and did lead, down many interesting byways.

For assistance in meeting the challenge presented by the life of Jonathan Worth, I am particularly indebted to Dr. Robert H. Woody, who offered incisive criticism all along the way, and to Worth's great-grandson, Jonathan Daniels, who provided both encouragement and information on the Worth family. I am grateful to the Duke University Graduate Committee of Publications and to Wake Forest College for aid in the publication of this biography.

RICHARD L. ZUBER

Preface

Contents

Jonathan Worth

A Biography of a Southern Unionist

· I ·

Ancestors and Influences

JONATHAN WORTH'S FAMILY TREE is planted firmly in the soil of Massachusetts' Nantucket Island. The first Worth in America, Jonathan's great-great-great-grandfather, William, left England in 1662, and visited Nantucket in that year. He settled on the island, working at first as a sailor, and in 1665, in the first marriage ceremony performed there, he married Sarah Macy, whose father was one of the ten original proprietors of the island and its first settler. William Worth established a family tradition of public service when he became the first justice of the peace of Nantucket. Other governmental positions he held were clerk of court, recorder and assistant justice of the colony, and, after 1680, clerk of the Court of Admiralty. The first manuscript record of births, deaths, and marriages for the island is in his handwriting.[1]

Three generations passed. William's descendants continued to live on Nantucket, following the trade of whaling. They became devoted members of the Society of Friends, the peace-loving sect commonly known as Quakers. Then about the middle of the eighteenth century, there was an exodus of Friends from the island to the counties of North Carolina now named Guilford, Randolph, and Alamance. Their most prominent and prosperous settlement was at New Garden, in Guilford County, near the city limits of the present city of Greensboro. Settled about 1750, New Garden grew rapidly and eventually became a sort of headquarters for the Quakers of North Carolina—and for the southern members of the Society of Friends.[2]

Among the immigrants from Nantucket to the New Garden settlement was Jonathan Worth's grandfather, Daniel. He was a tough young sea captain who had been on at least five long whaling voyages. Six years before the beginning of the American Revolution, Captain

Daniel moved with his wife to the vicinity of New Garden and settled near Guilford Court House. In 1769, he was received into the New Garden Monthly Meeting from the Monthly Meeting on Nantucket.[3] He was a hardy soul, if his life span is a fair indication of his vitality, for ninety-one years passed before he was buried in 1830 in the Quaker cemetery at Center, Guilford County.

Captain Daniel Worth's seventh child was born on May 19, 1776, at a time when a young America was breaking her allegiance to the Worths' native England. Following the Quaker custom of naming children after characters in the Bible, Daniel named his son David. Little is known of David before a notation appeared in the minutes of the Deep River Monthly Meeting for September 3, 1798, that "David Worth of Center and Eunice Gardner appeared at this meeting & declare their intentions of marriage with each other, the young man is directed to produce a certificate to next meeting seting forth what is needful on the occasion."[4] The Quakers were deeply solicitous about their young people, and it was customary for the Society to keep a close watch over their activities; this was particularly true of marriages. Two months after the declaration of intentions by David and Eunice, the women's minutes of the bride's congregation announced that "the Friends appointed to attend the marriage of David Worth with Eunice Gardner report it was orderly accomplished."[5]

David Worth's bride had an ancestry similar to her husband's. Her father, Stephen Gardner, born of a Quaker family on Nantucket, was received into the New Garden Monthly Meeting from the Nantucket group in 1773.[6] Thus, both of Jonathan Worth's grandfathers were Quakers who came to North Carolina from Nantucket in the early 1770's.

After their marriage in 1798, David and Eunice Worth established their home in the community of Center, some ten miles south of Greensboro, on the line between Guilford and Randolph counties; their house was one mile from the Quaker meeting house at Center. This village was one of the numerous settlements that sprang from the original nucleus of Quakers at New Garden. The first "day meeting" was established by settlers from New Garden in 1757, and by 1773, Center had reached the status of a Monthly Meeting. The growth of the settlement was slowed down when the American Revolution broke out and there was a minor exodus to the West around 1800, but in 1798, Center was a growing community of small farmers.[7] For several years, David Worth was a successful farmer himself.

The marriage was a happy one but the long shadow of tragedy fell across the Worths' homestead when their first son, Steven, died before he was four months old, their first daughter, Rachel, lived only two years, and their fifth child died in infancy. The third child, and second son, Jonathan, was born on November 18, 1802, and was followed by five brothers and four sisters over the next twenty years. Jonathan and all except one of the children who came after him lived and grew rapidly into happy, healthy children, but Steven and Rachel had died, so their father believed, because no doctor was available in Center. In 1815, after contemplating the deaths of his children for about fifteen years, David Worth took a step which was indicative of the man's enterprising character; at the age of thirty-nine he decided to become a doctor. Philadelphia was at that time acknowledged to be the leading medical center of the country, as it had been ever since the day of Benjamin Rush. One day in the summer of 1815, David Worth climbed into his sulky at Center, drove the hot, dusty roads to Philadelphia, and remained there until he had completed the medical course at Jefferson College.

When Dr. Worth returned to Center, he soon built up an extensive practice in Guilford and the surrounding counties. He might be seen riding a sturdy horse about the countryside at any hour of the day or night. Dr. Worth established what may have been the first hospital in North Carolina. Half way down the hill that separated his springhouse from his dwelling, he built a house where patients might come for treatment and recuperation; the nurses were Dr. Worth's servants.[8]

Such a man inevitably came to be popular among his neighbors, who sent him to the state legislature in 1820, 1822, and 1823. He also took time from his medical practice and farming to promote the schools of the neighborhood.[9] In all these activities Eunice Gardner Worth was a faithful helpmate. An excellent rider, she galloped her white horse about the countryside and assisted her husband as a nurse —and sometimes as a doctor; community tradition relates that she once saved the life of a child dying with diptheria by forcing air into his lungs through a sterilized goose quill. As a housekeeper and mother she is best remembered as a weaver of fine cloth and baker of bread, which was kept fresh in the cool springhouse. When neighbors' fortunes had taken a turn for the worse, many of her biscuits and fruit from the Worths' orchard appeared on their doorsteps.[10]

Probably the most significant fact about Jonathan Worth's parents, so far as their son is concerned, is that they were both Quakers and that they lived in an area heavily populated with Friends. Living in an environment that was pervaded with Quaker ideas and ideals, the young Jonathan naturally absorbed some of them. Indeed, the similarity of his matured views to those generally held by the Quakers is too striking to be overlooked.

Several attributes of the Quakers are relevant to the story of Jonathan Worth. Because of the attitude of the many people who neither understood nor appreciated the principles and practices of George Fox and the sect he founded, the Quakers found it necessary to habituate themselves to public disapproval and learn how to deal with it. Much of this disapproval stemmed from the well-known attitude of the Friends towards military service and war, a social evil they considered a flagrant violation of the principles and teachings of Jesus Christ. They refused to serve in the militia and finally managed to secure legal exemption from the state legislature, a privilege for which they paid a tax of two and a half dollars.[11] This feeling about the nature of war Jonathan Worth absorbed as soon as his mind became perceptive enough to take in an idea, and he held it until the day he died.

Another attribute of the Quakers that has some significance is their great concern for the education of their children. The Friends in North Carolina were very active in establishing schools to supplement the instruction given in their churches.[12] The first building to go up in a new settlement was usually a meeting house, but a school was never far behind in the order of priority. It was at one of these schools that Worth received his first formal education. In a third-person autobiographical sketch written for the North Carolina historian, John H. Wheeler, Worth wrote: "He received a fair English education at the neighboring old field schools, being much indebted to Wm. Reynolds, the benefactor of his neighborhood as a teacher, for correct instruction in English grammar and arithmetic."[13]

Until he was eighteen years old Worth remained on the farm

at Center and attended William Reynolds' neighborhood school. His
father then decided that he should enter the Greensboro Academy,
an institution established in 1816 on what is now Sycamore Street.[14]

Jonathan's first teacher at the Academy was the Reverend William
D. Paisley, a Presbyterian minister from Orange County, who had become Principal of the Academy at the January term, 1820.[15] The
curriculum of the Academy while Worth was in attendance included,
in addition to the basic courses—reading, writing, arithmetic—geography ("with the use of the Globes"), moral philosophy, rhetoric, and
logic. In the realm of the sciences there was natural philosophy,
astronomy, and mathematics. Major emphasis was on "the dead
languages," Latin and Greek. Worth forgot most of the Greek, but his
knowledge of Latin enabled him to spice his speech and writing to
the end of his life; he would explain a hurriedly written letter by a
postscript stating that the letter was an *"ante breakfast note written
currente calamo"*; or he might refer to his political enemies with
some epithet and add the phrase *"et id omne genus."*

Tuition at Greensboro Academy was not expensive, ranging from
twelve dollars a term for the science courses, through $10.50 for Latin
and Greek, down to five dollars for reading, writing, and spelling.[16]
To help pay these expenses Worth, who as a result of his training with
William Reynolds was a competent scholar in English grammar,
agreed to take a position as an assistant instructor in English. Notice
of his appointment appeared in the Raleigh *Register* on February 9,
1821:

The exercises of this Institution commenced on the first Monday of
January last, under the superintendance of the Rev. Wm. D. Paisley;
but as the English Language has heretofore been only partially taught,
the Trustees think it necessary to announce to the public that they
have employed Mr. Jonathan Worth, as an Assistant Teacher. No
young gentleman, we believe, sustains a fairer character than Mr.
Worth; and we can confidently pronounce him well qualified to discharge the duties of his station.

Even with his resources augmented by his assistantship it soon became apparent to Worth that he would have to leave Greensboro
Academy and set out to make his fortune on his own. His father was
unable to give him any assistance; although Dr. Worth had by this
time a firmly established reputation and a large practice, it was not

always easy to collect fees from his patients—and there were eight children to feed, not counting Jonathan. Faced with this financial crisis, Jonathan was forced to select a profession and start at it. His formal education came to an end after two and a half years at Greensboro Academy. He left there sometime in 1823.

At this time the law was generally considered to be one of the most honorable, if not the most lucrative, professions a young man might enter. A legal education opened doors that could be opened in no other way. It brought one into contact with the great men and leading families; it offered a means by which any young man who was willing to work hard could earn more than a decent living; and it was the calling which provided most of the political leaders of the state and nation. Whether these aspects of the legal profession were the ones which caused Jonathan Worth to decide upon a legal career is not certain, but they must have crossed his mind in that summer of 1823, when he made the decision to educate himself in the intricacies of the law.

There was nothing in North Carolina when Worth began his legal study that could be called a law school. Aspiring lawyers made their own arrangements with some prominent attorney or judge for a period of apprenticeship in practical legal matters. The student usually moved into the village, or sometimes into the home, of his preceptor. He used the teacher's books, helped with routine office work, observed the handling of cases, and learned "how to gather evidence, investigate authorities, draw pleadings, try a case in court, and appeal his case."[17] For these privileges the student paid tuition and expenses varying from a hundred to two hundred and twenty-five dollars a year.[18]

Having made his decision to study Blackstone, Kent, Chitty, and the other standard legal authorities under the guidance of some good teacher, Worth left Greensboro in 1823, and went to Hillsboro. Since he had acquired some teaching experience at the Greensboro Academy, he secured a position in a school near Hillsboro in order to pay his expenses. His selection of a teacher was probably the best that could possibly have been made, for he chose Archibald DeBow Murphey, a man who might legitimately be named as the greatest citizen North Carolina has ever produced. No choice Worth ever made was more important, or more indicative of the course his future life was to take, than his decision to place himself under the guidance and influence of

Judge Murphey. No man Jonathan Worth ever met left the impress of his personality and ideas upon him to the degree that Murphey did. In some eight years of association, Worth caught the spark of his spirit and came into contact with the prophetic ideas for the development of North Carolina that Worth and others eventually worked into the fabric of the state's political, social, and economic institutions.

Archibald DeBow Murphey has been called a prophet " 'crying in the wilderness' of economic despair,"[19] for North Carolina was indeed almost literally a wilderness during the last thirty years of Murphey's life, years which exactly coincided with Jonathan Worth's first thirty years. The state's economy was based primarily on small farms, where poor men scratched out of the soil a bare subsistence, using only primitive tools.[20] There was some commerce along the coast, but the state was severely handicapped by one of the roughest coastlines in the United States and by a lack of deep harbors. Only $1,328,271 worth of the state's products left these harbors in the year ending on September 30, 1816.[21] Much of the limited trade was carried on through neighboring states, for farmers living along the Virginia and South Carolina lines found it easier to haul their produce into Norfolk or Charleston than to Wilmington or Edenton. The roads these farmers had to travel were mud-soaked in wet weather and so dusty in dry seasons that a man might almost stifle. Manufacturing, except on a very small scale, was nonexistent; here and there was a turpentine "still," and there were grist mills where the farmers and small planters could grind their grain, but the real beginnings of that industrial revolution which was starting in New England had not yet come to North Carolina. One reason for this, besides the fact that most of the people were too poor to be steady consumers, was a lack of capital; there were, in 1815, only three banks in the state—at Raleigh, New Bern, and Wilmington. Because of these conditions, which seemed to be imposed on the state by a malevolent Providence, many men packed up their few belongings, their wives and numerous progeny in their wagons and left the Rip Van Winkle state for the more promising lands of the west.

The state's material poverty was reflected in its cultural life during the years while Jonathan Worth reached manhood. Murphey reported to the legislature in 1816 "that at this time in North Carolina, the early education of youth is left in a great measure to chance. Thousands of unfortunate children are growing up in perfect ignorance of their moral and religious duties."[22] Parents were little better informed than their ignorant offspring. There were few newspapers or magazines for their edification, and if there had been many, they would have been unable to read them. A few children attended the scattered academies if their parents were able to send them, but if a man like Dr. David Worth could not keep his son in school until he completed the courses, one can imagine how it was with the impoverished farmers. The only available solution to this appalling problem was the initiation of a system of schools supported by the state, but few men were willing to admit this in 1815. Instead of a ground swell of popular clamor for the abolition of ignorance, a deep-seated antipathy prevailed against the idea that all children should be educated at public expense.

It is obvious from these remarks that North Carolina was indeed "in the wilderness" in these years while Jonathan Worth was trying to get started in life. Much of the credit for the reform movement which began in the late 1830's and continued to the Civil War must be given to Worth's law teacher and friend, who formulated an economic and educational policy for the state in a series of reports and memorials to the legislature in 1816 and 1817. One of Murphey's reports, written in 1816, asserted that "the true foundations of national prosperity and of national glory, must be laid in a liberal system of Internal Improvements, and of Public Education; in a system which shall give encouragement to the cultivation of the soil; which shall give force to the faculties of the mind, and establish over the heart the empire of sound morality."[23]

When the next legislature met, Murphey presented to it a detailed plan for a system of public instruction which resembled in several particulars the scheme promoted in Virginia by Thomas Jefferson. The report recommended first that sufficient funds be made available. There was to be a policy-making board of six commissioners called the Board of Public Instruction. The system Murphey envisaged was to consist of primary schools in every county, ten academies throughout the state to prepare students for the university, and an asylum for the deaf and dumb. The state would have paid the salaries of the teachers in the primary schools—one hundred dollars a term—and one-third of the salaries in the academies. The plan contemplated the promotion of superior students only, and it specified the courses which should be taught in the primary schools, the academies, and the University.[24]

Twenty-three years later Jonathan Worth was to be one of the key figures in putting a modified version of this system into operation.

The second major scheme designed by Archibald D. Murphey to help North Carolina rid herself of her unbecoming reputation as a slumbering giant was an extensive system of internal development projects. His ideas on this subject were summarized in a report submitted to Hamilton Fulton, an English civil engineer hired by the state in 1819 to examine the feasibility of various projects proposed before that date. The great object was to build transportation facilities for carrying produce to market and for importing goods from abroad. The coast needed to be improved by deepening the inlets, cutting channels through the sand bars, and building a coastwise canal system to carry the products of the Tar, Neuse, and Roanoke River basins to Beaufort, where there was a good harbor. Murphey proposed that obstructions be removed from the inland waters of the major rivers, and that a canal system unite the Yadkin, Catawba, and Cape Fear rivers; this canal system was expected to build up Wilmington and Fayetteville as commercial centers. The extreme west, where there were no navigable rivers, might be penetrated by a system of roads and turnpikes. Finally, Murphey tacked on to his suggestions to Fulton a proposal to improve the health and wealth of the southeastern counties by draining the malarial swamps there and converting them into farm lands.[25] Murphey's ideas were too advanced to be generally adopted at the time he first formulated them, but Jonathan Worth readily absorbed them.

Worth's relationship with Murphey became more than that of an erstwhile law student, for among the members of Judge Murphey's household during the time Worth was teaching and studying law at Hillsboro was a pretty teenage girl named Martitia Daniel. A native Virginian, she was a daughter of the judge's sister, and his ward. Martitia had dark hair and large eyes under level brows. Naturally she caught Jonathan's eye, and before he left Hillsboro he was in love with her and had asked for her hand in marriage. She gladly consented and they were married at Murphey's estate, "The Hermitage," on April 20, 1824;[26] he was twenty-two years old, she seventeen. Two days later the newlyweds appeared at the groom's home in Center for the wedding of his oldest sister, Ruth, to Sidney Porter, who had lately moved from Connecticut to North Carolina and established residence in Greensboro. There was much gaiety about "the plantation," for it was not often that a brother and sister were married at the same time; "the brother's infare served as a wedding reception for the sister."[27] One interesting result of Jonathan's marriage to Martitia was that the Quakers "disowned" him for marrying outside the Society. The Friends were still rigid in their belief that Quakers should marry only members of their own sect, and since Martitia was a member of the Presbyterian Church, Jonathan had to be dropped from the rolls of the Center Monthly Meeting; he never belonged to any other religious denomination.[28] Worth's marriage to Murphey's niece naturally added a link to the chain of association between the two men. They also practiced law together, but only in a few cases.[29]

In 1829, Worth became engaged in the business of gold mining with Murphey, whose fortunes had sunk to a very low point as a result of a series of business reverses. The great man, sick and broken in body, but not in spirit, wrote optimistically to his good friend and former student, Thomas Ruffin, about the prospects of this mining venture with his young friend. He had seen a French chemist, identified only as M. D'Auvergne, "flux three oz. of common Ore and get 8 grains of pure Gold." Murphey was erecting four furnaces and mills to wash the gold ore. He expected to spend a hundred dollars for the furnaces and mills and get a return of six hundred dollars a week.[30] By September, 1829, M. D'Auvergne had not yet made a fortune for Murphey and Worth, and in January, 1830, the judge was "broke," from which one may infer that the mining venture was not paying to the extent the operators had anticipated.[31] In spite of the unpromising outlook the mine was still in operation in August, 1830, when Murphey ordered corn and flour for his and Worth's families and for the gold mine "at Gibson," in the southern part of Guilford County. Worth probably did most of the supervising, for Murphey indicated in his order that "Mr. Worth will be at the mine" to receive the provisions.[32]

After Worth completed his course of study and observation with Murphey, he obtained a license, in December, 1824, to practice law. A month earlier he and his brother-in-law, Sidney Porter, had bought, for seven dollars, a town lot in Asheboro, a village in which the county seat and court house of Randolph County were located. Commonly called "the spring lot," the piece of property was adjacent to the lands of Benjamin Elliott, who became Worth's friend and business associate.[33] Sometime between the day Worth secured his license as a lawyer and May, 1825, he and Martitia moved to Asheboro; it is probable, though not certain, that they lived on "the spring lot."

Asheboro, which was located almost exactly in the geographical center of North Carolina, was a quiet settlement of perhaps fifteen houses and a store or two centered around the county court house. As late as 1850, the population of the village included only 102 white citizens, and in 1890, a complacent resident noted that "this quiet country village, encircled by the hills of pine, in unpretentious simplicity, has stood for a hundred years, without assuming an air of town life, unafflicted with burglars, tramps, or insurance agents, in the enjoyment of the greatest of earthly treasures, contentment and health."[34] The Worths remained in this calm setting for almost forty years, from 1825 to 1863.

It is possible to catch only occasional glimpses of Worth as he began to put down roots in a new environment. At the May term of the county court in 1825, he was appointed overseer of the road from Asheboro to Hasket's Creek.[35] Overseeing was a task that a man might expect at one time or another, for the only way the roads were maintained was for the counties to appoint work crews and overseers to do whatever work was necessary.

It did not take Worth long to discover that earning a living by solving other people's legal problems was not easy. The figure of "the struggling young lawyer" was as common then as it is now. Most beginning practitioners of the legal art had a difficult time, if the financial returns from their practice mean anything. Bartholomew F. Moore, the lawyer who became famous in the case of the *State vs. Will*—in which Moore secured an acquittal of the slave, Will, on a charge of murdering his overseer—earned only seven hundred dollars in his first seven years of legal practice. Daniel G. Fowle, who became a judge and governor of the state, received only sixty-four dollars for his first year of work as an attorney. Both Moore and Fowle were better lawyers than Worth, whose income must have been low indeed.[36]

Worth himself later explained why he did not quickly become successful in his chosen profession during these first years. Speaking in the third person, he said: "Owing to extreme diffidence and the total absence of anything like oratorical flourish, others, not more learned, took the lead of him in practice. Notwithstanding his great need of professional gains his painful diffidence made him almost prefer to lose a fee rather than make a speech."[37]

Worth's reluctance to speak before juries hindered his success to the extent that he was compelled to supplement his income by engaging in occupations that did not require eloquent speeches. Sometimes he did the clerical work of the Court of Pleas and Quarter Sessions for Randolph County; the minutes of the Court for the May term, 1826, are in his handwriting. He also began to augment his resources by buying and selling land, a trade in which he soon displayed a flair for business. The first land trade Worth made, after he bought "the spring lot," came in February, 1825, when he purchased an unspecified amount of land at a sheriff's sale. He got the land for twenty-five cents, when no one else bid higher for the property.[38] The next year he acquired ten acres from John Henley[39] and sold to George Hoover the two town lots on which Asheboro's local tavern stood and a hundred acres of property adjoining the tavern.[40] These transactions were only the beginning of an extremely lengthy series of land trades. Worth's name appears very frequently in the deed books; the Register of Deeds must have become tired of seeing him.

When Jonathan Worth celebrated his birthday in November, 1830, he could look back across twenty-eight years and reflect upon what he had achieved. It was not yet much, but he had at least laid some foundations. He was married to a good wife, had studied law with one of the best lawyers of his time, and had begun to acquire the material things which are the outward signs of success in life.

· II ·

Attachment to the Union

———◆———

JONATHAN WORTH'S CAREER as a public servant began in 1830, when he decided "as a means of overcoming his repugnance to public speaking, to become a candidate for the legislature, hoping the canvass might give him more assurance."[1] There were at that time no regular political party organizations in the district around Asheboro. Whoever wanted to run simply announced his intentions and rode about the country making speeches at the crossroads stores and acquainting the voters with his views and qualifications. In Worth's first political campaign, about which there is little information extant, he was one of six candidates for the House of Commons and two for the Senate; one man, Abraham Brower, ran for both houses and was elected to both. On election day Worth got 710 votes, more than any of the other five candidates for the House.[2] These 710 votes represented an expression of faith from the citizens of Randolph County that remained unbroken until thirty-five years later, when the Civil War had dissolved political allegiances and forced Worth into strange associations.

Before 1835, the legislature met annually, convening usually about the beginning of the third week in November and remaining in session until a few days after the beginning of the new year. In 1830, opening day was November 15, three days before Worth's twenty-eighth birthday. Before the end of the session he had drawn the political spotlight of the state upon himself by offering a set of controversial resolutions denouncing the doctrine of nullification, which was then being discussed throughout the country. It was at this juncture, when Worth had been in political life only two weeks, that he made a clear exposition of the principle that guided his political actions throughout the remainder of his life. That principle was a love of and attachment to the federal union and the government which ruled it. His conduct in this crisis thus becomes particularly significant.

The background of the nullification crisis can be told in more than one volume, or stated briefly in a paragraph. It resulted from the "Tariff of Abominations," a protective measure passed by the Congress of the United States in 1828. The seaboard states of the South despised this tariff, placing blame on it for the complex economic ills that were beginning to plague the section. As a defense against the Tariff of 1828, and other possible oppressive measures, John C. Calhoun formulated his famous *Exposition and Protest,* an extremely able defense of the doctrine of nullification; and Robert Y. Hayne, United States Senator from South Carolina, expounded Calhoun's doctrines in an equally famous debate on the nature of the Union which occurred in January, 1830. Later in that year the South Carolina legislature summarized the arguments of the nullifiers when it resolved that the general government was limited by the federal constitution of 1787; that the states had created the central government; that the central government was becoming more and more absolute; and that South Carolina could nullify the tariff by simply interposing the authority of the state against the United States.[3]

This was dangerous doctrine indeed, and it seemed to please South Carolinians, but their neighbors to the immediate north would have little or nothing to do with it. There were some exceptions, to be sure. The New Bern *Sentinel,* for example, favored nullification, but the editor of its local rival, *The Spectator,* deplored the doctrine. He wrote in May, 1830, that "we do not believe that one man in a hundred in the New Bern district is willing to prevent, by force, the collection of duties on imports at New Bern, even though the Tariff should be declared perpetual." The editor feared that a civil war would result if South Carolina attempted interposition, and he pointed out that, in the event of hostilities, "the General Government, with one sloop of war, could annihilate our whole commerce, foreign and coastwise."[4]

There were expressions of disapproval of South Carolina's pet theory by the people themselves, as well as by the newspaper editors. Henry M. Wagstaff, student of the state rights movement in North Carolina, examined the toasts made in celebration of Independence Day on July 4, 1830, relevant to the question of nullification. By this means he determined that popular sentiment in North Carolina was strongly opposed to nullification. At Worth's home town, Asheboro, the orator for the celebration argued that "he who wantonly engenders a feeling of hostility between the States instead of soothing it to harmony is a traitor to his country. Let no such man be trusted."[5] Later in the course of the crisis the Greensboro *Patriot* praised the pacific tone of Governor Montford Stokes' remarks to the opening session of the legislature of 1831 on the subject of nullification and boasted that the governors of North Carolina, unlike those of South Carolina, never would be guilty of asking the legislative body of the state to oppose the laws of the United States.[6]

When Governor John Owen delivered his message to the General Assembly in November, 1830, he asked for a "solemn protest" against protective tariffs.[7] A few days later, November 22, the representative in the House of Commons from the port town of Edenton, Samuel T. Sawyer, introduced resolutions declaring the tariff laws of 1824 and 1828, "partial and oppressive in their operations upon the Southern States."[8] These resolutions, which merely denounced the tariffs without making any mention of the doctrine they had stimulated in South Carolina, did not please Jonathan Worth, who proceeded to draw up his own and introduce them on November 29, 1830. More significant as a statement of Worth's views on the nature of the Union than of his temporary disapproval of the tariff laws, they were in these words:

Resolved, that although the Tariff Laws as They now exist, are unwise, unequal in their operations and oppressive to the Southern States; yet this Legislature cannot concur with the extreme, violent and dangerous remedy to which the South Carolina doctrines of nullification manifestly tend,
Resolved, that in the sentiment "this union must be preserved," we recognize principles which challenge the approbation of every republican, and which promise to save the republic from disunion and anarchy.[9]

On the day Worth brought these resolutions before the House of Commons, that body ordered them to be printed and laid them on the table. They remained on the table until December 31, when the House called them back to the floor at ten o'clock in the morning and engaged in a furious debate on them that lasted until "a late hour" that night. The only modification of the resolutions was the addition of the phrase, "in the opinion of this legislature," to the first resolution, an action which changed Worth's blanket condemnation of the existing tariff laws to a mere opinion that those laws were unjust and oppressive. After this slight modification the representatives from the eastern counties of the state began an assault on Worth's denunciation of the South Carolina doctrine. George Blair, of Chowan County, moved indefinite postponement, but lost his motion, twenty-eight to eighty-eight. The representative from Halifax, Jessie A. Bynum, tried to strike out the express disapproval of nullification and simply "deprecate" any subversive doctrine, an attempt the House also struck down. Charles G. Spaight, New Bern's delegate, also wanted to strike out Worth's declaration that nullification was unconstitutional and state instead that North Carolina was too strongly attached to the Union to make use of such a dangerous theory; when this attempt failed, Spaight asked the House to throw out the whole resolution on nullification, but the legislators disapproved by a twenty-four to ninety vote. Still another approach to Worth's controversial first resolve was to limit its scope to a criticism only of those tariffs levied on essential items. Finally, after a long, hectic day the House approved Worth's condemnation of the nullification theory, eighty-seven to twenty-seven, and his statement of attachment to the federal union by a unanimous vote.[10]

On the last day of the session Charles G. Spaight, who had attempted to weaken Worth's anti-nullification resolution in the debate of December 31, entered into the journal of the House a lengthy protest against the resolution. He was opposed to its adoption because he interpreted it to mean that no right of nullification existed. Interposition of the authority of the individual states is not only a right, but a sacred duty, Spaight argued, but he conceded that such action should be used sparingly—only after a long series of encroachments on the rights of the state by the central government. To fortify his argument, this particularistic representative of the state rights school of political theory gave examples of circumstances in which a state might employ nullification in defense of its interests: if Congress should interfere with the relation between master and slave, or if it should attempt to prescribe where the legislature should meet to elect United States Senators, then it would be the clear duty of the state to declare the law of Congress unconstitutional and refuse to obey it. Finally, Spaight closed his protest by borrowing some of Thomas Jefferson's phrases about suffering "while evils are sufferable" and "a long train of abuses and usurpations." The final touch was a ringing declaration that the condemnations of posterity would fall not on a state which nullified and caused war, but on the usurping Congress which caused all the trouble by enacting oppressive legislation.[11]

Worth's resolutions on nullification and the nature of the Union failed to pass in the Senate, which was not yet sufficiently irate about South Carolina's actions to join in denouncing them as unduly precipitate. The Raleigh *Star* reported to its readers that the House of Commons had passed the Worth resolutions "after a very animated and interesting debate," but that in the upper house "for want of time to discuss them, they have been subsequently laid upon the table . . . with an understanding that they shall not be taken up again this session."[12] This action of the Senate prompted the *Western Carolinian,* a Salisbury paper, to grumble that "the Senate has given the enemy much room to talk."[13] Criticism of the Senate for failing to act on the resolutions was only one aspect of the general approbation with which they were received. The most influential paper in Worth's home district praised the resolutions and reminded South Carolina that "the cord of private friendship is but an attenuated thread, compared with the lion grip which binds North Carolina to the Union."[14]

Interest in the tariff question remained strong throughout the state during the summer of 1831. There were numerous public meetings to elect delegates to an anti-tariff convention scheduled to meet in Philadelphia on September 20. The minutes of these local meetings stated most of the objections which were raised against protective tariffs during the course of the nullification crisis. Among the criticisms of the protective system were assertions that it gave undue advantage to one pursuit over another by favoring industry at the expense of agriculture and commerce; that protective tariffs, as opposed to those levied for revenue only, were unconstitutional; that they were particularly oppressive to the South; and that North Carolina had never given its consent to be taxed by the methods employed in a protective system.[15]

Backed by popular sentiment at the grass roots level, the legislature of 1831-32 passed through both House of Commons and Senate resolutions condemning nullification as unconstitutional, revolutionary, and subversive to the principles of republican government. When in 1832 the South Carolina legislature passed an ordinance nullifying the provisions of the hated "Tariff of Abominations" and the Tariff of 1832, another series of mass meetings in North Carolina denounced the Ordinance of Nullification and endorsed the anti-nullification resolutions of the North Carolina legislature. Popular interest in the problem of the tariff and the political theory it produced died out after Congress passed a compromise tariff measure and President Andrew Jackson threatened to use force if South Carolina tried to implement its ordinance by obstructing the collection of the tariff at its ports.[16]

Jonathan Worth's clear denunciation of the doctrine of nullification was only one of several expressions of a nationalistic outlook he made during his first term in the North Carolina legislature. Another expression of his faith in a strong central government came when the House of Commons took up for consideration President Jackson's veto of a Congressional measure appropriating money to assist in the construction of a turnpike from Maysville to Lexington, Kentucky; the basic issue raised by the veto was the extent of the powers of Congress. The question came to the floor of the state legislature on November 22, 1830, when Samuel T. Sawyer, Edenton's representative in the House, introduced resolutions approving the president's veto of the turnpike bill. Sawyer interpreted the veto as an expression of the idea that Congress should not have unlimited powers to appropriate money for internal improvements.[17] The House took up Sawyer's resolutions on January 4, and added to them others approving "the general policy and prominent measures of the present administration" and calling for Jackson's re-election in 1832. These clearly political resolutions, which passed by an overwhelming majority of ninety-seven to nine, were too strong a dose for Jonathan Worth to swallow. Consequently, he voted with the minority of nine,[18] a move which stamped him for the remainder of his political career as "a Whig of the original panel," for opposition to the policies of Andrew Jackson was the one doctrine on which all Whigs could agree when the party was formed four years later.

When one takes a superficial view of Worth's attitude towards President Jackson by comparing his position on nullification with his stand on the resolutions approving the veto of the turnpike bill, the young legislator's actions appear to be inconsistent; in the first case he took the side of the president, but in the second he was diametrically opposed. The inconsistency proves, on closer examination of the issues involved, to be more apparent than real, for in both instances Worth took the position that the best interests of the country would be promoted by an extension, or at least a forceful demonstration of, the powers of the central government; it was the strong-willed president who was inconsistent.

Worth had another chance to demonstrate his consistency on the question of Congressional power in relation to internal improvements before the legislature adjourned. The governor had requested in his message that the Assembly ask Congress for funds to open a ship channel from Albemarle Sound to the Atlantic Ocean, only to have his suggestion pounced upon by the nimble guardians of state rights. The delegate from Halifax County, Jessie A. Bynum, introduced resolutions on December 2, labeling Congressional appropriations for internal improvements within the boundaries of a single state a "direct and palpable violation" of the United States Constitution. North Carolina's money, according to Bynum, should not be used for impolitic and inexpedient projects not authorized by the Constitution.[19] Here again was the question argued in the debates over the veto of the turnpike bill, and again Worth took the nationalistic position when he moved to postpone Bynum's resolutions indefinitely and voted unsuccessfully against their final adoption.[20]

One more problem on which Worth's early views are not only interesting but significant came up for discussion in his first session in the legislature; this problem was Negro slavery. In the years 1830 and 1831, there occurred in the South a sharp increase of interest and concern about slavery, an increase which probably stemmed from the fact that abolition-minded persons in the North were beginning to step up the tempo of their activities. A wave of hysteria swept over the South late in 1831, after a Negro preacher named Nat Turner led a slave uprising in Southampton County, Virginia, uncomfortably near the border of North Carolina, in which some fifty-five white persons were slaughtered. Some persons were also alarmed because of the nationalistic tendency inherent in the growing powers of Congress, as it was demonstrated in Congressional appropriations for internal improvements and federal participation in banking ventures. The major issues of the day—nullification, internal improvements, and slavery—were far from being separate questions; they could all be tied up into a neat package by any man who devoted much thought to them. Nathaniel Macon, North Carolina's most eminent guardian of the status quo and a large slaveholder, saw these relationships clearly: ". . . if Congress can make banks, roads, and canals under the constitution, they can free any slave in the United States," Macon opined to his friend Barlett Yancey.[21]

It was simply an historical accident, the date of his birth, that brought Jonathan Worth into the state legislature for the first time when views like those of Macon were floating about and when an alarmed people were beginning to enact more stringent laws to avert the possibility of an insurrection by their slaves. Towards all these measures Worth's attitude was one of coolness. On December 13, 1830, he moved unsuccessfully to postpone indefinitely a bill "to prevent free persons of color from hawking and peddling outside their own counties," a measure designed to prevent free Negroes from serving as liaison agents in slave plots.[22] He voted against postponing a bill to authorize Aquilla Day, a free Negro, to reside in the state, but the measure was postponed in spite of his efforts.[23] On another important matter relating to slavery, an act to prohibit the circulation of seditious publications, his record was similarly liberal, as he voted with the small minority who opposed a limitation on the circulation of reading matter.[24] Worth did not vote when the House considered and passed an act to prevent the intermarriage of free Negroes with white persons or slaves.

It is not necessary to look beyond Worth's ancestry and his environment around Asheboro in seeking reasons for his outlook and actions on the slavery problem while he was a member of the legislature in 1830 and 1831. His father, David Worth, was for many years active in the North Carolina Manumission Society, a Quaker organization that centered its activities in Guilford and Randolph counties.[25] One of Worth's brothers was named Thomas Clarkson, after the English Quaker of that name who led a movement in the 1790's against the use of sugar produced by slave labor.[26] This naming must certainly have reflected Dr. Worth's feeling about human bondage. Even if the older Worth's views did not influence his son, those of the young legislator's constituents did. Probably no county in the state, not even Guilford, had a larger proportion of Quakers among its population than Randolph. When the South began to cry out against the abolitionists and began to make life difficult for persons who openly declared their lack of enthusiasm for the "peculiar institution," many Quakers left the area around Worth's home and went to the Middle West, particularly to Indiana. Among the emigrants were three of Worth's sisters who married Quakers and moved to the Hoosier State.

One of the girls, Miriam, married Barnabas Coffin, a member of the family whose name is almost synonymous with the abolition movement. William Clark, husband of sister Louisa, was also strong in his anti-slavery views.

Slavery, nullification, the powers of Congress—these were the great questions during that first legislative session of Jonathan Worth's public career. The members had accomplished little except to pass resolutions on national political questions and make long-winded speeches, a practice which provoked the editor of the Salisbury *Western Carolinian* to note that "the members seem to have a repugnance to the transaction of any business."[27] Benjamin Swaim, crusading editor of the Greensboro *Patriot,* was even more disgusted with the legislature. Living in a section that needed good roads, he was particularly annoyed by Jessie Bynum's resolution stating that Congress could not contribute to the building of roads and canals in the interior of a single state; he was also irked by the passage of a law requiring Quakers to stand muster on militia day or be subject to a fine. Waxing sarcastic about "this assemblage of profound statesmen," Swaim announced his relief at their departure from Raleigh and summarized their achievements in these terms: ". . . North Carolina stands just where she did on the third Monday in November last —But mark her dejected look—she is fifty five days *older,* and thirty-five thousand dollars *poorer,* than when the last swarm of vultures commenced preying upon the small remains of her vitality."[28]

Worth served one other term in the legislature during the 1830's, when his constituents re-elected him to the House of Commons in August, 1831. November found him back in Raleigh to sit for another fifty-five days listening to discussion of the same issues that had been considered in the session of 1830. The Governor reported that "the excitement which seems to pervade a sister State, upon the subject of the Tariff, has effected little change in the opinions of the citizens of North Carolina. With regard to the policy of that measure, there is, so far as my information extends, a perfect union of sentiment."[29] This was only a polite way of saying that the tariff operated unequally and was contrary to the interests of Southern agriculture. The chief executive encouraged the passage of measures to secure a more effective police force and state militia to deal with the danger of slave revolts— a danger that had been intensified in the summer of 1831, when Nat Turner led his uprising in Southampton County, Virginia.

Since Worth's course in the legislature of 1831 was so similar to that in the session of 1830, it requires no detailed attention, except in a few particulars. In the earlier session a bill had been passed that made the teaching of slaves to read and write illegal. At that time Worth tried unsuccessfully to limit the prohibition to writing only, feeling that the slaves should be allowed to read. When this bill came up again in 1831, he supported parliamentary maneuvers to repeal part of it. He opposed a bill "for the better regulation of the conduct of negroes, slaves, and free persons of color," but supported an amendment to an act of 1816 "for the more speedy trial of slaves in capital cases."[30] The latter action may have been influenced by Nat Turner's insurrection, but there is no evidence on whether it was or not.

The spirit of Archibald Murphey, who had only a few months to live when the General Assembly of 1831 convened, was apparent when the legislators considered two bills to charter railroads in the interior of the state. Worth, of course, backed the chartering measures. When the bill to incorporate the North Carolina Central Railroad Company was on its third reading, David Outlaw, of Bertie County proposed to revoke the charter at any time the company asked for funds from the federal government. Worth voted against this limitation, and for a change found himself on the side of the majority.[31] The House publicly recognized Worth's interest in the movement for internal improvements, which was then beginning to receive more widespread support and enthusiasm, by placing him on the committee appointed to deal with that subject.

A clear-cut sectional division between the delegates from the eastern and western counties marked the legislatures of 1830 and 1831, and Worth, representing a western county, quite naturally took the side of the West. There was a conflict of interests between the sections lying roughly east and west of Raleigh—with some exceptions—that had its roots far back in the colonial and revolutionary periods of the state's history. Economically, the East was richer than the West, being the area where the largest plantations were located. It had better transportation facilities than the West, and these facilities served a smaller population than lived in the western country. Politically, the East was dominant because the Constitution of 1776 provided for representation by counties, and the East refused to create more counties in the West, even when that area became more populous. These geographical and political facts go far towards explaining why the men who opposed Worth's resolutions on nullification and his stand on internal improvements and slavery were easterners—Sawyer from Edenton, Bynum from Halifax County, and Spaight, who attempted to strike out the resolution on nullification, from New Bern.

The sectional conflict came into the open—not for the first time—when Alfred C. Moore, delegate from Surry County, introduced into the House of Commons on December 28, 1830, resolutions declaring the system of representation by counties unequal and directing the people of the state to vote at the next election for or against a constitutional convention to correct the inequalities which had arisen under the Constitution of 1776. Worth again found himself on the losing side when the representatives of the East succeeded in postponing Moore's resolutions. The question appeared again in the session of 1831, when James Whitaker, a mountaineer from Macon County, again called for a constitutional convention to be convened. The changes Whitaker desired the convention to make reflected the dissatisfaction of the West with the existing political system; if the people called the convention, Whitaker's resolutions contemplated the biennial election of senators, representation in the House of Commons on the basis of federal population, election of Commoners biennially by the free white men of the state, and a provision that the legislature meet every two years instead of annually. Worth favored these proposals, but the East guarded its dominant position by defeating the order for an election to determine whether the convention should be called.[32] It was not until 1835, when Worth was temporarily out of political life, that the delegates of the people assembled in Raleigh and added amendments to the Constitution of 1776 that revised the political system in the ways Whitaker had proposed, and struck a compromise between the two sections by giving the East control of the Senate and the West a majority in the House of Commons.[33] Had Worth been in the convention he would have supported these constitutional reforms, for he was still young, progressive, and a westerner.

Voting records can be cold statistics, but if one reads them in conjunction with a general knowledge of the man who casts the votes they may be quite revealing. The foregoing analysis of Jonathan Worth's ayes and nays in his first two sessions as a legislator makes at least three things clear: His resolutions on nullification are indicative of his firm attachment to the federal union of the states; his opposition to the repressive police measures designed to control Negro slaves exhibits a liberal attitude acquired from his family connections and constituents; and his consistent support of projects designed to improve the economic condition of the state, regardless of whether the projects were state or national in scope and origin, reveals a patriotic and personal interest in the economic welfare of North Carolina, as well as the influence of Archibald D. Murphey.

· III ·

The Making of a Conservative

DURING THE NINE YEARS from 1831 to 1840, Jonathan Worth was not a candidate for any elective office, but he was busily engaged in activities which helped to determine his course when he returned to the political arena in 1840. Worth himself told the story of these nine years in two short sentences: "In the beginning of 1831 he resolved to quit politics and devote himself to his profession. He soon went into a lucrative practice and paid off all his debts, and steadily accumulated property till the year 1840, when he was almost forced again to become a candidate for a seat in the Senate of the State Legislature on the Harrison ticket."[1] These two sentences left much untold.

Mrs. Worth may have had something to do with her husband's decision to quit politics, for the nights of November and December, when the legislature met, are the longest nights of the year. Martitia did not go to Raleigh with Jonathan when the Assembly met. During the session of 1831, she went to Center and remained with Worth's parents. On Christmas Eve of that year, Dr. Worth wrote to his son that Martitia ". . . was doseing in sleep and conceived herself to be at home siting on the carpet with her little twains playing around her when she heard the ratling of the stage and the same moment Mr. Marsh came running to inform her of your arrival when she sprang from her situation and ran with such speed to meet you as strained her back which caused her to awake but the pain in the back continued to fret her some."[2] Seven days earlier Martitia had given birth to twins, a girl and a boy. The girl was named Eunice Louisa and the boy David Gaston, probably after his grandfather and the great jurist William Gaston. When the twins were born the Worths already had two daughters, Roxana Cornelia and Lucy Jane, who had been born in 1826 and 1828, respectively. With a family increasing rapidly Worth had to forego the pleasures and trials of political life and turn his attention to rearing the children and building up his law practice and material fortunes.

When Worth returned to Asheboro from Raleigh in January, 1832, he was deeply in debt. Some of these debts were in connection with cases in which he had incurred expenses as the guardian of minor children; these obligations were secured by his father, David Worth. Others went back to 1824, when Worth had borrowed several hundred dollars to establish his home and legal practice in Asheboro. For these debts he had given notes, promising to repay them in 1826, but by January, 1832, he had managed to pay only fifty-four dollars and keep up payments of the required interest.

This was the nadir of Worth's fortunes. He began to extricate himself from his difficulties by mortgaging practically everything he had. On January 30, 1832, he signed a deed of trust to Barnabas Coffin for 161 acres of land on Abrams Creek in Randolph County, his interest in a tract lying partly in Guilford County, and his interest in the Moses Gibson mine in Guilford; this mine, in which Worth held four shares out of five on a twenty-five year venture, was the same one he had operated with Archibald D. Murphey. In case Worth did not fulfill the specification of the deed of trust, he stood to lose personal property including his horse, saddle and bridle, five hogs, seven head of cattle, all his pork and corn, beds and other furniture, and all his books. The conditions of the deed were such that if Worth paid all the debts before April 1, 1832—only two months in the future—title to the specified property would not pass to Coffin. But if Worth failed to pay, or could not get substitute securities, all the items and land were to be sold at auction in Asheboro on the seventh of May.[3]

With his back to the wall, Worth managed to find new securities for his debts and eventually paid them by working diligently and borrowing money from his close friends. George C. Mendenhall, a member of the most outstanding Quaker family in Guilford County, stood firmly behind Worth's ventures as security for his loans, and John Motley Morehead, later governor and railroad builder, was a constant creditor. Worth gratefully acknowledged Morehead's assistance in a letter to Morehead's son many years later:

When I became a member of the bar of North Carolina, I was very poor. I had no wealthy relative. I had married a wife poor as myself. At that time your father's pecuniary condition was far better than mine. He loaned me money when he knew I had no present

means for payment, and it was long before my talent, not of pre-
cocious order, enabled me to pay. *He* did not mortify me by asking
for payment before I was able to pay—and *I* did not delay payment
when I was able to make it. Cordial relations always existed between
us.[4]

An upturn in Worth's fortunes came in 1833 when he secured the
position of Clerk and Master in Equity for Randolph County. Since
Worth's law teacher had been a specialist in equity practice, which he
considered "the application of the rules of Moral Philosophy to the
practical affairs of men,"[5] it is likely that Murphey's student was well
qualified for the duties of Clerk and Master. His name appears in the
minutes of the Court of Equity for the first time at the March term,
1832, when the court awarded him forty dollars for taking depositions
and making a report. On May 26, 1833, the court accepted John
Daniel's resignation as Clerk and Master and appointed Jonathan
Worth to succeed Daniel. Benjamin Elliott and George C. Mendenhall
served as his securities when Worth gave bonds to the court for ten
thousand and four thousand dollars; the first bond was to assure the
safekeeping of the records, the second to secure the payment of any
money that might come into the Clerk's possession. After the court
accepted the bonds, Worth took the required oath of office and began
a tour of duty that was to last twenty-five years.[6]

The Clerk and Master in Equity occupied a position which could
prove advantageous to any young lawyer. He was basically an executive officer of the superior courts, appointed by the judge in whose
riding he lived, for a term of four years. He had to take the same
oaths and give the same bonds as a regular clerk of the superior court,
and was subject to the same penalties for malfeasance. The main
function of the Clerk and Master was selling real estate or other
property when sales were ordered by the Court of Equity to satisfy
judgments in civil suits. He was liable for all money that came into
his hands from such sales, and he had to be very careful that the
sales were made in accordance with the orders of the court. Other
duties included keeping "a fair and distinct record of the proceedings
of the court," caring for the documents involved in suits, and administering oaths to witnesses.[7] When a case arose, normal procedure was
for the Clerk and Master to make an investigation and file a report.
The parties to the case could file exceptions to his report, and the
judge of the Court of Equity would either sustain the Clerk and

Master, refer the exceptions to him for further examination, or submit the case to a trial by jury in one of the regular courts.[8] The court met in March and September and lasted from one day to a week, depending on the number of cases to be heard. There was usually a different judge for each term.

This seemingly insignificant office, Clerk and Master of the Court of Equity for Randolph County, was important to Jonathan Worth in several ways. Most obviously, it provided an additional source of income. It also gave him his first experience as an executive officer, and enabled him to meet many of the most influential judges of the state, among them Frederick Nash, John Dick, Thomas Settle, and Richmond M. Pearson. Most important of all, Worth's duties as Clerk and Master acquainted him with the status of various pieces of land in Randolph County and constantly impressed upon him the sacredness of property rights, one of the tenets of his emerging political philosophy.

Even before Worth secured the position as Clerk and Master he had begun a rise into the ranks of the landed gentry by a series of land trades in the late 1820's. From that time on, the trail of his dealings in real estate became a veritable labyrinth, but one can get some idea of them by perusing the carefully preserved deed books of Randolph County; between 1824 and 1864, the name of Jonathan Worth appears as a grantor or seller, 256 times, and 79 times as a grantee or buyer. The disparity in number of the two types of transaction may be explained by the fact that many of the sales Worth made were in connection with his work as Clerk and Master instead of personal exchanges. Another complicating factor is that when Worth signed bonds as security for his friends, a practice he often followed, his name appeared in the deed books as a grantor. But in spite of these complications, it is possible to ascertain that in his forty years as a citizen of Randolph County, Worth sold or leased in thirty strictly personal transactions, 1450 acres of land, at least eleven town lots, and a grist mill.[9] These figures serve only as a general indication of the extent of Worth's activities as a land trader, for he was also a buyer and seller in adjacent counties, and many transactions never found their way into the deed books, or were not recorded until many years after they were made; Emerson Lineberry, for example, bought eighty-one acres from Worth in 1843, but did not register his purchase until early in the 1880's.

The manner in which Worth conducted his real estate dealings shows something of the enterprising character of the man, for he acquired land in almost every conceivable way. Many of the larger tracts he bought at sales in which the county sheriff had been ordered to sell a person's land for the payment of debts—there was not yet a homestead exemption law in North Carolina to prevent the sale of a debtor's home. A similar source of acquisition was the trustee's sale, at which a designated trustee sold lands he had held as security for the performance of some obligation. Then there were regular purchases from men who simply wanted to sell their land, and once Worth secured a grant of eighteen acres from the state.

From the character of some of the transactions by which Worth became a large landowner one might conclude that he was sometimes cold-blooded in his business dealings. A case in which he forced the sale of the land and personal property of three of his debtors demonstrates clearly his insistence on the obligation of a contract. In 1844, Lucy and Solomon York and Joab Parks owed Worth $526. The Court of Equity delivered in March, 1844, a judgment in Worth's favor against the three debtors and ordered the sheriff, Hezekiah Andrews, to collect from their property the $526 and the cost of the suit. On June 5, the sheriff executed the order by seizing one hundred thirty acres of Lucy York's land and the cattle, hogs, crops, and household property of Solomon and Lucy; he also took "a crop of corn and oats" from Joab Parks, who had no other property. When Sheriff Andrews sold the personal property at auction he received only $46 for it. In September, the Court of Equity ordered him to sell a hundred and thirty acres of Lucy York's land, and Worth bought them for $301.[10] The last event in this unpleasant episode came in September, 1845, when Worth sold the land formerly belonging to Lucy and Solomon York to James Stout for $550.[11] The end result was that the debtors lost their property because of their inability to pay their debts and Worth emerged $277 poorer; if he had not brought suit and forced the sale he would have lost the entire debt. The answers to the questions of ethics raised in the case can best be left to the moralists, but it does illustrate Jonathan Worth's belief in the sanctity of a contract.

Land trading and legal practice were not the only things which helped Jonathan Worth to rise in the world of men and affairs. As he began to pay off his debts in the 1830's and to increase the number of his clients, his business and commercial interests began to multiply.

Whenever the county court met for its August term, the merchants of the county paid for a license that entitled them to sell merchandise in the county for one year. Worth first purchased a merchant's license from the court in August, 1835; each year thereafter he paid four or six dollars and renewed the license.[12] Little is known about his early ventures as a merchant, but one can gather from advertisements Worth ran in the local newspaper that he operated only one store, at which he sold general merchandise and a great variety of patent medicines which allegedly could cure anything from the common cold to rheumatism. Worth himself never made ridiculous claims for the healing powers of his medicines and the quality of his goods, but copied in his advertisements the manufacturer's laudatory descriptions and indicated that "the above named goods can be purchased at my store in Asheboro."[13] The actual operation of the store was in the hands of a responsible clerk, since Worth himself was usually busy with his law practice.

Soon after Worth moved to Asheboro he began to work himself into the small circle of men who dominated the political machinery, the economic affairs, and the social life of the town and county. Year after year the same men held the county offices, though occasionally an "outsider" would break into the charmed circle. Just as Jonathan Worth was the Clerk and Master in Equity for many years, Hugh McCain was the perennial Clerk of the County Court, and George Hoover was elected sheriff time and time again. The roster of delegates to the state legislature from Randolph County lists the same names year after year.[14] These were public-spirited men who identified the welfare of the county and state with their own personal interests, and no public obligation was too small for them to perform. When Asheboro needed a warning bell put up the county court ordered Worth, Hugh McCain, and John B. Troy to hang the bell and to draw money to pay for it; they were detailed also "to examine the court house and see if any repairs are necessary."[15] When the court house began to fall down, because of defective construction, Worth rebuilt it in 1835; he did the work so well that the building was still in good condition in 1890.[16] Worth also served as a town commissioner for Asheboro and as a member of the county finance committee; the latter duty was an early acknowledgment of the ability to deal with public monies that later served him well at a higher level of public finance.

The same political leaders and public servants began a movement in the early 1830's to develop cotton manufacturing in the county. Water power was essential to the success of this enterprise, and nature had been kind to Randolph in this respect, for the headwaters of two rivers, the Deep and the Uwharrie, ran through the county from north to south. The Deep River was particularly well adapted to the establishment of industries requiring a steady source of water power because it had a sharp drop of 549 feet in one ten mile stretch lying a few miles northeast of Asheboro.[17] Five cotton mills appeared on this stretch of the Deep River between 1830 and 1850.

Worth was a member of the group which secured the charter for the county's first cotton mill, the Cedar Falls Manufacturing Company, from the legislature of 1828.[18] He helped Hugh McCain, Jessie Walker, and Benjamin Elliott take subscriptions to the stock of the new company; this was slow, but successful. The factory opened in 1836 on land along the Deep River where Benjamin Elliott had formerly operated a grist and flour mill.[19] Two years later, in 1838, another factory opened on Deep River, at Franklinville, with John B. Troy as president, and Hugh McCain, Elisha Coffin, Jessie Wheeler, and Henry Kivett as directors. About 1850, the factory burned but soon was rebuilt and named the Franklinville Manufacturing Company. Four members of the Coffin family combined with George Makepeace, Minerva Mendenhall, and others in a company that built the county's third cotton mill at Island Ford in 1845. Worth's brother-in-law, William Clark, and his friend Jessie Walker, who was a member of the group that had built the factory at Cedar Falls, were instrumental in harnessing the power of the Deep River for a mill that opened in 1848 with the name of Union Factory, and William Clark as its general agent. The pre-Civil War industrialization of Randolph County was completed when Isaac H. Foust and three partners built the county's fifth cotton mill in 1850, "a short distance below where Sandy Creek empties into the river."[20]

The aspect of this early movement to industrialize Randolph County which is most relevant to an understanding of Jonathan Worth is that almost all the men who participated in it were his close friends. Many of them were active also in county and state politics and in broader movements to promote the economic and social welfare of the state. Between them and Worth there was a clear community of interest in the affairs of the county, state, and nation. Economic development and business ventures were almost a religion to these men, who "dreamed that the roar of spindles would be the noblest music of the river."[21] The Reverend Braxton Craven, President of Trinity College, which was located during its early years in Randolph County, once actually dedicated a cotton mill to the glory of God and to His service. During the course of his remarks in the dedication ceremony he spoke of the pioneers in the industrialization movement— in glowing phrases of approbation suitable to the occasion, of course. Part of Craven's comment on Worth was in these terms:

He was emphatically a worker, he knew no idle moments or amusement. He was a staunch, honest man, and the excitement of political life, in which for many years he acted a prominent part, and the love of money, common to most men, and every influence that turns men from the right, all failed to place one stigma upon Jonathan Worth. Among all the honored dead, he stands as a peer with the best. He had much to do in inaugurating the first movement of progress in this county.[22]

Craven can be forgiven if he overstated his case on such an occasion, but what he said was essentially true. Jonathan Worth and the other small-scale capitalists of his circle of acquaintances did indeed love money and what it could buy for them, but to interpret their commercial and business ventures purely in terms of economic self-interest would be less than just.

Worth's personal and political associations extended far beyond the limited boundaries of the county where he made his home. He was well acquainted with the men who were most active in the establishment of cotton mills around Fayetteville. Among this group of his friends was C. B. Mallett, who was a leader in the formation of the Phoenix Manufacturing Company, a factory established on Cross Creek outside Fayetteville in 1839. Edward L. Winslow and Edward J. Hale were among the incorporators of the Rock Fish Manufacturing Company, which was in 1840 the largest manufacturing establishment south of Petersburg, Virginia;[23] both of them had either business or political connections with Worth.

Besides the sharp drop in the Deep River near Asheboro there is one other geographical feature of North Carolina that throws light on Worth's business and commercial affiliations. If one lays a ruler on a straight line connecting Asheboro with the port of Wilmington, the line also passes through Fayetteville, which is almost exactly equidistant between Asheboro and Wilmington. Northwest of Asheboro an extension of this interesting line strikes through Winston-Salem and touches the edge of the city of High Point. All these places were beginning to display interest in business and commercial matters during the years that Jonathan Worth was most active in building up his own fortunes and serving his state as a public officer. Another interesting feature of the line, which might be called for convenience the "Asheboro-Wilmington commercial axis," is that the Deep River and the larger river into which it flows above Fayetteville, the Cape Fear, followed it closely on their way to the Atlantic Ocean at Wilmington. Fayetteville became the major shipping point for farm produce and manufactured goods from the country around Asheboro and the lands north and west of Fayetteville lying along the line from Asheboro to Wilmington. Wilmington was of course the point from which produce and manufactured items were exported after they had been sent down the Cape Fear River from Fayetteville by barge or steamboat.

Nothing tied Worth's interest to the Asheboro-Wilmington commercial axis more strongly than his intimate association with his four younger brothers. John Milton, Thomas Clarkson, Joseph Addison, and Barzillai Gardner were, like their older brother, men of conservative temperament and wide business interests. John Milton studied medicine in Kentucky, but his primary occupations were farming, mining, and merchandise venturing, in and around Asheboro; in many of these ventures brother Jonathan joined him.[24] The three other brothers, when they left the family home at Center to make their fortunes in the business world, posted themselves strategically along the Asheboro-Wilmington commercial axis. Addison moved to Fayetteville, where he engaged in a series of partnerships selling general merchandise and acted as general agent for a steamship line that operated on the Cape Fear River between Fayetteville and Wilmington. Brother Barzillai thought at first of earning his living by making daguerreotypes—an occupation which was then new—but after marrying Mary E. Carter in 1845 and conducting a general merchandise store with brother Jonathan in Asheboro, he went into a shipping and commission business in Wilmington with the fifth brother, Clarkson. When all these arrangements became relatively permanent, the family had its members stationed very advantageously for business and commercial purposes. Two brothers, Jonathan and

Milton, remained in Asheboro; one, Addison—the middle man—was posted at Fayetteville; and Barzillai and Clarkson gave a symmetrical touch to the arrangements by settling in Wilmington. There was an uncommonly close bond of friendship among this band of brothers. They were always ready to come to each other's assistance; they corresponded with and visited each other frequently, and they naturally exhibited great interest in matters of concern to the whole family of Worths.

Worth's personal and business connections with the pioneer industrialists of Randolph County and his political dependence upon them and upon the farmers of his district made it natural that he should be actively interested in the movement to improve transportation facilities in the state. One student of the development of manufactures has pointed out that in their efforts to get their goods to market "the inland mills were at a decided disadvantage."[25] The farmers of Randolph also needed a convenient means of getting their surplus produce to market at Fayetteville; in 1840, they were getting from their lands nearly three hundred thousand bushels of corn, seventy-eight thousand bushels of wheat, eighty thousand pounds of tobacco, eighty-one thousand pounds of cotton, and smaller quantities of oats and wool.[26]

Being a student of Archibald D. Murphey as well as a citizen of the western section of the state, Worth participated enthusiastically in the movement to improve the state economically which moved with increasing impetus from the middle of the 1830's to the outbreak of the Civil War. On June 30, 1838, he attended a local meeting in Asheboro to select delegates to a convention on internal improvements that was scheduled to meet in Greensboro on July 4. At the local meeting he introduced resolutions approving the acts of the last state legislature on the subject of internal improvements "and more particularly of the project of constructing a railroad from Fayetteville to the western part of the state."[27] After those in attendance at the meeting expressed approval of Worth's resolutions and the idea of a larger convention in Greensboro they appointed Henry B. Elliott, Elisha Coffin, Jessie Walker, Hugh McCain, and Jonathan Worth to represent them at Greensboro.

When the convention met at Greensboro on July 4, 1838, its main interest was in the construction of a railroad from Fayetteville to the western part of the state. Although the members suggested no particular route for such a road, one may suppose they hoped it would come up through Asheboro and Greensboro. The convention also devoted some of its time to a discussion of the development of port facilities along the coast. When the delegates decided to make the convention a continuing body they selected Worth a member of the General Committee, a group charged with the responsibility of determining how funds for internal improvements could be raised and whether it would be expedient for the state to embark upon a general program of internal improvements.[28]

The personnel of the convention at Greensboro is of some interest, since it consisted primarily of Worth's conservative friends. Among the delegates were Judge John M. Dick, John A. Gilmer, and two men who served the state as its first Whig governors, Edward B. Dudley and John M. Morehead; Dudley, who represented the Wilmington area, was president of the meeting. The Fayetteville cotton manufacturer, C. B. Mallett, also appeared. The Randolph County industrial interests had delegates present in the persons of Henry B. Elliott, Jessie Walker, and Worth.

The project of a railroad from Fayetteville through the western counties was Worth's favorite among the many schemes for internal improvements that were proposed in the thirties and forties. Others interested in the project secured a charter from the legislature of 1836 and began to take subscriptions to the stock, but the project moved slowly. A meeting was held in the Randolph County court house on February 4, 1840, to open the books of the company to persons who wanted to subscribe to stock. Jessie Harper was chairman of the meeting, and Worth served as secretary. An agent from the state's Board of Internal Improvements delivered a sales talk which "abounded with arguments calculated to induce the people to subscribe for the stock."[29] The road would be especially useful to the western counties, the salesman argued. Worth also spoke before he opened the books to subscribers. These speeches must have been effective, for within two days ten thousand dollars was promised. Unfortunately, many of the subscriptions remained only promises, and the Fayetteville and Western Railroad died before it was fairly well born. Later in the decade, the 1840's, the promoters turned their attention to a less expensive project that would serve the same purpose, a plank road, and were successful in completing it.

Most of the disciples of business enterprise and economic development in North Carolina in the two decades before 1850 gave their allegiance to the Whig Party, which was formed in the year 1834 around the men in national politics who opposed the policies of President Andrew Jackson. Jackson had antagonized many men by his unrelenting war on the second bank of the United States and his views on internal improvements, as expressed in the veto of the Maysville Turnpike bill. Jackson's chief opponent in the political wars of his administration was Henry Clay, Senator from Kentucky, master of the art of compromise, and champion of national banks, internal improvements, and protective tariffs. Because the great Kentuckian advocated the program which Worth so firmly believed was essential to the economic progress of the nation, Worth became "an ardent admirer" of Clay.[30] If he ever had a political god, Clay was that deity.

The Whig Party appealed to Jonathan Worth because it was essentially a party of conservative men who held views similar to his own. The *National Intelligencer,* the Whig party organ at Washington—and one of Worth's favorite newspapers—once commented that "conservatism is the principle [sic] element of which our party is composed, and when we find that feeling it should be cherished."[31] This conservative tendency of the Whigs would by itself have been sufficient to attract Worth to the party; expressed in a concrete legislative program by a man of Henry Clay's stature, the attraction was overwhelming.

The above generalizations on the Whig Party are dangerously broad, for the party was composed of many diverse elements, but it seems safe enough to say that it was more active in promoting those projects in which Worth was interested than the party of Andrew Jackson. There was a state rights wing of the party, the importance of which has been overestimated by writers looking for the causes of the Civil War. This element of the party had no appeal whatsoever for Worth, whose views on federal relations were very clear during the nullification crisis when he denied the validity of the theories on which the arguments of the state rights faction of the party depended.[32]

The Whig Party in North Carolina defies generalization even more than the national organization, for few of the remarks one can make about the Whigs at the national level or the Whig party in the South are applicable to the party as it existed in North Carolina. The major differences between the state party and its counterparts may be seen in a sentence by the leading authority on the state's history: "The North Carolina elements of opposition to Jackson, chiefly the small-farmer west and the commercial area of the East, identified themselves with the national Whig party whereas the plantation, slaveholding, aristocratic East was staunchly Jacksonian."[33] Aristocrats supporting the Democratic Jackson, western farmers opposing him— these are strange political facts indeed! Yet the facts are not so startling when one considers the need of the western farmers and the commercial and business interests for internal improvements and compares Jackson's views on the subject with those of Henry Clay. Worth's home county, Randolph, was an ideal sample of a North Carolina Whig stronghold, for in it were included a large number of small farmers needing a road or railroad down to Fayetteville and a number of men whose primary interest was in the development of manufacturing enterprises, the cotton mills along Deep River.

By 1840, Worth's fortunes were definitely on an upward swing. Since 1832, he had managed to emerge from his financial crisis and pay off the large debts that caused him so much consternation at the beginning of the decade. He was still Clerk and Master in Equity for Randolph County, and his legal practice was beginning to flourish. From the middle of the thirties he engaged in the merchandise business, and from the time he went to the two sessions of the legislature in 1830 and 1831, he was active in promoting the budding industrialism of Randolph County. Closely related to these activities was his participation in the efforts to secure better transportation facilities for the western part of the state, most particularly a railroad running west from Fayetteville. Because the Whig party seemed best designed to advance the welfare of the state and nation by promoting such projects and because of his great admiration for the leadership of Henry Clay and the leaders of the Whig Party, Worth became in these years a steadfast Whig. As his personal affairs continued to improve, he could find more time for politics, and by 1840, he was again ready to become a candidate for a seat in the state legislature. It was a most propitious year for a popular Whig to re-enter the great game of politics.

· IV ·

The Realization of a Dream

THE POLITICAL CAMPAIGN of 1840 was one of the most exciting in the history of American politics. The Whigs, unable to beat Andrew Jackson and his followers by the techniques they had used earlier, were forced to abandon Henry Clay, nominate a military hero of their own, and try to sell him to the electorate as a son of the frontier. They finally nominated General William Henry Harrison, aging hero of the battle of Tippecanoe, and selected for his running mate John Tyler of Virginia, who was calculated to appeal to the defenders of state rights.

Jonathan Worth was sorely disappointed when the Whigs shunted Clay aside and chose Harrison, but he and the other members of the party in Randolph swallowed their disappointment and worked enthusiastically for the hero of Tippecanoe. Throughout September and October, Worth spoke at rallies in and around Asheboro praising Harrison and the Whig Party.[1] The campaign was so exciting that even the women participated in the activities. At a meeting in Asheboro on October 30, Worth's teen-age daughter, Roxana, and Eliza Rose presented a flag to the enthusiastic gathering. One side of the banner was inscribed "Randolph! Thy Daughters Cheer Thee"; on the reverse side was "Harrison! the Star of the West." Worth and the editor of the local Whig paper made speeches. Then someone raised the girls' flag on a pole sixty-three feet high to fly in the breeze as a symbol of "Female approbation" of General Harrison. When the ladies presented the flag they sang verses composed for the occasion:

> Old Randolph! thy daughters do cheer thee,
> With hearts both loyal and true.
> A Flag we have to present thee,
> In honor of Tippecanoe.

We have no hard Cider to offer;
But our wishes shall ever be true;
We send our free approbation,
And shout for old Tippecanoe.[2]

When the Whigs called upon Worth in the summer to campaign for a seat in the state Senate he consented reluctantly and entered the race. At the August election he won by a wide majority; in Randolph County he received 777 votes compared to his opponent's 240.[3] Since the Democratic candidate had run on a ticket that included Martin Van Buren for President, Worth's overwhelming victory may have been an indication that the county was predominantly Whiggish in its sentiments, rather than a proof of Worth's popularity. In the election for governor the Whig candidate, John M. Morehead, beat the Democrat, Romulus M. Saunders, by a margin comparable to that by which Worth won, 1,290 to 343.[4]

During Worth's first two sessions in the state legislature he had sprung into prominence because of his resolutions on the doctrine of nullification. In the session of 1840-41, he was to occupy an equally prominent place, but in an entirely different type of legislation. Almost all his attention was to be devoted to writing and securing passage of the law which set up the machinery of North Carolina's recently established system of public schools. This was an achievement of which Worth was justly proud. Years later he boasted that the essential features of his measure "remained unchanged until the system of common schools was broken up by the late war."[5]

It would have been unnatural if Worth had not been interested in public education, considering that he was a protégé and disciple of "the father of public education" in North Carolina, Archibald D. Murphey. It was Worth's good fortune to return to the legislature at a time when public opinion was becoming more receptive to Murphey's ideas and when the state had developed its resources to the point at which it could begin to give those ideas a practical application. Worth probably acquired some of his interest in educational matters from the Quakers, to whom he belonged by birthright and sentiment, if not by active religious affiliation. His father, David Worth, was another possible source of influence, for Dr. Worth had been actively interested in the establishment of schools around Center. Add to all these facts the additional one that Worth himself had taught at Greensboro

Academy and at the school outside Hillsboro while he was studying law with Murphey and the reasons for his promotion of education as a legislator become apparent enough.

Even before he came to Raleigh in 1840 Worth had been a leader in promoting an academy for girls at Asheboro. In 1839, he had four daughters old enough to educate, but there was no suitable place near home for them to attend school. Early in 1839, the citizens of Asheboro decided that their daughters needed a school. Worth was one of five commissioners appointed to raise funds for the project; the other four were Alfred H. Marsh, George Hoover, Hugh McCain, and J. M. A. Drake. By the end of the first week in February the commissioners had secured pledges of between three and four hundred dollars—about half enough to build the necessary building.[6]

The project advanced rapidly and by June the first "exercises" of the academy were ready to begin. The trustees had imported MISS ELIZA RAE, whose name always appeared in boldface capital letters in the newspaper advertisements of the academy, to serve as the first teacher for the new institution. Miss Rae must have been quite versatile, for in addition to teaching the basic subjects such as spelling, reading, and arithmetic she was expected to instill in the young ladies of Asheboro and vicinity some knowledge of rhetoric, needlework, philosophy, and "Music on the Piano." To secure for their daughters the privilege of pursuing this curriculum the girls' fathers had to pay fees varying from six dollars for spelling to twenty dollars for piano lessons.[7] The classes were held in "a House large enough to accommodate sixty scholars, built and completely finished off (with the exception of painting), with twelve large glass windows, and every part of the materials of the best quality; . . . and furnished too with the necessary seats, tables, and a fine Piano."[8]

The residents of Asheboro were proud of their academy. Worth and his fellow trustees boasted of the "distinguished qualifications" of Miss Rae, the healthy atmosphere of Asheboro, and the reasonableness of the charges for tuition. Benjamin Swaim, who at that time was editor of the local newspaper, called the academy to the attention of potential patrons, emphasizing that the girls would fare well physically as well as mentally: "Our provisions," he said, "are mostly of the domestic kind—plenty of cheese, Butter and Milk, from the cool Recesses of the Dairy."[9] Most of the students boarded in Asheboro, for the school had no dormitory.

Unlike most of the academies that were founded in North Carolina in the eighteenth and nineteenth centuries, Randolph Female Academy had a relatively long and useful life. In 1842, Asheboro also built a school for boys, and the two academies were combined about 1853. Most of the teachers who followed Eliza Rae were graduates of Miss Willard's Seminary in Troy, New York. Among them was a girl named Julia Stickney, a native of Sandy Hill, New York, who personified the genteel tradition of nineteenth-century womanhood and loved to write letters reflecting a romantic temperament nourished by reading the English romantics. Worth's daughter Adelaide wrote in 1853 to her brother, David, who was then about to complete his studies at the University of North Carolina, that "Miss Stickney has quite a school and it fills the Academy quite full."[10] Adelaide reported further that the number of pupils was twenty-six, eleven of whom "goes from our house every day"; five of the eleven were Worth's daughters, the other six boarders kept by Mrs. Worth. The family's attachment to the Academy became even closer when David married Julia Stickney after he graduated from the University in 1853.

The conditions which made it necessary for North Carolinians to establish private institutions like Randolph Academy were much the same in 1838 as they had been in 1783. The children of those parents who could afford to hire teachers for a neighborhood school or pay tuition at an academy were the fortunate ones. The poor still lived in ignorance of even the rudiments of formal education. But the state had begun to show signs of educational life, chiefly as a result of the propaganda efforts of men like Archibald D. Murphey, Dr. Joseph Caldwell, the first president of the University of North Carolina, and various legislators who introduced plans for a public school system throughout the 1820's.[11] When Worth made his first appearance on the state educational scene in 1840, two important steps had already been taken. The legislature had created an educational fund in 1825 and enacted the state's first public school law in 1839. Worth's school law of 1840 must be set against the background of these earlier acts to make its outlines clear.

The nature of the law of 1825 may be seen in its official title, "An Act to Create a Fund for the Establishment of Common Schools." The first section of the act listed the sources from which the fund was to be created and maintained: dividends from stock held by the state in the Banks of New Bern and Cape Fear which had not been formerly allocated to the support of internal improvements; dividends from stock in three navigation companies; taxes from the sale of licenses to liquor dealers and auctioneers; the balance of the money remaining in the state's Agricultural Fund; fees paid for entry into the vacant lands in the state, except the land belonging to the Cherokee Indians; proceeds from the sale or development of the swamp lands belonging to North Carolina; and future appropriations by the legislature. The act created a corporate body to be called the President and Directors of the Literary Fund to manage the money derived from the sources of income listed in the first section; it consisted of the Governor, the Treasurer of the State, the Chief Justice of the Supreme Court, and the speakers of the Senate and House of Commons. The President and Directors secured broad powers to invest the fund in state or national banks and to increase or diminish it by buying or selling property belonging to the fund. The final section, and the one which led to the most divergent interpretations and arguments in subsequent debates on the intent of the law, specified that "whenever . . . the said fund shall have sufficiently accumulated, the proceeds thereof shall be divided among the several Counties, in proportion to the free white population of each, to be managed . . . as the Legislature shall hereafter authorize and direct."[12]

The twelve years after the passage of the law creating an educational fund were years of legislative indifference—one might say hostility—to the development of common schools, but the public was being prepared to accept them. Dr. Joseph Caldwell's *Letters on Public Education,* which appeared in 1832, was probably the most powerful argument for schools presented to the people since Murphey made his reports to the legislature in 1816 and 1817.[13] At Asheboro Benjamin Swaim helped to prepare the people of his section to accept common schools after he started publishing his newspaper, the *Southern Citizen,* in 1836. Early in 1837, he related an incident in which a Boston wood sawyer's son had beaten one of John Quincy Adams' boys for some academic medal. In Boston this was taken as a matter of course, but in Randolph County it was something to be marveled at. Swaim set before his readers as a model the school system of Massachusetts, which he described in detail and praised every time he mentioned it.[14]

It was apparent from the discussions of the proposals to establish common schools and from the union of the Literary Fund with the Internal Improvements Fund that education and internal improvements were inseparably connected in the thinking of progressive men; when it developed its economic resources, North Carolina could support a system of public schools. In Archibald Murphey's mind, schools, canals, and turnpikes were only parts of a comprehensive plan to advance the total welfare of the state. After Murphey died, Benjamin Swaim expressed his concept clearly in these words: "We go for improvements of every description. . . . They essentially aid and promote each others advancement. But if you intend permanently to improve the internal condition of a state or country, there is no way to begin right, but to lay the foundation first; and that can only be done by instituting some systematic method of diffusing light and knowledge among the common people."[15] Swaim even went so far as to say, in the same article, that the Fayetteville and Western Railroad would not be dying for lack of subscribers to its stock if the people along the proposed route had only been more enlightened in their cultural life.

Despite all the talk about the dependence of a public school system upon prior development of the state's economic resources, it was a gift from the federal government rather than improvement of the North Carolina economy that made state support of common schools possible and undermined the arguments of those who were opposed to education because it would be too expensive. The gift, amounting to $1,433,757, came in 1837 when Congress decided to distribute among the states a large surplus the federal government had acquired from the sale of public lands in the West. With this welcome grant—which did not necessarily have to be spent for public education—and the existing resources of the Literary Fund at its disposal, the legislature of 1838-39 enacted the first law passed in North Carolina providing support of educational institutions by public funds. Archibald Murphey's dream was beginning to come true.

The act of 1839, written and sponsored by Senator William W. Cherry and Representative Frederick J. Hill, was surprisingly brief for a law designed to put into operation a project as large as a statewide school system. Passed in January, it directed the county sheriffs to inform the voters throughout the state that at the August elections they would be expected to vote on the question whether the county should have "school" or "no school." Those who were willing for the county officials to levy a tax equal to one half the amount which might be allocated from the state's Literary Fund should vote for schools.

If a county acted favorably at the polls the county court would then choose five to ten superintendents to put the system into operation. Duties imposed on the county superintendents by the law included selection of three to six committee members for each district; dividing the county into districts not over six miles square; and numbering the districts and reporting their numbers and natural boundaries to the county court for registration. If a superintendent refused to perform his duties after accepting appointment, the county court could fine him fifty dollars and send the money to Raleigh to be added to the Literary Fund.

The method of school finance provided by the law of 1839 was a combination of local taxation and state allocations from the Literary Fund. After a county voted to accept money from the state, the county court was left with no choice except to levy a tax that would be equivalent to twenty dollars for each district in the county. The money raised in this way was to be sent to the district committees by the chairman of the Board of Superintendents. The state would double the money raised by local taxation, for the law of 1839 appropriated forty dollars to each district in the counties that had voted for schools, levied the twenty-dollar tax for each district, and erected a school house in the district "sufficient to accommodate at least fifty scholars." The chairman of the Board of Superintendents had to certify to the state treasurer that the required conditions had been met before the treasurer could send money from the Literary Fund.[16]

The state-wide election to decide which counties would accept money from the state and inaugurate a school system was scheduled for the first week in August, 1839. Through the spring and summer there was wide discussion of the proposed system in the newspapers, in political speeches, and no doubt in parlors and country stores. Benjamin Swaim printed the law without comment on February 8. Two weeks later he invited readers to send in their views, *pro* and *con*. There was some adverse criticism that the bill did not extend far enough. "It will be recollected, however," Swaim wrote, "that by the time we get under way, to the extent of the present act, another Legislature will be in session, ready to extend the system in a manner calculated to meet the views of the people."[17] In general, the reaction to the bill in Randolph County and throughout the state was favorable.[18]

Most of the counties in the state adopted the system in August, 1839, although seven were not yet ready to accept it. The vote in Worth's home county was 847 to 512 in favor of establishing schools,[19] and it became the duty of the County Court of Pleas and Quarter Sessions to appoint the county superintendents. When this was done at the November term, Worth was among the list of appointees. The superintendents in turn chose Worth as their chairman, a post which he was to hold continually for the next twenty-three years. The superintendent's minutes show that he was faithful to his duties, for they are repetitive in two respects: there was almost always an entry, "Present, J. Worth . . .," and each year he was unanimously appointed Chairman of the Board of Superintendents.[20]

Through the early months of 1840, Worth and his fellow superintendents began their efforts to reduce to a workable system the scheme provided by the law passed in February of the previous year. It was at this point, if not earlier, that Worth became painfully aware of the inadequacies of the first public school law. Many of the flaws in the act had been pointed out during the summer of 1839, but they are best summarized by an authority on the history of the public schools, M. C. S. Noble, who wrote ninety years later with the benefit of hindsight:

There was little said about schoolhouses or how to provide them. . . . There was nothing said about teachers—who should employ them or what their qualifications should be. There was no mention as to when the schools should begin or what subjects should be taught after they had begun. There was no provision for a central controlling head of the system to guide and direct either the county superintendents, the school committeemen, or the teachers. No duties were assigned to the district committeemen other than the very vague and indefinite statement that they were to assist the county superintendents in matters relating to the schools in their districts. In fact, the Act was very weak from every point of view, so far as organization and administration were concerned.[21]

Worth's role in the development of the ante-bellum school system was to transform the law of 1839 into a practical plan by working out many of the numerous administrative problems that inevitably appeared when the system first began operating.

With almost a year of frustrating experience as county superintendent behind him, Worth went to Raleigh in November, 1840, to serve his first term in the state Senate. An appointment to the Com-

mittee on Education placed him in a position where he could influence
the course of legislation on the subject of the common schools; as
it turned out, he not only influenced the law, he wrote it.

Early in the session the Senate directed the committee "to inquire
if any, and what alterations are expedient in the act for the establishment of Common Schools, and report by bill or otherwise." The
committee was probably more capable than the average legislative committee—among the members were two future governors of the state,
Worth and David S. Reid, and a United States Senator, Willie P.
Mangum. Worth wrote the report required of the group and submitted it to the Senate on December 17. Everyone on the committee
felt that the act of 1839 needed amending, Worth reported, "but great
diversity of opinion prevails as to the best plan of amending it."
Unfortunately, he did not describe the diverse opinions, but many of
them appeared when a bill submitted with the report came up for
approval of the two houses of the legislature.

The committee discovered by its research that the probable annual
income of the Literary Fund established in 1825 was $137,544, most of
which came from dividends on stock in banks, interest on loans to
railroad companies, and dividends on stock in navigation and turnpike
companies. Worth calculated that if there were 185,427 white children in the state, each one could be backed to the amount of $1.10
a year from the Literary Fund.[22] After giving this information to the
legislature, Worth then criticized the use of a fund as the sole means of
supporting a school system. He argued that direct taxation should be
used at the county level to supplement the meager funds flowing from
Raleigh. How else could the interest of the people be aroused except
by taxing them? Nor could the schools operate "a sufficient length of
time" on the money provided by the Literary Fund.

Still on the subject of taxation, which was of course a crucial
issue, Worth's report suggested a basic change in policy from that of
the original school law. That law had given the county courts no
choice as to whether or not they should levy school taxes, but the committee proposed now to make the levying of the school tax optional.
The theory behind this was that the county court "almost always re-
flects correctly the popular will of their county, and that they will
always impose a tax where the voice of the people sanctions it; and that
it will prejudice the cause to collect it where it is disapproved." Worth
and the committee hoped that the desired effect could be achieved by

stirring up a friendly rivalry between the counties; if some counties levied a tax the others would follow a policy of "laudable emulation."[23]

The bill Worth submitted to the Senate with his report passed its first reading on December 19. Six days later, on Christmas Day, the Raleigh *Register* reported, in a discussion of the proposed school bill, that "three or four different Plans are before the Legislature, and there seems to be a fixed determination not to adjourn, without doing something effectual in this important matter." On December 29, a lengthy parliamentary fight over the school bill began on the floor of the Senate—a debate in which education was subordinate to politics. The squabbling politicians seemed more concerned with guarding the interests of their own sections than in establishing a better system of public schools.

The debate broke out when Senator William B. Shepard, representing the eastern counties of Pasquotank and Perquimans introduced an amendment to the first section of Worth's bill that called for the distribution of the proceeds from the Literary Fund to the counties on the basis of their federal population instead of using the white population as the basis, as Worth had proposed. Shepard's amendment obviously was sectional in its implications, for the East, which had a larger number of slaves than the West, stood to gain a larger share of the money in the Literary Fund if distribution on the basis of federal population were adopted. The West had the larger white population, would have more children to educate, and was ready to oppose Shepard's proposal with all the strength it could muster. But in spite of the efforts of the men who represented western interests, Shepard got his amendment through the Senate by a vote of twenty-five to twenty-one; Worth, of course, voted with the minority.[24]

Soon after the Senate adopted the Shepard amendment the westerners began a series of efforts to repeal or modify it in such a way that it would be more palatable to themselves and their constituents. Senator Alfred Dockery tried unsuccessfully on January 4, 1841, to have the words "federal population" struck out of the first section and replaced by phraseology providing that half the funds should be distributed equally among all the districts of the state and the other half "in the ratio of white population."[25] Another proposal, by the senator from the mountain county of Rutherford, called for distributing money received from the federal government on the basis of federal population and funds from other sources according to the number of free whites in the various counties. Worth opposed Dockery's scheme and favored the one introduced by the senator from Rutherford, but both of them went down before the power of the eastern forces, who successfully maintained their position through this and subsequent debates on the system of distribution.

Senator Matthew R. Moore entertained the Senate with a powerful speech on January 4, in which he summarized the arguments of those who favored distribution of school money on the basis of federal population. Although the act that created the Literary Fund fifteen years earlier had provided that the proceeds of the Fund should be divided among the counties according to their white population, Moore insisted that the provision did not constitute a pledge and was not binding on subsequent legislatures. A law of 1837 vesting title to the state's swamp lands in the President and Directors of the Literary Fund and authorizing them to hold the lands in trust as a source of income for a future school system had made no mention of the problem of distribution.[26] Furthermore, the school law of 1839 called for the money in the Literary Fund to be sent directly to the school districts, forty dollars to each one that complied with the law, regardless of the number of children or whether they were white or black. The East, Moore's argument continued, had contributed more to the growth of the Literary Fund by paying more taxes than the West and should be rewarded by receiving a larger share of the money. The Senator pointed out that the Senate was faced with three alternative plans of distribution: the money could be paid out on the basis of white population, the amount of taxes paid to the state, or the federal population. He then fortified his arguments in favor of the latter plan with statistics showing what proportions of the total available funds each county would get under the various plans; the intermediate figure for fifty-nine of the sixty-eight counties was the number of dollars the counties would receive if the federal population were used as the basis of distribution.[27] Justice was on the side of the men who favored the system of distribution Worth had written into the law originally, but Moore and others stated their arguments so forcefully, and backed them with so much voting power, that federal population became the basis of distribution of school funds in 1841 and remained the basis until after the Civil War.

The debate over the system of distribution overshadowed the more important sections of the bill that attempted to improve the inadequate administrative machinery created by the school law of 1839. The sheriffs were directed to hold new elections in the counties which did not vote for schools under the law of 1839 to determine whether the voters had changed their minds. No superintendents could be appointed until a majority of the people had voted to accept money from the Literary Fund, but if a county voted "No Schools" its share of the fund could be invested in the stock of state or national banks or loaned to individuals at favorable rates until the county decided it wanted public schools.

The law of 1839 had barely mentioned that there was to be a school committee in each district to assist the superintendents in establishing the new system. Worth, with an eye for detail and an awareness from his own experience that the functions of the district committees needed to be defined, wrote into his bill six sections explaining how the members of the committee were to be chosen and what they were expected to do. As soon as a district was laid off, three committeemen were to be elected by the free white men in the district who were eligible to vote for members of the House of Commons. The superintendents had control of these elections, appointing election officials, designating when and where the elections should be held, and declaring the winners. The superintendents also could appoint committeemen if the districts failed to elect them. Once the committee was elected and organized, its first duty was to purchase a site and build a school; under the law each committee was made a body corporate for the purpose of buying and selling property. Another duty was to report to the county superintendents the number and names of all white children between five and twenty-one years old living in the district. Probably the most important obligation imposed on the local committees by the law was the task of locating teachers and contracting with them "for such time as the monies to which said district may be entitled will permit." The superintendents determined how many teachers were needed in each district after they had received the reports on the number of children compiled by the committeemen. Since each district made its own arrangements with individual teachers, there was no uniformity in the length of the school terms taught in the state, or even in the counties. Worth made no effort to specify what should be taught in the schools, although one section of his bill authorized instruction in "any branch of English education."[28]

Worth's school law of 1841 differed in several particulars from the act passed in 1839. It changed the system of distribution of the school funds from a district basis to distribution among the counties according to their federal population; this was against the will of the author of the legislation. Instead of requiring the county courts to levy taxes to support schools, the second law merely authorized them to raise money by taxation. Finally, Worth's bill expanded the functions of the superintendents and outlined in some detail the duties of the district committeemen. It laid down the principles that were to guide the men who were working at the administrative level where most of the actual work of establishing schools was done.

Besides his work in the Committee on Education, Worth demonstrated his interest in educational matters in other ways. He voted to purchase a library for the state, secured incorporation of the trustees and library of Union Institute, and voted for a loan of ten thousand dollars to Wake Forest College, a new Baptist institution. As a recognition of his concern for the educational welfare of the state, Worth's fellow legislators appointed him a trustee of the University of North Carolina[29]—an appointment that was confirmed biennially for the next twenty-eight years. But it was his authorship of the public school law which brought the greatest recognition and praise.

On the day the legislature adjourned the Raleigh *Register* called the school bill "decidedly, the most important measure of the session" and referred to Worth as "a gentleman, of whom it may be said without punning, that his modest *worth* affords the surest guarantee of his future distinction." The editor saw a good prospect for the future of the common schools, and predicted the appearance of a populace capable of understanding and appreciating "Free Government."[30] The Greensboro *Patriot* noted in its comments on the new school bill that "its detail bears evidence of indefatigable industry; and it has brought the provisions of law to the greatest possible perfection, till further experience shall indicate what may be yet defective."[31] The Raleigh *Star* also extended plaudits to Worth by reminding its readers that "the able Senator from Randolph" had written the school law and defended it in the legislature. This seemed to the *Star* to deserve some thanks—perhaps "some post in the public service." An interesting comment by the editor of the *Star* was one in which he described Worth's manner of public speaking in the heated debates over the school law: "Mr. Worth is not one of those pepetual [sic] noisy and frothy declaimers, who speak for the sake of acquiring a transient degree of admiration; he speaks to the question under consideration, and that in such a manner as to enlighten and convince the judgment of his hearers."[32] Apparently he had not entirely conquered the "extreme diffidence" that plagued him in the early years of his practice as a lawyer.

It is relatively rare when a man goes to the state capitol, writes a law, then returns to his home district to assume the responsibility of putting the law into effect, but this was the case with Jonathan Worth and the public school act of 1841. A detailed account of his activities as County Superintendent would be almost as difficult to read as his duties were to perform, but some brief remarks on the functioning of the system in Worth's home county will serve to illustrate how the law of 1841 operated and how it was modified and expanded in later years.

Before Worth went to Raleigh in 1840, the county surveyor of Randolph, working for the superintendents, had divided the county into twenty-one school districts with boundaries running nine miles north and south and four miles east and west; the superintendents agreed that further subdivisions could be made at a later date. For each of the twenty-one districts the Board of Superintendents appointed six local committeemen, giving three to the northern half and three to the southern half of each district, and instructed them to call public meetings in each district to decide upon a location for a school.[33] There were some disagreements about where the buildings should be located, but after tempers calmed down, the schoolhouses began to appear in the districts. The people paid for most of the school buildings by voluntary contributions, preferring to use the money received from the state for teachers' salaries.[34] In 1841, the superintendents voted to begin subdividing the original twenty-one districts, and the number increased rapidly; there were fifty-nine by 1846, sixty-one in 1848, sixty-five in 1852, and seventy-one when Worth signed his last report as County Superintendent in April, 1861.[35] The increase in the number is in itself not important, but it indicates the number of schools that were being built.

Worth had to deal with minor squabbles over election of committeemen, location of schoolhouses, and division of districts, in addition to having charge of all the money that paid for the schools in the county. In March, 1842, the superintendents decided to distribute available funds to the districts according to the number of children in them; districts with less than ninety children were to have one teacher, the others two. Four months later they reduced the base figure to eighty and adopted the policy of making increases in funds paid to the districts directly proportional to the number of pupils. Every district having eighty children or fewer was then entitled to money sufficient to hire one teacher, but if a district had a hundred and twenty children it received one half more than the amount required for one teacher.[36] When the legislature of 1854-55 passed a law requiring the superintendents to distribute the money equally among the districts, Worth wrote to his friend Calvin H. Wiley that he and the other superintendents considered the act "so flagrantly unjust and unreasonable that we are extremely reluctant to carry it out" because the number of children ranged from twenty-seven in the district that had the fewest children to a hundred and sixty-eight in the largest.[37]

Finding teachers who were properly trained was almost impossible, since there was no institution in the state designed specifically for training them. In an effort to make sure that the teachers employed were not incompetent, the legislature of 1846 authorized the superintendents to examine persons desiring to teach in the public schools and to issue certificates to those found capable and qualified. After Randolph County started examining teachers, Worth served on almost every examining committee. At one time he and A. J. Hale were the only members. They graded the teachers from "1" to "5" in six categories—spelling, reading, writing, arithmetic, grammar, and geography—before issuing the teacher his certificate. The committee had also to report the details of each school term to the Chairman of the Board of Superintendents before the teacher could draw his salary.[38] Because it was so difficult to secure qualified teachers, Governor Charles Manly recommended that the counties employ more women, whose "soft and gentle manners, purer morals, greater tact in instructing young children and taming the wild and stubborn, fit them in a peculiar degree for this office."[39] The superintendents in Randolph apparently heeded the Governor's advice, for the number of female teachers in the county jumped from one in 1853 to eleven in 1855; during the latter year forty-six males were licensed to teach in Randolph.

Under Worth's school law of 1841, the common school system grew rapidly, but it suffered many growing pains, and the legislature was forced to experiment constantly with new methods. Governor Manly, who was probably the most education-minded chief executive of the ante-bellum period in North Carolina, painted a dark picture of the condition of the public schools in his message to the legislature of 1850. The roadsides were dotted with deserted schoolhouses, their appearance marred by broken doors and tall grass growing in the school yards; children of the wealthy were going "elsewhere" to school; children of the poor stayed at home to help with farm work; and "a general listlessness prevails."[40]

Most of the problems could be traced to one glaring flaw in the system, the absence of a strong central authority to formulate school policy and co-ordinate the efforts of subordinate officials throughout the state. Worth had recognized this basic weakness as early as 1846, when he wrote to the President and Directors of the Literary Fund that "the system is working pretty well in this county—but a general superintendent for state ought to be appointed, to supervise and regulate the system."[41] Finally, thirteen years after the passage of the original school law and eleven years after Worth began outlining the mechanics of the system, the legislature created the office of General Superintendent of Common Schools and elected one of its members, Calvin H. Wiley, a novelist-lawyer from Greensboro, to be the first incumbent. Under his leadership the system developed into probably the most effective one in the South. Worth worked closely with Wiley, who was his personal friend as well as his immediate superior in the business of school administration. Sometimes he complained of the tiresome paper work involved in his job, frequently he made suggestions to the general superintendent about how the administration of the schools might be improved, but on the whole Worth was delighted as he observed the realization of Archibald Murphey's dream that some day North Carolina would cease to be a land of ignorance.

· V ·

The Politics of Failure

———•·•———

WHEN WORTH RETURNED to Asheboro after serving his third term in the state legislature, he was returning to the obligations of private life that were to occupy his time for the next seventeen years, for it was not until 1858 that he went back to Raleigh to serve his people through the trying years of the Civil War and Reconstruction. The years from 1841 to 1861 were his happiest ones. The struggles of the young lawyer and politician were behind Worth and the golden years of life as country gentleman, farmer, lawyer, and merchant lay ahead of him as he rode home to Martitia and the children in January, 1841.

He did not immediately give up his ambitions to serve the state as a public officer, but waited to forego the excitements of active campaigning until he had been beaten in two campaigns for a seat in the United States House of Representatives. These races, one in 1841 and the other in 1845, demonstrate some of Worth's methods as a practical politician and his intense devotion to the principles of the Whig Party.

Early in 1841, Worth began considering whether he should run for Congress against Abram Rencher, a Whig who had represented Randolph, Rowan, Chatham, Davie, and Davidson counties in the House of Representatives from 1829 to 1839, when he was defeated by Charles Fisher of Salisbury, the most powerful Democrat in the district. Fisher decided not to run again in 1841 and lured Worth into a battle with Rencher by promising him that the Democrats would not run a candidate if he came out against Rencher. The Democratic Congressman also supplied Worth with some campaign ammunition: a copy of a letter from Rencher to "a thorough nullifier" which was supposed to prove that Rencher could not be relied upon, and a statement that the former Whig Congressman had collected almost a thousand dollars of taxpayers' money by falsifying the number of miles he had traveled back and forth to Washington between 1829 and 1839.[1] It was Fisher's "candid opinion" that Worth could beat Rencher or any other Whig who might be a candidate. Fortified with Fisher's promises and half convinced that Rencher was not a sincere disciple of Henry Clay, Worth came to the decision to oppose his fellow Whig. He then secured from the sergeant at arms of the national House of Representatives a true copy of the payments to Rencher for mileage while Rencher had served as a member of Congress; the statement showed that Worth's opponent had listed the distance from his home in Chatham County to Washington as four hundred thirty miles.

Some of Worth's friends were disturbed by his decision to run against Rencher, feeling that an intra-party battle would do the Whigs more harm than good. One of them told Worth plainly that Rencher would beat him, explaining that Rencher had got a head start in the campaign and that as a result of his longer political experience he was better acquainted with the voters. Furthermore, Worth's adviser insisted, the alliance with Charles Fisher would be harmful, since "anything that savors of Fisherism is odious and consequently unpopular."[2] By the time Worth got this sound advice he was already too deeply involved in the campaign to withdraw his candidacy.

The election of Congressmen was scheduled for the second week in May—unusually early that year because a special session had been called and the members had to be chosen before it convened. Rencher began making speeches throughout the district about the first of April. Later in the month he and Worth traveled together from one county court to another engaging in joint debates and discussions.[3] In his speeches Rencher explained that he had not campaigned against Charles Fisher because he had been in bad health and that he had supported Harrison instead of Clay for the Presidency in 1840 because he felt that the general had a better chance to win than the leader of the party. He advocated the repeal of the Independent Treasury Act passed in 1840, rechartering a national bank, and the continuation of a moderate tariff.[4]

Rencher, by advocating a program which would have been approved by Henry Clay himself and which was essentially the same as Worth's, took all the sting out of Worth's charges that he was not a constant Whig. This forced Worth to begin an attack on Rencher

himself, rather than the policies he favored. He published the copy
of Rencher's letter which had been supplied by Charles Fisher in an
effort to prove that Rencher had remained neutral in the presidential
campaign of 1840. He maintained, in a circular published two weeks
before the election, that Rencher's friends had not reported fairly
the proceedings of a district convention at Asheboro on April 12, at
which there was strong opposition to Rencher's becoming the Whig
candidate.[5]

Worth considered Fisher's allegation that Rencher had collected for
excess "mileage" as a member of Congress a very serious charge "directly affecting Mr. Rencher's integrity as a public servant"—and he
told the voters so in his campaign circular. He checked the local post-
master's books and found that the distance along the mail route from
Pittsboro, near Rencher's home, to Washington was listed at 319 miles
in one book and 324 miles in another; his opponent had collected
money for a trip of 430 miles. In these figures Worth thought he
had a good case, but Rencher explained that members of Congress
were entitled to collect mileage based on the distance from their homes
to Washington by the nearest water route. Worth in reply insisted
that they were expected to base their figures on the distance along
"the most usual road," which in this case was the mail route through
Richmond and Fredericksburg. "If the law allowed a member 40
cents per mile on any route he might choose to go," Worth joked,
"it might suit some members to take shipping on the Pacific and sail
around Cape Horn to Washington."[6] Only the election could determine whether Worth had convinced the voters of Rencher's lack of
integrity. He was of course playing a dangerous game by telling the
people that they had elected an unfit man to five terms in Congress.

Five days before the voters went to the polls Worth became uneasy
about his chances of winning. He wrote to Charles Fisher on May 8,
in a letter marked "confidential," that the Democrats were not supporting him, as Fisher had expected they would. Some of Fisher's
friends did not know the Congressman was backing Worth, and the
uneasy Whig asked him to post men at the polls to inform the voters
whom Fisher was supporting—"If I don't get the Democratic vote I
shall be beaten," Worth told his powerful supporter. He reported
also that the Whig leaders were stirring up resentment against him
because of the coalition with Fisher. By some peculiar reasoning
Worth did not consider his union with Fisher a coalition, and he was

disappointed with those Whigs who had abandoned him because of the unnatural alignment with a Democrat. The Whigs, Worth said, "are determined to go against me though I should prove Rencher had pocketed fifty times more than he has."[7]

The election on May 13, 1841, proved that Worth's fears were justified, for Rencher beat him easily, winning four of the five counties in the district. It was apparent that Rencher's head start in the campaigning west of the Yadkin River had given him the advantage there, as Worth's friends had suspected it would. Randolph County stood firmly by her favorite son, giving him a substantial margin, but the neighboring counties of Davidson and Chatham threw in their lot with Rencher.[8] One of Worth's political allies in Salisbury had an explanation of the results when he notified Worth that Rencher had won there by a margin of 205 to 182: "The result is most unexpected to me but to be accounted for by the alarm of the Whigs at Fisher's support of you." The reporter noted also that "the same indefinite sort of apprehension prevailed" among the Whigs of Davie and Davidson counties.[9] Worth believed that he had lost the election because he failed to convince the people that Rencher was not firm in his attachment to the policies of Henry Clay, who was the idol of the district,[10] but it seems more likely that his defeat resulted from the unorthodox alliance with Charles Fisher and the absence of any real differences between the views of the two opposing candidates.

After his loss to Rencher in May, 1841, Worth remained active in the affairs of the North Carolina Whigs. When the party leaders of Randolph County met in November, 1843, to appoint delegates to a state convention in Raleigh on December 7, Worth was one of the three men who drew up the customary resolutions; these endorsed Henry Clay for President and William A. Graham for Governor in 1844. He was also one of the delegates to the state convention.[11] Throughout 1844, he eagerly promoted the fortunes of Clay. In July when the Whigs around Asheboro heard that a prominent Democrat, Judge Romulus M. Saunders, was planning to make an address at the next term of Superior Court they asked Worth to invite Willie P. Mangum, the leading Whig in the state, to answer Saunders publicly. In extending the invitation to Mangum, Worth explained that "great apathy prevails among the Whigs of this county" and that the Clay Club of Asheboro thought Mangum's appearance in the county would stir up enough interest to arouse them from their lethargy.[12] Worth extended the invitation at the request of the individual members of the Clay Club, who knew that he was personally acquainted with the great Whig senator. It was apparent from the invitation that he was the acknowledged leader of the Whigs in his area.

After Worth ran for Congress in 1841, the Democrats got control of the state government and redistricted the state for Congressional elections. Under the new arrangement his county was included in the fourth district with Guilford, Davidson, Montgomery, Stanly, Anson, and Richmond. The district formed a compact geographical unit, but the Whigs of Guilford County complained that the redistricting was done "with the intention to suppress the will of the people of North Carolina in the national councils, and to weaken Whig influence by means of collisions among themselves in the heavy Whig districts."[13] One of these family "collisions" occurred in 1845 when Worth again opposed another Whig, General Alfred Dockery, of Richmond County, for a seat in the national House of Representatives.

No candidate had announced his intentions to run for the House before the first week in April, 1845. At that time the men most frequently mentioned as candidates were Governor John M. Morehead, James T. Morehead, and two of Worth's colleagues in the legal profession, Ralph Gorrell and George C. Mendenhall; all four were from Guilford County. Henry B. Elliott and Worth were the prospects from Randolph and General Dockery was the likely candidate from the southern half of the district. The nomination was equivalent to election if a Whig opposed a Democrat, for the district was solidly Whig.[14]

There was some feeling in the southern half of the district against the call of a nominating convention—a device which was then relatively new and still suspected of being a tool of the professional politicians. "Procul Iste," writing in the Fayetteville *Observer*, argued that no convention should be held, certainly not at Asheboro, and that if Governor Morehead were not nominated there was bound to be a clash between two or more Whigs for the seat in Congress. The anonymous article of "Procul Iste," written in Dockery's home county, reflected a fear that the more populous northern half of the district would be dominant in a district nominating convention. The Greensboro paper was for a convention, and certain that no one would be so foolish as to oppose the nominee of a "full and fair" convention.[15]

In spite of the objections to a convention, twenty-three Whigs met in Asheboro on the seventh of May to name the official Whig candidate.[16] Sixteen of the twenty-three were from either Randolph or Guilford, although each delegation had the same number of votes as its county had members in the state House of Commons; this system gave Guilford three votes to one for Richmond. The "delegate" from Davidson County, a Mr. Long, was not a delegate from a county convention, but an interested spectator; as the only citizen from Davidson at the convention he cast the county's two votes. Two of the twenty-three delegates were Worth's brothers, but "from motives of delicacy" they did not vote after the first ballot.

Governor Morehead and Ralph Gorrell had written letters to the convention declining to run, and after these were read the selection of the nominee began. George C. Mendenhall got five votes on the first and second ballots to three for Worth, two for H. B. Elliott, and one for Dockery. Worth gained Elliott's two votes on the third ballot, tying him with Mendenhall, and Dockery retained his single vote from his home county. Finally, Worth got the vote which had formerly been cast for Dockery and was nominated over Mendenhall by six to five. At the afternoon session of the convention Worth accepted the nomination in a speech in which he said that the honor came as a surprise to him. He had not sought it, and it would require "considerable sacrifice" for him personally, but for the sake of the party he allowed his name to be presented to the voters.

Worth was clearly the choice of the leaders of the Whig Party to carry their banner into the campaign, but when General Dockery returned from a trip to the western part of the state, where he had been during the nominating convention, he announced that he was running for Congress as an independent Whig candidate. He and Worth published a schedule of joint meetings to be held throughout the district between July 15 and the date of the election in August. In addition, each candidate announced the times and places where he would appear alone; Dockery scheduled four individual speeches to Worth's two, but he cancelled one and met Worth in joint debate in Asheboro on August 5. Dockery apparently campaigned more intensively than Worth, who was busy, as usual, with his personal affairs. Five of the eight joint debates and almost all the individual appearances were in the northern half of the district.[17]

The summer of 1845 was a miserable one for political candidates.

On July 23, the temperature in Greensboro was a little over a hundred
degrees, and the sweltering editor of the *Patriot* suggested that the
local citizenry adopt Georgia's fashion of dress for hot weather,
"which is said to consist of a shirt collar and a pair of spurs."[18] In the
uncomfortable heat Worth got a dose of campaigning sufficient to last
him thirteen years.

Compared with the fierceness of the weather, the race between
Worth and Dockery was a tame affair; it was a contest between friends
and was conducted accordingly. Both men consistently advocated the
Whig program, but Dockery made the nominating convention an issue.
In a typical meeting between the two men Worth explained that he
approved the convention, while claiming that he had nothing to do
with calling it.[19] He asserted that he would not have run if he had
known there would be a contest, acknowledged Dockery to be a good
Whig, and asked the voters to select their candidate "on the ground
of their personal and public merits alone." In effect, Worth was in the
position of having to apologize for being a candidate. Dockery answered cordially that he was not opposed to nominating conventions
in general, but he criticized the one at Asheboro which had nominated
Worth, claiming that it was not fairly representative of the sentiment
of the district. The General claimed he had "in effect" entered the
race in March, that the first he heard of a convention was when he
returned from his western trip. In his discussion of public issues he
tried to instill a bit of vigor into the local party members and "sustained his character as a bold Whig." Worth then got up and apologized for running, saying he never dreamed that Dockery had expressed
an intention to run as early as March. He chided Dockery good
naturedly by surmising that Dockery would have accepted the nomination of the convention if it had been offered. "Gen. Dockery replied
that if he had come out under the nomination of that convention, he
should have considered himself a used up man."

The most interesting episode of the campaign occurred when a
man from Greensboro named George B. Crowson started a rumor that
"Jonathan Worth is in the habit of letting negroes come to his table
and then eat with them as one of his own family. . . ."[20] Crowson
claimed he derived this startling information from his brother, A. S.
Crowson, who lived in Asheboro only a few yards from Worth's house.
Verification of such a rumor could prove disastrous to a political candidate, even in 1845.

When David Caldwell, one of Worth's supporters in Greensboro, heard the tale about Worth's eating habits, he immediately took steps to put an end to it. He wrote to John Sherwood, of Asheboro, and asked him to get a certificate from A. S. Crowson denying that he had started the rumor and declaring it false. Crowson, who was not only Worth's neighbor but his personal friend as well, was quite willing to sign the following unpunctuated statement:

I understand that a report is in circulation in the county of Guilford that Jonathan Worth is in the habit of letting Negroes come to his table and that he eats with them and allso that I am referred to as being the auther of the report I hear state that I have no recollection of ever stateing or hearing any sutch thing and I am very certain that it is false come from who it may as I have lived right opposite him for better than 2 years and am certain that I should have known it if it had been the case.[21]

Sherwood, in returning Crowson's certificate to Caldwell for use in dispelling the rumor, branded the reports of Worth's fraternization with his slaves as "a low, contemptible, malicious, and wilful *lie*. . . ." No one would believe such an outrageously wild story, said Sherwood, unless he belonged to that group mentioned by Hudibras in his couplet: "Convince a man against his will, he's of the same opinion still."[22]

It is not likely that the rumor changed the opinion of many voters on election day—it was not widespread—but Worth's selection as a candidate by the Asheboro convention helped to reduce his chances of beating Dockery. Since the people were assured that a constant Whig would represent them no matter who won, many failed to vote at all; only a few ballots over 7,000 were cast in the seven counties composing the fourth district. Of this total Worth received 3,135 to his opponent's 4,078, winning only two counties and four of eleven precincts. The Greensboro paper explained the result by noting that "the fact of Mr. Worth's nomination by a convention was made to bear against him to an extent which influenced a number of votes."[23] Worth's weakness as a public speaker also weighed against him on the political balance, as Dockery evidently got the better of him in their joint debates. At the three polling places where they spoke together and for which specific results are known, Dockery won by 119 to 30, 74 to 41, and 84 to 33. Needless to say, the collision between two staunch Whigs delighted the Democrats, one of whom reported to

Democratic President James K. Polk that "in the next district . . . the regular Whig nominee (Worth) is defeated by Gen. Dockery—This will produce some family jars hard to reconcile."[24]

The president's informant overstated the facts, for the two Whigs remained on good terms and the district continued to scorn Democratic candidates for public office. But after the "family jar" of 1845, Worth never again became a candidate for Congress against either Whig or Democrat; twice was enough.

· VI ·

Among Family and Friends

———•———

THE BEST THING THAT WAS LEFT to posterity from Worth's two unsuccessful campaigns for a seat in Congress was a pen portrait of him written by an unidentified person who had observed him in a debate with Abram Rencher during the campaign of 1841. When the editor of the Greensboro *Patriot* published the sketch, he commented that it was drawn with "extraordinary truth"; it was certainly the best description of Jonathan Worth ever written by one of his contemporaries. Here, then, is Worth as he appeared in 1841, a few months before his thirty-ninth birthday:

Mr. W——, . . . is short in stature and stoops in the shoulders. His arms are short, with a hand of short fingers. He seems not to have bestowed a thought on the acquirement of the graces of attitued [sic] or gesture; perhaps because his good sense informed him it would be labor lost on a physical frame so ill adapted by nature for the pleasing exhibition of these oratorical accomplishments. His voice is any thing but melody. His lungs seem to have very little to do with the business of speaking: his articulation appears to be produced by some machinery placed in the neighborhood of the *glotis,* and altogether incapable of being modulated into anything like emphasis or cadence. Yet, with this strange machinery alone, directed by an acute and penetrating mind, he is enabled to produce considerable effect on his hearers. Mr. W's head is large, covered with a suit of jet black hair, with a dark grey eye sunk deep under a fine forehead. I am no phrenologist . . . but I look upon his as a calculating head.—He seems indeed to possess wonderful facility in subjecting every thing to the test of his arithmetical standard. Whether the subject have reference to finances, space and distance, time or locality, things present or things past, all must submit to this yankee process of calculation, and receive from his plastic hand the apparent impress of critical accuracy and rigid economy.[1]

The writer was being satirical when he spoke of Worth's calculating mind; he obviously had reference to the attack on Rencher's collection of excess money for mileage, to which Worth had indeed devoted considerable calculation. Yet, in spinning his satire, the observer caught sight of the arithmetical quality of a mind that dealt with the affairs of daily life in terms of their most minute details. His observation that Worth insisted on critical accuracy and rigid economy was constantly being proved by the methodical habits of the man he was describing.

Worth was indeed the type of man who kept his eye on every penny that came into his hands or even passed his way. His accounts were kept very carefully; it is possible to examine them for hours without finding an error. When a merchant tried to overcharge him he would protest, question whether the price was not exorbitant, and ask for an explanation—and a reduction.[2] He believed in saving everything. If the pages of his letter book stuck together, causing him to leave a blank page, he would write on it later. This sometimes got his letters out of order, but it saved a sheet of paper.

His Quaker frugality was only one characteristic of a many-sided, complex personality. It never quite developed into parsimony, but, on the contrary, was balanced by a warm generosity and the open-handed hospitality that was expected of Southern gentlemen—and almost ruined some of them. He frequently showered his daughters with such expensive gifts as silver sets and sofas, and less expensive items like subscriptions to *Harper's Magazine*. In 1858, he told brothers Clarkson and Barzillai that he wished "to buy for Roxana a cotton gin and screw to be worked by water power of sufficient size to pick her cotton and that of her neighbors."[3] Roxana had married John McNeill in 1848 and had three fine daughters, but when her husband "fell suddenly and died in a few hours" in March, 1857, she and the children came back to Asheboro to live with her parents, and Worth worked for many years to settle the McNeill estate.[4] His generosity extended far beyond the immediate family to cousins, in-laws, and nephews. Mrs. Worth had a sister, Lucy Baldwin, who lived in Willimantic, Connecticut. After Lucy's husband died, Worth made elaborate arrangements for her to come for a visit, paid her expenses, and arranged for an escort and the shipment of her baggage. He then invited her and her children to stay permanently at the Worth home in Asheboro.[5]

Several times Worth helped establish his relatives in business and tried to keep them out of debt by fending off their creditors and lending them large sums of money. It was in this way that he became instrumental in setting up the drug store in Greensboro that later became famous as the boyhood haunt of the writer O. Henry, whose real name was William Sidney Porter. Worth helped his nephew, Dr. A. S. Porter, out of debt in 1852 after he had failed as a druggist. Porter's friends wanted to see him get a fresh start, but none of them was willing to supplement good wishes with cash loans. Worth came to his rescue and set him up in another "apothecary shop" by lending him a thousand dollars to buy his stock.[6]

There were occasions when Worth's generosity to his nephews ended in misfortune. In the early fifties he set up David Porter and a man named Hatfield Ogden in the business of carriage making. David had no skill in building carriages, and Ogden was brought in as a partner because he could supply this deficiency. "Ogden spent more in furniture and the expenses of his family than his income warranted —took his wife's sister to live with him—got her with child—of course producing strife with his wife—and ran away to avoid his creditors and the frowns of the community."[7] He had spent more than his half of the firm's earnings. But in spite of all Ogden's shortcomings Worth helped clear up his affairs after he left the country—keeping his communication with the departed carriage maker a secret. Five years later the carriage business was again in financial trouble. Worth checked the books of the firm and, believing it to be worth more than it owed, helped it with money. The largest creditor failed and Worth lost a large part of what he had loaned the firm; there was little prospect of getting it back. Worth asked his nephew's creditors to hold off because "he is industrious and sober, but has a rising family to support requiring all his earnings."[8]

Worth always sought to stay on good terms with everybody he knew, for he was a peaceable man who disliked personal controversy. When he had offended a man, or thought maybe he had, he usually made an apology and expressed regret that amicable relations had been disturbed. An instance of this occurred in 1850, just after Worth had argued a case in court involving his friend John B. Troy. Someone, in a talk with Troy, misrepresented one of Worth's remarks made during the trial and Troy wrote to Worth asking for an explanation. Worth replied: "I have not now and never had an unkind feeling

towards you and deeply regret that anything should have occurred on
the trial to wound your feelings. I am confident you misapplied the
remarks to which you refer."[9] Another time Worth tried to repair a
friendship with J. M. Coffin, a friend who suspected him of luring away
one of his overseers and some of his field hands. Worth denied that
he had done this, told Coffin that he had expressed his unwillingness
to hire the overseer without Coffin's consent, and explained that he had
made it clear to the overseer that he was not to bring any of the laborers
when he came to work for Worth.[10]

Throughout his life Worth was forced to indulge in a mild form
of duplicity in order to maintain his good relations with his friends,
neighbors, and fellow politicians. Frequently persons would ask him
for his opinion of some other individual with whom he was well acquainted. Upon receiving such an inquiry he sat down and wrote an
objective evaluation, but if he had anything unpleasant to say about
the person he was describing he would ask the inquirer to keep such
remarks to himself. The following letter, quoted in full, illustrates his
desire to stay in the good graces of those with whom he came in contact. The subject of the letter managed the hotel where Worth boarded
when he attended court in Montgomery County.

Thomas C. Holtsam, of Troy, Montgomery County, N.C., starts
North in a day or two to buy goods and has requested me to say to
you that he is good for any reasonable bill—I think he is worth from
$5000. to $10,000. more than he owes and his property consists of a
Hotel in Troy and other real estate, and negroes:—He is what our ex-
centric [sic] friend Geo. C. Mendenhall calls "our blessed landlord"
and for this reason I would not incur his displeasure, but I desire
in justice to you to tell the *whole* truth—He acquired his property
by inheritance—He is intemperate, gambles moderately—is a great fool
and has no business qualifications—and if he lives a few years, will fail
—I think the bills he may make this trip will be paid but probably after
suit.

If you decline to credit him, please put your refusal on grounds
which will leave me all right with our "blessed landlord."[11]

Worth's judgment of Holtsam appears to have been sound, for six
months later the innkeeper was being pressed by his creditors—and
Worth was defending him in court.

In his home life Worth was a model husband and father; no wife
and children could have desired a better man to love them and to
watch over and protect their interests. The family lived in a com-

fortably large two-story frame house on the highest hill in Asheboro. Outside was a large yard filled with shade trees and surrounded by a neat picket fence that seemed designed to help shut off the premises from the world. Inside, there were large, well-furnished rooms, carpeted floors, and several fireplaces, before which the Worths could spend the long evenings of winter. The smoke from their cheerful fires escaped through three ivy-covered chimneys and drifted through the bare branches of a giant tree that seemed to stand as a guardian over the house.

The size of the family grew, as Jonathan and Martitia had eight children over the twenty year period from 1826 to 1846. After Martitia gave birth to "the little twains," David and Louisa, in December, 1831, while Jonathan was away in Raleigh, four more daughters came: Elvira Evelina in 1836; Sarah Corinna in January, 1839; Adelaide Ann in December, 1842; and Mary Martitia in September, 1846. By the time Mary was born, Roxana, the oldest child, was about ready to get married; she wedded John McNeill in April, 1848. The next two daughters after Roxana to get husbands were Lucy, the second daughter, and Elvira, who married two brothers from Chatham County, Joseph John and Samuel Spencer Jackson, in 1849 and 1856, respectively. David married Julia Stickney, the teacher at Randolph Female Academy, a few days after he graduated from the University of North Carolina in 1853.[12]

The bonds of affection between "Pa" and "Mama," as the parents were invariably called, and the children, and between the children themselves, were uncommonly strong. This may be seen in one of the few extant family letters from the period before the children were grown and married. Written by Lucy Jane to David, who was away in school at Lexington, it gives a few glimpses into the everyday life of the Worths: Mama was recovering from some household accident, but Lucy had been deeply concerned about her; Uncle Milton had eaten dinner at the house on his way to the North last Saturday; the chemistry lesson at the Academy was excessively long and difficult; and Mama was sending some sweetcakes to improve on the menu at David's school. The letter, like most of those written by the Worth girls to each other and to David, was signed "Your affectionate Sister."[13]

Acting as patriarch and family conciliator among his wife and children, Worth frequently displayed his skill in the delicate art of human relations, a talent which served him well in public as well as private life. When two of David's children died in 1858, David was offended because he thought his sister Corinna had not displayed her grief in the manner expected under such circumstances. Corinna was deeply hurt when she discovered that David was offended by the passivity of her actions. Worth tried to assure David that "she makes no ostentatious display of her kind feelings, but they exist with her as strongly as any of your sisters." Corinna wrote David two letters in an effort to restore friendly feelings between them but David refused to answer. His father scolded him for his refusal in words which give a great deal of insight into Worth's relations not only with his children but with other men as well: "You should have answered her —If she has not succeeded in making a satisfactory explanation you should have given her kind admonition—If she explained satisfactorily, you should have said so."[14] The type of straightforward, plain speaking he urged on his son in a situation involving only members of his own family was characteristic of Worth's own dealings with his fellow men, and a quality he greatly admired.

Worth was a man who greatly deplored suffering; he could not bear to see or hear anyone in pain. Once when his daughter Louisa was painfully ill he wrote a long letter to the best doctor he knew, a specialist in Philadelphia, asking for advice. The local doctor was doing all he could to help the girl, but his treatment seemed to produce more harm than good, and Worth objected to its use. He begged the eminent doctor for relief for his screaming daughter. Louisa had been ill for a long time when her suffering became intense late in 1851. Her case seemed to be "within the reach of remedies," but Worth could not submit to the severe one being used, or would not without an opinion from Philadelphia sustaining it. He spent a great deal of money and declared himself willing to exhaust his resources to cure Louisa,[15] but in spite of everything he and the doctors could do, Louisa died at the age of twenty on February 2, 1852, and was buried in the town cemetery near the Worth home. Worth noted in his Bible that she died of consumption, but it was apparent from some of the symptoms he described to the doctor in Philadelphia that her pain came from what was then euphemistically referred to as "female trouble," possibly a cancer of the womb.

The doctor who had treated Louisa before Worth began writing to Philadelphia expressed concern after her death that the Worths had lost confidence in him. Jonathan denied any loss of confidence, but explained that his hopes for his daughter's survival had been raised by letters from Mrs. Worth and Louisa herself. The death came as a greater shock than it would have otherwise—for shattered hope is worse than no hope at all. "You must not suppose," Worth said, "that myself or wife or any member of my family entertain any unkind feeling towards you."[16]

The death of Louisa Worth produced another incident that helps reveal the man who was her father. When he began writing desperately to Philadelphia the doctor there prescribed cod liver oil—among other medicines—but it was not available and Worth sent to Philadelphia for it; since there was no apothecary shop in Asheboro, other prescriptions had to come from Greensboro. Nine months after Louisa died, the cod liver oil had not reached Asheboro, but Worth was trying to find out what had happened to it. After he found that it had been shipped by Adams Express Company and delayed in Richmond,[17] he never forgave the express company, and he used other means of transportation when they were available.

Worth reared his children in a way that enabled him to place great confidence in their moral character and judgment when they no longer had the guidance of their parents close at hand. When Adelaide, for example, left Asheboro to attend Oakland Female Institute in Norristown, Pennsylvania, her father wrote to the Reverend Grier Ralston, the master of the Institute, to "let her have money whenever she wants it. . . . I am opposed to extravagant expenditures and desire that she may use no more money than may be necessary for her comfort and making her feel that she is not inferior in dress. etc. to your pupils generally." Worth also authorized the headmaster to allow Adelaide to go into Philadelphia or wherever else she wanted to go, but he hoped that she would remain on the campus if she needed to study. "She has always been a dutiful and discreet child and I have no fears that she would in any way act improperly out of your school during vacation," the father concluded.[18]

As the head of a large and ever increasing family, Worth was always ready to give out words of encouragement and advice, and it pleased him greatly when they were remembered and followed. After he made some remarks emphasizing the value of punctuality to one of his sons-in-law he promised that "If you act on them and live to have my experience you will still more value and approve them"; he also encouraged the young man to read Robert Burns's advice on the subject and to commit it to memory.[19] Another virtue he admired and advised his children to follow was perfect candor in their dealings with others, especially when personal feelings were involved.

Not all the people who lived on Worth's home place were white, and those who were black were of course not members of the family by blood, but no discussion of the Worth family would be complete without some mention of slaves and slavery. In many ways the bonds between the Worths and their Negroes were stronger than the legal tie that bound them to each other. Adelaide once wrote David that Roxana had brought on a visit a three-year-old Negro girl. "You can ask her who she belongs to and who she loves she will say she loves Miss Martitia and belongs to her. . . . She is a great amusement for us children. . . . She will not leave Ma hardly one minute, she cried because she wanted to go to church with her on Sunday, her name is Francis."[20] From such comments as this it is clear that the legal relationship of superior-inferior was clearly understood, but there is no indication that Worth ever took advantage of his legal superiority in a manner harmful to his slaves.

The number of slaves Worth owned increased gradually from 1830 to 1860, but, like most of the people in his section of the state, he never acquired many; only 10 per cent of the population of Randolph County consisted of slaves, while the figure for the nearby counties of Guilford, Davidson, and Forsyth was less than 20 per cent.[21] Worth himself reported only one slave to the census taker in 1830, but as his financial status improved and he acquired more lands he could buy more Negroes. By 1850, the number had grown to ten, six of whom were males and four females.[22] The total had reached fourteen before the Civil War came, but of this number five were over fifty years old, one was blind, and two were children; two were mulattoes, the others black.[23]

It would not be surprising if Worth, because of his Quaker ancestry and environment, had been an opponent of slavery instead of a slaveholder. One possible explanation of the fact that he did buy slaves and work them on his farms and in his household is that the Quakers of North Carolina had adopted the practice, peculiar to that state, of holding slaves under a system by which certain individuals held the slaves as agents of the church. The slaves were virtually free, although legally they retained the status of slaves. Judge William Gaston advised the Quakers on the legality of the system they devised, and it lasted until the Civil War.[24] In effect, this legal device sanctioned slaveholding—so long as it was beneficent and humane. Worth did not hold his Negroes as an agent of the church, but it was easy to rationalize his buying and selling slaves when his mother's church was doing the same thing, and when his treatment of his slaves was humane. He taught them to read and write, or had them taught—in violation of a law forbidding instruction of Negroes which he had opposed in the legislature in 1830. After the war he corresponded with his former slaves, in mostly friendly letters about members of the family. It would be impossible to determine which of his incoming letters were from the Negroes he had owned if he had not put such an endorsement as this on them: "Stephen (of color)."[25]

Whenever Worth needed to sell a slave he tried to find a buyer who would be suitable to the slave being sold. When he sold some land in 1860, and no longer needed all his men, he offered to sell Wiley, whom he described as "oldish, rheumatic, a fair rock mason," for $650, or Jordan for seven hundred dollars, or Julius for $850. He expressed his unwillingness to sell Julius, who was "an uncommonly desirable servant," unless he consented to change masters;[26] when Julius expressed a desire to remain in the family, Worth sold him to his son David. About the same time, he sold a slave named Emanuel to the man who owned Emanuel's wife. When the new owner complained that Emanuel was unable to work after he arrived at his new home, Worth explained that Emanuel was in good health but that "he was greatly elated at getting to his wife and I expect walked too fast."[27] This dead-serious explanation was probably as correct as it was unconsciously humorous, for Worth tried to keep his Negroes in good health. When one of them, a girl thirteen or fourteen years old, was going blind from the effects of scrofula, he wrote to one doctor and proposed that he treat the girl on "no cure, no pay" terms, and asked the doctor to hurry, "as I propose to consult or send her to some skilful occulist [sic] soon."[28]

Although Worth himself was kind to his slaves and took good care of them, he sometimes had trouble with overseers who were not as gentle as they might have been. Once Worth hired some of Mrs. Ann Alston's slaves and some of them complained to her that Worth's overseer had used "undue severity" with them. Worth had learned earlier that the slaves were satisfied with his foreman, but he had his son-in-law, Sam Jackson, to investigate the complaint after Mrs. Alston inquired about it. Then he assured the owner of the slaves that "they shall be well treated in all things."[29] Six months later he had to relieve the overseer of his position for hitting a slave with an ax. One can see Worth's self-interest struggling with his humane spirit in his decision to "fire" the overseer, who was essential to the success of a turpentine distillery he was then operating.[30]

As Worth's slaves became older and more burdensome and as it began to appear to him that the institution of slavery was about to be used as a pretext for dissolving the federal union, he began to doubt whether slavery was really as valuable as its defenders asserted it was. The following business note reveals Worth's emerging doubt, as well as the deep concern he almost invariably displayed for the personal happiness of the people he owned: "I have thought for some time past that I never would buy another negro at any price, but your boy Daniel and my woman Eliza seem to be so much attached and importune me so much that I have concluded to offer you $1200 for Daniel. . . . I sold one lately, quite as good a smith as Daniel, much larger and about the same age, at $1400. . . . I do this only to keep him and his wife together."[31]

Notwithstanding the fact that Worth was beset with doubts about the institution of slavery, he never reached the point of condemning it openly as a feature of the social and economic system of the South. Influenced by his relations with his own slaves, which give the lie to the ugly picture of slavery painted by the abolitionists, it was easy for him to look upon the South's peculiar institution as an arrangement which was beneficial not only to masters but to their slaves as well.

· VII ·

Lawyer and Businessman

DURING THE DECADE of the 1850's, Jonathan Worth was an extremely busy man. He spent much of his time with legal matters as a full-time practicing lawyer and as Clerk and Master in Equity of the superior court. Various business ventures—merchandising, mining, distilling turpentine—and farming consumed large portions of his time. He was still Superintendent of Common Schools for Randolph County, and after 1856, he carried the additional burden of being General Superintendent of the Fayetteville and Western Plank Road, the ribbon of pine that finally linked Asheboro with Fayetteville. As if he did not have enough to occupy his time, he campaigned for a seat in the state Senate in 1858 and served another term at Raleigh. Two months after this busy decade ended he wrote to his friend J. M. A. Drake: "You know I have had more to do than I could well perform for years—Four months of last year consumed in electioneering and service in the legislature imposed on me more than I could do—I have not yet got up."[1]

While Worth was engaged in a variety of enterprises and activities, it was as a lawyer that he spent most of his time and earned most of his money, for the law was his basic occupation. The County Courts of Pleas and Quarter Sessions met four times each year and the superior court judges visited each county twice a year to hear the cases which were above the jurisdiction of the county courts. Like most other lawyers of his day, Worth rode about from one county and superior court to another, which was possible because the courts were held in successive weeks within a judicial district. In May, 1858, for example, he had to be in Randolph County for the first week of the month, at Fayetteville the second week, and at Harnett County court on the third Monday. He was frequently gone from home for weeks at a time, and his family sometimes worried about him; riding the circuit on horseback was always strenuous and sometimes dangerous. Lucy Jane wrote to David in 1846 that "Papa started to Salisbury court yesterday morning he will not be at home before the last of the week. I fear he had an unpleasant ride yesterday the wind blew very hard. I expect the Yadkin was so high that he could not cross. I hope not though."[2] But in spite of the swollen rivers, the hard work, and the long absences from his family, Worth visited the county and superior courts regularly until 1862.

The territory in which he practiced varied from year to year, but it always included Randolph County. He did not begin going to the courts of Moore and Montgomery counties until about 1855, but he rode as far west as Rowan and as far south as Cumberland at one time or another. He would accept claims for the collection of debts, when a creditor held a note, for any county in the state, provided the creditor would sign the note or notes over to him. In this way Worth could sue for collection in the quarterly courts of the various counties. But in cases where the notes were held against men who could not be sued, or in the case of persons with an open account, he would accept collection suits only in Cumberland, Harnett, Moore, Montgomery, and Randolph counties. These were the counties in which he attended court most frequently and where he had contacts extensive enough to make the difficult collection cases easier.[3]

Somewhat handicapped by his natural diffidence and his inability to expound in the grand fashion of some of his contemporary lawyers, Worth developed a simple and direct courtroom manner that was effective and suited the personality of the lawyer himself. This manner, which was similar to that of his teacher, Murphey—though not nearly as powerful—was best described by Marmaduke S. Robbins, a schoolteacher and lawyer from Asheboro who knew Worth for many years and served with him in the legislature:

He was not generally regarded as a very eloquent advocate, as the phrase has it; . . . though less noisy and ostentatious, he had a method of addressing a jury that was probably quite as effective in influencing them. He was not tedious nor elaborate as most of his brother attorneys; but was plain, straight, and so pointed that no one need fail to understand his reasoning, and the result to which it led. This, together with his well recognized honesty, integrity and truthfulness known to belong to him, gave him an influence with both jury and court, probably not inferior to any other lawyer . . . in the courts of this county.[4]

Worth made up for his lack of eloquence and legal brilliance by close attention to the details of the cases he managed and by jealously guarding the interests of his clients. Once when he represented a man named Richie in a suit against Trinity College, Braxton Craven, the president of the college, asked him to postpone the case until the next term of court. Worth was surprised at Craven, who was a minister, for asking him to do such a thing, for in a lawyer's view it would constitute a breach of fidelity to his client. He told Craven the proper course would be to ask the plaintiff, instead of his attorney, for a continuance of the case.[5]

When Worth failed to win a case, he was not inclined to give up the fight if he thought a judgment had been wrong. When he lost a case in 1858 involving the Virginia common law because Judge Romulus M. Saunders ruled that he had cited an irrelevant precedent, he wrote to one of his friends, an able lawyer, asking for advice and giving the details of the case. He also wrote to a lawyer in Virginia for information, declaring: "I intend to be better prepared next trial."[6] After Judge Saunders made the adverse ruling, Worth continued the case from one term of court to another, hoping that Saunders might be replaced by another judge who would see the matter differently.

Many suits handled by Worth in the courts dragged out over several months, and sometimes for years. In August, 1858, he obtained a judgment in the county court in the case of *Hamlin* vs. *Hamlin*. The judgment was appealed to the fall term of superior court, scheduled for September, but since the docket was heavily loaded Worth informed his client that the case was not likely to be heard before the spring term, March, 1859. "I expect to get the money," Worth said, "but the Lord only can tell when. They will postpone as long as possible."[7] In the 1850's, the great delay in getting suits through the superior courts caused many people to make assignments of debts due to them to other persons so that jurisdiction could pass to the county courts. This method of securing judgment took only half the time required to collect a debt by means of a suit in a superior court, and Worth suggested to Ralph Gorrell, who was then in the legislature, "whether it would not be better so to amend the act [on assignments] that we may do directly what we now do by indirection."[8]

The suggestion was characteristic of Worth's dislike of the indirect approach to any problem, whether it was a complex legal case, or the simplest relation of his daily life. He liked to get things done without any wasted time or effort.

By far the largest part of Worth's work as a lawyer was in cases in which he was hired to collect debts due to merchants and businessmen. This was important in the formation of his political and social views, for it brought him into frequent contact with men of property, with whose interests he had to identify himself, and with whom he naturally was in sympathy because he too was a merchant and businessman. Collecting debts was onerous, since much of the business of the ante-bellum period was conducted by the use of informal notes. These were plain, unprinted slips of paper specifying in writing a principal, a date due, and the amount of interest to be paid. Transactions with them became quite complicated, for they were negotiable instruments and sometimes had several endorsers. It could be a minor research project to trace the history of a single note.

One of Worth's most interesting debt collection cases involving the use of notes was one in which a firm in New York hired him to collect $250.74 from a storekeeper named D. P. Clark. Clark could not pay when Worth called on him, but he held notes on his customers sufficient to cover part of the debt to the wholesaler in New York. Worth had him endorse these notes, which were small enough to be collected in a proceeding before a justice of the peace, and then placed the claims into the hands of the proper court official for collection. Worth did this because he believed there was a better chance of collecting the amounts due from Clark's debtors than from Clark himself. The most remarkable aspect of the transaction is that all the parties involved had given notes, and the small debtors ended up owing money to a mercantile firm in New York instead of to the local store.[9] Many small business men in the South became indebted to northern merchants, and as a consequence probably half of Worth's clients were wholesalers in Philadelphia or New York City. As a result of his law practice and his own business affairs he built up extensive connections in those cities, and he visited them in the intervals between court sessions.

Normal procedure in debt collection cases was for the creditor to turn the papers certifying the debt over to Worth, who tallied up the debt, including notes and interest, and deducted his commission, arriving at the total amount due to the creditor. The debtor then made payment directly to Worth, rather than sending it to the firm demanding payment. The lawyer was at the same time trustee for the debtor and business agent of the creditor. For these services Worth's fee was usually 5 per cent of what he collected. If his commission was unusually large he would explain how he had arrived at the figure, and sometimes he apologized to his clients for taking so long to secure judgments in their favor; to one he said, "I have used the utmost diligence and more than earned the commission charged."[10]

Worth had to be a fair student of human behavior in order to handle collection cases most effectively. He studied the character and habits of those against whom he was acting before he made a move, and from his observations he gained a knowledge of men and their actions and thoughts that was extremely valuable to him not only in his law practice but in his career as a politician. If a man was very conscious of his status in a community, Worth was reluctant to sue him, but would use the threat of a lawsuit in such a way as to induce the debtor to pay off. "It is very seldom," he once explained to an impatient creditor, "that the interests of the creditors are best subserved by legal process. The dread of it or some other means are almost always more efficient."[11] Because of the differences he found between individual men, Worth did not always follow a set procedure in the cases he handled, but asked his clients to allow him wide discretion as to what steps should be followed when the outcome of a suit was doubtful.

Worth never made a large fortune by practicing law, but he earned enough to support his family comfortably and had some left over for investments in land and various business enterprises. Although it is impossible to ascertain his total income from his legal practice, it is possible to determine the amount of his salaries and fees for a few sessions of court; these varied widely. At the term of court held in Montgomery County in July, 1859, he earned a hundred and sixty dollars for his week of work, but at the court in Montgomery during February of the next year he collected only thirty-five dollars for his services. From ten sessions of court in Randolph and Montgomery counties between July, 1859 and April, 1860, his total salaries and fees amounted to $878, an average for each court of $87.80.[12]

Worth continued to practice law up to the very eve of the Civil War as if nothing unusual were going on in the world about him.

After the firing on Fort Sumter he was still communicating with his clients in the North and looking after their interests in North Carolina. Many of them were deeply concerned about the controversy long before any fighting started. Worth assured one firm in New York City whom he represented: "You will have your usual trade from this quarter for the present, but if you would keep up friendly relations, remove our just grounds of suspicion by electing conservative men to Congress and to your legislature."[13] He of course lost his Northern clientele when the war broke out in earnest, but he continued to practice on a limited scale throughout the war period. Shortly before the beginning of the sectional conflict he took his son-in-law, Sam Jackson, into the law business as a partner, and when it became necessary for him to remain in Raleigh after he was appointed Public Treasurer, Jackson remained in Asheboro to manage the large practice his father-in-law had built up by forty years of diligent effort.

Although Worth's profession was that of the lawyer, he was at heart a businessman. From the time he bought his first acre of land when he was in his early twenties to the day he died he never lost interest in the business world in general and his own numerous enterprises in particular. His mind was so constantly filled with the details of his own private affairs that one is forced to wonder how he found so much time to cope with the problems of other people. In fact, he was so deeply engaged in business by 1850 that he was sometimes forced to neglect his law practice.

Worth secured his first license to operate a general merchandise business in 1835, but little is known of his early ventures as a merchant. In 1846, he ran a series of advertisements in the *Randolph Herald* that show something of the variety of his enterprises at that time. One of his advertisements announced the dissolution of a partnership in general merchandising with his brother Addison, asked the customers to pay off their debts at May court, and announced the receipt of goods which would be sold for either cash or produce. There was an indication of Worth's conservatism where money was concerned in his notice to his customers that "we have not promised long term credits to our customers because we knew we could not give such credits."[14] A second advertisement informed the readers of the *Herald* that Worth had hired a blacksmith, Hiram Elliott, to work at his shop in Asheboro, and that produce would be received in payment for the smith's work. Worth had purchased some unfinished buggies, wagons, and carriages from the carriage shop of William Lawrence, which were to be finished by a skilled workman and sold. He also had some rosewood and mahogany, from which he would make furniture to order. In addition to carriage materials and furniture, he sold such items as New Orleans molasses, Kings Mountain iron and castings, number one mackerel, and coffee from Rio.[15]

The partnership with brother Addison that Worth mentioned in his advertisements was closed in September, 1850; it had begun in November, 1844, run a little over a year, closed temporarily, and then commenced again in March, 1846. Addison performed the actual operations of the business, selling the merchandise and keeping some of the accounts. For these services to the partnership he collected a salary before the profits were divided. Jonathan calculated that the actual profits from the venture were $3,081.56, an amount he thought very good, "considering that we traded on borrowed capital."[16]

Worth took great pains to make sure the partnership was closed on equitable terms. He had provided the house in which the store operated, a clerk for the firm and his board, and various legal services. Each partner was responsible for the transactions he had made. It turned out that Addison owed the firm money when the partnership was closed, as indicated in the close-out agreement Jonathan asked him to sign:

On a final settlement of the firm of J. and J. A. Worth this day made it appears that my profits are $1027.18 of which sum $1,022.79 are to be placed to my credit on the books of the firm to balance my account, and the remaining $4.39 I have this day received. J. Worth is to pay the remaining outstanding debts of the firm including two bonds to Jesse Harper amounting to $1500. principal money; and he is to retain to his own use all he can collect of the remaining debts due to the firm. This 12 day of Sept. 1850.[17]

After Addison signed this agreement he still owed his brother $1,649.45 on notes and sums he had borrowed, and Jonathan asked for a note covering this amount. The business closed with the brothers on good terms, although Addison naturally was disappointed that his returns were almost nonexistent. The story of the partnership, if it shows anything, shows that Worth was at least a better businessman than his brother Addison, that his business relations with his brothers were "strictly business," and that he could make money without having to work hard for it; he was a capitalist on a small scale. The partnership with Addison was only one of several similar joint ventures in which Worth was engaged during the twenty years before the Civil War. In 1850, for example, he was in business with brother Barzillai selling general merchandise.[18]

In his business affairs Worth was willing to sacrifice to please his customers. When one of them complained about some planks he had bought at Worth's sawmill, Worth offered to meet the man and straighten out the matter, and he promised to select the next shipment personally. Worth said that if the customer had not received his entire order, and was not satisfied, he would prefer that the purchaser buy his lumber elsewhere, rather than be dissatisfied.[19] Better to lose a customer than have him unhappy was one of the axioms in Worth's philosophy of business.

The most striking, and probably the most significant, feature of Worth's business affairs in the 1850's is the extent to which he was dependent upon wholesale merchants and capitalists in the cities of the North, particularly New York and Philadelphia. His private enterprises bound him to the North even more than his law practice, for it was there that he purchased most of the finished goods he used and sold, and there he secured credit with which to operate his several ventures. To study in detail his commercial dependence upon his friends in the North would involve much of the history of the economic differences between the two sections north and south of the Mason-Dixon line—an interesting, but tangential, story. Worth's dealings with his favorite firm in Philadelphia, David Springs and Company,[20] will give some idea of the nature of his connections with the northern cities in the 1850's.

David Springs and Company, like most of the other merchants Worth dealt with, was a wholesale supply house. It was through Springs that Worth bought most of the general merchandise he sold at his stores. Since Worth was a steady customer of Springs and a personal friend, the latter often served as a liaison man between Worth and other business firms in and around Philadelphia, a service that sometimes required the delicacy of a diplomat; it was no easy chore to explain to another merchant why a customer in North Carolina had stopped trading with him. When Worth became dissatisfied with Ford and Company after he had to buy something at retail prices because Ford had not filled an order promptly, the trouble of straightening out and closing Worth's account fell on Springs.[21] Worth inadvertently

omitted putting sufficient funds in the bank at Salem to cover a note
to Ford given to close out his account, and in his embarrassment he
asked Springs to pay off the note for him if Ford was not willing to
wait until he could draw a check and get it to Philadelphia.

Worth used David Springs as his financial agent when he paid off
his debts to northern merchants in 1851. In May, he sent a check on
the Leather Manufacturers Bank of New York to Springs with directions to pay off a Philadelphia confectioner to whom Worth owed the
modest sum of sixty dollars; the remaining forty dollars was to be
applied towards paying a large note against Worth held by Springs,
to whom he owed "more than I owe to all my Northern creditors."[22]
Worth sent a check later in the year for $4,000, from the Merchants
Bank in New York, to liquidate not only his large debt to Springs,
but all his small ones as well; these included $275 to Uriah Hunt and
Son, $210 to Maris and Company, $145 to Caleb Cope and Company,
and almost $300 to three other merchants. While he was settling these
debts, Springs neglected to credit Worth with an amount that another
of Worth's merchant friends had paid Springs on his account, and
Worth asked Springs to correct the error by paying the amount to
still another firm, William T. Howell and Company. Business of this
kind was endlessly complicated, but Worth managed to keep many
of the details in his mind, and he gained valuable experience that later
was useful at the higher levels of public finance.

Occasionally Worth secured money he needed in his legal practice
from northern sources. In 1852, for example, he paid off some heirs
he had represented in a suit by giving them a draft on David Springs
and Company for $220.23. When this amount turned out to be more
than was needed to pay what was due, Worth, after depositing the
money, asked Springs to buy him a pair of spectacles. That Worth's
age was beginning to show was apparent in his request for the spectacles, a note which also casts some light on the state of optometry in
North Carolina: "Buy for me a pair of first rate glasses. . . . I am 50
years old—and my vision as good as usual at that age. If you will cut
two or three extra glasses some of them would be likely to suit. I am
greatly handicapped for want of a pair, but can find no decent ones
hereabouts."[23] The spectacles were not to be shipped by Adams Express Company, which Worth branded "a villanous concern"—probably
because of their failure to deliver Louisa's cod liver oil before she
died. As Worth grew older and his eyes weaker, he relieved them with

a solution known as "Baker's eye water"; even this had to come from Philadelphia.

Worth relied upon Springs for many other purely personal services, and there was a bond of genuine friendship between the two men. When Adelaide came into Philadelphia from the school she attended at Norristown, Springs helped entertain her, and he transmitted money from her father to Grier Ralston, the master of Adelaide's school, to be used for her various needs. Most of the clothing for Adelaide and the other women in the Worth family came from the clothiers in Philadelphia; it was necessary for them to dress well because they had risen into the upper social class and because their father was the leading public figure of the county in which they lived. Once when Worth ordered twenty-four pairs of calf or goat skin high-quartered ladies shoes from David Springs he explained that they were for "the better set of people to wear on little public days" and that his daughters wore them to school in the winter.[24] Worth himself had a tailor in Philadelphia from whom most of his own clothing came. He ordered it sight unseen, or went to Philadelphia for his fittings, or sent for various garments by his brothers, who frequently visited Philadelphia. To Milton he wrote in 1858, just before the summer election campaigning began: "I find I must have a summer suit. . . . I prefer black color—assist Leon Berg and Company in selecting the material—and say to them I have grown a little since they took my measure, around the waist and abdomen—The Waistband of the pants and the vest should be a little more roomy—say an inch."[25] He almost invariably ordered black clothes, though occasionally he left the choice of color to David Springs or brother Milton. Underneath his suit coat he wore a white shirt that was often obscured by a double breasted vest which buttoned up to the chin. It required "a hat suitable for a N. C. Senator, No. 7½" to protect his head from the sun and to lend dignity to an appearance that was quite somber. It is small wonder that people never ceased to think of him as a member of the Society of Friends, who were noted for their plainness of dress.

Worth sent orders to David Springs for various categories of goods to be sold in his store, specifying in some instances the firms from which they were to be purchased. Springs might pay for them with a draft on a bank in New York where Worth had built up credit, or Worth might send money directly to Philadelphia. The orders usually specified the point or points to which the goods were to be directed—

almost always to one of the Worths at Wilmington and then on to brother Addison at Fayetteville by way of the Cape Fear River. A typical order from Philadelphia included ready-made clothing, cloth, umbrellas, candies, pecans—as if they had to come from the North— figs and "raisons" from David Springs, and Kossuth hats at $7.50 each from George Henderson and Company; these hats were extremely popular after the leader of the Hungarian Revolution of 1848 received a rousing welcome in the United States in 1849. In the shoe line, Worth called for thirty pairs of russet brogans at eighty-five cents and two dozen pairs of ladies heeled shoes for seventy cents each. The wholesale druggist, J. M. Maris and Company, was to supply madder, blue vitriol, "opodelsook," Horseman's Hope, Godfrey's cordial, and Davis's Pain Killer.[26]

Worth was almost always in debt, but it was because of the credit system of doing business rather than any lack of financial acumen in him. One reason he did so much of his buying on credit was the scarcity of efficient banking facilities. He promised, in 1851, when one of his creditors started pressing him, that payment would be forth-coming and explained that "I have the money but it may be a week or two before I can get a check."[27] He would allow his debts to increase for a year or two at a time, then be induced by some financial upturn or political crisis to pay them all at once. In March, 1850, while the great sectional debate over the Compromise of 1850 was going on in Congress, he wrote to one of his brothers who was in New York at the time and asked him to pay off all his debts in the northern cities; the itemized list he sent showed debts amounting to over fifteen hundred dollars.[28]

Many of Worth's debts were in the form of notes he had given whenever he needed to raise money in a hurry, but in some cases he was in no hurry to pay back money he raised in this way. The most remarkable—almost incredible—story of one of Worth's notes involves a slip of paper he gave Noah Rush in 1852 with this inscription on it: "One day after date I promise to pay Noah Rush, Sr. one hundred and twenty seven dollars and ninety five cents for value recd. Feb. 17th 1852. J. Worth";[29] Worth was giving Rush this note to refinance the balance on still another note, signed originally in Worth's personal financial crisis of 1832; five years after Worth re-financed the twenty year old debt in 1852 he paid $28.33 on the note of that date, and still later, in May, 1858, he wiped out eighty-four more dollars of the debt to Noah Rush. But the total amount of the note was not paid until 1867, thirty-five years after the original transaction. This sort of negligence was connected with the fact that gentlemen simply did not press each other for small personal debts when times were good and money was plentiful. But after the Civil War, when many fortunes had been liquidated, little slips of paper signed in the affluent ante-bellum years began to crop up. One of Worth's pre-war creditors, J. M. Coffin, wrote him in 1867: "I . . . find a note for $200. . . . dated Sept. 16th, 1846. I also find one more note which you wrote yourself the first week after Noah left the Ark, for $324.35." Coffin gave his recollection of the transaction for which the notes had been given and remarked, "It will take a Philadelphia lawyer to settle up such a concern."[30] Worth himself had a remarkable memory for the details of his hundreds of transactions, but he preferred to keep careful records rather than rely on it, as Zebedee Rush discovered when he asked Worth for the final payment on the note to his father, Noah. Worth had a receipt for one payment he had made, but he was certain he had made two payments. His certainty was confirmed when Sam Jackson rummaged through his note case and found the receipt for the second payment, made over nine years earlier. Worth's mind was full of a thousand figures, most of which would have been forgotten by a person who had no feeling for financial matters.

Next to Worth's general merchandise operations, the largest business in which he was engaged was that of distilling turpentine and rosin in the pine forests of Cumberland and Moore counties; these items were used in the production of naval stores and certain medicines. Under the name of J. Worth and Sons he began his first venture in this field in 1853. In his optimistic calculations he figured that for eight hundred dollars he could erect a distillery with a capacity of five thousand barrels that would produce in one season twenty-one thousand dollars worth of turpentine and rosin at an expense of less than nine thousand dollars—a most alluring prospect. An unusually good hand could produce three hundred barrels of turpentine in a season —from April to November—but the average for a single worker was about two hundred barrels. Worth expected to employ twenty-seven laborers to tap the trees, at a cost of two hundred dollars each, a distiller, and two assistant distillers. His calculations were based on New York prices—five dollars for a three hundred pound barrel of number one rosin and thirty-two cents a gallon for distilled spirits of turpentine.[31]

When the turpentine operations actually began, they proved to be quite different from what Worth had foreseen in his calculations. Instead of the twenty-seven laborers he had planned to use, the distillery in Cumberland County required sixty-three hired hands, including fifty men, two women, and eleven boys. The highest rate of pay for any man, except the distiller, was $175 a season; the average pay was $145 for seven months. Because of the many difficulties involved in the use of hired labor, Worth bought ten Negroes in 1855 from a company that had just finished using them to build a section of railroad. These ten slaves cost him $8450, which he borrowed and secured by a note, with brother Milton and George C. Mendenhall as securities. Worth rationalized his purchase of the slaves by reminding himself and Mendenhall that "they were to be sold and scattered, if I had not bought them."[32]

It soon became obvious to Worth that his vision of making large profits in a short time was to remain a vision, but he continued to distill turpentine and collect rosin. Once they were extracted they were sent to the firm of Rayner and Gilmer in New York for sale and the money was placed to the credit of J. Worth and Sons on the books of Rayner and Gilmer. Lack of information about the activities of his New York factor became one of Worth's many problems in financing his operations at the distillery. Not knowing whether the factor had sold or whether he still held recent shipments made it difficult to pay operating expenses conveniently. Worth asked Rayner and Gilmer to allow him to draw funds from them without knowing for certain that they had received and sold his turpentine and rosin. They consented, and thereafter he frequently wrote drafts on the factor when he had no money to his credit.[33] In Worth's correspondence with his factor he also explained some of his woes as a distiller. Leaky barrels were a problem, as Rayner and Gilmer discovered when some of Worth's barrels arrived empty in New York. The cooper who made the barrels blamed the still man for not sealing them properly, and the still man attributed leakage to the poor quality of the barrels. Another problem was the "low state of the river"—the Cape Fear; this made it difficult, sometimes impossible, for distillers in the interior of North Carolina to get their turpentine and rosin to Wilmington for shipment to New York.[34]

Worth struggled with the problems of distilling turpentine for over five years before he discontinued his operations, and, although the pines never made for him the large profits he had envisioned in 1853, they provided a tidy supplement to his income. He told brothers Clarkson and Barzillai after the end of the turpentine season in 1855 that the profits for that year were in the neighborhood of a thousand dollars and explained the disappointingly low returns by saying that "wages and subsistence have been entirely out of proportion to the value of turpentine." He expected to continue the business another year, the extent of future operations depending upon the cost of labor and the amount of profits made in 1855.[35] A month earlier he had asked a man who owed him a debt to "remember, I am a turp. maker, a class not overburthened with money."[36]

A number of miscellaneous small-scale projects rounded out Worth's business ventures in the 1850's. After he operated the Gibson mine with Archibald Murphey he never lost his interest in mining, an interest which was no doubt stimulated by the fact that there were small veins of gold under the soil of Randolph County; in 1846 "eight or ten" farmers in the county were extracting gold from their lands.[37] Not much is known of Worth's participation in gold mining, but it is certain that he once operated what was known as the Gray mine in Randolph, and in 1850, he paid off some of his debts to northern merchants in gold.[38] One incident in his career in mining shows his efficiency as a businessman. He bought a forty horsepower steam engine that had been installed to work a gold mine, but since there was not enough water available to operate the mine over six months a year, Worth decided to buy a circular saw, attach it to the engine, and use it to cut lumber when there was not water enough to wash the gold ores. He simply could not bear to see a forty horsepower engine standing idle when it could be put to some use, so he bought the lands around the mine, proposing to make, in addition to lumber, spokes and other wooden parts of carriages with which to supply the shops about Asheboro.[39] If Jonathan Worth had ever chosen to adopt a middle name it might well have been Enterprise.

On a trip to the Virginia mountains in late 1852 or early in 1853 to buy horses for hauling his turpentine, Worth heard talk of a rich vein of copper in Carroll County. The prospect looked so promising that Worth associated two of his brothers, his son, and a son-in-law with him and bought the copper ore on a conditional sale.

They went into the venture blindly, not knowing anything about the business of mining copper. Worth then wrote to his favorite merchant in New York to send him a book on copper mining, or any other aid they might be able to give him. In the course of his odd request to the merchant Worth remarked: "I always apply to you when I want anything done in New York, however incongruous to your occupation. I don't exactly know how far I may carry this before you will begin to think me a little troublesome."[40] Unperturbed by their ignorance, Worth and his associates mined the copper, with brother Milton actually supervising the operations. Later, Jonathan and Milton bought the lease, machinery, and other property of a mining company in Randolph County.[41] At various times Worth was engaged in business ventures with all his brothers, but since Milton lived nearer than any of the other Worth brothers, he was Jonathan's most frequent partner.

Besides his operations in merchandise, distilling, and mining, Worth made money on agricultural products and services. He bought herds of swine, killed the hogs and sold the pork when prices were high; he operated a grist mill; and he once bought twenty-two tons of guano to sell to the farmers around Asheboro. In the fifties his own lands included a five hundred acre farm in Moore County, which was farmed by an overseer, and large holdings in Randolph. Most of the products of his farms were small grains and cattle, rather than cotton or tobacco, a fact of some importance in determining his political affiliations—which were not with the cotton planters of the state. In 1859-60 he and Milton grew twelve hundred bushels of wheat, between seven and eight hundred bushels of oats, and enough hay to feed their livestock. All this was done without machinery. In April, 1860, they were considering whether to buy a reaper, mower, and thresher, but hesitated because their land was hilly and stony. Worth said that "we have not seen a mower and reaper."[42] Obviously, slaves were necessary for the production of large quantities of agricultural produce without the use of machinery.

The story of what Worth did with all the money he acquired from his business, commercial, and agricultural enterprises by his skill in financial matters and by sheer hard work is a story as fascinating as the manner in which he rose from the status of debt-ridden young lawyer in 1832 to comparative affluence in 1860, but it is too long and involved a story to be told here. There was, of course, enough to enable the Worth family to maintain a standard of living that bordered on luxury. Some money was poured back into the particular venture that produced it. Then there was a complex of heavy investments in transportation facilities and industrial establishments. The most important of these were the Cape Fear Steam Boat Company, which Worth and his brothers practically owned; the Carolina City Company, a group formed to buy stock in the Atlantic and North Carolina Railroad Company and land along its route; the Fayetteville and Western Plank Road Company, of which Worth was general superintendent from 1856 to 1860; and the Cedar Falls Manufacturing Company, the cotton mill on Deep River for which he secured a renewed charter in 1858 and which he was serving as president at the time of his death.[43] Some of these investments, particularly those in the steam boat company and the cotton mill, paid good dividends, while others—the plank road company, for example—were bitter disappointments. But in general, his skill in making money and using it wisely was far greater than that of the average businessman. It was the development of that skill through forty years of varied enterprise that eventually resulted in his elevation to the highest financial office in the state.

· VIII ·

Roads of Iron and Pine

EARLY IN THE YEAR 1858, Worth's conservative friends among the
Whigs of Randolph and Alamance counties lured him away from his
personal affairs back into active political campaigning when they asked
him to represent the two counties in the state Senate. Worth was reluctant to run, but considering the other potential Whig candidate,
Dr. William B. Lane, unfit to serve the district, he yielded to the request of the Whig leaders and became a candidate. In May, before
Lane announced that he would be a candidate, Worth asked the Whig
Congressman from his district, John A. Gilmer, to persuade Lane
that a contest between two Whigs would be detrimental to the interests of the party. He also expressed to Gilmer a fear that Lane "will
talk about aristocracy,"[1] an issue which could be raised because the
state had abolished the freehold qualification for electors of state
senators the year before. Worth was not deeply concerned about Lane's
appeal to the nonfreeholders, but some of his friends expected Lane
to draw the vote of that class.

If John Gilmer ever said anything to Dr. Lane about not running,
it had no effect, for he soon announced his candidacy for the Senate;
a Democrat also announced, but since the district was solidly Whig,
Worth did not have to worry about him. The active campaigning,
which Worth found most distasteful, was confined to the month of
July, and at the election in August, Worth won over Lane by almost
a three to one margin. The result was so pleasing to him that he
lapsed into an uncommon manner of speaking when he reported it:
"I beat the old fornicator badly—I got 1605 votes—he 569."[2]

When he went to Raleigh in November, 1858, for his second term
in the state Senate, Worth rendered no service equal in importance
to his authorship of the public school law when he was in the Senate

in 1840 and 1841. Most of his time was spent on what he considered at the time the most important act of his public career, an investigation of the management of the North Carolina Railroad.[3] In the long perspective of history, that particular public act was not as important as his later work in the state treasury or his administration of the state government during the early years of Reconstruction. But the railroad investigation is, for several reasons, important to an understanding of Worth both as a personality and as a public servant. The fact that he suspected corruption and mismanagement of the railroad and worked so diligently to prove that these circumstances existed gives some insight into his character; especially revealing are his tenacity when he became convinced that he was right and his persistence in maintaining that conviction even when the evidence was weighing against him. More significant still, the investigation precipitated the bitterest political controversy in which Jonathan Worth was ever engaged. Since a man is likely to reveal the depths of his character when he is under attack, it is necessary to examine the railroad controversy in some detail.

The North Carolina Railroad Company, chartered by the legislature of 1848, was involved in state politics from the beginning of its existence. The state had lost money when it subsidized private railroads in the eighteen-thirties and forties, and as a result many politicians were wary of state participation in railroad building and management. When the chartering bill for the state railroad came before the state Senate in 1848, it squeaked through by only one vote, with the presiding officer breaking a tie. The vote in the legislature appeared, on the surface, to be along party lines, the charter receiving far more support from the Whigs than from the Democrats, but it was basically a compromise measure, with the vote actually being cast more on sectional lines than upon purely political considerations. "In general, there was a preponderance of votes for the bill among legislators from the central Piedmont and extreme western sections," the areas that stood to benefit most from the construction of the railroad.[4] The charter authorized the North Carolina Railroad Company, which it created, to build a line from the junction of the Wilmington and Raleigh Railroad and the Neuse River by way of Raleigh and Salisbury to Charlotte. The capital stock of the company was set at three million dollars, of which the state was to subscribe two million dollars after the private stockholders had subscribed the remaining one million and paid 5 per cent of their subscription. The charter thus made the state the major stockholder in a railroad that was expected to pay profits into the state treasury, and the interests of the railroad became in a real sense the interests of the state.

The company was organized in July, 1850, when the stockholders met at the Methodist church in Salisbury. They selected Walter Gwynn as chief engineer and told him to survey a proposed route for the line.[5] Politics must have entered into the choice of a route, for the road was built in a great curve rather than on a more economically direct route. C. K. Brown, the best authority on the history of the railroad, dug up the following quotation that is somewhat exaggerated but illustrates the point clearly: "Unless the road had gone to the home of Governor Morehead, had passed by Hillsboro, the home of Secretary of the Navy, Governor, and United States Senator Graham, and other distinguished men, had taken in the state capital in its route, and terminated in the midst of the descendents of the signers of the Mecklenburg Declaration of Independence, it could not have come into existence at all."[6] The work on the railroad was started in 1852. The state sank another million dollars into the road in 1855,[7] and in January, 1856, the first trains passed over the completed road.[8] The legislature came to the rescue of the company again the next year when it exempted $350,000 worth of coupon bonds from taxation and set the rate of interest on the bonds at 8 per cent.

Gradually the North Carolina Railroad Company slipped from the control of the Whigs and into the hands of the Democrats, a movement parallel to what was happening in state government. The Whigs, under the leadership of such men as John Motley Morehead and William A. Graham, had dominated state politics in the fifteen years prior to 1850; when the railroad bill passed the legislature, it was considered a Whig measure. But the Democrats came into power in 1850 and remained dominant until the outbreak of the Civil War. The same shift in power may be seen in the control of the North Carolina Railroad Company. After 1853, the state was entitled to appoint eight members to the board of directors of the company. In that year two Whigs and six Democrats represented the state, but in 1854 (and afterwards), all eight of the state's directors were Democrats.[9] The presidency of the railroad also shifted from the Whigs to the Democrats when John Motley Morehead was replaced in 1855 by Charles F. Fisher, a Democrat. Fisher, who served for six years

as president, had earlier been a Whig and had voted for Jonathan
Worth when Worth ran for Congress in 1840. When controversy
broke out, Fisher could claim that Worth, who led the assault on the
railroad management, was abandoning an old friend; this only served
to make a bad situation worse.

The basis for the investigation of the railroad was a clamor for
dividends that had started almost as soon as the road went into operation. The state, as a major stockholder, had sent a representative to
the stockholders' meetings, and he had demanded the payment of a
dividend in 1857 and 1858, only to be refused by the directors. It was
under these circumstances that Worth proposed an inquiry into the
management of the North Carolina Railroad Company to see why
no dividends had been paid and what the prospects were for future
payment.[10] The proposal to investigate was a part of Worth's job on
the finance committee of the Senate, for he was charged with the responsibility of finding additional sources of revenue for the state.
The state's investment in the railroad had promised to be rewarding
and Worth wanted to find out why no reward had come. There is no
evidence that he intended to set off a bitter argument with Fisher or to
drag the railroad issue into the political arena. But this happened
because the railroad was intimately associated with state politics;
it had been from the beginning, and would remain so.

Worth proposed in the Senate on November 29, 1858, "to raise a
joint select committee of five—three on the part of the Commons and
two on the part of the Senate, to enquire into and report on the general
management and financial condition and prospects of the North Carolina Railroad Company."[11] The committee was duly appointed and
began its work in December, 1858, when it addressed a letter to President Fisher requesting him to meet the committee on January 4, 1859,
along with his treasurer, bookkeeper, and the company's books. The
committee chose Worth as its chairman, probably because he had
proposed the investigation. On the date set for the beginning of the
examination, Fisher put in his appearance, along with Cyrus P.
Mendenhall, the treasurer of the company, and R. W. Mills, the bookkeeper. Fisher told the examiners he needed to be at work on the road
and the committee excused him. On January 8, Mills failed to show
up for the meeting of the committee; he stayed away all that week
keeping with him some of the books necessary for the investigation. It
turned out that Fisher had gone to Salisbury; from there he asked

the bookkeeper, Mills, to send him the journal of the directors, and Mills complied. On the fifteenth of January, Worth wrote to Fisher and "required" that his bookkeeper appear with his books. Two days later Mills appeared, explaining "that he had been engaged in supplying Mr. Fisher with materials for a report he was having printed in Salisbury."[12] In the face of these obstructions, the committee continued to examine such books as were made available. They did not exercise the authority vested in them to subpoena persons and examine them under oath, ostensibly because there was not enough time for such proceedings. The admittedly "imperfect inquiry" was finally completed and the report submitted to the legislature early in February, 1859.

In the meantime, Fisher worked hastily to head off the adverse criticism he expected to result from the report of the committee investigating his railroad. "His" is the appropriate adjective, for Fisher had a proprietary attitude towards the company. Any criticism of it and its policies he would interpret almost as an attack on his person. To soften the anticipated prick of his sensitive skin he submitted to the governor of the state a report of the railroad company's condition and its future prospects. Many of the facts and figures he needed for his report were in the books then being examined by the investigating committee headed by his old friend Jonathan Worth. He did not hesitate to have these books carried off to Salisbury. This move was interpreted by Worth as a deliberate effort to hinder the work of the investigating committee. What Fisher's real intentions were is impossible to determine. The most that can be said is that he selected a most inopportune moment to compile his statistics; but his feeling that he, as president of the North Carolina Railroad Company, had as much right to the books as a group representing an "outside" agency is understandable. At any rate, he took away the books and got ahead of the committee by submitting his report to the governor almost three weeks before the frustrated investigators could get theirs in to the legislature.

The report Fisher submitted to the governor[13] was what might be expected—a defense of Fisher's policies and a prediction of rosy prospects for the future of the railroad. After giving a brief history of the company, Fisher discussed the cost of building the road and explained why it had not yet paid dividends to the state. Nothing irritated him more than the clamor for dividends from "those so remote from it as to feel no direct benefits, and who enquire no farther than to ascertain that it has not paid dividends to the treasury."[14] No similar enterprise could make such a favorable report, with regard to cost and condition, asserted Fisher. The matter of the company shops evidently troubled him, for he went to great lengths to explain their size, and particularly their location, a point which had come in for question. Fisher was quite willing to accept sole responsibility for the administration of the company's affairs. The most important part of his report, so far as the controversy with Worth is concerned, was his rationalization of the failure to pay dividends and a promise that the road would begin paying returns on the state's preferred stock in the next year.

The next stage in the controversy opened when the investigating committee submitted its report to the legislature on February 8. This lengthy document, signed by two Whigs and two Democrats, concluded simply that "this road has been badly managed—by the President and Directors—in the particulars which we have been able to examine, in the time and under the circumstances, herein set forth."[15] The report was, basically, a charge of failing to manage efficiently the funds invested by the state. The "circumstances" affecting the work of the committee included the press of legislative duties and the obstruction by Fisher in carrying away the company books during the course of the examination.

When the report of the committee reached the floor of the Senate, there was some parliamentary sparring about whether extra copies should be printed for each member, but the issue was postponed. Fisher then got hold of the committee report and felt compelled to repudiate it publicly. He drew up a long reply,[16] and it was this document which set off the personal recriminations between Worth and Fisher that continued for over a year. In the "Reply" Fisher consistently referred to the report of the committee as "the chairman's report," ignoring the fact that it was signed by three other legislators, two of them Democrats. The committee had criticized the company for running an extra express train. The tone of Fisher's "Reply" may be seen in his remarks on this matter: "The chairman's section on the Express train . . . is really so absurd throughout, and displays such unmitigated ignorance of the subject, that I cannot undertake to mend its blunders or correct the misstatements."[17] With regard to the excess wood found by the committee, the offended president said that he had stopped all contracting for wood except where the supply was inadequate, and that he had reduced the price paid for wood by twenty-five cents a cord, a considerable saving; he also tried to shift responsibility for the bad management of wood contracts to John Motley Morehead, the ex-Governor and former president of the railroad. Fisher challenged Worth to find one unnecessary building at the company shops[18] and accused him of exaggeration and of failing to make proper inquiry and examination. Worth "did not enquire to learn, but to censure," Fisher said. Continuing his biting criticism of Jonathan Worth, Fisher self-righteously maintained that it was only his own generosity that had made the investigation possible, arguing that "the charter of this corporation gives no authority to the legislature to make any such inquisition"[19] and that he could have refused to co-operate or surrender the books of the company. Towards the end of his "Reply" he became exceedingly sarcastic when he rendered his thanks to the chairman of the investigating committee for directing attention to the condition of the North Carolina Railroad.

Worth might have been able to disregard Fisher's "Reply" and let it die unnoticed if Fisher had not sent it to the Speaker of the Senate, Henry T. Clark, and asked that it be read on the floor. This request led to "a very undignified reign of pandemonium"[20] after Senator Pool moved that the communication be read. The reader had reached the third page, where the "Reply" stated that Worth was not able to appreciate some particular courtesy extended by Fisher, when Senator Leach, of Johnston County, interrupted the reading and objected to the paper as "disrespectful to the Senate."[21] The fiery Josiah Turner, Jr., Whig Senator from Orange County and a good friend of Worth, encouraged Leach to break up the reading. The account of this incident given by William Holden, the partisan editor of the Democratic Raleigh Standard, presented a most unfavorable picture of the Whig Senators on this occasion. According to Holden, Leach spoke "violently and furiously," and Turner goaded him on by voice and gesture, shouting "Go on, Leach!—that's right, Leach!—stop the reading, Leach! —it is an outrage on the Senate!"[22] Several Senators called Turner to order and one moved that he be taken into custody by the doorkeeper. Turner then "rose and defied the Speaker and Senate to take him into custody, using expressions of a violent and inflammatory character."[23] After several hours of debate Fisher's communication was withdrawn and order restored. Worth then rose and tried to make a personal explanation to the Senate, but the Senator who had first introduced the "Reply" objected and Worth had to remain silent.[24] Earlier in the debate Fisher's advocates had argued that since Worth's report had been printed by the Senate without a reading, the "Reply" should also be printed without reading. Worth then got the floor and "insisted that there was a marked distinction between printing without reading, a report of a committee and a paper from any person not officially connected with the Senate, and distinctly urged that it be read in order that we might see what it was before offering it to be printed."[25] As it turned out, the communication was not read at all, but hostility was engendered on both sides of the political fence.

Fisher was enraged because he had not been heard in the Senate, and he brought the debate out into the open when he published the "Reply" to the committee report in Holden's *Standard,* adding an appendix that explained his views in very strong terms. He labeled the offensive report as a "Bill of indictment," the scene in the Senate as an "ex parte hearing," and branded the whole proceeding as a *"conspiracy* to defame my administration." The Senate was called a "Star Chamber" and Worth's report "contemptible." When the controversy reached the newspapers it became more acrid than before, and persons other than Fisher and Worth were drawn into the verbal battle. Using the Raleigh *Register* as their organ, the Whigs struck back at Fisher. Senator Leach, in a public letter, wanted to know why Fisher had assailed him and proposed—with tongue in cheek, perhaps—that a committee be selected to inquire into the public and private behavior of himself and Fisher and render a verdict. "I hope, and believe," said Leach, that "the committee would not find your character in as bad a fix as they found your road."[26] Leach admitted stopping the reading of Fisher's communication to the Senate and that he had been encouraged by Josiah Turner; he acknowledged that he had talked rather loudly in the Senate debate but confessed that "I can't think I was heard half as far as Senator Brown, who spoke in your favor."[27]

Worth had remained on the sidelines up to this point, but he became irritated when Holden published an article stating that Worth was "mistaken" concerning the circumstances under which Fisher's communication to the Senate had been presented. Holden denied that Senator Ashe had made a motion to print the "Reply" without reading it. Worth was "surprised that on this point there should be any misapprehension."[28] Holden later admitted that Worth was correct, but in the same article he revealed his delight that Fisher had again blasted Worth in the columns of the Salisbury *Banner*. Holden also made public in his paper the fact that Worth had bought from him five hundred copies of the committee report. "Mr. Worth appears to be determined that the results of his investigation of the affairs of this corporation shall be widely known," Holden remarked.[29] Worth thought that, since this transaction was a personal one, the report of it should not have appeared in the *Standard*.

When the Greensboro *Patriot* announced that gentlemen "unconnected with Mr. Worth" had subscribed for a thousand copies of Worth's report, Holden simply gloated. He immediately branded the subscribers as "the party" and claimed that he had drawn an admission of this from the Whig editors of the *Patriot* by implying that Worth was paying for the distribution of the report. To clinch his argument that the Whigs were making the railroad question a party matter he quoted an article from the Wilmington *Journal* which, in his opinion, "hit the nail on the head": "It is evident that the whole thing amounts to an attack on Charles F. Fisher; that it springs from, and is engineered by, a clique at Greensborough; that it is pushed forward for political effect, and to make party capital. We speak this in view of the *animus* displayed, and from an inspection of the earmarks. No one can have watched the course of things without seeing this."[30]

These charges that Worth was using the railroad issue as a political club to smite the Democratic Party do not appear valid now, although it is easy to see how the Democrats might have thought so in 1859. Worth apparently entered upon the investigation with no motive other than his desire to secure much needed money for the state. But, unfortunately, Fisher chose to make a big issue of the investigation and dragged it into the political struggle between the Whigs and the Democrats. Worth then accepted the challenge, while consistently asserting both publicly and privately that he was not motivated by political considerations and that he was not a member of any clique whose purpose was to make political capital of the railroad question. He did, however, see the value of the issue for the Whigs. In his view Fisher's "Reply" and the articles in the Democratic newspaper were "the most insolent attempt by a party majority to degrade and insult a minority of which I have any recollection in legislation."[31] The Democrats were, he thought, playing into the hands of the Whigs by defending Fisher and attacking the report of the investigating committee. Worth had so much confidence in the soundness of his report that he said "I think I am in a coat of mail that the Devil and Democracy can not pierce,"[32] but he was pushed into a corner by the continued attacks of Fisher and his party; and, worst of all, his personal honor and integrity were being questioned. In the face of all this, Worth might better have ignored what was going on. Instead, he determined to defend himself. The earnestness with which he labored to secure the approval of his friends and constituents was almost compulsive.

Worth worked long and diligently on his reply to the paper Fisher had presented to the Senate. On February 22, 1859, in a letter to John W. Syme, the editor of the state's leading Whig paper, the Raleigh *Register,* he promised to reply publicly to Fisher and asserted that "any sensible man who will read the report of the committee . . . and this communication which . . . singles me out as the object of Mr. Fisher's malice, will see that not a fact in the report is met by anything but the *ipse dixit* of Mr. Fisher. . . ."[33]

By March 2, Worth had finished his defense of the committee report and submitted it to the *Register* for publication. He perceived that it was too long to be read by casual readers, but regretted that he had not been able to reply to all Fisher's insinuations.[34] The article appeared in the *Register* two weeks later, on March 16, 1859. Moderate in tone, it did not attack Fisher personally, although Worth saw evidence of "a sad defect of memory" in some of the remarks Fisher had made. He gave the background of the investigation of the railroad, asserting that he decided independently to ask for an examination of the general prospects of the road after he heard his constituents complaining of the management. This was of course a denial that the investigation was part of a plot engineered by the Whig clique in Greensboro. As evidence of the non-partisan character of the committee's work, Worth pointed out that the wood contracts had been examined on the proposal of a Democratic member of the committee.[35] "We unanimously regarded our duty as one wholly disconnected with party," Worth said, and he would not have bothered to reply to Fisher at all if it had not been for the fiasco in the Senate. He had presumed on that occasion that the Speaker knew what was in Fisher's communication before he introduced it to be read and printed, but this had not been true. Finally, Worth's defense reviewed in great detail

Fisher's "Reply" and asserted that Fisher refused to co-operate with the committee. In this round of the battle Worth's conduct had been more gentlemanly than that of Fisher, for he had at least kept his eyes on the basic issues rather than upon the personalities involved.

Worth's counterattacking article appeared on March 16, 1859, and the first phase of the tedious recriminations was over. During the cooling off period that followed, the editor of the Hillsboro *Recorder* gave a fairly levelheaded evaluation of what had been going on: "It may, perhaps, be admitted that Mr. Fisher has been too bitter in some of his remarks as applied to the chairman of the committee; but the impression made upon our mind from the imperfect perusal which we have been able to bestow upon that report seems in some measure to justify his warmth of feeling."[36] There were too few editors who were willing to see both sides of the case. Even this one went on to say that "the examination of the committee was too superficial to be useful, and displays more of a disposition to find fault than is consistent with even handed justice."[37] Holden collected all such unfavorable remarks from the papers he read and spread them through the pages of the *Standard*. Unfortunately for Worth, the allegation that the work of the committee was not sufficiently thorough had some truth in it; the committee had acknowledged this and apologized for it, but Worth's opponents used it as a club with which to beat him and to repudiate the entire work of the committee.

Worth became tired of the argument by April, 1859, and decided to pay no further attention to Fisher. "Anything further would be mere personality which would disgust the public," he said.[38] He changed his mind, however, for he reopened the controversy in October, 1859, when he published an article over the signature "Plebs" in the Greensboro *Patriot*. Exactly what caused him to change his mind is impossible to determine, but the most likely explanation is that Fisher was overwhelmingly re-elected by the stockholders of the North Carolina Railroad Company at their annual meeting held in July. What hurt Worth most was that many of the prominent Whig stockholders voted for Fisher. Even John Motley Morehead, Fisher's predecessor as president of the railroad, voted for Worth's opponent. Morehead's action was incomprehensible to the crusading Worth, who considered the re-election of Fisher as a personal rebuke to him and a triumph for the Democrats. Once again he was on the defensive and renewed the controversy in October after he heard rumors that the

Greensboro *Patriot* was planning to drag the mud-splattered railroad issue into the open again. It was then that he wrote his nine column article and published it over the signature "Plebs."

The issue Worth now seized upon to renew his argument with Fisher was a construction contract Fisher had made with the Western North Carolina Railroad Company, the line that was supposed to join with the North Carolina Railroad and give the western part of the state a railroad on which they could ship their products to the coast. The people of Burke County had trouble raising $220,000 required to build their part of the road from Hales' Store to Morganton. They had promised to pay fifty thousand dollars and Fisher had agreed to subscribe the remaining $170,000, provided he was given the contract. This arrangement was made and work started. The subscription by the justices of Burke County for the fifty thousand dollars worth of stock was upheld by the state Supreme Court in December, 1858. A committee of the legislature, chaired by David Outlaw, investigated Fisher's contract and found that some irregularity existed, but not as much as had been expected.[39] In the "Plebs" article Worth called upon Fisher to resign as president of the North Carolina Railroad Company, because it appeared to him that Fisher was using his position as president of one road to make unearned profits as a contractor on the other line. Large amounts of money for shop work were due from the Western North Carolina Railroad to the North Carolina Railroad, but they were not entered on the books of the latter company. Worth thought the work might have been for Fisher's personal benefit, a suspicion he was forced later to retract publicly.[40] He alluded to the possibility that Fisher had partners in the contract, but he quibbled later, "I did not pretend to *know* that he had any."[41] The article also went over the earlier controversy, but Worth spent most of his time talking about the Fisher contract. He had felt the ground slip from under him when the North Carolina Railroad began paying dividends to the state earlier in the year, undermining the assertion of the investigating committee that the road had been mismanaged. All that Worth could do now was prove that he had been right about Fisher's incapacity to manage a railroad. In this attempt he was unsuccessful.

Worth explained to his friends that he had written the "Plebs" article incognito because he believed that the public would attribute it to "personal ill feeling" if the author were known. But his anonymity did not survive very long. Fisher stamped into the office of the *Patriot* and demanded to know the name of the writer. James A. Long, the editor of the paper, refused at first to reveal Worth's name to Fisher "if it was wanted to hold up the writer to the animadversions of the press," but when the indignant Fisher specified that he merely wanted to denounce the author personally, Long gave him the desired information. Fisher then violated his promise to Long by publicizing in the Salisbury *Banner* the fact that Worth had written the article over "Plebs."[42] Fisher felt that Worth's anonymous article was an unwarranted intrusion into his personal affairs, and demanded satisfaction of the type sometimes resorted to by ante-bellum Southern gentlemen. But the pacific Worth ignored the challenge and refused to declare his sentiments on dueling.[43] Fisher did not press him further.

Fisher was the only man who had ever treated Worth with such personal disrespect, and Worth could not bring himself to give up the struggle to vindicate himself. He must have realized gradually that his position was not as tenable as he kept telling himself it was, and in his uneasiness he began to grasp at straws. He had made the attack on Fisher's contract without seeing it, relying for information on the report of the committee that had investigated the contract in 1858. In an effort to find out what was in the contract he wrote to David Outlaw, the chairman of that investigating committee, and four days later to Fisher himself, requesting a copy. Finally he received two copies through the mail from anonymous sources. These copies seemed to confirm in his mind the allegations he had formerly made. The estimates on which the contract was based were far too high, in Worth's opinion. Fisher was not bound to construct a specified amount of "turnout," although the estimate had been 8 per cent. The grades on the road could be changed, reducing the cost of construction, but a specified sum would still be paid. This is how the matter looked to Worth. "All this is a palpable fraud on the state," he said.[44] But this does not seem to have been the case. The contract had been arrived at openly between Fisher and the Western North Carolina Railroad Company; it had been investigated by the legislature, and found to be somewhat irregular, but not fraudulent; and the Supreme Court of North Carolina had ruled on certain aspects of the negotiations, upholding them as legal. How then can Worth's tenacity be explained?

The answer seems to be that he remained convinced that he was right, even in view of all the evidence to the contrary. There was just enough validity in his arguments to convince him that he was performing a public service by exposing the poor management of railroads in which the state had invested a great deal of the people's money. Many of his friends encouraged him to go on with the battle. To one of these, Victor C. Barringer, a professor at Davidson College, he expressed appreciation for a note of approval and said that "an occasional cheer such as yours will nerve me with greater vigor."[45] The support of his close friends and his conviction that he was right may have been the only reasons Worth continued to drag the railroad issue through the mire of newspaper publicity, but he was motivated also by a very human failing, the inability to admit that he was wrong, or at least that he might have gone too far. He never admitted to himself or to his friends that this was the case. On February 10, 1860, over a year after the investigating committee had reported its findings to the legislature, Worth fired the last open shot in the controversy, a nine-column article in the Greensboro *Patriot* which went over the same ground he had covered previously, but added nothing new. As late as June, 1860, he was still trying to get a bar of Fisher's iron weighed, in an effort to show that the railroad president and contractor was profiting by using cheap materials.[46] Nothing resulted from this effort.

The most important result of the dispute with Fisher, so far as Jonathan Worth's political career is concerned, was that it influenced greatly his decision to run again for the state Senate in 1860. When the "politicking" for the senatorial nomination became intense Worth pointed out to the Whig leaders of his district that "omission to sustain me will be called by Democracy as a virtual repudiation of my course, and will deter any other from the unpleasant and laborious duty of looking into the management of our public works."[47] Worth had gotten himself into such a position in the railroad debate that he came to feel the personal need for the party to sustain him; he would not have run, he said, except for the "peculiar position" he occupied That peculiar position resulted from Worth's sincere belief that Charles Fisher was unfit to manage the North Carolina Railroad In the attempt to prove the soundness of his belief, he lost a bitter and most distasteful argument that occupied much of his valuable time for a year and a half. But in losing that argument he revealed the tenacit of his personal convictions, his strong individuality, and a great concern that anyone should consider him anything but an honest man. Worth's concern for his personal reputation was exceeded only by the extreme sensitivity of Fisher. Both men were convinced that they were honest citizens—and they were, essentially—but both felt compelled to prove it.

During the time when Worth was engaged in the unseemly dispute with Charles Fisher over the North Carolina Railroad he was involved in an entirely different way with another of the state's important arteries of transportation, the Fayetteville and Western Plank Road Company. During the late thirties and early forties he had participated in the effort to build a railroad from Fayetteville towards Asheboro and Salem, but that effort had failed. The parties who had wanted the railroad then turned their attention to the possibility of laying a road of heavy pine planks. The legislature of 1848-49 granted a charter for the proposed road, and by 1852, the Fayetteville and Western Plank Road Company had laid ninety-one miles of plank and was paying a dividend of 3½ per cent. When it was completed from Fayetteville to the Moravian settlement at Bethania, it was a hundred and sixty miles long, by far the largest and most important of the plank roads that were built in North Carolina.[48] Since the road ran through Asheboro, Jonathan Worth took a deep interest in its welfare from the very beginning, for it would provide him quicker and cheaper transportation to Fayetteville. Better still, it opened up several avenues of enterprise and investment to him.

Worth was quick to seize upon the business opportunities provided by the construction of the plank road between 1850 and 1855. In the fall of 1850, he and his brother Milton contracted to build a section of the road on the west side of Haskett's Creek in the vicinity of Asheboro. After collecting all the money he had available and calling in what he could get from his debtors, he plunged headlong into the relatively simple tasks of road building. Most of his time in the early months of 1851 was consumed in this activity. Before the building started he wrote his brother Clarkson: "I have great confidence in our plank road contract. We have succeeded in getting a good hold on timber at moderate rates—and think our net can't fall short of $10,000 —and hope to make it much larger."[49] Actually his profits fell short of his expectations because he had to replace a leased sawmill which burned, but he and Milton still made enough money to more than repay them for their time and effort. By early 1852, they had completed their section of the road.

Another way Worth benefited from the Fayetteville and Western Plank Road was by setting up a general merchandise store along its route. In 1852, he was in a partnership with Oren A. Burgess that operated a store in Moore County at which Burgess, the active partner, sold such items as finger rings, thread, and "fancy looking glasses" to the workmen who were building the road; he called this business his plank road store.[50] Judging Worth by this type of activity and by the earlier construction contract, it is apparent that *carpe diem* was more to him than an empty Latin phrase he had learned at Greensboro Academy. The man could literally smell opportunity about him; all he had to do was sniff the wind as it blew through a forest of pines.

The building contract and the plank road store were peripheral to the activities of the Fayetteville and Western Plank Road Company, but Worth was also very active in the affairs of the company itself. At the stockholders' meeting of 1850, he was elected a director in the company and served on one of the committees. He corresponded frequently with the president and fellow directors, offering advice—usually sound—on the administration and policies of the road. When the road was divided into three sections for administrative purposes, Worth took charge of the section from Carthage to High Point. Sometimes he advanced his own money to pay part of the expenses of his section, but he disliked doing this because he had "no idea of being entangled in the web of innumerable accounts."[51]

The web enmeshed Worth even more closely when he became the first general superintendent of the entire road at the spring meeting of the stockholders in 1856. A matter of "personal delicacy" had arisen before the meeting when he heard that his friend H. B. Elliott wanted the position, but after Worth offered to step aside and it became apparent that Elliott was not a serious candidate for the job, Worth got the appointment.[52] For the next four years—until his resignation in 1860—it was his responsibility to see that the road was kept in good repair and to supervise the collection of tolls. He also ended up keeping the "innumerable accounts." These duties, for which the pay was four dollars a day, consumed four or five months of Worth's time each year, but added five or six hundred dollars to his income.

The plank road never prospered under Worth's supervision, for by the time he took over the management inexorable economic circumstances were operating against the success of the road. Probably the most important of these circumstances was the fact that the North Carolina Railroad was completed shortly after the Fayetteville and Western Plank Road began operating. Since produce could be shipped much faster on the railroad there was a steady decline in the amount of tolls collected along the plank road. The president reported to the stockholders in 1857 that "the great diminishment of tolls is owing to two causes—the short crops and the completion of the North Carolina Railroad."[53]

With these constantly diminishing tolls Worth had to pay an ever growing series of repair bills. Even in 1852, the planks were beginning to need replacement, and by the time Worth took over the road the job of keeping it in good order had become exceedingly troublesome. The planks were wearing thin, and the dirt which was piled around the ends and over the tops of the planks to prevent decay had washed away in many places. When Worth started "dirting" the road he soon realized that the tolls were not sufficient to pay for the work. After "an extraordinary freshet" in August, 1857, damaged both the bridges and the road, Worth began experimenting with stone surfaces, but plank remained the favorite paving material. As the planks got thinner he began to economize by ordering two and a half instead of three inch boards "upon the idea that they will fit in better with the old plank, thin now by use—will probably last as long as 3 in.—and will cost less."[54] Things worsened towards the end of the fifties as the timbers on the bridges began to weaken and fall off. In the fall of 1860, a man sued the company for the cost of a team of mules that had drowned when the animals became frightened and backed through a spot where the railing of the bridge was missing—"the water being deep below." When Worth wrote to James Morehead to hire him as counsel for the company, he explained that he had kept the road "in as good repair as its income will permit."[55]

In spite of the difficulties in keeping the road repaired, collecting tolls from persons who tried to avoid paying them, and competing with the North Carolina Railroad, Worth managed to get the company out of debt by 1860. But by that time he was weary of his duties and tired of hearing complaints about the condition of the road. Particularly annoying to him were demands by the stockholders and directors in

Fayetteville, who tended to dominate the company, that their part of the road should be maintained in good order at the expense of the rest of the road. Some stockholders also complained about what Worth called his "trifling compensation." The grumbling, the minor disagreement with the Fayetteville interests, and more important, election to another term in the state legislature, caused Worth to tender his resignation as superintendent of the Fayetteville and Western Plank Road in October, 1860.

· IX ·

The March of Madness: Secession

THE STORY OF THE FIRST FIFTY-EIGHT YEARS of Jonathan Worth's life—
from 1802 to 1860—is essentially the story of a happy man rearing his
family, building up his material fortunes, and contributing his modest
talents to the betterment of his native state in the role of public
servant. After 1860, the story becomes a tragedy, for Worth was caught
up in the vortex of a war he hated from start to finish and in the
vicious political struggles of the period of restoration following that
war. Worth was strongly attached to the southern way of life, but in
1860 and 1861, he did not cherish that way of life so highly that he
was willing to dissolve the federal union in an attempt to preserve it.
If there is any central theme in the story of Worth's last ten years,
it is one of his efforts first to save the union from dissolution and then
to help restore it after it had been destroyed.

Worth's course of opposition to secession was foreshadowed by his
resolutions in the legislature of 1830, when he went on record as a
proponent of the view that the nation established in 1787 must be
preserved at almost any cost; this view never changed, for Jonathan
Worth was not a man who readily adapted his sentiments to changing
circumstances. His consistent moderation on the subject of federal-
state relations may be seen in a review of his attitudes in some of the
portentous events in the decade before the secession crisis.

In 1850, Worth strongly supported the compromise measures
adopted by Congress after the long debates over whether the territory
acquired from Mexico in the Mexican War should be made into slave
or free states. Later in the year he expressed himself on the dominant
issues in these terms:

I am sorry to see the legislature occupying so much time with
slavery resolutions. Vermont and South Carolina have gone mad on

the two opposite extremes. I hope North Carolina will keep cool—I yet hope there is too much patriotism and good sense among the masses of people both North and South to rush into nullification, secession or revolutionary measures and I would not . . . threaten retaliatory measures against *all* the non-slaveholding states, for the folly and madness of Vermont and the proceedings of a few meetings of monomaniacs.[1]

In the same vein Worth said that it would not be fair to a majority of the people of the North to condemn them in legislative resolutions until it became quite evident that they were flagrantly violating the Fugitive Slave Act passed by Congress to appease the South. Daniel Webster, Lewis Cass, and other northern statesmen should be given time to prevail upon the good sense of the northern people, Worth thought; if they could not, "then will be time enough to determine on the proper course for us to adopt." He felt that residents of the slaveholding states, regardless of their views on slavery, could not condone northern nullification of the Fugitive Slave Act, but he was unwilling to adopt the assumption that the people of the North would not obey the law.

By 1852, Worth was disgusted with party politics at the national level, believing that it had become "common in our leaders to look rather to the availability of a candidate than to the correctness of his principles,"[2] but he remained intensely interested in politics. Though still a steadfast Whig, he decided that if the Democrats ran Lewis Cass for president and the Whigs nominated Winfield Scott, he would vote for the Democrat because Scott had not taken a firm stand during the crisis of 1850. "My attachment to the Union is much stronger than my attachment to party," Worth said after the nominating conventions had met, "hence I thought both parties ought to have nominated . . . those who, in the late turmoil, had the moral courage to breast the storm while its issue was uncertain."[3] Worth had no use for quibblers, in 1850 or any other time.

After 1850, the next major sectional crisis on which Worth's views are ascertainable resulted from Stephen A. Douglas' Kansas-Nebraska Act, the central feature of which was that settlers in a territory could determine whether they would or would not allow slavery when the territory became a state. Worth approved this basic principle—then called "squatter sovereignty"—but he deplored the "abominable frauds" in the Kansas elections held to determine the status of Kansas when it entered the union; the fight to preserve slavery in Kansas he referred to as "fighting for a shadow," since the territory was unfit for an economy based on slaveholding.[4] During the legislature of 1858, Worth and his best political and personal friends tried unsuccessfully to have a resolution adopted denouncing the expulsion of Senator Douglas from the Congressional committee on territories as "an act of petty and party tyranny, which must, upon reflection, cause more mortification to those Senators who rejected him, than it can to the distinguished Senator rejected."[5]

The slavery problem came closest home to Worth when his first cousin, Daniel Worth, was thrown into the Guilford County jail in the winter of 1859-60 to await trial on a charge that he had violated the law of 1830, forbidding the circulation of incendiary publications. Daniel Worth was an old man—sixty-seven years old—when he was confined to an uncomfortable jail and threatened by lynch mobs. A Methodist minister, he had lived for many years in Indiana, but he returned to Guilford County in 1857, began teaching slaves to read, and spread copies of Hinton Rowan Helper's hated book, The Impending Crisis. In a letter to the editor of the National Era, written in July, 1859, he described his work in North Carolina in a way which gave the impression that he was trying to stir up abolition sentiment in the state. The editor of the North Carolina Presbyterian advised Worth to leave the state, but he continued his work zealously.[6] After the authorities of Guilford County issued a warrant for him, he surrendered and went to jail.

When Jonathan Worth heard that Cousin Daniel was in the lion's den, he began working to prevent the full application of the law of 1830, under which Daniel had been arrested; by the terms of that law the prisoner was subject not only to imprisonment, but also to whipping and confinement in a pillory. Worth was horrified at the thought that an aged minister should be whipped, and he realized that such treatment would serve to make his cousin a martyr in the eyes of other abolitionists, who would take advantage of the situation in their antisouthern propagandist activities. With these thoughts in mind he wrote to the editor of the North Carolina Presbyterian, George McNeill, giving his reasons why Cousin Daniel should not be whipped and seeking indirectly, through the editor, to secure the influence of Thomas Ruffin, the most respected judge in the state, against the full application of the law. Worth suggested that the prisoner should be convicted—he was clearly guilty—but that he be allowed to leave the state instead of being whipped or rotting away in the Guilford County jail. Because of his relationship to the abolitionist preacher and the nature of his offense, Worth asked McNeill that his intervention in the case not be revealed to anyone except Judge Ruffin.[7] As soon as McNeill received Worth's letter requesting Ruffin to use his influence he sent it directly to the judge without commenting on it at any length.[8]

When Daniel Worth came to trial the courts followed the plan his cousin had outlined in the indirect letter to Judge Ruffin by allowing him to escape the harsh penalties of the law. Twice he was convicted and twice he appealed to the state Supreme Court. He received a sentence of one year in prison, but was never subjected to the indignity of whipping. After the second conviction in Guilford County, while his second appeal to the Supreme Court was pending, Daniel Worth raised money for bail—three thousand dollars—left the county jail, and headed for the more congenial atmosphere north of the Mason-Dixon line.[9] There he lectured publicly to raise enough money to repay the men who secured his bail.

Relieved by the outcome of Daniel Worth's trial, Jonathan Worth turned his attention once again to state politics; his particular interest in the early months of 1860 was in the district senatorial election. There was a standing agreement between Randolph and Alamance counties that the senator from the district which they formed should be alternated between the two counties. Since Worth was from Randolph, and had been warmly supported in 1858 by the Whigs of Alamance, he was determined not to be a candidate in 1860, unless the Alamance Whigs drafted him. In February, he promised his support to a prospective candidate from Alamance, Dr. E. F. Watson, but at the same time he told Watson that he would run if the Whigs wanted him as their candidate. When the "politicking" became intense Worth pointed out to his Whig friends that "omission to sustain me will be called by Democracy as a virtual repudiation of my course" in the railroad controversy, damaging the Whigs' hopes of recapturing control of the state government.[10]

Dr. Watson declared himself a candidate for the Senate before the middle of April, but when the Whigs of Alamance met in May and unanimously nominated Worth for re-election he considered the nomination "so flattering an endorsement" that he could not refuse to accept it. Watson withdrew from the race and left the field open to Worth.[11]

After accepting the nomination, Worth decided to emphasize in the July campaign the question of ad valorem taxation of slaves and other property, an issue that the Whig Party throughout North Carolina hoped would help them regain control of the state in 1860; they had been excluded for ten years. Under the Constitution of 1835 slaves were not taxed according to their value, but were subject to a capitation tax equal to the amount paid on three hundred dollars worth of land. The whole tax system was inequitable, favoring the commercial interests at the expense of landholders. In 1852, Governor David Reid had recommended ad valorem taxation of all property except slaves, but no reform was made. Six years later, when Worth was in the Senate in 1858, Moses Bledsoe, a slaveholding Senator from Wake County, attempted unsuccessfully to have the finance committee write the ad valorem principle into the biennial revenue bill. Those who favored Bledsoe's measure pointed to the inequality of taxing land more than slaves, claimed that people had left the state as a result of the existing tax system, and insisted that ad valorem taxation was working well in other states where it was being used. The opponents of a tax on the value of property argued that it would fall heavily on the poor and noted that it was a basic principle of contemporary political economy that capital should not be taxed.[12] Worth supported Bledsoe's effort at tax reform by legislative action, and after it failed he backed a constitutional amendment providing for ad valorem taxation of slaves.[13] Thus, Worth's selection of taxation as his campaign issue in 1860 was based on an expressed conviction that slaves should be taxed according to their value. Emphasizing the tax question, "with a light touch on national politics," he campaigned throughout July and easily won the senatorial election early in August. During the next three months he prepared himself for one of the most exciting legislatures in the history of the state. In the election for governor, a secession-minded Democrat, John W. Ellis, beat his Whig opponent, John Pool, by a narrow margin. The Democrats also won thirty-one of the fifty seats in the Senate and sixty-five of the hundred and twenty seats in the House of Commons.[14] Since the Democratic party was generally considered the secession party, the election was a great disappointment to Whig Unionists and a portent of what might happen if the radical wing of the Democrats gained control of the legislature.

Two weeks before the legislature convened in November, Abraham
Lincoln, who received a minority of the total popular vote in the nation, was elected President of the United States, and the cotton states
of the deep South were threatening to secede from the Union.
Throughout North Carolina the question of federal relations was on
the lips of every man who was even remotely interested in politics.
From the discussion several different theories emerged as to the appropriate course for North Carolina to follow in its relations with the
government in Washington. There were still some men who expounded Calhoun's theory of nullification. Another group, the secessionists, believed that a state was free to withdraw from the Union,
which they felt was only a loose confederation. A third school held
that the states did not reserve the right of secession when they ratified
the Constitution of the United States, but insisted upon the right of
revolution if their constitutional rights were infringed. A fourth idea
was that "the states bore about the same relation to the general
government that counties bore to a state."[15] Worth held no brief for
nullification or secession either as abstract political theories or as
practical methods of securing a redress of the South's grievances. Disregarding the academic differences between the various plans and
theories being discussed, he looked upon any method of overthrowing
the authority of the United States government or taking the South
out of the Union as revolutionary. He consistently referred to
secession itself as a revolution; though there was technically a difference
between the two, the academic distinction was unimportant to the
practical-minded Worth. All he could see was that the application of
either theory would result in the dissolution of his beloved Union.

The legislature convened in Raleigh on November 19, 1860, and it
soon became apparent that the secessionists were going to dominate
the Democratic majority. They managed to have a leading secessionist, Thomas L. Clingman, elected to the United States Senate, and they
"decapitated" William W. Holden, editor of the Raleigh *Standard*
and former leader of the Democratic party, by depriving him of the
office of state printer, a plum he had nibbled for many years. Holden,
like many prime movers in revolutions, had cried loudly for southern
rights and for secession until the crisis came; then in 1860, he pulled
up his tent and staked it in the camp of the Unionists. Worth commented on the election of Clingman to the Senate that it "awakens

painful reflections in every lover of Union, whose patriotism raises him above the influences of party."[16]

In the Senate, Worth consistently opposed any measure that appeared militant and supported any step that might help stem the tide of revolution. On December 10, Bedford Brown, Senator from Caswell who had emerged as the leader of the Unionist element, introduced a resolution appointing Thomas Ruffin, Weldon H. Edwards, William A. Graham, and William N. H. Smith to attend the convention of the people of South Carolina on December 17; the delegation was to express the sympathy and concern of North Carolina for her sister state, but was to ask the South Carolina convention "to suspend any action by which secession from the Confederacy shall be accomplished, and await a common consultation through a convention of all the states. . . ."[17] When Senator John M. Morehead tried to have this resolution sent to the legislature's Committee on Federal Relations, Worth voted against such action and spoke in favor of Brown's proposal to send a commission to the South Carolina convention. He said that sending the commissioners would only be a performance of duty, that it would in no way compromise the dignity of North Carolina.[18] W. W. Avery, an avowed secessionist from Burke County, moved two days later to add to Brown's resolution one which stated that the federal government could not coerce a seceding state, and Josiah Turner, Jr., a Whig Unionist, tried to amend Avery's amendment by saying that no state could engage in war or collect import duties without the consent of Congress, and that it was the duty of the general government to collect duties at all the ports in the country. Worth voted against making these amendments to the Brown resolution the special order of the Senate, and Brown withdrew his original resolution when it was still entangled in a web of amendments only three days before the beginning of the convention in South Carolina.

The Senate rode roughshod over Worth, Alfred Dockery, John M. Morehead, James G. Ramsey, and other Unionists when they tried, on December 17, to delay a bill "to provide for the purchase of arms and munitions of war."[19] The next day Worth moved that the arms bill be printed and that consideration of it be postponed until January 7, 1861; this dilatory motion failed by a vote of forty to five, as even many of the Unionists opposed it and favored arming the state immediately. In the one-sided debate over the arms bill, Worth said that he was opposed to hasty legislation, that if arms were bought the legislature should carefully control distribution of them, and that he objected to the high prices the state would have to pay for war materials.[20] While Worth was attempting to give the senators time to consider what they were doing, the proceedings were interrupted for an announcement that two commissioners from Alabama had arrived in Raleigh "to confer with the State of North Carolina upon the subject of our federal relations."[21] After this announcement Senator Avery had the rules suspended and the arms bill rammed through. Efforts of the Unionists to adjourn failed. On the final vote only Jonathan Worth, J. G. Ramsey, and L. Q. Sharpe, Senator from the western district including the Unionist counties of Wilkes and Iredell, voted against the appropriation of money to arm the state.[22]

Worth's spirits began to fall as he saw the more conservative Democrats falling under the influence of the secessionists and the state beginning to raise volunteers and supply them with arms. Only those who openly and unconditionally favored disunion were advocating secession for existing causes, but Worth feared that, as tension mounted, "in bringing the Abolitionists to their senses we are likely to lose our own."[23] It began to appear to him that the increasingly powerful secession leaders were more interested in breaking up the Union than in securing a redress of their grievances against the North.

While the legislature was in session and during the recess for Christmas, public meetings throughout the state were expressing the will of the people of North Carolina for the guidance of their representatives in the public councils. At Asheboro on December 28, between eight hundred and a thousand persons, both Whigs and Democrats, met to discuss the deepening crisis and to express their opinions in a series of resolutions. The first step was to appoint a committee to draw up the resolutions. While the committee was out Worth addressed the meeting, explaining his course in the legislature before Christmas, and the crowd approved heartily. After his speech the committee on resolutions reported and the meeting approved the following resolutions: that secession, "for any causes now existing," would be suicidal; that if extremists broke up the Union it would be to North Carolina's advantage not to take sides with the North or South "but to be one of a Central Confederacy to consist of conservative states North and South, to be known as the 'United States of America' "; and that a national convention, rather than a series of state conventions, should be called to consider the sectional alienation between the

North and South. The meeting gave formal approval to Worth's actions in the Senate and the similar course of its representatives in the House of Commons on the bill to arm the state, and adjourned with a declaration that "all men who love their country . . . should . . . unite for the salvation of the Union and the Constitution."[24] It is clear from the character of the resolutions approved by the meeting that when Worth opposed disunion he gave voice not only to the dictates of his own conscience but also the will of a majority of his constituents. There was a striking similarity and a well-balanced interaction between the senator's opinions and those of the people he represented. He undoubtedly wielded a powerful influence in the formation of public opinion in the secession crisis, and the climate of opinion in turn helped to guide him. Underlying the views of both Worth and his people were the economic and political facts that the population in and about Randolph County held relatively few slaves, that it had been consistently Whig for twenty-five years, and that the area was still inhabited by many Quakers whose religious principles were opposed to war. There is little to wonder about in the fact that Jonathan Worth was a conservative Unionist in the greatest constitutional crisis he ever had to face.

Early in January, 1861, a delegation of citizens from Wilmington requested permission from Governor John W. Ellis to take possession of Fort Caswell, an ungarrisoned United States military post on the Cape Fear River, but Ellis refused to allow the occupation of the fort.[25] In the Senate, Josiah Turner, Jr., introduced resolutions calling upon the governor to tell the Senate whether anyone had consulted him about taking over Fort Caswell and other federal posts in the state, and whether he knew of any plan to occupy them. Worth favored Turner's resolutions, but W. W. Avery succeeded in having them tabled.[26] An organized company of citizens seized Fort Caswell on January 10, but Ellis made them evacuate it the next day. Later, Turner introduced another resolution in the Senate approving the governor's action in forcing the evacuation and stipulating that those who voted to table the resolution of approval "by so doing justify the seizure of Fort Caswell and . . . declare to the world that North Carolina should dissolve her connection with the United States of America."[27] When the Senate refused to approve the evacuation, by defeating Turner's resolution twenty-four to twenty, it was apparent that the secessionists had the upper hand, by this time the Unionists could not even get through a resolution requesting the governor to raise the United States flag over the capitol building.

After Christmas the legislature spent most of its time debating a bill to call a convention of the people of North Carolina. When the Senate began its discussion of the bill Worth was one of its most active opponents; Josiah Turner, Jr., John M. Morehead, and David Outlaw were equally active in opposition. Their main pleas were that the people should be allowed to decide whether a convention should be called, and that if one were called, the delegates should not be elected until after the inauguration of Lincoln on March 4; Worth tried to postpone the meeting of the convention—if one were called—until March 18.[28]

During the debate on the convention bill, Worth jotted down some of the remarks he prepared for delivery to the Senate. These remarks indicated his willingness to call a convention only if its actions were subject to approval by a subsequent vote of the people of the state, but he was not willing that the legislature itself should call a convention to deal with federal relations, "because the Constitution authorizes the General Assembly to call no such Convention."[29] He pointed out forcefully that the only convention which the legislature could call to deal with national affairs was the type of convention authorized in Article Five of the United States Constitution—the section which outlines the amending procedure and allows the state legislatures to call conventions for amending the Constitution. Worth noted also that the states which had met in convention had seceded from the Union, branded the doctrine of secession "a ruinous heresy," and predicted that "a new Republic founded on it would be based on Disintegration." Secession, he declared, was a revolutionary doctrine, and his constituents were not ready to resort to revolutionary measures.

Most of the Unionists' demands were written into a bill which passed on January 29. The act called upon the people of North Carolina to vote whether or not they wanted a convention, and to elect a hundred and twenty delegates to represent them if the convention were approved. No action of the convention, which was limited to actions on federal relations only, was to be valid until it was approved by consent of the people.[30]

The convention bill was by no means an extreme measure, but John M. Morehead entered against it a protest which was signed by

Worth, Turner, Alfred Dockery, and three other Unionists. The main complaint of the protest was that the bill did not allow enough time for the voters to discuss the issues facing them and to decide upon a course of action: "Whilst the bill purports to submit the important question to the people, the submission is illusory and hasty, without any sufficient reason for such precipitancy, without time for consultation, and for forming mature conclusions after prudent deliberation. . . ."[31]

In the short interval between the passage of the convention bill on January 29 and the day scheduled for the election, February 28, 1861, both secessionists and Unionists tried to convince the people of the soundness of their views. The secessionists favored the call of a convention while the Unionists were divided in their opinions as to whether one should be called or not. The secessionists maintained that the Republican party would destroy slavery if the South stayed in the Union, and the Unionists insisted it would be destroyed in the war that would follow secession. The Unionists fired a whole salvo of arguments that would be hard to overcome on February 28: southern senators could block unfavorable legislation and refuse to confirm objectionable appointees of the federal government; the Supreme Court favored the South, and a new president could be elected before the present court was changed; if secession succeeded it would become more difficult to secure fugitive slaves; the proposed new confederacy would be so similar to the United States that there was no use in having a new government; and, geographically, the South was bound to the North so closely that economic self-interest favored continued Union.[32]

Worth formulated his own arguments and issued them to his constituents under the title, "Mr. Worth's Address to the People of Randolph and Alamance."[33] The address was a clear expression of Worth's patriotic nationalism and of his conservatism in constitutional and legal matters. Written shortly after the passage of the convention bill, it announced the content of the bill and explained that Worth had voted against it because of the constitutional objections he had stated in the Senate and because he feared "it may do much mischief." He looked upon the proposed convention as "a modern invention of South Carolina, to bring about a sort of legalized revolution." Worth then quoted the article of the Constitution of the United States which prescribes the amending procedure, and interpreted it to mean that the founding fathers did not believe "the great fundamental law—the

Constitution—should be lightly altered." The article Worth quoted
outlined a means of amending the constitution which had never been
used and which he thought was perfectly designed to fit the present
situation, the call of a national convention. Such a convention, he
felt, would "compose the National commotions."

Worth then warned his constituents that a convention in North
Carolina would be exceedingly dangerous, and that they should not
be deluded by the secessionists' claim that the convention would try
to save the Union. "Believe not those who may tell you this convention is called to *save* the Union," said Worth. "It is called to *destroy*
it." North Carolina would still have time to rush into a revolution
after all constitutional remedies had been exhausted and all efforts
at compromise had failed. Finally, Worth closed out his plea for the
Union in these terms: "I content myself with saying that I have carefully read all the debates in Congress, and I see no sufficient reason for
abandoning the counsels of the Father of his Country, and the Government under which we have become the freest and most powerful nation
of the earth, and launching, probably through civil war, upon the dark
sea of experiment." Apparently Worth's address had a powerful
effect, for on February 28, the citizens of Randolph County voted
against the call of a convention by an overwhelming margin of better
than fifty to one.[34] In the state as a whole the anti-convention forces
won an uncomfortably close victory, 47,323 to 46,672; on this result
Worth later commented that "everybody attributed to me a larger
share of the credit or discredit of defeating the call of a Convention
than to any other man in the State."[35]

The defeat of the call for a convention was followed by a series of
events beyond the control of any individual—events that dragged a
reluctant state down the long road to disunion and civil war. The
newly formed Confederate army attacked Fort Sumter on April 12,
and forced the Union garrison to surrender a day later. President
Lincoln, facing the crisis with practically no army, called upon the
loyal states for seventy-five thousand troops, but Governor Ellis
refused to send any from North Carolina. When Virginia seceded
from the Union on April 17, isolating North Carolina from the
United States, Ellis called a special session of the legislature to meet
in Raleigh on May 1 and determine what should be done. As Worth
prepared to return to the center of events in the state capital he
gloomily remarked to his brothers that "the hotspurs of the South,

aided by a silly administration at Washington, have at length precipitated the nation into universal ruin."[36]

Governor Ellis' proclamation calling the legislature into extra session referred to Lincoln's call for troops as a "high handed act of tyrannical outrage . . . not only in violation of all constitutional law, but also in utter disregard of every sentiment of humanity and Christian civilization. . . ."[37] When the legislators met on May 1, the governor sent in a message recommending the organization of ten regiments of state troops, expenditure of the balance of the three hundred thousand dollars appropriated for arms in December, the erection of coastal defenses, and the call of a convention with "full and final powers" to take North Carolina out of the Union. Before the day was over both houses had passed a bill calling the convention; it did not provide for ratification of the convention's action by an expression of the will of the people.

Worth voted for the convention bill on its first reading, but after the third reading he moved this amendment: "Provided, That any amendment made to the Constitution of the State by said Convention, or any treaty or agreement annexing or confederating this State to any other State or Government, shall have no validity, until ratified by a vote of the people of the State. . . ." When the Senate refused to add this amendment to the convention bill and brought the bill to its final vote, Worth, Josiah Turner, Jr., and L. Q. Sharpe were the only three men who cast their ballots against it.[38] They were, in fact, the only three men in the entire legislature who made a final effort to defeat the call of a convention—for the House of Commons passed the bill unanimously.

After the legislature passed the convention bill and began enacting a series of measures to prepare the state for war, it was apparent that North Carolina was getting ready to leave the Union, but Worth made one final effort to prevent hasty action by the secessionists. On May 3, he introduced a curious resolution designed to place control of the state in the hands of the governor's council between the time the legislature adjourned and the convention met. He proposed to add five members to the council, give it both executive and legislative power, and the authority to lend money or make drafts on the treasury for the purpose of defending the state. If Worth's plan had been followed, the general assembly would have chosen the five extra members of the council and immediately adjourned. The scheme apparently was designed to prevent Governor Ellis, who inclined towards the secessionists, from taking radical measures in the few remaining days before the convention met. Like almost everything Worth did at this time in the Senate, the scheme failed;[39] the secessionists would probably have dominated the council anyway.

While the legislature was still in session Worth had to rush home to Asheboro for two days to attend court. His mind was so preoccupied with the crisis facing the nation that he found it difficult to pay much attention to the affairs of daily life. After weeks of sober reflection he had come to the conclusion that the best way to avoid a terrible civil war was for the South to present a solid military front. "In this view," he informed his friend Cyrus Mendenhall on May 6, "I shall take the stump tomorrow and urge our young men to volunteer."[40] With this shift in his anti-war tactics came the painful necessity of explaining his new course to those who had firmly supported his Unionist position up to that time. Again he drew up a circular, "To the People of Randolph County,"[41] outlining his position and asking them to unite in an effort to save the Union. He still believed that the doctrine of secession was absurd and he told the people so, but he spent most of his words on a severe criticism of the policy of the Lincoln administration in the period shortly preceding and immediately following the bombardment of Fort Sumter. Worth was basically sympathetic to Lincoln's view that the laws of the United States must be executed and federal property in the seceding states protected, but he felt that the president had undermined the Unionists of the South by employing a policy of coercion. He argued that Lincoln should never have tried to use force, because "it would result in a bloody civil war" and "because I thought Congress had indicated, by refusing to pass a force bill, that it was inexpedient at that time, to use military power to retain or regain the public property, through the agency of a sectional President. . . ." Worth's mind flew back over the years to the nullification crisis of 1833 and recalled that in that crisis the great men of the day "held that extraordinary Legislation was necessary to enable the executive to suppress . . . rebellion." Since Congress had adjourned without passing any extraordinary legislation to authorize Lincoln's policy of coercion, Worth interpreted the president's actions as an inexpedient violation of the will of Congress. Thus reasoned an ardent lover of the Union—"rendered impotent to resist the current of Revolution"—as he called upon the young men about him to take up their arms and prepare for whatever should happen next. "I think the South is committing suicide," he told his son David, "but my lot is cast with the South, and being unable to manage the ship, I intend to face the breakers manfully and go down with my companions."[42]

On May 20, 1861, a convention of a hundred and twenty delegates met in Raleigh and unanimously voted North Carolina out of the Union. There was general agreement that the separation had to take place—the state was in such a position that it had no choice—but on the question of how the state should leave the Union there were two schools of thought, the secessionists and the revolutionists. The latter group, composed principally of Whig Unionists like Worth, favored a resolution of separation introduced by George E. Badger which declared simply that North Carolina was no longer a member of the United States of America. The Badger resolution did not satisfy the secessionists, who substituted and passed an ordinance introduced by Burton Craige, that not only declared North Carolina an independent state, but also repealed the act by which the state had ratified the Constitution of the United States. Badger's resolution was based on the age-old right of revolution, Craige's on the theory of state sovereignty which lay at the heart of the doctrine of secession. When the delegates signed the Craige ordinance on May 21, North Carolina was leaving the Union for a period of seven long and bitter years.[43]

· X ·

The First Year of the War

———•—•———

"THERE ARE FEW MEN in so unhappy a frame of mind as myself,"
Jonathan Worth confided to his brothers when it became obvious to
him that the Union could not be saved.[1] In his public utterances he
managed an appearance of hope, but his family and close friends knew
that his mind and heart were filled with despair. He could see no man
among the leaders of the North or South who did not seem to be
motivated by selfishness. Even if the Confederacy were successful, he
mused, it was not likely that it would long hold together. It would
be built on the fatal doctrine of secession, and from it would spring
an endless variety of petty republics—possibly monarchies—based on
"the European plan of preserving government by the cartridge box, instead of the ballot box." By May, Worth believed that the only way
war could be averted was for the United States to recognize the Confederacy and allow the seceded states to depart in peace, but he also
felt that it might be better to have a war than to establish in the South
a government based on the pernicious doctrine of secession. "This
continent ought to be a *united* Government," he said.[2]

As he brooded over the condition of the country, Worth was especially bitter towards the political leaders in both sections. Disgusted
with Abraham Lincoln, he called the president a fool because he had
misjudged the relative strength of the secessionists and Unionists in
the South and followed a policy that made it impossible for the
Unionists to exert any influence in preventing war. Yet, he had no
faith in the leaders of the Southern Confederacy. It seemed to him
that ambitious and selfish politicians in both North and South were
plunging the nation into war, using slavery as a pretext for promoting
their own selfish ends. In formulating this theory about the underlying cause of the impending struggle, Worth spoke in moral terms:

the virtue and order of those opposed to war would be unequal to the ambition and selfishness of those whose political and economic fortunes would be promoted by a war. While he dismissed slavery as the underlying cause of the coming conflict, he was worried about the fate of the black man of the South: "If the civil war is protracted and Northern troops sent among us they will ultimately incite insurrection. The poor negroes will be killed."[3]

Another aspect of the situation in May, 1861, that was exceedingly distasteful to Worth was what he thought of as the triumph of Democracy—the party he had consistently opposed for over thirty years. He firmly believed that the Democrats were the war party, and that most of the men of virtue and intelligence in the state were the Whigs. Events forced him to become the vassal of a party he strongly opposed. He saw that opposition to the North had for the moment obliterated divisions among the politicians in the state, but he realized that this was only a temporary harmony that would soon disappear amid the stress of wartime politics. The day after North Carolina seceded, Worth noted that his reluctance to bow under the yoke of triumphant Democracy made him "particularly obnoxious to low, mean democrats about home."[4]

Wallowing in pessimistic despair, far from convinced that the cause of the South was a just cause, and despising both abolition and secession, Worth cast his lot with the South. His devotion to the Union was strong, but the ties that bound him to the South—his home, his family, his friends, and his state—were stronger. It was a choice he had hoped he would never have to make, but when the fateful moment came he was not hesitant, and once he made the decision he worked as earnestly for the South as he had worked to save the Union.

When in June, 1861, he began to induce the young men of his county to volunteer for service, Worth became involved in the first of a long series of episodes that contributed to his dislike of the war. His nephew, Shubal G. Worth, was trying to raise a company, and a rumor reached the ears of Captain Robert Gray, who was also raising a company, that Worth was using his influence to assist Shubal at the expense of Captain Gray's organization. The rumor forced Worth into explanations to Captain Gray; he denied the rumor—a "colorless falsehood"—and promised that in future recruiting activities he would assist in the effort to raise two strong companies.[5]

When the companies were forming in Randolph and some soldiers, accustomed to having slaves for personal servants, began seizing free Negroes to serve them in the field, Worth did all he could to save the Negroes. One new recruit seized a free Negro who had been working for Worth, and sent Worth a request to forward his clothes; the Negro, an eighteen-year-old boy named Henry Stith, was to serve the soldier in camp and the field. This illegal seizure, and similar cases, irritated Worth, who felt an obligation to the boy who had worked faithfully for him. He retained John A. Gilmer to have Henry returned. Worth expressed to Gilmer the fear that there was only one step from the seizure of free Negroes to the confiscation of slaves for use by the military authorities. But he was not willing to incur "public odium" by having the boy brought back. He instructed Gilmer, in effect, to sound out public opinion on impressment before saving Henry Stith from being dragged off to the army; if bringing the boy back would arouse hostility to either Worth or Gilmer, Worth was willing to let him go.[6]

Later in 1861, Worth wrote to Captain Leigh Andrews requesting that a Negro boy seized by Andrews' men be released. He enclosed an order of the Adjutant General of the state to show that the boy was taken unlawfully.[7] The episode was repeated early in 1862, when soldiers carried off a free Negro named Lewis, who had a wife, two small children, and a crop of wheat and oats in the ground. In requesting that these Negroes be released, Worth invariably spoke of them as men of good character, and interpreted the seizures as infringements on their personal rights.[8]

Late in the summer of 1861, Worth had to return to Raleigh for another extra session of the legislature. He sat for the first few days listening to complaints that the convention elected in May was still in existence and to discussions whether Henry T. Clark, the Speaker of the Senate, should continue to act as governor, a position he had held since John W. Ellis died in July; in spite of some protests, the convention continued to act until 1862, and Clark stayed on as governor.[9] Most of the work of the legislature was concerned with financing the war, and it was at this session that Worth became the recognized expert in this field. He found that he wielded more influence than he had expected, particularly after the Democrats publicly recognized his financial abilities by making him chairman of the committee responsible for drawing up an extremely important revenue bill; he sus-

pected that they had extended this honor to him so they might avoid
"the labor and odium of a bill to increase the taxes."[10]

During the summer the state convention had adopted an ordinance
requiring that both lands and slaves should be taxed ad valorem. As
the chairman of the finance committee, Worth made sure that the
ordinance would be put into effect by reporting to the Senate that the
finance committee "do[es] consider it expedient to tax slaves ad
valorem" and by writing the ad valorem principle into the revenue
bill he introduced on September 4.[11] Since the taxation of slaves
according to their value had been adopted, Worth thought that horses,
mules, cattle, and certain other items should also be taxed—a measure
which would arouse opposition in the West. One faction in the legislature, led by Burgess S. Gaither of Burke, a western county, was
reluctant to raise taxes to pay the state's expenses, preferring the issue
of treasury notes. Worth, more concerned with maintaining the
credit of the state and preventing inflation than in catering to
the traditional anti-taxation sentiment of the people, wanted the
state to follow the policy of "pay as you go"—and the only way
this could be done was by increased taxes. When the revenue bill
came before the Senate he managed to have several items added to the
list of taxables, after a long debate in which he had to do some tactical
compromising.[12]

Long before the legislature met it was apparent that the state
would have to go deeply in debt if it were to maintain its own little
army. The convention had turned the state's forces over to the Confederacy, but at Governor Clark's suggestion the legislature authorized
the maintenance of ten regiments for state defense. How to pay for
them was a problem—the state was already in debt when the war
started. Worth reported the opinion of the finance committee that a
resolution calling for the issue of state bonds was inexpedient,[13] and
the committee decided to issue treasury notes instead. There was disagreement between the two houses over the legislation necessary to
authorize the issue of the treasury notes, and a committee of conference recommended that a tax of two cents should be levied on each
hundred dollars worth of land and slaves to pay the principal and
interest on the loan authorized by the bill. At first, only the interest
would be paid from the tax, the balance of the proceeds from the
levy going into the state's Sinking Fund to pay off the principal when
it became due. The House of Commons refused to accept this pro-

posal to levy a tax, the Senate was too stubborn to recede, and another conference committee met. Speaking for this second committee, Worth recommended that the Senate recede, and a revised bill passed on September 20.[14] It authorized the state treasurer to issue a million dollars worth of notes ranging in denomination from five to one hundred dollars; in effect, the state would be printing its own money. What this all amounted to was that the legislature was authorizing a loan of a million dollars without making adequate provision to repay it. In spite of his participation Worth was disgusted. It was the type of proceeding that caused him to grow weary with the General Assembly; he considered the body a sorry group, "incompetent to discharge its duties."[15]

The war measure Worth opposed most strongly in 1861 was a stay law hidden behind the innocent-sounding title, "a bill to alter the jurisdiction of the courts of the state."[16] When the bill first appeared in the regular session of the legislature, Worth delivered one of his lengthier speeches against it. Denouncing the proposed measure as unconstitutional and inexpedient, he read to the Senate a decision of the state Supreme Court to prove his basic contention that incidental stays—those incident to changes of jurisdiction—were legal and that other stays were not.[17] When the slightly disguised stay law reappeared in the second extra session of the assembly and was passed in both houses, Worth entered into the journal a protest in which he summarized his arguments against the bill to stop the collection of debts. The protest was a clear statement of conservative principles that would have pleased an old Hamiltonian Federalist. Its major points were that the bill was not designed for the purpose it stated, but "to hinder and delay creditors in the collection of debts due to them"; that it was unconstitutional because it impaired the obligation of contracts; that similar stay laws passed during the Revolutionary War had been detrimental and, as a result, legislative bodies were deprived of the power to alter private contracts; that the law was an inadequate means of effecting a desired end; and, finally, that it was a legislative threat against the judiciary—implying "the power to abolish the judiciary department of the government whenever the General Assembly shall deem it expedient to do so. . . ."[18] Worth's firm opposition to stay laws in general and this one in particular may be accounted for by remembering his extensive connections with the creditor class, the fact that he was a lawyer, and his innate conservatism in matters financial; but he also believed that stay laws were detrimental to debtors, because in the long run they tended to weaken the credit system. With reference to the law passed in August, 1861, Worth called it "abominable" and reported to his brother Addison that "the stay law deranges everything. There is not a man here, rich or poor, who ever indulges in the luxury of cursing, who does not curse everybody who voted for it—and those who don't curse, use terms as nearly equivalent as good morals will allow."[19]

Late in September, 1861, the extra session of the legislature adjourned and Worth returned to Asheboro to continue his legal practice and to look after his personal affairs. That fall the realities of a wartime economy began to impinge upon him in a manner that affected the size of his purse and led to considerable grumbling. Debts were stayed and prices were beginning to rise. He usually bought a large stock of provisions for his family and slaves after the crops had been harvested and the hogs butchered. Early in December, pork was selling at ten dollars for a hundred pounds, and Worth expected to buy what he needed at that price, but some farmers in the county got contracts for the sale of pork to a military commissary lately established at High Point for $13.50. This made it impossible for Worth to buy pork for his own use without paying the prices offered by the commissary's agents.[20]

Actually Worth had little cause to complain about the high price of pork, for he was himself beginning to capitalize on the need for provisions by buying meat and selling it at a profit. In the fall of 1861, he formed a partnership with Nathaniel Steed and Sam Jackson in what he called "my beef enterprise."[21] The partners bought twenty-five thousand pounds of beef that had been pickled in salt brine, and Worth began negotiating with Captain Thomas D. Hogg, an agent of the state, in an effort to sell the beef for use by the military. This proved to be an aggravating transaction, wrapped in many yards of what is now called "red tape." Before meat could be sold to the commissary department it had to be approved by a government inspector —who was not always easy to find. The government also required that the meat be salted more heavily than it would have been salted for use by civilians; this of course reduced the margin of profit that could be made. Prices were not uniform throughout the state, so Worth tried to select his market carefully. In trying to sell the beef, he became so annoyed he called the state's meat inspector a fool because "he

requires more salt than can do any good."[22] He finally decided, because of the difficulties involved in selling to the commissary at High
Point, to send the meat to his son David at Wilmington for sale to
the commissary of subsistence in that city. How much money he made
cannot be ascertained, but shortly after the last of the beef was sold he
received from Hogg, the purchasing agent, a draft for $720.45.[23] After
Worth sent the beef to Wilmington he explained to Captain Hogg that
he sent it there because he could not get it inspected at High Point
and because he "did not wish to be regarded as a speculator in provisions."[24] A month later he was buying large quantities of bacon and
dried beef.

The commodity which interested Worth most was salt. In December, 1861, his brother Milton accepted the office of state salt commissioner, and Worth himself was the county salt commissioner for Randolph County. Salt was an essential item, particularly in wartime
when so much meat had to be preserved for the use of soldiers. Before the war most of the salt used in the South came from either Europe
or the West Indies, but after Lincoln declared a blockade of the Confederacy in April, 1861, the price of it began to spiral to a point where
it appeared that the average consumer would not be able to buy it,
and the states were forced to begin manufacturing it.[25] In North Carolina, the state convention enacted the necessary legislation, and Milton
Worth accepted the position as the state's first salt commissioner;
under him there was a commissioner for each county.

When Jonathan Worth heard that brother Milton had been appointed salt commissioner, he wrote: "In the undertaking in which
you are embarked our family reputation for energy and success is involved, and I will sustain you to the utmost of my ability."[26] At the
same time he refused to participate in a joint commission with his
brother, but he offered this friendly advice: ". . . have all your accounts
in condition to defy malevolence itself"; afterwards he did assume
several responsibilities in connection with the manufacture of salt.

When Milton began organizing the salt works, Worth carried out
his promise to help in any way he could to make the operations a
success. Early in 1862, he assisted Milton by visiting the area around
Currituck Sound, appointing an agent there, and buying boilers in
Norfolk, Virginia, to be used in boiling salt from sea water. A bushel
of salt could be extracted from sixty gallons of water taken from wells
on the banks of the sound. He reported that "individuals are making

some three hundred bushels per day in Currituck."[27] He further assisted by appointing agents to distribute salt produced on the coast in the various counties; there was one agent for each tax district.

At first there were three salt works, one on Currituck Sound, one near Morehead City, and one at Wilmington, but the Union forces captured the sounds and cut off Morehead City in 1862, leaving the works at Wilmington the only one in operation. It was eight miles above the city and twenty miles from the mouth of the Cape Fear River. Worth, fearing that Wilmington might also fall to the enemy, asked the state geologist to examine an old salt spring near Wadesboro to see if it could be used in the event that it was needed,[28] but, fortunately, Wilmington did not fall until late in the war, and the salt works continued to operate there. By December of 1862, brother Milton could boast to Jonathan that he had provided twenty-one thousand bushels of salt to seventy-five counties, at an average cost to the counties of $3.50 a bushel. This was achieved in spite of an epidemic of yellow fever that struck Wilmington in the fall of 1862 and forced the operations of the salt makers to be suspended for several weeks. When the work at Wilmington stopped, Jonathan Worth began negotiations to procure salt for Randolph County from Saltville, Virginia, where the state had made arrangements to get salt, but he resigned as county salt commissioner to return to the legislature before the first wagon train headed for Saltville.[29]

Intensifying other troubles at this time, the Worths had a personal sorrow, for one of the victims of the yellow fever epidemic in Wilmington was Clarkson Worth. The close little band of brothers had been broken for the first time.

In December, 1862, an incident occurred which created antagonism between the salt commissioner and the Confederate general in charge at Wilmington and resulted later in open warfare between the Worths and the general. The commander, W. H. C. Whiting, came to Wilmington to supervise and erect additional defenses for the city, and in his eagerness to get his work done he ordered a hundred and fifty of the laborers at the salt works to help fortify Wilmington. Milton naturally was furious. A few days later General Whiting called him to his office and said, "I understand you have too many men at your works, and have also learned that you are on that account making the salt cost the State more than any salt that is made hereabouts."

Milton replied heatedly, "If any one has told you that I have too many hands and that my salt costs more than that made by private parties they told you a d—— lie." The two men glared at each other for a few silent moments; then the general turned to his adjutant and countermanded the order which caused the strained relations. Milton's son, Shubal, reported the scene to his Uncle Jonathan, who held General Whiting in low esteem from that time on.[30]

Worth made several efforts to assure that the salt works would have an adequate number of workers. In March, 1862, he asked Governor Vance to excuse from military service any Quaker who was willing to work as a salt maker or hire a substitute to work for him. Vance agreed to this, and a few weeks later the state convention passed an ordinance providing that if a Quaker could produce a certificate of membership in the Society of Friends and would pay a hundred dollars to the sheriff of his county he was exempt from military service; if he was unable to pay the hundred dollars the governor could send him to the salt works or to one of the state's hospitals to act as a nurse.[31] This plan of Worth's served the double purpose of keeping his Quaker friends out of the army and providing a source of labor for the salt works, but the Quakers refused to co-operate, until he had convinced one of their leaders, Allen M. Tomlinson, that the salt works were out of range of enemy ships, that there was "ample opportunity to escape," that the climate was salubrious, and that the "hardest work is cutting and splitting cord wood" for the boilers.[32]

The salt commissioner devised an additional plan by which Quakers could pay him a commutation of eleven dollars a month instead of sending a worker; payment of the money supposedly exempted one from conscription. In April, 1862, Aaron Newlin, a Quaker, received an order from the Adjutant General of the state troops, James G. Martin, to report for military service. Newlin then sent Worth eleven dollars to pay a substitute at the salt works, indicated that he expected to continue paying the price of commutation each month, and asked Worth to intercede for him. Worth informed General Martin that Newlin was paying a substitute and that if this was not acceptable Newlin would go to the salt works in preference to the army.[33] The Quakers who were unable to raise the price of exemption clearly were faced with an ugly choice—the army or the salt works.

The case of Aaron Newlin gives some indication of how Worth felt about uprooting men from their homes and sending them off to war. He believed that a man could use any legal means of staying out of the army without losing his honor, and he applied this notion in several cases in which his own interests were involved. This was particularly true after the Confederacy passed a conscription law in April, 1862, that made all men between the ages of eighteen and thirty-five subject to service in the Confederate Army. The details of the conscription law reached Worth on the same day he heard of the fall of New Orleans and Fort Macon, and before the effects of the triple blow had worn off he wrote to his friend, Alfred G. Foster, a member of the state convention:

The gloom thickens to a mind like mine, which has at no time been able to see a bright spot in the future, whether our arms are successful or unsuccessful. If unsuccessful we shall be in no better condition, I fear, than were the English after the conquest of William the Norman. If successful, we shall be an impoverished, demoralized and waste nation. Democracy and the Devil still have dominion, in any event I can see.

If our enemies should fail to overthrow us in arms our Legislation would ruin us. With all our men from 18 to 35 called to camps of instruction at this season, famine is inevitable . . . an adequate supply of wheat cannot be made and the harvest must be saved.[34]

He also told Foster the convention should exempt from military service everyone who was making salt, whether they were working for the state or not.

Before the Confederacy began to resort to conscription, Worth had become President of the Cedar Falls Manufacturing Company. After Congress began making exceptions to the Conscription Act he took steps to keep employees of the Cedar Falls cotton factory out of the army. Following prescribed procedures, he drew up a statement to be signed by the superintendent of the factory, George Makepeace, certifying that certain employees were "absolutely necessary" to the successful operation of the company. It also certified that the company had been supplying the state with large quantities of cloth and was at that time under contract to deliver fifty thousand shirts and drawers for use by the army.[35] This statement served its intended purpose, the workers remained at Cedar Falls, and the factory continued to supply the state.

The successful attempt to keep the employees at Cedar Falls out of the Confederate army was achieved by perfectly legitimate means, but when Worth made an effort to keep one of his farm overseers from being drafted he consciously evaded the conscription laws. The situation that required this evasion arose in April, 1862, when Worth bought a six hundred acre farm from Cyrus P. Mendenhall. After Worth looked at the farm as a prospective buyer he wrote to Mendenhall that "we found the barn rotten, the house old style, a good deal of the place much worn and much of the wood land very poor," but he bought it anyway.[36]

The caretaker of the farm was a man named Wyatt Jordan. Worth retained his services on the same terms he had worked for Mendenhall, sent two slaves to the farm, and instructed Jordan to give them five pounds of bacon and a peck of meal each week and to get them a good milk cow. When the two slaves arrived Jordan's status changed from caretaker to overseer.[37]

Through the summer and fall of 1862, Jordan worked the farm. Then in October, it began to appear that he would be drafted into the army. Worth wanted to have his overseer exempted from conscription, but under the provisions of the Confederacy's unpopular "twenty nigger law" this could only be done if there were at least twenty slaves under the overseer's supervision. Worth could not afford to buy enough slaves to raise the number on the farm to twenty, but there was one chance of meeting the provision of the conscript law and keeping Jordan out of the army: some planters in the eastern counties of the state wanted to move their slaves out of the way of a possible enemy attack and were willing to hire them out rather cheaply. Worth made plans to talk with some of the eastern slaveholders in the legislature about hiring additional hands when he went to Raleigh—if Jordan were not drafted before Worth could get to the capital city.[38] He also set his cousin Hiram to searching for available Negroes.

By the last of October, Hiram had found enough slaves to bring the number on the farm up to fourteen. Worth then rounded out the required twenty by sending a woman, three children, and two men from his home place in Asheboro. Feeling very uneasy about evading the conscript law in this way—which was, strictly speaking, legal—he told Jordan that the law was "going to be very unpopular" and asked him not to tell anyone about their scheme to have him exempted. Worth admitted that he entered into this plan not only for Jordan's sake—he was a husband and father—but in the hope that Jordan, by good management, might avert a loss of profits.[39] It is to Worth's credit that he did at least comply with the letter of the law, as some others did not bother to do. This was in accordance with his unvarying policy of obeying the laws of the land, however unwise or inexpedient he considered them to be; of laws in this category there was an unending stream throughout the war period. His prediction to Jordan that conscription would be unpopular proved to be based on more than one man's personal disapproval, for in October, 1862, Randolph County was beginning to be plagued by "some fifty or more" deserters and men who were evading conscription. A few of these men were no better than desperadoes, and the militia was out chasing them.[40]

Eighteen sixty-two was another election year, and while Worth was busy managing his farms, helping with the production of salt, and trying to keep his friends out of the army he had to consider whether he should try to get elected to the legislature for another term; since it was the privilege of Alamance County to send one of its citizens to the Senate that year he would have to run for the House of Commons. In May, he wrote to William J. Long, one of his conservative friends:

My mind has been painfully exercised for some time on the question whether I ought to be a candidate for the Commons. . . . Unbridled Jacobinism is soon to become disunion if conservative men shrink from breasting the storm of popular frenzy. . . . Only one of us ought to run. Which of us can render most service to the public? I am fairly certain you can. The opposition to me amounts to malignant personal hatred. . . . I do not doubt that I can be elected, but I regard it as doubtful whether I can do any good against the furious feeling which I believe will grow out of it.[41]

Early in July, after Long decided not to be a candidate and several other men encouraged Worth to enter the race, he announced his candidacy.

There was no time to conduct a regular campaign, for an overseer at Worth's farm in Randolph—not Wyatt Jordan—had been drafted, leaving his employer with the duties of supervising the farming. Worth was fairly certain that he could be elected, but he made a special effort to secure the votes of the men in the army. His political opponents in Randolph, mistrusting him because of his strong Unionist position in the secession crisis and his lack of enthusiasm for the war, began what he called an "effort to prejudice the army against me."[42] They brought up the old charge that he had made it difficult

for some companies to enlist men, by encouraging enlistments ex-
clusively in his nephew's company, and blamed him for certain acts
of his brother Milton. As a colonel in the militia, Milton had secured
the release of a man who had been forced by a mob to join a company. "I had no more to do with it than the man in the moon," Worth
said of Milton's act.[43]

Two weeks before the day the army was to vote in the field Worth
wrote a letter to the commanding officer of each company from the
county—there were eight—announcing that he was a candidate for
the House of Commons and stating that he would be gratified if the
soldiers would vote for him. He admitted that he had opposed the
war until hostilities became unavoidable, and that he earnestly desired
peace "as soon as it can honorably be made," but he insisted that after
the war began he encouraged the people of the South to present a
united front and did everything he could to promote the welfare of
the soldiers in the field. In one letter Worth expressed the hope and
conviction that the soldiers from the county knew him too well to be
deluded by false rumors about his loyalty.[44]

On election day Worth got only thirty-two votes from the soldiers
of Randolph County, bearing out his suspicion that his course had been
misunderstood; most of the soldier vote went to Marmaduke Robbins
and Thomas Winslow, who received ninety-eight and forty-seven ballots, respectively. But when the ballots of those persons remaining at
home were added to those of the army men, Worth won the election
easily, receiving more votes than five other candidates combined.[45]
He was gratified that those who had been in the best position to observe
his actions had overwhelmingly sustained him, but little did he
suspect that he had just been elected to the North Carolina legislature for the last time.

· XI ·

The Wartime Treasury

BEFORE WORTH LEFT ASHEBORO to attend the legislature of 1862, he received information from an intimate friend, Isaac H. Foust, that the political faction which supported and elected Zebulon B. Vance for governor in the August elections was considering Worth as its candidate for state treasurer. The same news came from William A. Graham, the most distinguished of the former Union Whigs, ex-governor, and Secretary of the Navy. When Worth heard from Graham he replied: "You say many of my friends are speaking of making me Public Treasurer. It originated with my friends. I had not thought of it. If my friends, without my seeking shall confer the appointment on me I will accept it, having some confidence that I could discharge the duties of the place properly."[1] After Worth wrote to Graham it was a foregone conclusion that he would be nominated for state treasurer when the legislature met in November.

The question of who should be treasurer was deeply involved in party politics. By the fall of 1862, two factions had emerged in the state, differing mainly in their attitude toward the war and the policies of the Confederate government. Worth was the candidate of the Conservatives, the less enthusiastic party. His opponent, D. W. Courts, who was already serving the state as treasurer, was supported by the Confederates, the party which was associated in the minds of the Conservatives with the former secession Democrats. Wartime politics centered around the question of the extent of opposition to or support of the Confederacy. The difference between the opposing factions was only one of degree and method, as both sides actively supported the struggling Confederacy—at least during the first two years of the war.

There were varying points of view on the prospect of Worth's election as the highest financial officer of the state. Martitia and the chil-

dren took a great interest in what "Pa" was doing when he was away
in Raleigh. They moaned when the majority voted against him and
shared his triumphs when he won some minor victory. When the
rumor was going around that he was about to be elected treasurer,
Adelaide wrote that one of the neighbors "knew Col. Fisher would turn
over in his grave" if Worth were elected.[2] On the day before the election William W. Holden, who was then allied with the Conservatives,
wrote in his *Standard:* "We sincerely trust that Mr. Worth will be
elected."[3] The editor pointed out that Worth was a loyal supporter
of Governor Vance, identified Courts, "in word and deed," with the
Confederates, and claimed that his re-election as treasurer would be
an embarrassment to the governor.

The Confederates naturally saw matters in a different light. One
disgruntled opponent of Worth made this biting remark: ". . . I learn,
they have decided in caucus that Courts is to be beaten. And whom
do you suppose has been selected for Treasurer? Jonathan Worth of
Randolph!!—as I was informed yesterday. The heart sickens at the
sight of such doings."[4] Courts himself, who stood to lose his job if
Worth were elected, reported to Thomas Ruffin that almost everyone
expected Worth to be the choice of the legislature, but in an effort
to head off his removal Courts asked Judge Ruffin for a lengthy letter
"rebutting the charge of favoritism to political friends in handing out
eight per cent Treasury notes and bonds."[5]

Whether Courts's management of the treasury was partisan and
illegal, or whether it was based on a misunderstanding of the law, is
debatable, but the legislature of 1862 used his handling of bonds and
treasury notes as the grounds for not re-electing him to office on December 3, 1862. In the voting Jonathan Worth won by 52 to 42 in the
House of Commons and 27 to 19 in the Senate.[6] William Holden expressed the gratification of the Conservatives at the result of the election and repeated his opinion that Worth was better qualified than
Courts to manage the treasury, but the Confederates cried "proscription."

Although Worth's election meant that he would have to move
from Asheboro to Raleigh, the family was pleased with his new position. Mrs. Worth wrote: "I feel very much gratified at your election
and am proud of your high standing in the state. You must make
haste and come home that I may congratulate you in a more cordial
manner." Adelaide remarked teasingly about the new position of

honor that "it was a blessed thing that people did not always trust to *appearances* or you would never have been elected Treasurer in that old, white, greasy hat." Mary was anxious to move to Raleigh because the schools were better there than they were in Asheboro.[7] Worth's many friends in Randolph County were also pleased with his election but saddened with the thought that the Worths would be leaving Asheboro. They had depended on Jonathan Worth for many things, and looked to him as the best representative of their interests. The sheriff said he did not know what the county would do without Worth, and Gaius Winningham, a neighbor, commented that "the bull cow of Randolph is gone and the cattle will scatter."[8] Worth terminated his services as a legislator for the people among whom he had lived for almost forty years when he resigned from the House of Commons, effective December 20, 1862.[9] Martitia and the children came to Raleigh a few weeks later.

In normal times the state treasurer performed several important functions. His basic task was supervising the collection and expenditure of the state's money, and keeping detailed accounts of the state's financial transactions. At the time Worth took office the money was divided among three entirely separate accounts, the Public Fund, the Literary Fund, and the Sinking Fund. The treasurer also served as an adviser to the legislature on financial policy, submitting suggestions about the collection of revenues and the maintenance of public credit; these suggestions were based on the treasurer's knowledge of general economic and financial conditions and upon carefully drawn estimates of the future income and expenditures of the state.

The task of performing the normal peacetime duties outlined above was enough to keep any man busy, but in addition Worth had the burden of administering a complex mass of financial legislation designed to finance North Carolina's sizable war establishment. Indeed, the story of his administration of the treasury is basically an account of how the exigencies of the Civil War affected the financial policy of the state and of the methods by which the treasurer administered that policy and helped to formulate it.

The basic policies Worth administered were already laid down before he became treasurer. Almost all of them were shaped by the one great overriding consideration—the war. Two weeks after Lincoln was elected the state owed over ten million dollars, most of which was for railroad bonds and investments in other internal improvements. The interest on the debt and the normal expenses of operating the state government required an outlay of $728,424 in 1859-60, but the income for that year was only $618,964.[10] The legislature had created a sinking fund in 1857 to pay off the debt. The major source of income for the fund was dividends on railroad stocks, and there was a fair prospect that the debt would be retired as the railroads grew and paid larger dividends. Then the war came.

Legislation designed to meet the needs of a state at war began to come out of the legislature even before the war started when the General Assembly authorized the issue of three hundred thousand dollars worth of bonds in January, 1861; Worth strongly opposed this measure,[11] but he supported later measures passed to raise money for soldiers and supplies. The basic fiscal policies of the war period emerged from the first extra session of the legislature in May, 1861, and the first session of the convention, which was in session from May 20 to June 28. On May 11, the legislature appropriated five million dollars to be used during the next two years. The treasurer had to raise this by issuing treasury notes or borrowing money from the banks of the state in return for 6 per cent bonds on which interest would be paid annually. In case the banks refused to lend money to the state, the treasurer could issue notes up to the five million dollar maximum; if the banks were willing to make loans on the specified terms, the treasurer was to alternate issues of notes and loans from the banks. The banks had suspended specie payments in November, 1860, and the law promised that no bank which loaned money to the state would be required to resume specie payments until the state paid back what it borrowed under the terms of this basic defense act.[12]

Subsequent legislation by both the legislature and the state convention continued the policy of raising money by issuing treasury notes and bonds and borrowing from banks. In June, 1861, the convention added two hundred thousand dollars to the amount of notes that the treasurer could issue and raised the authorized amount of bank loans to three million dollars.[13] The legislature again raised the amount of notes that could be issued when it authorized the treasurer, in September, 1861, to issue a million dollars in notes of large denominations and eight hundred thousand in notes of denominations less than one dollar.[14] Three months later the convention gave further authorization for the issue of notes "not exceeding at any one time, three millions of dollars." This particular issue of notes was both interest-bearing and fundable in 6 per cent, thirty year bonds. The notes could be used to pay state taxes, and after they returned to the treasury they could not be reissued, but others might replace them.[15]

The two most important financial measures of 1862 were a funding act passed by the convention in February and "An Act to Provide Ways and Means for Supplying the Treasury" passed on the day Jonathan Worth became Public Treasurer, December 20, 1862. The funding act made the notes authorized in the previous December and those appropriated for the payment of the Confederate tax fundable in 8 per cent, twenty year bonds or 6 per cent bonds maturing in thirty years. It also provided for two more issues of notes and declared that taxes were payable in either of the following currencies: North Carolina treasury notes; Confederate treasury notes; bank notes of banks recognizing and using North Carolina treasury notes; and gold or silver coin.[16] The legislation at the end of the year 1862 authorized Worth to issue four and a half million dollars in treasury notes and five million dollars in 6 per cent, twenty year bonds.[17] The act authorizing these issues was part of a concerted plan to convert the growing debt of the state into 6 per cent bonds running twenty years. In February, 1863, Worth was directed to stamp "fundable only in six per cent bonds" across the face of treasury notes he received which were formerly fundable in 8 per cent bonds. These notes could be reissued, provided the total amount of notes in circulation did not exceed six and a half million dollars.[18] After February, 1863, the legislature authorized two more issues of treasury notes and two bond issues to supply the wartime treasury, but there was little change in policy except that treasury notes issued after December, 1864, were made fundable in 1876 instead of in 1866.[19]

There was considerable disparity between the amount of notes and bonds authorized during the war and the amount actually issued, but the cumulative effects of wartime legislation pertaining to notes and bonds may be summarized in a few figures. The treasurers had authority to issue $14,176,555 in bonds, but less than thirteen millions were issued for purposes of carrying on the war. Even more treasury notes could have been issued, as some twenty million dollars worth were authorized, but in actual practice Courts and Worth put only eight and a half million dollars in circulation; of this amount they had withdrawn $3,261,000 before the war ended, leaving in circulation

$5,246,000. A little over three million dollars of the treasury notes were funded for state bonds.[20] From these figures it is apparent the state relied primarily upon the issue of bonds to raise money during the war period, and to a lesser extent upon treasury notes.

Worth was as conservative in the issue of bonds and treasury notes as the conditions of a war economy would allow him to be. Because each issue put the state deeper in debt, he was reluctant to issue notes and bonds unless such action was absolutely necessary. Early in 1863, the resources of the treasury began to get low and he sold $110,500 worth of bonds to individuals and $971,500 worth to the commissioners of the Sinking Fund; those sold to individuals brought a 5 per cent premium. When Worth could pay expenses in Confederate notes he did so, in preference to issuing state notes or bonds.[21] Worth employed the services of the same broker Courts used, Lancaster and Company of Richmond, to sell North Carolina's bonds. The procedure was for him to send the bonds to Richmond, where the company sold them in the open market and sent the proceeds back to Raleigh. Selling in the money markets of Richmond, the state's bonds had to meet competition from other types of securities and were subject to general market conditions. For this reason the treasurer had to pick the most propitious time to throw his bonds on the market. When Worth put his first issue of bonds on the Richmond exchange to be sold, North Carolina sixes were selling on very favorable terms. On February 18, 1863, they were selling at 26 per cent premium above their par value. There was a sharp increase in premium on North Carolina sixes during the first week in March, resulting from a sudden demand by blockade runners for the bonds and a rise in the gold market at New York.[22] The high premiums made Worth's first bond sale quite successful.

There are two possible explanations for the fact that North Carolina's bonds sold at a premium over Confederate bonds in 1862 and 1863. In general, Worth and his predecessor at the treasury were more conservative in their management of the state's finances than the struggling Confederate treasury could afford to be. Underlying everything else was the simple fact that if the South lost the war the Confederacy would pass out of existence and the state of North Carolina would not. These same factors also explain why the state had a good credit rating in financial circles almost to the end of the war.

North Carolina's treasury notes also were worth more than their par value, but Worth did not issue any during his first few months at the treasury, except some small ones for fractions of a dollar and some three dollar bills. By June, 1863, state notes were being sold in Raleigh at the following premiums: non-fundable notes, at 10 per cent; notes fundable in 1866, at 27 per cent; and notes immediately fundable, at 40 per cent.[23] Worth soon discovered that, because state treasury notes were selling at a premium—in terms of Confederate money—they did not always serve the purpose for which they were designed, to serve as a circulating medium. This was particularly true of some notes of small denominations authorized in December, 1863. By the time Worth got the notes printed they could be sold at a 50 per cent premium over Confederate notes. He did not even bother to have them signed, for they would only have been hoarded.[24]

A minor difficulty in using treasury notes was that it was hard to get paper of good quality on which to print them, especially in the later years of the war. The scarcity of engravers and lithographers in the Confederacy was also a problem. North Carolina's notes were printed in New Orleans by the firm of J. Manouvrier until New Orleans fell to the Union in April, 1862. For a few months Courts could not get notes and was forced to borrow in order to pay demands on the treasury. Finally, he made a contract with J. T. Patterson and Company, of Columbia, South Carolina, for the printing of the notes.[25] When Worth became treasurer he continued to use the services of Patterson.

Worth never did like treasury notes—they reminded him of the assignat of the French Revolution and the paper money issued during and after the American Revolution. They were inflationary in their effects, and Worth believed they tended to destroy the state's credit. Furthermore, the differences in value between state and Confederate notes could be embarrassing, as witnessed in the following letter from Worth to one of his friends:

I am now prepared to let you have the $3500. you deposited with me, in N.C. Treas. notes. At the time I accepted the deposit and made the promise to exchange, the N.C. notes were not worth any premium above the notes deposited by you. The $3. bills which I am now ready to let you have, are worth 27 per cent.—premium. Although the transaction is a perfectly fair one, as it turns out unfortunately for the State, both you and I would probably be censured, if the newspapers knew it. It is inexpedient to be put on the defensive for a justifiable transaction, and therefore it need not be known to the public.[26]

But regardless of Worth's dislike of paper money and the occasional embarrassments arising from its use, financial necessity compelled him to rely upon treasury notes almost to the end of the war.

Next to bonds and treasury notes, the state's largest source of income during the war period was a series of bank loans that began in May, 1861, and continued through February, 1863. During the month in which the legislature first authorized these loans, May, 1861, the banks promptly responded to the state's need for money by patriotically turning over $523,342 worth of their assets. The total loans for July of that year were also over a half million dollars, but the largest amount borrowed in one month was in December, 1862, when the state secured over a million dollars from seven different banks. The Bank of North Carolina was by far the largest contributor to the state's war effort, and to it belongs the credit for the largest individual loan, $393,933, in December, 1862; the Hillsboro Savings Institution, which made the smallest loan, $3,750, probably possessed more patriotic ardor than cash. Shortly after Worth became treasurer, the state also secured six loans from individuals who had money to spare, but this policy lasted only two months. The comptroller's reports do not show any loans from either banks or individuals after February, 1863. In the total picture of wartime finance the loans from individuals were insignificant, but the amount borrowed from the banks of the state amounted to $7,675,753, only a little less than the amount issued in treasury notes.[27] Worth reported to the legislature in May, 1864, that the banks had accepted $2,665,500 in payments on loans, but he was thwarted in his efforts to repay the total amount of the loans because the banks became quite particular about the type of currency they would accept from the state.[28] At the end of the war over half of the debt to the banks was still unpaid, and the banks were holding state bonds as security.

In normal times, taxation was the state's primary source of annual revenue, but during the war it ran fourth behind bonds, notes, and loans. The largest part of the revenue in the ante-bellum period came from a tax of one-fifth of 1 per cent on real estate and some items of personal property. Within a month after North Carolina left the Union, the state convention—which continued to act until 1862— began raising taxes. It subjected all free males between twenty-one and forty-five years old to a capitation tax equal to the tax on land worth three hundred dollars and declared that both lands and slaves should be taxed according to their value. Land and slaves of equal value were taxed at the same rate, but the value of slaves had to be determined by the legislature on the basis of age, sex, and other personal characteristics.[29] Worth's revenue law of September, 1861, gave legislative confirmation to the action of the convention[30] but because of defects in his law tax collections did not increase greatly during 1861 and 1862. Before Worth resigned from the House of Commons in 1862 to become treasurer he reported another bill which his successor at the treasury called "the best Revenue Bill ever presented to a legislative body in North Carolina."[31] This law raised the tax on real property and slaves to two-fifths of 1 per cent ad valorem, and taxed money invested in manufacturing companies, county and state bonds, and cotton and tobacco held by speculators. It raised the poll tax and improved the earlier clauses on property taxes by establishing a system for determining values.[32] Under this law, which Worth was responsible for administering, tax collections for the next year increased by 159 per cent.[33] The sources from which the largest amounts of revenue were derived under the tax laws of 1862-63 were slaves, land, solvent debts due, and liquor dealers; these were followed in order by taxes on dividends and profits from manufacturing companies, brandy, money on hand, and town property.[34] It is obvious from this list that Worth was not one of that category of gentlemen representatives who refused to tax those items in which they had a personal interest. The total amount of taxes due for the fiscal year ending in September, 1863, was $1,873,000; this was over a million dollars more than the taxes listed two years earlier.

The war, and particularly the occupation of the coastal area by the Union army, created problems for the treasurer, the tax collectors, and the taxpayers. Some slaveowners were subjected to double taxes on their slaves when they moved from the eastern counties to avoid losing their slaves to the enemy. The sheriffs of some of the counties to which the owners removed tried to collect taxes on the slaves brought into their counties, but the legislature provided that taxes should be paid in the county in which the slaveowners maintained a legal residence.[35] The last session of the state convention directed sheriffs of counties in control of the enemy to settle their tax accounts with the treasurer for monies collected up to the time the Union forces invaded and disrupted their collections. The treasurer was relieved of the duty of bringing legal action against sheriffs who failed to pay the amount of taxes for which they were charged, and citizens of invaded counties could not be prosecuted for failure to list their property.[36] In 1864, the Assembly authorized Worth to receive partial payments of taxes from counties held by the enemy.[37]

Occupation of North Carolina by Union troops was not nearly as troublesome to Worth in his efforts to keep the state supplied with money as the fact that the state was a member of the Southern Confederacy. In his role of treasurer, he inevitably felt the effects of the Confederacy's financial policies and was compelled by the duties of his position to stay in close touch with Richmond. He had distrusted the leadership of the Confederate authorities from the very beginning of the war, and his financial relations with the central government only served to increase his antagonism and his disgust with the war.

Worth's first unpleasant experience with the Confederacy began shortly after he entered the treasurer's office, when he started trying to collect a large debt from the Confederate treasury to pay North Carolina for clothing supplied to the state's troops in the Confederate army. In 1861, the governor had entered into a peculiar logistical arrangement by which he agreed that North Carolina should provide clothing to its soldiers, and a legislative resolution of September 20, 1861, authorized him to draw from the state treasury amounts sufficient to buy "winter clothing" for the troops; the Confederacy agreed to reimburse the state. Whether the legislature's resolution was intended to remain in effect after the winter of 1861-62 was not clear, and the governor continued to buy clothing. Worth was never able to find out how much was spent under the resolution because in the state's accounts all expenditures for the army were thrown into one great amorphous category, "Military Appropriations," but when he became treasurer the Confederate government owed North Carolina between five and six million dollars.[38]

On the day Worth became treasurer, the General Assembly authorized him to hire an agent to collect the mounting debt from the Confederacy. If and when he collected the debt, the treasurer was directed to use the money to pay off the holders of the state's 8 per cent bonds who were not willing to exchange them for 6 per cent bonds payable in 1893. The Assembly also directed Worth to begin paying back the money borrowed from the banks of the state in 1861. If he were not able to use the money from the Confederacy in the ways directed, he could, after consultation with the governor, spend it as he thought best.[39] This act gave Worth a strong incentive for pressing the state's claim—if he did not get it he would have to put the state further in debt by selling bonds or issuing notes.

Worth's first step in trying to collect the debt came in January, 1863, when he wrote to William T. Dortch, one of North Carolina's Confederate senators, that the Confederacy owed North Carolina six million dollars for clothing, cavalry horses, and other supplies. He explained to Dortch that Captain William B. Gulick, an agent of the state, had just secured the auditing of $1,289,495 worth of the vouchers on which the state's claim was based, but this amount was not paid because the Confederate Congress had made no appropriation to cover it. Worth reported that he could not meet the demands on the state treasury "if this money be not received very promptly," and asked Dortch to push an appropriation through Congress as quickly as he could.[40] Dortch called the attention of the Secretary of the Treasury to the debt and asked him to include it in his request for appropriations.[41]

After Worth began writing to Richmond about the debt the Assembly ordered the state auditor to "prepare the accounts of the disbursements of North Carolina, because of the war"; this was in reality an instruction to audit the state's account against the Confederacy.[42] On February 6, 1863, the legislature also repealed the directive to Worth requiring him to pay off the holders of the state's 8 per cent bonds and the banks who had loaned money to the state, and informed Worth that the money collected from the Confederacy for clothing and cavalry horses should be used to meet the more pressing expenses of the treasury.[43]

Under authority of an act passed in December, 1862, Worth appointed Patrick H. Winston, a Bertie County lawyer and former member of the legislature, to prosecute the state's claim against the Confederate treasury. The vouchers upon which the claims were based were very numerous, but Winston collected those that were still in Raleigh and headed for Richmond.[44] The efforts of Worth and Winston were soon rewarded, for the Confederate treasury sent Worth $1,289,000 on February 19, 1863; later in the year he received another $1,631,777. By the first of July, the North Carolina treasury had on hand over nine hundred thousand dollars worth of Confederate money, and this enabled Worth to avoid further issues of state notes and bonds, except for small amounts.[45] The Confederacy still owed

North Carolina about four million dollars in November, 1863. The Confederate auditor at Richmond was still examining vouchers and approving payments at that time, but in May, 1864, Worth informed the legislature that all the debt had not been paid because the clerks responsible for auditing the vouchers had been compelled to serve as soldiers in the defense of Richmond.

The dilatory procedure of the officials and clerks in Richmond was enough to drive a man mad, thought Worth, but he had to tolerate it. Then, in the early months of 1864, he became extremely annoyed with the Quartermaster General of the Confederacy about a new policy adopted with reference to the money owed by the Confederacy to North Carolina. In January and February of 1864, the state supplied over seven hundred thousand dollars worth of clothing to its troops; as usual, the Confederacy had to pay the state for them. But at the same time Congress devalued the currency by a third, and the Quartermaster General decided that he would reduce the amount of North Carolina's claim by one-third. Worth was outraged by this decision. Calling it "monstrously unjust," he asked the legislature to make an "indignant remonstrance" against the policy of the Quartermaster General,[46] and succeeded in having a resolution introduced in the Confederate Congress asking the Secretary of the Treasury to explain why the Quartermaster General adopted such a policy.

The aggravating difficulties in collecting the debt from the Confederacy and his belief that North Carolina should not have participated in the arrangement that resulted in the debt finally led Worth into a scathing criticism of some of the methods by which the state had secured supplies since the beginning of the war. He admitted that the measure to clothe the troops was necessary in 1861, but by 1864, he questioned seriously whether the burden should not be shifted directly to the Confederacy. He also held strong reservations about the state's policy of operating its own blockade running ship, the "Ad-Vance," a speedy vessel that carried cotton through the federal blockade and brought in supplies from Nassau and Bermuda. Worth spent Christmas Day, 1863, writing a long letter to the editor of the Charlotte *Democrat*, William J. Yates, in which he discussed the relation between state finance and the state's logistical arrangements and denounced the clothing establishment and the blockade-running operations. The gist of his diatribe may be seen in the following passages:

Much of the legislation of the State, essentially affecting our Finances, has been secret. This has crippled my ability to make a comprehensive and clear exhibition of our real and prospective condition. The legislation under which the Executive has bought the Advance and perhaps other ships—by which he is conducting an immense mercantile operation—buying, importing and selling, not merely clothing for our troops and munitions of war but sperm oil, tin, liquor and assorted merchandise—the means by which he raises specie in Europe by which to make these purchases—at what prices sold and in what media paid for—are a sealed book, not only to the public, but to the chief financial officer of the state.

This trade, together with our clothing department and State military establishments, in my opinion, will ruin our credit, if long continued. . . . The State . . . can get nothing so cheap as the Confederacy and consequently is not re-imbursed for her expenditures. . . . The competition enhances prices without increase of supply.—I regard it as a Quixotic liberality.

. . . Governor Vance is performing his novitiate as a merchant and, as many a new trader, evidently forms his connections and commences using the supposed profits without taking the trouble of adding up long columns of figures, making estimates and deductions of expenses, etc.[47]

Worth went on with an outline of the history of the clothing establishment, insinuating that it supplied the state's military officers with fine clothing—"and who knows at what rates?" He cited figures from his latest annual report to show that the state was spending over five million dollars a year on its military establishment beyond what the treasury was receiving and predicted that this amount would never be reimbursed to the treasury. After citing his facts, Worth told the editor it was "high time the attention of the Genl. A. and the public was directed to them," but he asked Yates not to reveal the source from which the facts came if they were used in a newspaper discussion. "The *expediency* of keeping up these establishments is not a legitimate matter for me to discuss as Treasurer," Worth opined. It is clear from this remark that the treasurer was in a hopeless situation: he was himself without power to change the policies of which he disapproved, even though he believed they were wrecking the treasury and ruining the state, but he soon decided to use what influence he had over the legislature to have some changes made.

There was to be a special session of the legislature in May, 1864. Before it met Worth expressed the hope that no appropriations would be made for the war establishment of the state. He reiterated his view that the clothing establishment and the blockade running operations were pets of Governor Vance and that they caused an unnecessary drain on the resources of the treasury. "I deem them suicidal to the State, without any compensating benefit to the Confederacy," he told Thomas Ruffin, who, as a commissioner of the Sinking Fund, was also deeply concerned about the worsening financial condition of the state.[48] The General Assembly and the treasurer were still largely ignorant of what was going on in the state's war establishment, and Worth realized that if he spoke out he would be criticized for interfering in matters which were not directly concerned with his department, but he determined to ask the legislature to make some changes in the arrangements he had been attacking privately.

When the legislature met Worth reported to it the alarming increase of the state debt, which had already reduced the premium at which state bonds and notes could be sold. He told the legislature that the best way to stop the debt from increasing was to revert to the policy followed by the state convention in the early months of the war of letting the Confederacy control and pay for state troops supplied by North Carolina. This policy had been gradually modified in a way that required more state expenditures. In arguing against the dual supply system which Worth believed had been wasteful and detrimental to the interests of the state, he asserted that "military operations are more efficient and less expensive when directed by one head and one government, than when under different commands, and supplied by competing Commissaries and Quartermasters."[49] Worth urged that the state turn its military establishment over to the Confederacy, stop wasting money on efforts to enforce the Conscription Act for the War Department, and use taxation instead of bonds to raise money; by these means the increase in the debt could be stopped, he said.

The Assembly responded to Worth's recommendations by declaring that "in all cases hereafter no money shall be drawn from the public treasury for the military establishment of this state upon the warrant of the Governor, but specific appropriations shall be made by the General Assembly for each department of the said military establishment, and the Treasurer shall keep his accounts accordingly."[50] Later in the year the Assembly required Worth to report what amounts were being drawn for clothing and the amount reimbursed by the Confederate government. He also had to report the names of clothing agents appointed by Governor Vance and the sums drawn by each of these agents.[51]   As for the blockade running, Worth did not have to worry after September 10, 1864, that the operation of the "Ad-Vance" would longer interfere with his bookkeeping, for on that day the vessel fell into the hands of the Union navy.[52]

The difficulties that plagued Worth's effort to collect the Confederacy's debt to North Carolina for clothing and supplies seem insignificant when compared with the problems created for him by the Confederacy's financial policies.   Very trying circumstances arose early in Worth's administration of the treasury from a funding act passed by the Confederate Congress in March, 1863. The act provided that Confederate notes issued before its passage could be funded in 8 per cent bonds if the notes were issued before December, 1862, or 7 per cent for those issued later. Notes issued by the Confederacy before December, 1862, were fundable in 8 per cent bonds if they were funded before April 23, 1863. Between April and August, they could be funded at 7 per cent; after August 1, notes of this class could not be funded. Notes issued *after* December 1, 1862, but prior to April, 1863, could be funded in 7 per cent bonds until August 1, 1863, and afterwards in 4 per cent bonds.[53]

The Confederacy was compelled to pass the funding act in an effort to drive out of circulation some of the currency it had issued. Congress was attempting to diminish the supply of currency by placing limits on the time when notes could be funded; by making some notes not fundable at all after certain dates; by taxing money; and by levying a tax in kind to secure provisions for the army, instead of buying provisions with treasury notes.[54] All of these methods failed— because the Confederacy itself was failing. In the meantime, Jonathan Worth had to struggle with the effects they might have on North Carolina.

The Confederate legislation of March 29, 1863, the Funding Act, caused Worth more anxiety and annoyance than any other public law he was required to administer during his term as Public Treasurer. By an act of the state convention passed in February, 1862,[55] he was required to receive Confederate notes for state taxes and other debts owed to the state. When the Funding Act passed Congress, Worth believed that it would achieve its object, diminishing the supply of Confederate treasury notes, but he feared that much of the old issue would not be funded and would rapidly depreciate; this fear was justified by the subsequent history of Confederate notes. Worth could visualize streams of the depreciated "old issue" pouring into the state treasury when the sheriffs started turning in their tax monies in October, and he would have no alternative—they had to be accepted. To add to his woes, the legislature of Virginia passed an act which specified that only the new issue of Confederate notes would be received for taxes in Virginia, and as a result the old issue was beginning to flow across the state line from Virginia into North Carolina. No doubt the Virginia legislature acted in an effort to drive the old issue out of circulation, but Governor Vance looked upon its measure as a "partial repudiation of Congress."[56] If Worth accepted the old issue he would lay himself open to the charge of filling the treasury with money that was becoming worthless.

Worth pondered the problem and sought advice before he took any action. He secured opinions from former governor William A. Graham and from Judge Bartholomew F. Moore that he had the authority to order the county sheriffs not to accept the old issue of Confederate currency when they began collecting taxes, but he was afraid to act on this advice because, by his own interpretation of the state law, the treasurer had no such power.[57] It appeared to Worth that an act of the General Assembly was the only means by which he could be relieved of his embarrassment. Since the Assembly was not in session, he asked Governor Vance to convene the Council of State for the purpose of considering whether the legislature should be called, and if it were called, what action should be taken with regard to the Confederate Funding Act.[58]

Before Vance called the Council of State to meet, there was considerable public discussion as to whether a session of the legislature should be held—it would be expensive. There were three schools of thought on the matter of the currency. One held that Worth had the power to refuse the old issue as payment of taxes; a second group maintained that the Funding Act and the act of the Virginia legislature would make no difference in the value of the old issues; still another school of thought was that Worth could trade the old currency to the Confederate treasury for new.[59] Vance asked the Supreme Court for an opinion on the extent of Worth's powers in accepting or rejecting the old issue and the chief justice replied that "the Judges are unanimously of opinion that the Treasurer of the state has no power under the ordinance of the convention in question to instruct the sheriffs of the state not to receive Confederate notes in payment of public taxes."[60]

After hearing all this discussion and conflicting opinion, Worth was still uncertain what course he should follow. With the governor's permission he asked the presidents of the banks in the state "to consider . . . whether, after the 1st August next, they would receive as currency Confederacy non-interest bearing notes, dated prior to April 6th, 1863." At a conference with Worth, the bank presidents were unable to tell Worth whether they would accept the old issues after August 1. Earlier Worth had written to the Confederate Secretary of the Treasury, Christopher G. Memminger, asking whether he would exchange new issue for the old notes held or to be received by North Carolina. Memminger replied that he was not authorized to make the exchange, and tried to assure Worth that "the currency of neither class is affected by the legislation of Congress further than by making a difference in their relative value."[61] Were not all the notes, regardless of when they were issued, backed by the Confederate government, asked Memminger. Finally, Worth sought advice from the treasurers of the other Confederate states in a letter asking what they proposed to do about the depreciation of old issue when time came to collect the states' revenues. The only treasurer to reply promptly was John Jones of Georgia, who quoted Governor Joseph E. Brown's view that "questions merely pecuniary having a tendency to damage the credit or depreciate the currency of the Confederate States should not be entertained," and informed Worth that Georgia would accept for taxes all issues of Confederate treasury notes.[62] No one with whom Worth consulted gave him much consolation.

At last Governor Vance acted upon Worth's recommendation and called the legislature to meet in a special session in July, 1863. Like Governor Brown of Georgia, Vance was unwilling that the legislature should take any action which smacked of repudiation of Confederate currency; consequently, he recommended that the state continue to receive all issues of Confederate notes for taxes and other debts to the state, feeling that "if one issue . . . be good, then all are good."[63] Vance also submitted Worth's views on the currency to the special session. In a letter to Vance, Worth had recommended that the legislature suspend the collection of taxes until after Congress met again, and that the old issues not be received until the state could ask Congress to repeal the Funding Act or exchange the new notes for the old ones. The treasurer also asked the legislature to formulate some rules for him to follow in disbursing Confederate currency from the treasury. The following question is typical of those he faced as a result of the diversity of currencies: "Is each claimant to be entitled to demand any class of Confederate currency in the Treasury, which he may prefer; or is he the treasurer to pay out the poorest, or the best, first?"[64] Worth's final recommendation was that the taxes for 1863 be paid by August 1—two months earlier than usual—and that the treasurer be allowed to fund before August 1 all old issue received in the collection, August 1 being the deadline for funding set by the Funding Act.

When the legislature met, the main item of business was a currency act. The committee on the currency recommended that all Confederate notes should be received, that the sheriffs should collect as much of the taxes for 1863 as they could gather before July 28, at which time the tax monies were to be submitted to the treasurer. The old issue could then be funded in 7 per cent Confederate bonds. The committee was strongly motivated by patriotic considerations; no breach of faith with the Confederacy or with North Carolina's sister states could be permitted. The members perceived that, to some extent at least, the credit of the Confederacy was the basic issue.[65]

On July 3, 1863, the legislature converted the recommendations of Worth, Vance, and the committee on the currency into law when it directed the sheriffs to turn in all the tax monies they could collect by July 28, and instructed the treasurer to fund that portion of the taxes paid by old issues in 7 per cent bonds. In an effort to increase the amount of tax collections above what was normal, the legislature offered tax collectors an extra commission of 1 per cent above what they usually received, on all money collected before July 28. Acting under these provisions of the currency act, the sheriffs collected and Worth funded $1,564,000 of the old issue.[66]

The Assembly also helped to clear up the confusion about the relative value of various issues of Confederate currency by declaring that, so far as the state was concerned, any issue was equal to all others after July 28, 1863. The treasurer was authorized to sell at par or for a premium the 7 per cent bonds received from the funding of the old issue, the resulting money to be used for paying regular expenses.[67] This act, which relieved Worth temporarily of his mental anguish about receiving depreciated currency, was at the same time a public declaration by the North Carolina legislature of its faith in the fortunes of the Confederacy. Ironically, the battle of Gettysburg was in progress at the moment the act passed, and Vicksburg surrendered within twenty-four hours.

Not everyone had as much faith in Confederate money as the members of the legislature expressed, as may be seen in the attitude of some of the county courts towards certain appropriations. The best example is an appropriation of one million dollars made in 1863 for the relief of soldiers' families. When it was made, the treasury did not have sufficient funds to pay the entire million dollars, so Worth decided to pay it to the counties in four installments. Before these installments were due, the treasury began to receive an abundance of Confederate treasury notes from Richmond as a partial payment for clothing North Carolina had supplied to its troops in the Confederate army. Worth determined to pay the appropriation for soldiers' families with the money received from the Confederate treasury, but several of the county courts made it quite plain that they preferred to be paid in North Carolina treasury notes. Jones County, for example, directed one of its commissioners to return the Confederate money the county received in its first installment and asked that "the funds due said county of Jones, be paid in the treasury notes or current funds of the state. . . ."[68] Worth refused to comply with the request of the county courts to pay them in state notes. He explained to Governor Vance that if he issued state notes, such an act would be equivalent to borrowing money when it was not needed. Why increase the debt of the state by issuing notes and bonds when there was plenty of Confederate money in the state's vault waiting to be used? The only counties entitled by law to payment in state currency were those under the control of the enemy's army. Worth construed this provision to mean that all other counties could be paid in Confederate money.[69] He persisted in his refusal, and continued to hold on to the state's notes as long as he could.

Some county officials responded to Worth's policy of paying appropriations and debts to the counties in Confederate money by hoarding warrants and drafts with the hope of collecting them in sounder currency some time in the future. This was particularly true of payments to county school boards and to the commissioners administering the act for the relief of soldiers' families. The legislature remedied this situation by resolving that drafts to the school boards

and the commissioners of relief funds should be paid "only in Confederate Treasury notes. . . ."[70]

Depreciation of Confederate currency presented a number of other
problems for Worth to solve. It became very difficult for him to pay
off the 8 per cent bonds issued by the state early in the war, because
no one wanted the Confederate money in which he made it a rule
to pay the state's debts. Since almost everyone was willing to
accept state treasury notes, Worth recommended to the Assembly
that he be authorized to pay off the 8 per cent bonds with state notes,
when the bondholders did not want Confederate money.[71] The Assembly responded by authorizing the issue of three million dollars in
treasury notes to be used in paying off the coupons from the bonds.[72]

There was one way in which depreciation of Confederate currency
was helpful to Worth in his efforts to raise money for the state. Because state bonds could frequently be sold at a high premium in Confederate money, he was able to realize considerable profits from selling
them. Both state and Confederate currency depreciated at about the
same rate until late in 1862, when the state money began to be considered more valuable; the highest premium for which it could be sold
in terms of Confederate money, came early in 1864, when the premium
reached 150 per cent.[73] After that time the premium dropped, but in
November, 1864, five months before the war ended, Worth reported to
the legislature that he could buy $1,850 worth of Confederate money
with a state bond valued at a thousand dollars.[74]

Even the insane felt the effects of depreciation. "It is impossible
to make estimates with reasonable approximation to accuracy," Worth
reminded the legislature in asking them to replace money he had paid
to the Lunatic Asylum when that institution's funds proved to be
insufficient to meet expenses in 1863. Administrators of the state's
governmental departments had to submit estimates of their expenses
before appropriations could be made, but runaway inflation resulting
from depreciation made it impossible to determine what they would
have to pay for goods and services at a short time in the future, and
it was not uncommon for them to run out of money before new appropriations could be made. Worth's normal procedure when a department or institution of the state exhausted its funds was to advance
the necessary money and depend upon the legislature to ratify his
action.[75] This procedure might have gotten him into trouble if the
Assembly had been unco-operative, but it never did.

Worth believed by 1862 that "whatever may be the issue of the war, Confederate money must be nearly useless at the end,"[76] and he conducted his personal financial affairs accordingly, but in his role of Public Treasurer he had to appear as a believer in the value of Confederate money and securities. He expressed his real views in these terms:

As you ask for my opinion confidentially whether I would sell land or negroes for Confederate money or bonds, I will give it. I would not unless I could use them to pay debts, or purchase other property more desirable. I regard real estate as far the best investment that can now be made. . . . You are not at liberty to communicate this opinion to any body—It is my duty as Treasurer and my wish as citizen to sustain the credit of Confederate currency by every means I can honorably use; but as you ask my opinion as a friend, I give it candidly, but in strict confidence.[77]

After almost a year at the treasury Worth thought that "if something be not speedily done vastly to diminish the volume of Confederate currency, that it will soon cease to answer the purpose of money."[78] But he was helpless. The only agency that had power to solve the problem of depreciation—if it were subject to solution—was the Confederate Congress. Worth felt that neither repudiation nor voluntary funding of former issues could stabilize the currency; the only hope lay in increased taxation, but even that hope was a slender one.

The Confederate Congress attempted once more to cope with the depreciation problem when it passed, on February 17, 1864, a compulsory funding act. This compulsory act embarrassed Worth's administration of the state Treasury almost as much as the voluntary funding act tried in 1863. The new legislation offered persons holding Confederate treasury notes two choices: the notes could be traded for new ones, three dollars of the old being worth two dollars of the new, or they might be funded into bonds bearing 4 per cent interest and payable in twenty years.[79] The Funding Act also authorized the Secretary of the Treasury to issue five hundred million dollars worth of 5 per cent bonds, which were to be free from taxation, and pledged certain export and import duties to pay the interest. Congress allowed the states to fund their Confederate treasury notes in 6 per cent bonds, but the bonds to be issued to the states were neither made tax-free nor the interest guaranteed. Worth thought the distinction made in favor of the bonds to be issued directly by the Confederacy a case of rank discrimination against the states: "None of these provisions, tending to give credit to these bonds, attach to the bonds which the States may take . . . ," he told the legislature.[80] This discrimination against North Carolina and other states further intensified Worth's exasperation with Confederate financial policy.

When the first telegraphic account of the Funding Act reached Raleigh it failed to mention that the state could fund its Confederate notes in 6 per cent bonds after the act went into effect, and Worth interpreted the action of Congress to mean that the act had simply devalued Confederate currency by one-third; the state, he thought, was about to lose a third of its Confederate money. If Worth ever went into a panic, he did then. Dashing madly about the capitol building, he rounded up an "extraordinary force" of clerks, had them separate all the Confederate money from the Sinking Fund, and immediately invested it in 6 per cent bonds. When a copy of the Funding Act arrived and Worth saw that he would have been able to do the funding at a more leisurely pace, he realized that he had resorted to "unnecessary haste."[81]

Worth had been opposed to compulsory funding from the time it was first bruited about in the fall of 1863. In November, he told his son-in-law, Sam Jackson, that the plan subsequently adopted by Congress "has for its basis a monstrous breach of faith, and its operation will overwhelm half the taxpayers in the Confederacy."[82] He felt that a compulsory funding act would also destroy some of the weaker banks in North Carolina, and this made it necessary for those personally interested in financial matters to mend their speculative fences. The treasurer went on to advise Jackson that the banks with the best chance of survival were the Bank of North Carolina and the Merchants Bank at New Bern; it would be safe to "lay up" their notes, he said.[83]

One embarrassment Worth had to face as a result of the compulsory Funding Act of 1864 was the fact that certain large debts were due to the state. Ordinarily this would be very pleasing to anyone managing a state's funds, but it was a frightful prospect for Worth— what if he should be paid in the currency devalued by the Confederate Congress? The Atlantic and North Carolina Railroad owed the state one hundred and fifty thousand dollars it had borrowed in 1856; the Raleigh and Gaston Railroad another fifty thousand dollars; and the city of Raleigh, forty-nine thousand. When the Council of State met, as it had done in 1863, to determine whether the legislature should be called to deal with the currency problem, Worth told the members of the Council that he was not willing to receive payment of these large debts in the depreciated currency.[84] After the Council went home, the railroad companies tried to pay Worth what they owed. He refused to receive payment, assuming responsibility for disregarding the literal terms of the act making all Confederate notes valid for debts in North Carolina. As usual, the legislature subsequently approved his conduct and declared it "just."[85]

The problem of how to fund the Confederate notes held by the state still remained. When Congress passed the Funding Act the North Carolina treasury had about seven hundred thousand dollars in Confederate currency; of this amount, $450,000 was in the Sinking Fund and could not be funded unless the legislature authorized such action. If Worth assumed the power to fund the notes, he could invest them in 4 per cent bonds, or, under the twelfth section of the Confederate Funding Act, he could invest in 6 per cent bonds. Between these two courses Worth at first considered the purchase of the fours better policy for the state. The main consideration was to buy the ones which would command the largest amount of currency when sold in the open market; since the sixes would not sell, Worth preferred to rely on the fours. The sixes would not sell because the Confederacy taxed them 5 per cent and because they would not be acceptable for taxes.

Worth stated his preference for investing in the 4 per cent bonds in a letter to Governor Vance on February 27, 1864, seven days after the Confederate Congress passed the compulsory Funding Act.[86] In the same letter he pointed out to Vance that the treasurer would not have the option of funding the state's Confederate notes after April 1, 1864, and he strongly urged that Vance call the legislature to authorize the funding. Another reason Worth suggested for calling the legislature was that the treasurer was still obligated to accept all Confederate notes for payment of taxes.[87] This policy would have to be changed, but if the legislature did not meet until its regular meeting in May the taxpayers could not receive sufficient notice that old issue would not be acceptable for taxes at its face value; collections began in July.

When the Council of State met to decide whether Vance should call the legislature into session before its scheduled meeting, Worth had changed his mind about the wisdom of funding the Confederate treasury notes in 4 per cent bonds. Instead, he had concluded that Congress might "modify the act as to allow the states to exchange the currency on hand on the first day of April at par, for the new issue, or to invest in the preferred class of bonds authorized. . . ."[88] In an effort to secure modification or repeal of the Funding Act, Worth corresponded directly with delegates in Congress, stating his views and asking that the act be modified, but when the North Carolina legislature met in May, Congress had taken no action.[89] Worth then had to recommend what the state should do with the old notes. He suggested that all except the hundred dollar bills should be traded for new notes, the state receiving only two-thirds of the value of the old issue; the hundred dollar bills could best be invested in 6 per cent bonds. The problem of tax money Worth proposed to solve by receiving old issue at two-thirds of its par value, and new issue at the amount written on its face. The adoption of this policy would of course require a repeal of the act passed in 1863, requiring the treasurer to accept all issues of Confederate money at their face value. The legislature responded to Worth's recommendations by adopting those reducing the value of the old issue to two-thirds of its face, and repealing the law of 1863 which made all Confederate notes equal to the amount printed on them.[90] For Worth's guidance in getting rid of the old issue, the assembly gave him three alternatives: he could exchange it for new issue, fund it in bonds, or pay debts with it; but when he used it to pay expenses it was worth only two-thirds of its face value.[91] This meant, in practical terms, that if the treasury had some work done for which the charge was two hundred dollars, it would have to pay three hundred dollars for the work if old issue were used.

The decision of the legislature in 1864 not to accept the older issues of Confederate Treasury notes at their face value for payment of debts to the state was the opposite of the decision made after Congress passed the Funding Act of 1863. The explanation of the difference in policy may be found not in a diminished faith in the Confederate government, but in the necessity to conform to the provisions of the Funding Act of 1864. Congress had simply devalued some of its currency by one-third, and North Carolina could not afford to accept it as equal to the newer currency.

When the assembly granted Worth discretion as to how he was to dispose of the old Confederate notes, the bond market was very uncertain, so Worth decided that, if he possibly could, he would trade in the old notes for new notes instead of buying bonds for resale. He asked the Confederate Secretary of the Treasury to take half of the old issue North Carolina owned for new notes, giving full credit for the old issue, and to reduce by one-third the other half of the old issue owned by the state and give new issue in notes for it. By such a transaction North Carolina would get in new issue five-sixths of what it had in old; this would have been ready cash instead of bonds. The attorney general of the Confederacy ruled such a transaction illegal and Worth began to search for another solution to the funding problem. Finally he had the idea of funding half the old issue for new notes and taking an option on 4 per cent or 6 per cent Confederate bonds to an amount equal to the remaining half of the old issue. This arrangement seemed to the Secretary of the Treasury to be legitimate and he approved. The new issue was to be stored with the Confederate depository in Raleigh.[92]

Even after this settlement was made, Worth had to prod the Confederate officials to make them keep their part of the bargain by placing the better class of money in Raleigh. Late in September, 1864, he informed the Secretary of the Treasury before the sheriffs began turning in the tax monies that much of the taxes would be in old issue. The treasurer emphasized the necessity of being able to exchange currencies as soon as possible after the old issue came in.[93] Claimants against the state had already stopped accepting the old issue as payment for services. Worth therefore encouraged the Secretary of the Treasury to store the new issue in the depository at Raleigh, so Worth could go there and trade in the tax money for the usable new issue.

The Confederate officials promised to deposit the new money in Raleigh, and the difficulties arising from the Funding Act of 1864 came to an end.[94]

When the first session of the legislature of 1864 convened in November, it was time to hold another election for Public Treasurer. Worth had performed his duties quite ably, and there was little doubt that he would be re-elected. Almost exactly two years to the day from the time of his first election the legislature chose him for a second term; there was no opposition candidate. Worth had little to say about the election, except that it was "a compliment, considering the difficulties I have encountered."[95]

The prospect facing Worth as he entered upon his second term

was bleak indeed. In spite of all he or anyone else could do, the
state was deep in debt and going deeper. Worth reported shortly before his election that the treasury was operating under a deficit of
over three and a half million dollars, and that almost twelve millions
would be needed in the fiscal year 1864-65. The state debt had increased by $5,216,905 during the year ending on September 30, 1864,[96]
and amounted to a total of $31,442,440. Against this debt, which
Worth feared was mounting to the point at which state credit would
be destroyed, the state held certain securities, sufficient to reduce the
amount of the debt to $21,443,940, but these securities were in the
form of bonds which might never be paid; included among the bonds
were some issued by the state and held by the commissioners of the
Sinking Fund, bonds of several railroads held by the state, and Confederate bonds held in the Sinking Fund.[97]

The Assembly appropriated almost ten million dollars in December, 1864, to pay for military bureaus, salt works, asylums, soldiers'
families, and civil expenses during 1865, but the potential resources
of the treasury totaled only five million. Worth was uncertain that
he could acquire even the first five million he needed, for the legislature expected him to sell Confederate bonds held by the state and
to collect money which was still due from the Confederacy for clothing. The second five million was to be raised by issuing two and a
half million more dollars worth of Treasury notes and selling an
equal amount of state bonds. Worth preferred to begin by selling
bonds.[98]

The bond sale proved to be one of Worth's most successful ventures as the wartime treasurer of North Carolina—and his last one,
too. In January, 1865, he kept an eagle eye on the bond market, and
as soon as he detected an upward trend in the price of North Carolina bonds he ran the price even higher by advertising a new issue
of state bonds and rejecting the bids. By these measures he was able
to sell the bonds at 200 per cent of their par value, and the state
made a handsome profit of four hundred thousand dollars. This profit
made it possible for Worth to pay some of the pressing bills of the
treasury and to struggle on a little while longer.[99]

During the last two months of the war, when the Confederacy was
preparing to breathe its last gasp and North Carolina was fearfully
anticipating General Sherman's entry into the state, Worth was still
trying to make ends meet at the treasury by collecting money from

the Confederacy for clothing and supplies; Richmond still owed Raleigh three million dollars. The Assembly directed that when the clothing establishment received the three millions they should be turned over to the treasury, but the money from the Confederate treasury came in dribbles, and the state officials who received the money from Richmond would not pay Worth until they got the entire amount. Since Worth felt that he could "get along" until the taxes were paid in if the Confederacy would pay what it owed the state, he asked William A. Graham, who was then in the Confederate Senate, to do some prodding in the necessary places. "Otherwise," Worth feared, "the State credit will be almost destroyed by the vast amount of bonds I shall be forced to put in the market."[100] Fortunately for Worth's reputation as treasurer and for North Carolina, he never sold many bonds or issued any treasury notes after January, 1865, and the state kept its high credit rating to the very end of the Civil War.

Given extraordinary discretionary powers to manage the state's resources at the most trying period in the financial history of the state, Worth had exercised his powers in the manner of the conservative business man he was. A treasurer who was more inclined to be a spendthrift could have sold more bonds and issued more paper money than Worth did, but he never liked to put himself or the state in debt unless it was absolutely necessary to do so. He constantly urged the legislature to shift the burden of war financing to the shoulders of the Confederacy, and from beginning to end he favored increased taxation as a source of revenue instead of bonds and paper money; but this sound advice went unheeded, except for the fact that the state legislature kept raising taxes as long as the people could pay. In the words of a specialist on the state's financial history, Benjamin U. Ratchford, "the state assumed too much of the burden of war financing"; "the convention and the legislature were too free and too loose with credit and too sparing with taxes"; and, finally, "the influence of Treasurer Worth was consistently exerted in favor of conservative financing."[101] Innate hostility to the Confederate government, as well as conservative financial views and concern for his own state, undoubtedly affected Worth's administration of the treasury. It was almost as if he were acting under the assumption that if the Confederate government insisted on fighting that accursed war, it ought at least to pay the expense.

· XII ·

This Accursed War

———•———

WHEN WORTH BECAME PUBLIC TREASURER late in 1862, he decided
to move to Raleigh, since his new duties would keep him there most
of the time. After surveying the real estate situation until January
17, 1863, he bought a large house on the south side of Lenoir Street
for five thousand dollars. The Worths had been accustomed to living
in gracious comfort, and they still would, for "Sharon"—as the new
house was named—was quite the equal of the home in Asheboro.
Located in "the extended city limits" of Raleigh, it was soon well
furnished with pieces from the house at Asheboro. The dwelling was
surrounded by a spacious yard and garden which together covered
eight acres. At the back of the property, separated from the yard by
a Spanish oak and a fence, was a vegetable garden which became one
of Worth's favorite projects.[1] After buying the new place, Worth
moved Martitia and the children to Sharon in January or February,
1863.

At Sharon, life went on much as it had in Asheboro, with Worth
pursuing a variety of personal enterprises to keep the family in the
comfortable style to which it had become accustomed, Mrs. Worth
supervising the activities of the household, and the remaining daughters—Corinna, Adelaide, and Mary—biding their time until some suitor
should come along. Their prospects, in spite of the shortage of young
men, were fairly good, for the Worths moved in the highest social
circles of the city, by virtue of Worth's position in the state government and his more-than-moderate means. Corinna was not long in
waiting. She married Dr. William C. Roberts, a frail young druggist
from Edenton, in March, 1864, and honeymooned in South Carolina
and Georgia.[2]

There was a regular outburst of weddings in Raleigh about the
time Corinna married. Adelaide wrote Major William H. Bagley, a

lawyer, editor, and soldier from Perquimans County who had recently become her suitor, of an elegant reception at the Governor's Mansion for one of the couples: "Every luxury of good old times was there—It is wonderful what changes come over people—before the war it was *unheard* of for people to go to a party and indulge their appetites to any great degree. At the Governor's it was different, it looked like a real *"snatch and grab"* game, and nearly all seemed to have gone into the supper room for the *sole* purpose of *eating.*"[3]

The guests at the wedding party snatched and grabbed because the luxurious foods "of good old times" were no longer as abundant as they were before the war; and even when they were available, prices were beyond reason. Worth's mother, Eunice, who by 1864 was eighty-three years old, expressed a desire for some good coffee, a stimulant "essential to her comfort." Worth told his brothers of their mother's desire and proposed that each of the brothers contribute a hundred dollars and send her as much coffee as their contributions would buy. Thus inflation had affected the state to the extent that an old woman in her eighties could be expected to drink four hundred dollars worth of coffee.[4] David Worth informed his father from Wilmington early in 1863 that "we are almost starved out here" because Confederate General Whiting had been seizing country produce and taking farmers' wagons to haul materials for fortifications, and the farmers had stopped bringing food into Wilmington to sell.[5]

There were cases of destitution in the state, particularly among the families of soldiers who were away from home fighting while their fields lay fallow. When the legislature appropriated money for the relief of soldiers' families, Worth, in his role of treasurer, had to be responsible for the distribution of the funds. This was not as difficult as some of Worth's regular duties, but troublesome situations appeared occasionally. In the case of Craven County, for example, it was impossible, because of the federal occupation, to comply with the exact terms of the relief act. Before Worth would pay out any money to the county officials who were to manage the relief money at the local level he required them to fill out a long affidavit stating the circumstances of their case and outlining a plan for the distribution of the funds.[6] From the other end of the state, at Burnsville, Governor Vance received complaints that the relief money sent there had been distributed equally, rather than to the destitute, "which gives a great deal of the money into families . . . that are independent livers."[7]

Vance passed this and similar complaints on to Worth, who made
every effort to see that the relief act was administered fairly.[8]

Although Worth and his immediate family never actually suffered
between 1861 and 1865, the war brought with it a number of personal
inconveniences that constantly exacerbated Worth's dislike of the war
itself. Early in the war he bought some iron from a factory in South
Carolina, but several months passed before he could get it shipped;
the railroads had to give priority to military supplies.[9] When Worth
sold some bacon to the state in 1862, his horses were being used for
planting corn, and he could not hire wagons to haul his bacon. In
June, 1864, he practically had to beg to have some wood sent to him
by rail.[10] Conditions finally reached the point where Worth even had
to reduce his consumption of alcoholic beverages. He drank moderately—rye whiskey, brandy, and scuppernong wine he made on his farm
at Asheboro. In June, 1864, he offered to trade some lead pipe to
H. E. Colton for brandy. "Send the brandy *soon*," he urged Colton.
"Nothing else would have tempted me. I am *over dry*."[11] Colton
balked at Worth's terms and tried to get a better bargain, but Worth
reminded him that both lead pipe and brandy were equally scarce in
the Confederacy and added: "I would like for you to have [the pipe],
and you touched the vulnerable place when you offered me liquor for
it, but I am not dry enough to get up to your figures."[12] The following note tells what happened to Worth's drinking habits as a result
of the endlessly aggravating war:

I requested you to send me [a] keg of whiskey, without regard to
price, but it did not occur to me that it would cost so much as $100.
per gallon. I have no income which will warrant me in indulging in
the luxury of drinking good whiskey at this cost. If you have not
sent it off, please don't send it. I can't pay my taxes, etc. and continue
my habit of an occasional drink. If I have occasioned any inconvenience or cost to you in procuring a keg, let me know the amount and
I will remit it.[13]

As Worth hinted in his note about the whiskey, taxes were high
during the war, and they continued to go higher as the war dragged
on into its third and fourth years. Although Worth favored heavy
taxes as a means of financing the war machines of the state and Confederate governments, the increase caused him to grumble occasionally. At tax-collecting time in 1864, he reported to his son-in-law, J. J.
Jackson, that "my State and county tax here and in Chatham is $2324.

—My corporation and Confederate tax much larger, besides tithes and besides my boat and factory stock, the tax on which is paid by the corporations. Frightful!!!"[14] Payment of the "tithes"—a tax in kind levied by the Confederacy on 10 per cent of the farm produce of the South—was particularly troublesome. The amount of produce Worth owed the Confederacy from his Chatham County farm for 1864 included seventy bushels of corn, thirty bushels of wheat, twenty bushels of oats, and over a ton of hay and fodder.[15] He failed to deliver the corn, oats, and forage at the required time and had to pay their cash value to the Confederate official responsible for collecting the produce. He had also to pay an extra 50 per cent for paying the tithe in cash instead of produce; the value of the produce and the forfeiture amounted to $843.[16] When Worth instructed Samuel Jackson to pay his tithes he said: "I am so confined here that I cannot give proper attention to my personal affairs and hope some indulgence will be extended to me if I have neglected the prompt compliance I always wish to give to the laws of my country, however unwise or oppressive I may regard them."[17]

High taxes, high prices, and depreciation created more inconveniences than real hardship for Worth during the war period, but it is ironic that while he was being largely successful with state finance he had to borrow money to buy provisions for his own family. His salary as treasurer, seventy-five hundred dollars a year in 1864,[18] depreciated by January, 1865, to the point where it was not worth over a hundred and fifty dollars a year in hard money. To add to his woes, the Confederate and state governments had made his corporation stock "about worthless" by heavy taxation, and the fact that he could not secure an overseer for one of his farms made it "more than worthless."[19] But in spite of these difficulties, Worth's dignity kept him from complaining much about his salary.

Worth's statements about his personal financial hardships must be taken lightly, for when he had to borrow money it simply meant that he was temporarily unable "to provide for the urgent wants of [his] family, without materially encroaching on the earnings of former years. . . ."[20] He did actually have to borrow money and barter goods during the hard war years, but it was not because he had no money; it was because his "earnings of former years" were tied up in an intricate knot of business finance—in cotton, real estate, and state bonds.

The principal business in which Worth was interested during the war was cotton manufacturing and speculation in cotton. As president of the Cedar Falls Manufacturing Company, and as a large stockholder, he naturally took an interest in the welfare of the company and promoted it as much as he could.[21] When the General Assembly and the Confederate Congress taxed cotton manufacturing heavily, Worth thought up a scheme to reduce the amount of tax the company would have to pay. Since the stockholders in Cedar Falls were authorized to receive their dividends in the products of the company, he proposed that the general superintendent, George Makepeace, sell to him products of the company to an amount not exceeding the next probable dividend. Worth would then hire an agent to sell the cotton products secretly at a profit of 50 to 100 per cent. "I see nothing morally wrong with this," Worth told Makepeace, "and only propose to conduct it secretly to avoid unjust clamor."[22] The Confederate tax on cotton amounted to one-sixth of all profits, and the state took all profits over 75 per cent made after January 1, 1862. Worth's idea was to sell to the stockholders at a low rate, thereby reducing the taxable profits of the company; the stockholders could in turn sell their cheaply-acquired goods at a handsome profit. Everybody—except the Confederate and state governments—would benefit.

Worth's biggest cotton trade came in September, 1863, when Sam Jackson bought for him twenty-five thousand pounds of raw cotton from Ebenezer Ingram, an Anson County planter, and paid for it in Confederate bonds.[23] This began a disagreement that was to last almost three years when Ingram told Jackson that he would not deliver the cotton, because of "the want of validity in the funds I received."[24] By October, 1863, Jackson, in competition with the state's purchasing agents, was buying cotton to sell wherever he could get the best price for it. He wrote to Worth and asked him to see the state purchasing agent in Raleigh, describe the cotton, and see how much the state would pay for it. Then Worth was to advise his son-in-law whether to sell the cotton or hold it until a better opportunity came. "I think . . . that I can make something by the transfer to the state," Jackson said.[25]

While Worth watched the cotton markets closely he also kept an eye on the bond market and invested money in state bonds. In April, 1863, he offered to pay Kemp Battle a 15 per cent premium in Confederate currency for five thousand dollars worth of bonds Battle had advertised for sale.[26] He also proposed to Darius Starbuck in January, 1865, that Starbuck buy between ten and twenty thousand dollars worth of state bonds, using Worth's money; it would have been unbecoming for Worth to speculate openly, since he occupied the position of Public Treasurer. Worth would then sell the bonds for Starbuck at a profit and they would divide the amount cleared on the deal. The treasurer, who was selling the bonds for the state, explained to Starbuck why he wanted the bonds: "The state does not pay me one sixth part of the expenses of supporting my family and I am forced to do something outside to make ends meet."[27] The transaction would have been a legitimate one, although some persons might have considered it questionable, but Starbuck was reluctant to join in and it was never completed.

Because of Worth's position, speculators frequently called upon him for advice, and he usually accommodated them with such information as he had at his disposal. Worth himself was wary of investing in anything except land and cotton, although he did put a small amount in the bonds of the state. He recommended to a Mrs. Andrews in Statesville when she asked for advice on sound investments that "in order to have two strings to your bow, I would . . . invest about one half in state bonds and the balance in cotton."[28] Rarely did he encourage anyone to invest in Confederate securities. In fact, by October, 1864, Worth had no faith left in the success of the Confederacy. To one inquirer about investments he wrote: "I deem all Confederate securities as not likely to be worth anything in any contingency that I can foresee. This is intended as a frank answer to your inquiry, and I desire that it may be deemed confidential."[29]

Heavy taxes on cotton and naval stores held by speculators, and the Confederate tax in kind on farm produce, the tithes, led Worth to the idea that the best investment one could make would be the purchase of lands on which nothing was being produced.[30] Accordingly, he bought several tracts of land during the war. As he explained to J. J. Jackson, his son-in-law at Pittsboro, "I had a good deal of currency a few weeks ago. My creditors would neither receive Confederate or any other paper currency—and to invest it as safely as I could, (for no solvent men would borrow it) I bought of C. P. Mendenhall the 600 acre tract on Cane Creek in your county."[31] Worth, his son David, and David's business partner, Greene Daniel, bought a farm in the Horry district of South Carolina in January, 1864, for twenty-four thousand dollars. The place had six hundred acres of rich swamp land, a hundred and fifty acres cleared for cultivation, and two thousand acres of pine forest. It had a two-story house and some outbuildings, but had not been cultivated since the war started. Worth did not expect to gain anything from this farm until after the war ended, and he offered to rent it for barely enough to pay the taxes.[32]

Two other investments rounded out Worth's purchasing of real estate during the war period. In the spring of 1864, Worth, George Swepson, Paris Benbow, Daniel Worth, and John Baxter bought three hundred acres on Long Island, New York; Baxter owned a half interest and the others one-eighth each. This same group of men also began buying bonds of towns outside the state that were growing up along the Mississippi and Missouri Railroad and bonds of the Covington and Lexington Railroad Company in Kentucky.[33] Worth purchased for his own use a farm of 188 acres six miles outside of Raleigh. The farm, for which he paid fifteen thousand dollars, was half cleared and had on it a small, neat dwelling, plenty of outbuildings, a good orchard, and fine water. "The place suits me well," Worth confided to Sam Jackson shortly after he bought it.[34]

While Worth was in a trading mood he sold his house in Asheboro to Sam Jackson, who had remained there to carry on Worth's law practice. It was not actually a sale, for Worth proposed that Jackson give him thirty-five hundred dollars—twice the amount it had cost Worth originally—and pay only the interest on that amount until Worth died. Then the principal was to be left to Jackson in Worth's will. Dr. Jack Hamlin tried to buy the place, but Worth wanted to keep it in the family: "I have a sort of sentimental feeling about it and don't want it desecrated by such an occupant as Jack," Worth said of the big house where he had spent the best years of his life and brought up his children.[35]

Worth began trying to sell his farm on Cane Creek in Chatham County for six thousand dollars about two years after he bought it. He insisted that part of the price he asked should be paid by a note redeemable in specie, or its equivalent, after the war. He needed money to pay some debts, and his knowledge of finance and economics enabled him to foresee that it would be scarce after the war and that debtors would have a difficult time paying what they owed. "I am growing old," Worth said—he was sixty-two in 1864—"and wish, if possible, to pay my debts before I die."[36] His reason for paying his

debts was even more clearly stated in his remark that "I want to pay
. . . before the Yankees get me and my money."[37] But the circumstances of war were against Worth, for the parties who held the notes
constituting his debts refused to accept "any currency whatever" for
them. Creditors found all sorts of excuses for refusing to accept payment but at least one finally took notes of the Bank of North Carolina
for which Worth had paid a high premium.

Worth had paid off all of his large debts in 1864 except three
thousand dollars in the form of two notes to Benjamin Moffitt, his
former neighbor at Asheboro, and to Moffitt's mother. "To pay these
two debts, which is nearly all I owe," Worth wrote, "I would sell
the house over my head, my property in Asheboro, or even my
farm. . . ."[38] He offered to sell the Cane Creek place on the condition
that the buyer pay off the debts to the Moffitts as part of the purchase
price.

Another reason Worth wanted to sell the farm on Cane Creek was
that he was having trouble with his overseer. In spite of everything
Worth could do, Wyatt G. Jordan, the first overseer, had finally been
drafted into the Confederate army, and Worth had been forced to
put the farm in charge of an undependable character named James
Russell. The Negroes on the place came to despise Russell because
he treated them badly and because he stole a third of their annual
supply of bacon. Worth feared dire consequences if Russell remained
on the place, but the overseer held the only copy of the contract he
had made with Worth. There was also the problem of finding a suitable man to replace Russell—only old men and disabled soldiers were
available.[39]

At last Worth found an excuse for deposing Russell. One of the
slaves on the farm, Joseph, ran away when Russell threatened to whip
him and came to Sharon, Worth's house in Raleigh. Quite indignant—
downright angry, in fact—about the conduct of his overseer, Worth
sent Joseph to live with one of his sons-in-law, and the next day told
Russell summarily, "I have no further use for your services," ordered
him to get off the farm, and replaced the notorious overseer with a
slave named Don.[40] Don was more satisfactory than Russell, but he
converted some of Worth's grain into liquor. Finally, Worth solved
his problems by selling the farm to his brother Milton shortly before
he bought the smaller farm at Raleigh. After Milton took the Cane
Creek place, Worth asked him if his overseer could attend to gather-

ing Worth's corn and fattening his hogs, so that Don might be brought to Raleigh to begin work on the farm there.[41]

When Wyatt Jordan left the farm on Cane Creek to go into the army, Worth promised to take care of his wife and child. This was in accordance with his practice of helping soldiers; he would purchase items for them in Raleigh and send what they had requested to the field. When Worth removed James Russell as overseer at Cane Creek he made the odd request that Russell take Mrs. Jordan and the child with him, but when brother Milton bought the farm Worth expected that the Jordans would be allowed to remain there. Worth wrote to Jordan, who had somehow got out of the Confederate army and was in Elmira, New York, to "give yourself no uneasiness about your wife and child. I will see that they do not suffer."[42]

While Worth did what he could to relieve the discomforts and worries of soldiers in the field, he did even more to keep men, especially Quakers and members of his own family, from becoming soldiers at all. This was probably to be expected of a former Quaker who still professed to have "as much abhorrence for war as any Quaker" and who regarded war as "wholesale murder."[43] In June, 1863, three Quakers, Nere Cox, Seth Cox, and Eli Macon, were taken from their fields and not given time to secure enough money to pay their exemption. When they arrived at Camp Holmes, the camp of instruction for North Carolina near Raleigh, they asked Worth to help them. He called upon Colonel Peter Mallett to allow the Coxes and Eli Macon to go home for ten days, under guard, if necessary, to raise the money they needed. If this were not permissible, Worth offered to loan the reluctant soldiers the fifteen hundred dollars required to keep them out of the Confederate army.[44] He also intervened in favor of Abijah and Charles Mason, two men who had been Quakers until they married contrary to the rules of the Society. They had become Methodists, but when the Confederate Congress exempted Quakers from conscription—they paid five hundred dollars each—the Masons claimed they still believed in the principles of their former religious denomination, the Society of Friends. When the enrolling officer accused Abijah Mason of becoming a Quaker only after the exemption act was passed, Worth knew better and told the enrolling officer that Mason "was raised under Quaker principles and will be worse than useless as a soldier."[45]

Worth also protested to Governor Vance against the removal of free Negroes from the farms of Randolph County to help build forts along the coast. He mentioned to the governor at least seven cases in which conscription of Negro laborers had resulted in hardship for his former constituents. The following representations are typical of what he said to the governor: "Rebecca Pearce is a widow—owns a good farm. Her only laborer—a free negro named Mose, is taken. Felix Walker, who has a good farm, and who is working at the State Salt works to avoid military service, has several children of tender years. His wife has recently become insane and is in the Asylum here. I am informed that Lewis Phillips, a free negro and his only hand, is taken."[46] After outlining these and other cases Worth asked that the free Negroes be allowed to return to Randolph County, where they could relieve some of the hardship and produce much-needed grain.

Paternal affection and concern caused Worth to worry about whether his son, David, would have to go into the army. When the war started David was less than thirty years old and in good health—a fine subject for conscription. After the conscription act passed, Worth strongly encouraged David to take charge of his widowed sister's plantation so he would be exempt under the provision of the law exempting overseers of twenty or more slaves from military service. David, fearing public censure if he took a job as Roxana's overseer, was reluctant to follow his father's advice, but Worth tried to convince him that evasion of the conscript law by any legal means was justifiable: "For public disapprobation, unless just, I have little regard, but I think intelligent public opinion would approve your course, even putting it on the ground that exemption was your object."[47] Under the original Conscript Act, David had hired a substitute and made arrangements to be replaced in the army until November 15, 1863. When he reported to his father that he had secured a few more months of freedom he said, "I feel very happy over it you may well suppose. I had about determined on going to Roxana's and take charge of her negroes but I saw that Congress would probably repeal that part of the Act exempting owners and agents of 20 negros."[48]

David received what amounted to a permanent exemption from the army when he replaced his uncle Milton as state salt commissioner in July, 1863, an appointment that led to one of his father's most serious disputes with the Confederate military authorities. Milton resigned because he felt that "it is just impossible to get along where the military have control of everything."[49] He had had an argument with Confederate General Whiting in December, 1862,[50] and early in January, 1863, Whiting seized the "flats" used to haul wood for the salt boilers across Masonboro Sound. Two weeks later the general impressed all the hands at the salt works for temporary service on fortifications.[51] The salt commissioner also had some difficulty with the state military authorities. Worth heard Colonel Mallett, the conscription officer, asking Governor Vance to have Milton supply a certified list of the conscripts at the salt works. Someone had informed Mallett that about a hundred men from Randolph County were employed there, but Milton had told Mallett there were only eight. It appeared to Jonathan Worth, from what he heard the conscription officer saying to the governor, that Mallett was trying to drag the salt workers into the army.[52] All this was too much for Milton; he resigned as salt commissioner in July, 1863.

Governor Vance asked Worth to find a successor for brother Milton, and the treasurer recommended his son David. Worth then wrote David, telling him that the governor "requested me not to let any body know about the vacancy as he would be besieged with a thousand applicants" and asking David to send a recommendation "from some body other than a near relative."[53] A few days later Vance appointed David as the state's second, and last, salt commissioner.

After David became salt commissioner, relations with General Whiting improved for a few months, but in the spring of 1864, they took a sudden turn for the worse. A raiding party of Union sailors attacked the salt works on April 21, set fire to some of the buildings, and captured forty-seven laborers. Whiting then ordered David to move the works from Masonboro Sound to a point on the Cape Fear River to be selected by Whiting. David refused to comply with the order, and sent it to Governor Vance with a statement that if the works had to be moved from Masonboro Sound the state might as well abandon them. Vance ordered the salt commissioner to continue his operations on the sound and asked General Whiting "by what authority and for what reason he had issued the aforesaid order" to move the salt works.[54] After Vance intervened in the clash between David Worth and General Whiting, the works continued to operate for a few weeks without interference from the Confederate military authorities.

Whiting's order to change the location of the salt works raised the delicate question of whether the elected officials of North Carolina or officials of the Confederate government were supreme within the state. William W. Holden, the editor of the Raleigh *Standard*, who had become increasingly hostile to the Confederacy and its policies, had this to say about the dispute over the salt works:

The order of General Whiting, addressed to the commissioner, to break up the works below Wilmington and to remove them to some other point, was most extraordinary. Gen. Whiting has nothing to do with these works. He had just as much right to order the removal of the two Asylums from Raleigh. Of course Governor Vance has *protested* against this order; but Gen. Whiting has shown a want of respect for him and for the State by addressing the Commissioner directly, and not through him. Mr. Worth is a *State* officer, and as such is subject to no direct order from a Confederate General.[55]

Jonathan Worth shared Holden's view that the location of the salt works was not the business of General Whiting, and he spilled a considerable amount of ink defending the salt commissioner and his laborers. After Whiting flatly ordered David to close the works early in June, 1864, claiming that some of the laborers were collaborating with the enemy, Worth wrote William A. Graham, North Carolina's Confederate senator: "Whether you can do anything to arrest this high-handed proceeding I know not, but I have thought it expedient to inform you of the facts."[56]

Worth also secured a letter of introduction from Governor Vance to the Secretary of War and started to Richmond to discuss the problem of General Whiting's interference with the salt works; but at the railroad depot in Raleigh he decided to abandon the idea of going to Richmond, because of the inconveniences, and possible danger, involved in such a trip. Instead, he submitted a detailed statement of the facts in the case to Governor Vance for transmission to the Confederate capital. These are the facts, as Worth saw them: General Whiting claimed that the men working under David Worth, mostly men exempted from military duty, were disloyal, that they had been communicating with the enemy and would continue to communicate if they were not removed from the area around Masonboro Sound. Whiting also believed that the salt works could be operated as well by slaves as by white "exempts," and he insisted that Negroes be enrolled for duty there. Worse still, the general would not allow the flatboats which hauled wood for the salt works to cross the waters of the sound. If Whiting were sustained in his actions, Worth claimed, the effectiveness of the salt works would be destroyed.

Whiting's refusal to let the flats cross the sound was particularly galling to Worth, for the use of them had been his own idea. It required sixty cords of wood each day to keep the salt kettles boiling. After more than two years of operation in the same location the wood supply in the vicinity was exhausted, and this presented the alternatives of moving the works, buying a large number of mules to haul wood, or building flats and hauling the wood across the sound. Worth had a flat boat built for experimental use, found that it worked well, and had constructed four more when General Whiting stopped them from operating. Whiting's objections were that the men at the works would use the flats to communicate with the enemy and that the sound had torpedoes in it. Several hundred cords of wood lay on the wrong side of Masonboro Sound waiting to be hauled across for use at the salt boilers.

Worth vigorously denied Whiting's allegation that the salt workers were disloyal, but suggested to Vance that a small force of soldiers be stationed at the works to watch them and to protect the works against enemy raids. He questioned the validity of Whiting's contention that slave labor could be used profitably in making salt, maintaining that the price of hiring slaves would be too high and that it was essential to keep the price of salt down to a level where the poor people of the state could afford to buy it. Worth further objected that there was no other eligible location for the salt works, that the cost of moving them would be prohibitive, and that the legislature had made no appropriation for moving the works.[57]

Moved by Worth's protests and his own indignation, Governor Vance had General P. G. T. Beauregard suspend the operation of Whiting's order to abandon the salt works. Late in June, Vance appealed to the Secretary of War, and when the governor threatened to ask for the removal of Whiting from the command at Wilmington, Whiting agreed to tolerate the salt works a few months longer. But on October 27, 1864, Whiting suspended the operation of private salt works along the coast. Three weeks later he ordered the men and teams to leave the state works on Masonboro Sound.[58] For all practical purposes, the production of salt on the coast of North Carolina came to an end. The governor protested vainly to the legislature,[59] but nothing was done.

Long before Worth's clash with General Whiting over the salt works, resentment against the Confederate government and hatred of the war had been building up in the mind of the old Unionist. He had to give up the produce of his farms to the Confederate government; pay outrageously high prices for food to replace what the government took away from him; and pay higher taxes than he had ever paid before. His Quaker friends had been dragged into military service against their will, and free Negro laborers taken from their farms. The war deprived him of an opportunity to display his financial talents under normal conditions, and his relations with the Confederacy in his position of treasurer were far from pleasant. All these things, plus his temperamental aversion to the horrors of war, caused Worth to sympathize openly with those who desired an early peace and to participate covertly in a peace movement that reached its most active stage in the year preceding the gubernatorial election of 1864.

In its political aspect, the peace movement was essentially a contest between Governor Vance and William W. Holden, the editor of the Raleigh *Standard*. Both had been Unionists at the beginning of the war, both were members of the Conservative party in opposition to those "destructives" who most avidly supported the South's war effort, and both were critical of Confederate policies. One difference between Vance and Holden was that Vance, while he jousted with Jefferson Davis about such matters as conscription, impressment, the suspension of habeas corpus, and infringements on state rights, was willing and determined to uphold North Carolina's honor on the battlefield. Holden, in contrast to the governor, openly attacked the Confederate government through articles in his newspaper and boldly cried for peace. Before the war there had been basic political differences between Vance and Holden which had been temporarily obliterated by their opposition to secession and their concern over some of the Confederacy's alleged infringements of North Carolina's rights and honor. Holden had been the leader of the Democrats, Vance a devout Whig. Vance was probably the more conservative of the two. Both were in a sense champions of the common people, but much of Vance's popularity derived from the fact that he was a war hero who represented the determination and pride of those persons who wished to continue the war. By 1863, Holden's enthusiasm for both the war and the Confederacy had disappeared—and in that fact lay the essential difference between Zeb Vance and William Holden.[60]

Worth's role in the peace movement was a difficult one, for his relations with both Vance and Holden were cordial, and he did not wish to antagonize either of them by identifying himself too closely with the other. As a member of the Vance administration he was in no position to publicize his pacific sentiments, but behind the scenes he supported Holden. He reported to his friend Jesse Henshaw, a prominent Quaker, that "Holden's bold position in favor of peace is hailed with joy by many," and asked Henshaw if he would find two hundred new subscribers for the *Standard* in Randolph County.[61] This was the only thing Worth did in 1863 to promote the growth of the peace movements. There was a series of public meetings in August, 1863, to discuss the possibility of a negotiated peace, but Worth had nothing to do with them; he could not decide for himself whether the meetings would help or hinder the cause of peace. He perceived that "they will be impotent and mischievous if the *army* is still for war to the last man and the last dollar" and advised his friends in Randolph not to participate in peace meetings.[62] Fearing that criticism of Vance would lead to a split in the Conservative ranks, Worth attempted to repress expressions of dissatisfaction with the governor.

When the peace movement began to create dissension in the Worth family itself, Jonathan became deeply concerned and wrote to his brother Milton a lengthy letter in which he made the following plea for unity within the family:

For a few months back I had been pained to hear of unpleasant bickerings between Sam. Jackson and you and Shubal, which I had labored to repress, growing out of a difference of opinion about the accursed war in which we are involved, which if not soon stopped will destroy everything worth living for. . . . Some weeks ago Albert [Worth] was here.—He detailed in presence of the family, many harsh things— very offensive remarks of yours in reference to Sam's extortions as a lawyer and his sympathy with the peace movements, and your apprehensions that I was not, according to your views, exactly sound. . . . If this war must destroy every thing else worth living for, let it not mar what has been our chief happiness heretofore—the genuine brotherhood of the Worths.

It would be more than unprofitable to mention the particulars of what has been reported as being said. Let it all be forgotten or understood as never having been uttered and if we differ in opinion about the war, it should not be suffered to grow into a canker destroying the enjoyments of our domestic relations.[63]

At the beginning of 1864, Worth took a trip to Whiteville to look at some swamp land he was planning to buy. After he returned to Raleigh, he told J. J. Jackson that the man who was selling the land "will give you a vivid picture of myself on an old negro's back, making a survey of his swamp. The sight kept his risibles in action till I left him."[64] Along the way to Whiteville and Wilmington, Worth talked politics, and it appeared to him that almost everyone he saw was "openly for re-construction on the basis of the Constitution of the U.S., if these terms can be obtained."[65] Favoring peace on almost any honorable terms, he had begun to feel that even William Holden did not go far enough in his pleas for peace. His desire for an end to the war became more intense as he became more disillusioned with the Confederacy. A month before the Confederate government suspended the writ of habeas corpus in February, 1864, he quoted to one of his Quaker friends, Allen M. Tomlinson, the old Greek saying that "Whom the Gods would destroy they first make mad," and went on to say that the Confederate Congress was "quite crazy . . . , their iniquitous measures are precipitating the end."[66] He told Tomlinson that there was some sentiment in the state for the call of a new convention that would secede from the Confederacy.

Worth believed that the only basis on which peace could, or should, be made was a restoration of the Union as it existed before the war; he would not listen to talk of North Carolina's seceding from the Confederacy and becoming independent or making a separate peace with the United States. Believing that the masses, both North and South, shared his views, and feeling that if the people would exert pressure on their leaders the war would soon be ended, Worth tried to mobilize public opinion by the use of petitions. Early in February, 1864, he sent a copy of a petition he had prepared to Darius H. Starbuck, an anti-secession Whig from Forsyth County who was trying to organize a movement to call a new state convention. Worth's petition, which he had submitted to Holden for approval, was the best concise expression of his attitude towards the peace movement and of the methods he wanted to employ in the quest for an end to the war. Asking Starbuck to keep the origin of the petition secret if he decided to use it, Worth sent him the following copy:

To his Excellency, Z. B. Vance, Govr. of N.Ca.

We citizens of ————— County, think that "all, save those who owe their riches to their country's ruin, suffer by the war," and that it is manifest that the authorities of the United States and of the Confederate States, authorised by the power of the Government to make peace, will not appoint Commissioners to open negotiations for this purpose. We wish to know whether peace can be obtained on honorable terms;—and as this cannot be ascertained through the regular channels of the Government, we respectfully petition your Excellency to convoke the Genl. Assembly without delay, to the end that they authorise a vote of the people upon the question whether a Convention ought not to be called in this State; and to authorise the election of delegates at the same time, (such election to be valid only in case a majority of the people shall vote for a Convention) with power to put on foot measures looking to a general peace, and with all the powers with which the people can invest it, with the limitations only that the power of such Convention shall cease within two years after the election of the delegates;—and that any action of said Convention, agreeing on a final treaty of peace; or altering the Constitution of the State shall not be valid until ratified by a vote of the people, at such time and under such regulations as said Convention may prescribe.

We also pray your Excellency to lay this, our petition, before the Genl. Assembly.

February 1864.[67]

The efforts of Worth and other Unionists to call a convention failed, for Governor Vance did not share their view that a convention would be the best method of negotiating for peace and he refused to call the legislature into session.[68]

Faced with the governor's refusal to co-operate, Worth did not give up easily his efforts to promote the cause of peace and a reconstruction of the Union. After his own petition failed to serve its purpose he came into possession of a peace circular signed by Bryan Tyson, a Unionist from Randolph County who lived in Washington, D.C., during the war and corresponded regularly with Confederate soldiers in Old Capitol Prison and the prison at Point Lookout, Maryland in an effort to promote Union sentiments among them.[69] The avowed purpose of Tyson's circular, which was designed for circulation in the North, was to unite the people of the North more firmly, thereby bringing a quicker end to the war and saving many human lives. Soon after the circulars were printed the course of the war improved—from a Northern viewpoint—and Tyson decided not to distribute his circulars. The writer, having abandoned his ambitious plan to unite the North, then decided that if the circulars were distributed in North Carolina they "might throw some light upon things South." Either Tyson or William W. Holden wrote the history of the petition on its reverse side and added a paragraph relating specifically to North Carolina which read as follows: "The day-star of the Union is looming up in the distance. Old North Carolina will soon take her position under the stars and stripes; and, one star plucked from the Confederacy, the remaining states would soon follow. Yes, if we will pull together, pull steadily, and pull long enough . . . the stars and stripes will wave triumphantly throughout the entire length and breadth of the land."[70] Tyson's circular authorized those who received it to use it in any way that would aid the Union. When Worth read the material printed on the back side of the circular, it conformed so closely to his own views that he had copies published and circulated them anonymously. This effort to rouse public opinion, or to give voice to it, proved to be a failure, just as Worth's own petition failed.

Equally futile were the treasurer's efforts to mend a break in relations between Vance and Holden that resulted from Holden's leadership of the peace movement and caused the editor to announce himself a candidate for governor against Vance in the election of 1864. Worth had great respect for the abilities of both candidates, and he regarded Holden "not as a traitor, but as an ambitious, flexible politician—as unscrupulous, but not more unscrupulous than democratic leaders generally."[71] Lacking enthusiasm for either candidate, Worth planned to vote for Vance, principally because Holden had shifted his position in the past too frequently to please Worth's demand for consistency; the editor had been both Whig and Democrat, secessionist and anti-secessionist. Seeking to avert a contest which might weaken the Conservatives and allow the most radical supporters of the war to edge their way into control of the state government, Worth asked Holden to withdraw his candidacy and let Vance run without opposition. He tried to convince Holden that "the difference between you on the questions of public interest [can] be narrowed down to the Convention question, an issue at present, not warranting a contest."[72] Holden was nothing, if not ambitious, and Worth appealed to his ambitions for the future by promising that, if Holden should withdraw, his political stock would be raised high, that "the Destructionists . . . would fall the flattest that ever party did fall," and that "you might be elected our next Govr., almost by acclamation."

Holden saw matters differently from Worth and refused to withdraw. Even before Worth asked him to give up the fight against Vance, arguing that the question whether a convention should be called was the only point at issue between the two men, Holden had pointed out several other issues. He explained to one of his political friends in March, 1864, that he was running against Vance because the governor was, in his view, the candidate of the faction which supported the war. It appeared to Holden that Vance had been on the side of the war party ever since he visited Jefferson Davis at Richmond in August, 1863. Other complaints Holden made against Vance were that his recent appointments had been "nearly all Destructives";[73] that he was not as diligent in protecting the laws of North Carolina from Confederate abuse as he pretended to be; that the pro-Confederate newspapers had approved a speech at Wilkesboro in which Vance toned down his criticisms of the suspension of habeas corpus; and that N. W. Woodfin, a leader of the "Destructives," had been in Raleigh to promise support of Vance by his faction.[74] These were the reasons Holden himself gave for remaining in the race against Vance. Worth attributed his failure to convince Holden he should not run to Vance's "impudence" in calling Holden a coward because of the way the editor acted when a mob of Confederate soldiers, angry about his peace articles, destroyed his newspaper press in September, 1863. The treasurer thought Holden could not withdraw from the gubernatorial race without confirming Vance's charge of cowardice, thereby bringing upon himself "positive degradation."[75]

After it became apparent to Worth that he could not reconcile Vance and Holden he remained on good terms with both of them but did not actively support either one. When Vance went to Randolph County in May, 1864, to make a campaign speech, he invited Worth, but Worth found it inconvenient to go. He liked to fish better than he liked politics, and he wanted to visit his daughter Roxana and go on his "annual fishing frolic" before the weather got too hot. He referred Vance to the leading Whigs of the county and offered his law office for a conference room. In advising the governor about what to say in his speech, Worth reminded him that "the people of Randolph are the most stable Whigs in the State," that they had voted 2566 to 45 against the call of the secession convention in 1861, and that Holden was very popular there. Worth supposed that most of the people there favored a convention designed to promote the cause of peace.

Remembering the strong Unionist sentiments of his former constituents, Worth advised Vance, who was opposed to a convention, that he should give the people of Randolph credit for the honesty of their convictions, and not condemn Holden severely.[76]

The election of 1864 demonstrated conclusively that the people of North Carolina had turned a deaf ear to William Holden's cries for peace. Vance, the popular soldier and eloquent orator, who insisted during the campaign that the South should continue to fight for its independence, beat Holden in all but three counties, receiving five times as many votes as his opponent; significantly one of the three counties Holden carried was Randolph.[77] Worth expressed no disappointment at the outcome of the election, even though it had become evident that most of the people of the state desired independence in preference to a return to the Union.

Throughout the fall and winter months of 1864-65, Worth labored with his duties at the treasury and waited hopefully for the end of the war to come. Peace resolutions introduced by John Pool, the Whig candidate for governor in 1860, failed in the fall term of the legislature, but by January, 1865, even the Confederate party was weary of the war. They proposed to the Conservatives that representatives be sent to Jefferson Davis to find out whether the president was making any efforts to negotiate a peace. Worth favored negotiations— "We are whipped and ought to make the best terms we can," he said late in January.[78] There were negotiations, at Hampton Roads, Virginia, between representatives of the Union and the Confederacy, but they failed because Lincoln insisted on a reconstruction of the Union and Jefferson Davis would hear of nothing short of independence for the South. Worth anticipated the breakdown of the conference at Hampton Roads, and bitterly criticized the Confederate leaders for insisting on independence. "Reconstruction is the only practical remedy," he believed, but "this with our present rulers is impossible."[79]

Even before the peace negotiations failed there were signs that the war would soon end. The prices of produce in Wilmington "declined wonderfully," and Worth told his son David, on February 9, that the price of a slave he had bought for one of his friends a few days earlier had dropped by fifteen hundred dollars—an indication of the declining fortunes of the Confederacy.[80] Randolph County, like some other counties, was swarming with deserters from Lee's army, and

Milton Worth wrote from Asheboro that when the Home Guard was called out to pursue them some members of the Guard refused to leave their homes, fearing that their houses would be robbed by the deserters. The military situation of the South grew worse as General Sherman led his army northward through Georgia and Grant prepared to drive the defenders of Petersburg and Richmond out of their defenses and chase them westward across the open fields of Virginia. Worth feared that if the Confederate army could not win a major battle the South would be vanquished and that emancipation of slaves and confiscation of other property would follow. He quoted a line of the poet Milton to explain why the people of North Carolina and the South did not begin to fight harder against the consequences they faced: "They feel as Milton represents Satan—'which way I fly is death.' "[81]

A few days after Sherman's army entered North Carolina it seemed to Worth "so apparent that we can hope for nothing from our arms, that I am astonished that the Government persists in making a show of fight, which, without a miracle, can result only in a further destruction of life and property."[82] No miracle intervened, and the relentless Sherman marched on towards Fayetteville and Raleigh. Worth, who had long since ceased to expect divine intervention in behalf of the South, began making preparations to save what he could of his own and the state's property.

· XIII ·

Guardian of the Public Property

THE OFFICIALS of the state government began to prepare for an invasion of North Carolina as early as July, 1863. Although there was no immediate danger at that time, some members of the legislature had foresight enough to see that the records and funds of the state would be widely scattered if proper provision for their care were not made. Accordingly, a resolution was passed calling upon Governor Vance to have boxes made into which the public papers, money, bonds, military stores, and other effects could be thrown and hauled away from Raleigh on short notice.[1] When General Sherman's army swept into North Carolina in March, 1865, Vance delegated to Worth the responsibility of carrying the state's property away from Raleigh and keeping it out of the clutches of the Union and Confederate armies, deserters, and robbers.

On March 4, 1865, Worth wrote to J. J. Jackson from Raleigh: "I cannot leave here. My whole mental and physical powers are employed in preparing for the security of the valuables belonging to the state and to myself if the enemy come here. . . ."[2] Worth had already made arrangements with Thomas Ruffin, a commissioner of the Sinking Fund, to secure the assets of the Fund, which was the pool for retiring the state debt. The treasurer suggested that he give each commissioner of the Fund a certificate stating the number, dates, and amounts of the bonds and stocks held by the treasury for the Sinking Fund; then if the enemy attacked Raleigh the original bonds and stocks could be burned.[3] The property of the treasury and other departments was thrown into boxes so it could be hauled away before Sherman reached Raleigh. No precise destination was arranged for the state officers when they fled the capital, and Worth was uneasy about where he would go. "Where is the place of Security to which I could fly?"[4] he wondered. There would probably be as much danger of being robbed by deserters from Lee's army as there would be from Sherman's men, he feared.

After Worth prepared the state's valuables for a hasty evacuation he remained in Raleigh, deeply concerned about the welfare of the members of his family who were in Sherman's line of march. David was at Roxana's plantation, and when a few Union raiders appeared there he "took to the bushes" to avoid being captured. The Yankee soldiers took six of Roxana's mules and four of her Negroes, but one of the slaves, Sam, who was at the rear of the party as it left, escaped and returned to the plantation when a sniper fired on the party.[5] The Worth house at Asheboro escaped damage, but Elvira wrote Mrs. Worth that "you ought to have seen us hiding meat, corn, etc. the other day. We heard that 4000 Cavalry were to pass here and we knew if they did we would be eaten out and so we went to hiding hay and provisions. Fortunately for us the Cavalry turned off. . . ."[6]

Brothers Barzillai and Addison, both at Fayetteville, were the most unfortunate members of the Worth family. A large arsenal at Fayetteville drew Sherman's army there, and when it arrived Barzillai's house, barn, and provisions went up in flames. Most of Addison's property was destroyed too, and the Yankees captured the steamboat owned by the Worths. Jonathan wrote J. J. Jackson that Addison wished "he had been Sampson with a cart load of the jaw bones of asses and he would have made piles of Yankees."[7] As for Jonathan, he lost his slaves, who were of course emancipated, and probably some provisions he was desperately trying to haul out of the enemy's way. If the Yankees ruined Worth's farm at Raleigh, he planned to move what equipment and animals remained to Roxana's plantation and put out his crops there, but it did not become necessary to put this plan into operation.

Three years after the war Worth lamented, with slight exaggeration, that "I lost by a war which I had no hand in bringing on . . . more than half my estate; and by good luck was not left insolvent as so many thousands of wealthier men were."[8] He was indeed more fortunate than those who had invested heavily in Confederate and state securities since 1861, for those securities became worthless after the war ended. The lands in which he invested in 1864 could not be destroyed, even by Sherman; the Cedar Falls factory escaped damage and continued its operations; the large quantity of cotton Worth bought for Confederate bonds in 1863 was delivered after the war ended;[9] and the Cape Fear Steamboat Company continued its operations after it recuperated from the loss of its facilities at Fayetteville and its boat was returned. After the shooting and burning ceased and the former slaves went their not-so-merry way, Jonathan Worth's assets still totaled well over twenty thousand dollars.

Early in March, 1865, Worth believed that after the "valuables" were hauled away from the capital the state officers, including the governor, should remain in Raleigh to help protect the town and the capitol, but Vance did not agree with this view. The treasurer's sense of duty to his family and his belief that he would be of more value to the state in Raleigh than anywhere else caused him to consider whether he should not stay in Raleigh, regardless of the governor's orders, but on March 23, he loaded the state records and the funds of the treasury into a railroad car and headed west on the North Carolina Railroad. Adelaide Worth wrote her suitor, William II. Bagley, that "Pa had to leave us. The parting cost us all many tears for we know not how long he may be away. . . . He would not leave us without some gentleman here and succeeded in getting Mr. Patrick Winston, Sr. to stay here."[10]

Worth and his party of fifteen or twenty clerks arrived in Greensboro on the morning of March 25, after two days of travel. There he "stationed" himself and the clerks in the branch office of the Bank of Cape Fear for a few days. At night, while the clerks stayed in the bank with the archives and funds, Worth slept in James T. Morehead's law office. Fearful that his wife would worry about him, he wrote her that he was faring well—a Major Sloan was furnishing rations—but that he had been "terribly busy" since he left Raleigh.[11]

After remaining five days at Greensboro, Worth returned to Raleigh, leaving the valuables in charge of his chief clerk, but he spent only one day at home before he had to rush back to Greensboro. A threatening column of Union cavalry under General George Stoneman was sweeping through the western part of the state from Tennessee. After Stoneman headed north into Virginia, Worth returned to Raleigh on the night of April 8.[12]

At Raleigh, Governor Vance was having a difficult time deciding what he should do when Sherman's army reached the capital. Former governors William A. Graham and David L. Swain urged Vance to secure a temporary cessation of hostilities and call the legislature into session to negotiate for peace with General Sherman. Worth first heard

of the plan suggested by Swain and Graham on Tuesday night, April
10. The next morning he suggested to Vance the course the governor
subsequently followed:

> On Wednesday morning, [Worth wrote], I saw Gov. Vance alone.
> He told me he could not concur in their plans—I suggested to him
> then whether he could not send Gov. Swain and Gov. Graham under a
> flag of truce to ask protection for the Capitol and a suspension of
> hostilities with the view to a general pacification. Gov. G. came
> in soon after, intending to leave for home by the next train. Gov.
> V. asked him if he would consent to go. He said being a member
> of Congress, he doubted whether the enemy would not hold him
> a prisoner—that he had left home suddenly and ought to return
> home to provide for the approach of the army. I urged upon him
> that he alone could save the Capitol from destruction—and that he
> ought to incur the hazard and inconvenience. At this state my duties
> compelled me to withdraw from the conference.[13]

After Worth left, Graham and Swain went out to meet General Sher-
man, who did not accept an armistice but promised that the town of
Raleigh would not suffer the type of damage his army had inflicted on
Fayetteville and upon Columbia, South Carolina.[14]

When Graham and Swain left Raleigh for their talk with Sherman, Worth took charge of a wagon train loaded with military supplies
that had been stored in Raleigh. The railroad train containing the
archives and funds of the treasury had fled from Greensboro to Hillsboro on April 9, when General Stoneman came back south out of
Virginia, and Worth now intended to meet the train at Morrisville,
load the archives and effects of the treasury on the wagons, and head
south where the Union army had already been. His plans went
completely awry. Before the wagons left Raleigh, the drivers employed
by the state deserted and others had to be found. By the time they
left Raleigh on Wednesday night, April 11, Sherman's advanced guard
was only six miles away. The roads between Raleigh and Durham
Station were so clogged with army wagons that the state's wagons did
not reach Durham Station until after sunset on Thursday, April 12.
That morning Sherman had entered Raleigh.

On the morning of April 13, Worth sent General Beauregard a
telegram from Durham Station asking what he should do next: "I am
here in charge of the state funds and archives with the state wagon
trains. Will you favor me with your opinion whether it will be safe to
endeavor to carry off the effects by the wagon trains in the direction

of Fayetteville or to fall back towards Greensboro, and if you advise the latter at what point do you advise?"[15] By this time Sherman's cavalry was too close for Worth to take a chance on sending the records and archives southward on the wagon train, so he moved with them first to Company Shops, on the railroad in Alamance County, and then on to Greensboro; the wagons with the supplies were left behind.

When Generals Johnston and Sherman began negotiating for peace and hostilities were suspended, Worth moved his train, which now consisted only of an engine, tender, and one passenger car, back to Company Shops to await the result of the negotiations. The presence of numerous camp followers and deserters in the vicinity made it necessary to keep the passenger car locked and the windows closed; inside it was stifling hot. Governor Vance had placed a bolt of fine English cloth on the train to be divided among the members of Worth's party as a reward for their services. Fear of robbery by deserters led Worth to secure from General Joseph E. Johnston the serv ices of a Georgia battalion commanded by a Colonel Bursey to serve as guards. One night while Worth was sleeping in the village near the shops, Bursey told the engineer of the train that his soldiers were about to raid the train, but that he could control them better if he had the bolt of English cloth to distribute among them. Worth's men refused to be bribed and armed themselves, but the Georgians did not attempt to break open the car. When Worth returned next morning and heard what had happened, he went to Colonel Bursey and made it plain to the colonel that if he could not control his men, Worth would have them sent back to the front and get a more disciplined battalion; this put an end to the threat of robbery.[16]

Besides threatening to break open the car containing the archives and funds of the treasury, Confederate soldiers seized all the state's property along the North Carolina Railroad between Haw River and Greensboro. When Vance protested to General Johnston, the general asked the governor to make a list of the state property taken by Confederate troops. Vance was unable to report exactly how much property had been taken, because the marauders who stole the property had in some cases taken the quartermaster's records. The state quartermaster at Graham told Vance that he had been forced by Confederate soldiers to surrender sixty-three hundred pairs of trousers, twenty-one hundred blankets, two thousand yards of jeans cloth, and a large quantity of leather. Local citizens then joined the soldiers in carrying away cloth and leather. Vance himself saw soldiers at McLean's Station "staggering under heavy loads of the plunder." The governor naturally protested against the issue of North Carolina's supplies to the Confederate army without compensation to the state. As he pointed out to Johnston, the state could never be paid for the supplies because the Confederacy was passing out of existence, and there was no possibility that any Southern state would help North Carolina pay the debt she had incurred in Europe to buy the supplies.[17]

General Johnston denied that the troops in his army were guilty of stealing property from the state and from private citizens. Most of the thefts he attributed to the disbanded troops of the Army of Northern Virginia, who were straggling homeward from Appomattox in threadbare clothing. Johnston's army itself was not free from these skilled marauders; food, especially, was not safe anywhere from Lee's hungry soldiers.[18]

Vance proposed to Johnston that Johnston deliver to the state authorities all Confederate property within the state, if and when the war ended; this was to be a partial payment of the Confederacy's large debt to North Carolina. Johnston declined to make such an agreement, stating as his reason the fact that the Confederacy was indebted to other states as well as to North Carolina and that its property should be divided "proportionally."[19]

Worth and Vance were in Greensboro when Johnston and Sherman reached their preliminary terms of surrender on April 18, 1865. Both Worth and Vance thought that General Sherman intended to use the governmental machinery which had existed under Vance for purposes of reorganization, and Vance wrote to Sherman, proposing to come to Raleigh and call a session of the legislature; the legislature could in turn call a convention to restore the state to the Union. Vance read the letter in which he proposed this plan of reorganization to Worth and Worth agreed to carry the letter to Sherman. After getting a passport from General Johnston, Worth set out for Raleigh, traveling on the railroad where it had not been cut, and by private transportation the remainder of the way. At Durham Station, General Judson Kilpatrick, Sherman's cavalry commander, told Worth that Sherman was about to leave Raleigh and would be gone by the time he arrived there. Kilpatrick sent a telegram to Sherman in which he explained Worth's business and asked Sherman to wait for his arrival, but Sherman left after referring Worth to General John M. Schofield, who was in command after Sherman's departure. When Worth arrived in Raleigh the next morning, Schofield told him the surrender terms agreed upon by Johnston and Sherman had been disapproved in Washington and asked Worth to inform Vance that none of the state officers would be allowed to retain their positions. Worth then asked Schofield if he would be willing to meet Vance in Raleigh and discuss the affairs of the state. Schofield declined, but promised to see the governor at Greensboro in a few days.[20] Severely disappointed at the way things had turned out, Worth returned to Greensboro.

Worth's last act in the series of tiresome events at the end of the war was to carry the state archives back to Raleigh. Governor Vance had received assurance from General Sherman that if the archives and funds of the treasury were carried back to Raleigh they would not be captured.[21] After Worth returned to Greensboro from his mission to General Schofield he loaded up the public records, carried them back to the military authorities at Raleigh, "and retired from office without a murmur."[22] His tour of duty as the wartime treasurer of North Carolina had come to an end.

Six weeks after the war ended, Worth was appointed treasurer and property agent in a provisional government established by President Johnson, but before he could become eligible to accept the appointment he had to secure a presidential pardon for his participation in the state government during the war. On May 29, 1865, President Johnson appointed William W. Holden as provisional governor of North Carolina[23] and issued a proclamation extending a general amnesty to the people of the South for their participation in the rebellion. There were fourteen categories of persons excepted from the provisions of the amnesty act. Worth was ineligible for a pardon until he made a special application because the thirteenth exception to the proclamation included all persons who held property worth over twenty thousand dollars. Governor Holden, whom President Johnson had asked to recommend approval or disapproval of special applications for pardon, favored the early pardon of Worth and recommended to Johnson that clemency be granted in order that Worth might become his treasurer in the provisional government.[24]

After Worth took the oath required by the Amnesty Proclamation, he wrote out an application to the president for a pardon.[25] The application stated that he had never believed in secession, and that he had voted and used his influence against the secession movement in

1861. Worth pointed out that he had held no office in the government of the Confederate States, but admitted that, as a member of the legislature of 1862, he had taken an oath to support the Confederacy. He asserted that his election to the legislature in 1862 had been "by an immense majority chiefly on account of his known repugnance to the Rebellion." The application ended with statements that the applicant had served as state treasurer to the end of the war and that he had taken the amnesty oath.[26] Before Holden sent the application to Washington he endorsed it as follows: "I respectfully recommend an *immediate* pardon in this case." The pardon was granted in July, 1865.

Worth must have been certain that he would be pardoned by the president, for he accepted the office of provisional treasurer before he started the process of securing executive clemency. Holden made the appointment and it was confirmed by a military order issued on June 12, 1865.[27] The *Standard,* Holden's newspaper, announced on June 10 that Worth had accepted the post of treasurer and property agent[28] for the provisional government. "In addition to the duties of Treasurer," the announcement said, "he will be charged with collecting and selling all the property belonging to the State—cotton, turpentine, and every other article of state property—and to investigate the condition of banks, railroads, asylums, and other public corporations."[29] When Holden announced the appointment of Worth, he praised the treasurer for his "judgment, energy, and integrity."

Much of the state's property had been seized by the Union army in the last weeks of the war, and Worth began trying to restore this property to the state soon after he took office as provisional treasurer. General Schofield, who commanded the Department of North Carolina immediately after the war ended, informed Worth that he would return the property held by the military authorities if Worth would ask for it in writing. Worth did make two written requests, but Schofield was relieved of command before he could fulfill his promise. The treasurer then applied to Schofield's successor, Major General J. D. Cox, who authorized Worth "to reclaim and take possession of all wagons, mules, and other property, lately belonging to the State, which may have come into possession of the United States forces, and which can still be traced or identified."[30]

After securing Cox's promise that the state's property would be returned, Worth sent an agent to Greensboro to reclaim a hundred and twenty bales of cotton held by a subordinate quartermaster

official. The quartermaster would not give up the cotton without an
order from Colonel James F. Boyd, the quartermaster of the Department of North Carolina. Boyd also refused to surrender the cotton,
questioning General Cox's authority to return it to the state of North
Carolina. Boyd promised to consult the Quartermaster Department in
Washington, but the last time Worth heard of the cotton which had
been at Greensboro, the Quartermaster Department had hauled it out
of the state.[31]

Before the war ended, the United States Department of the Treasury had begun sending agents into the South to take charge of captured and abandoned property, and Worth inevitably had some disagreements with these agents who were performing a function similar
to his own duties. Early in June, Worth received word that Colonel
David Heaton, an agent of the United States treasury, was removing
from the state eleven hundred bales of North Carolina's cotton at
Graham and Clarksville Junction which had been taken after General
Johnston capitulated to Sherman. Worth informed Governor Holden,
who then protested to Heaton against the removal of the cotton from
the state. Colonel Heaton justified his actions by giving Worth a copy
of the treasury department's regulations pertaining to captured and
abandoned property. Worth asked General Schofield to order the return of the cotton, but Schofield said that title had passed to the
United States and suggested that Holden write to President Johnson.[32]
The governor then wrote the president: "In view of the destitute condition of our people I beg you not to enforce confiscation of State
property."[33] Holden informed the president that the cotton Colonel
Heaton was about to remove had not been captured before the war
ended. Furthermore, Holden implored, General Schofield wanted the
cotton returned to the state, but could not issue an order to put his
wish into effect unless he received an order from Washington. Johnson
did not act immediately to stop the seizure and removal of property
from the state, for on June 17, 1865, the Secretary of the Treasury,
Hugh McCulloch, ordered his chief agent, Heaton, to send the cotton
claimed by North Carolina to New York—"without regard to State
claims."[34]

When it became apparent that more state property would be lost
unless Holden and Worth did something besides writing imploring
letters and making requests, Worth went to Washington to secure a
clarification of the status of North Carolina's property in the hands of

United States military authorities and treasury agents. He took to Washington a letter from Holden to the president and a letter from General Cox in which Cox stated that he had captured the state's cotton at Graham because he thought it belonged to the Confederacy. Worth tried to convince the president and his cabinet that the seizure of state property after the war ended was "unwarranted, in my opinion, by the act of Congress and not sanctioned by the law of nations—but at all events savoring of the rapacious and highly impolitic."[35] The president did not accept Worth's argument that the seizures were illegal, but the provisional treasurer's plea that further confiscation should stop had the desired effect: on July 8, while Worth was still in Washington, Johnson authorized North Carolina to take possession of all the state's property which had not been seized prior to that date.[36]

Worth also inquired in Washington about who was to pay the expenses of reorganizing the civil government of North Carolina. The state was badly in need of money to meet its normal operating expenses for the year 1865, and Worth hoped to collect and sell as much of the remaining property as he could in order to help pay these expenses. Secretary of State Seward promised that the War Department would pay the cost of *reorganizing* the state government—"as an expense incident to the suppression of the rebellion"—if Worth would submit an estimate of the costs of the reorganization; but the state was to pay its regular expenses from whatever sources it had available.[37] Upon Worth devolved the task of determining what civil expenses were, as distinguished from those incurred in the reorganization. This was embarrassing and difficult—to say the least—but Worth finally arrived at an estimate of $53,800, as the cost of the reorganization. When he submitted his estimate to the War Department, it was reduced to seven thousand dollars. Worth never knew what items in his estimate had been disallowed.[38]

When Worth returned from Washington, he began trying to collect and sell whatever property had not been captured, seized, or stolen. This proved to be one of the most "onerous" duties in which he was ever engaged, for the property, mostly cotton and rosin, was widely scattered. Besides the lots of cotton in North Carolina, there were stores of cotton in Georgia and Alabama which the state had bought during the last months of the war. The rosin was in pits and in warehouses throughout the state. The state had some goods in the West Indies which had been stored there when the Union navy put an end to North Carolina's blockade-running operations, and a sizable amount of state funds which had been sent to England. Soon after Worth became provisional treasurer he began appointing agents to hunt for state cotton and rosin and to sell it.

In an effort to find out how much property or money the state had in England, Worth sought information from John White, who had been the chief agent of the state in negotiations with English firms. White reported that J. H. Flanner, another of the state's agents, had taken the funds remaining in England—some twelve or thirteen thousand pounds—and gone to the continent for a grand tour.[39] White's report to Worth was not entirely without value, for it told what had happened to the goods belonging to the state which had been stored in the islands of the Caribbean and Bermuda when the blockade operations were stopped. They had been pledged as collateral security for a loan from Alexander Collie and Company about the first of April, 1865. When the news of the collapse of the Confederacy reached Bermuda, Collie and Company seized all the goods, approximately fifty thousand pounds in weight, for debts owed to the company by the state.[40] At the time Worth made his investigation in the summer of 1865, the goods from the West Indies were stored in English warehouses; presumably, Collie and Company later sold them, for the state never got them back.

Worth's efforts to collect the state's rosin and cotton were more successful than his attempt to bring funds back from England. In 1864 and 1865, one of Governor Vance's agents had bought most of the rosin lying west of the Wilmington and Weldon Railroad in Wilson, Wayne, Johnston, Sampson, and Harnett counties. Much of it was in deposits left on sites where distilleries had formerly been operated. Normally, it was not considered worthwhile to pick up rosin which had spilled and soaked into the ground, but the state was so hard pressed for money that Worth hired men to "resurrect the rosin."[41] With visions of securing for the state the proceeds from over thirty thousand barrels of rosin, Worth made contracts for having the rosin strained, barreled, and hauled to market. He managed the collection and sale as if it were one of his personal business ventures, and it soon took on the aspect of a family enterprise. He asked his brother Addison to take charge of the rosin which came through Fayetteville, and to ship it to David Worth and his partner at Wilmington on the barges of the Cape Fear Steamboat Company. From Wilmington the rosin was shipped to New York and sold through commission merchants, one of which was Dibble, Worth, and Company, a firm in which Barzillai Worth had recently become a partner.[42] The collection and sale of the rosin progressed slowly, but before Worth resigned as provisional treasurer, most of it had been "resurrected" and was headed to the markets of New York.

Cotton proved to be the most troublesome item Worth tried to collect and sell. Even after President Johnson promised that no more state property would be seized, some United States treasury agents in other states confiscated cotton that Worth's agents were trying to gather and sell; as late as October, 1865, Governor Holden found it necessary to protest to the Secretary of the Treasury when federal military officials confiscated some cotton belonging to North Carolina from a warehouse in Eufala, Alabama.[43] In Georgia, federal agents seized almost five hundred bales of cotton, seventy of which had already been collected by one of Worth's agents and prepared for shipment to New York.[44] The treasury agents and military authorities in North Carolina co-operated with Worth and relinquished most of the scattered lots of cotton in the state after President Johnson ordered them to turn it over to Worth and his agents. Once the cotton was collected it was sent, like the rosin, to New York to be sold. The firm which handled more of the cotton and rosin in New York than any other was Swepson, Mendenhall, and Company, a firm consisting of two of Worth's business friends from North Carolina, George W. Swepson and Cyrus P. Mendenhall.

The sale of one lot of cotton in New York required Worth's special attention. In February, 1866, after he had resigned as provisional treasurer, Cyrus Mendenhall wrote him a letter showing what Worth called a "villainous transaction."[45] According to Mendenhall, Dr. William B. Sloan, who had succeeded Worth as provisional treasurer, had sold over fifteen thousand pounds of the state's cotton to A. J. Jones, a state senator, for fourteen cents a pound below the price at which cotton was selling in the open market.[46] When Worth heard Mendenhall's version of what had occurred, he immediately wrote to Jones and Sloan and asked them whether they had made the alleged trade.

In response to Worth's inquiries, Jones and Sloan explained their questionable transaction. Some twenty or twenty-five bales of cotton belonging to the state had been shipped from Macon, Georgia, several weeks before, but it had not arrived in New York when Sloan got there to straighten up the cotton accounts. Sloan then determined to sell the missing cotton to Jones for thirty-three cents a pound if Jones would locate the cotton and pay the expenses of getting it to New York. Jones accepted the cotton at thirty-three cents and sold it the same day for forty-seven cents a pound; no money changed hands, but Jones was to make a profit of more than twenty-two hundred dollars. Sloan told Worth that he rescinded the transaction when he heard later that the missing cotton was in Alexandria, Virginia.[47]

Worth telegraphed Swepson, Mendenhall, and Company on March 5, 1866, that the state would not recognize the transaction between Sloan and Jones, and directed that the company turn over all money received for cotton directly to the state treasurer. On the following day Jones turned over to the treasurer the money he had received for the cotton. Although Sloan maintained that his trade with Jones had been rescinded, it was not until Worth started applying pressure that the state received the money it would have gotten earlier if the cotton had been sold on the open market.

In spite of all the difficulties with the United States Army, treasury agents, thieves, and individuals who were inclined to defraud the state, Worth's collection and sale of the state's scattered property resulted in profits large enough to pay the operating expenses of the government for 1865.[48] The value of his efforts may best be seen by considering that the state could hardly have met its obligations at all if the cotton and rosin had not been sold.

As the provisional treasurer, Worth also had to investigate the condition of the banks, the railroads, and the Literary Fund and submit his findings to the convention which met in the fall of 1865; the convention was to use these reports when it began to make legislation on the subjects Worth investigated. He addressed letters to the presidents of the banks and railroads, asking for the desired information and requesting that they answer by August 15, in order that reports could be compiled before the convention met. Worth himself had to make the report on the status of the Literary Fund.

The public school system was still a matter of great concern to Worth, who had labored for it in one way or another through most of his life. Now he found that the Literary Fund had assets of two and a half million dollars, but these assets were mostly in stocks and bonds of banks, railroads, and the state; they would not yield enough income to operate a school system until the state recovered from the war. "Is our system of Common Schools to be abandoned?" Worth asked. Not willing that the schools should be abandoned, he proposed that the state sell part of the swamp lands donated to the Literary Fund in 1825 by the act creating the Fund. He did not presume to recommend in detail how the lands might best be utilized, but suggested that Calvin H. Wiley, the Superintendent of Common Schools, could make a fruitful recommendation.

Worth had finished compiling the reports he had received, had written his report on the Common Schools, and had submitted them to the governor by the end of September, 1865. He continued to collect and sell state property for several more weeks, but on October 18, two days after he decided to become a candidate for governor, he offered his resignation as provisional treasurer.

· XIV ·

Fixed Star and Blazing Comet

———————

WHEN WILLIAM HOLDEN took office as provisional governor of North Carolina in June, 1865, he issued a proclamation in which he outlined a plan by which a regular civil government was to be provided for the state. A convention was to be called. It was expected to acknowledge the fact that the South had been defeated in war by repealing the ordinance of secession, abolishing the institution of slavery, and repudiating the state's war debt. The convention would arrange for the election of a governor, a legislature, and members of Congress. When the state officers were elected and had taken office and when the state's representatives were admitted to Congress, North Carolina would once again be a member of the Union. This policy had been formulated by President Lincoln and continued by Andrew Johnson.[1]

Soon after Holden outlined the president's policy for the restoration of civil government and a return to normal relations with the Union, there was talk of who should be the next governor. Worth's name was mentioned as a possible candidate as early as the middle of July, but to his surprise and dismay, he was being associated with a political faction he had always opposed, the former secessionists. He firmly denied that, even if he should allow his friends to nominate him for governor, he would depend upon support from the secessionists:

> The statement that I have written to Alfred Brown or to any body else, that I would probably be [a] candidate for Govr. and that I expected to be supported by the Secession war-party is false. There is no public man in N.C. whose whole public record is so completely at variance with the principles of that party. No one who so utterly opposed them in the zenith of their power. That I should feel any affiliation for them when time has demonstrated the correctness of my

views and the folly of theirs, would prove me deficient in common honesty or common sense.[2]

When Worth made this statement he was not interested in becoming the governor of North Carolina—as anyone's candidate. Apparently he did not seriously consider the possibility that he might be asked to run. He wrote no letters to political associates sounding out possibilities and asking for support, nor did he make any speeches in which he sounded like a prospective candidate. The idea that he might be called upon to run may have occurred to him, but he did nothing to encourage a movement for his nomination.

By the time the convention met in October, it had become apparent that Holden wanted to be elected governor; he had already tried to win that office twice and had been spurned both times, once by the leaders of the Democratic party in 1858, and by the people of the state in 1864. Holden's newspaper, the *Standard*, had been grooming him for the executive harness ever since he became the provisional governor. On October 2, 1865, the day the convention assembled in Raleigh, the *Standard* summed up its admiration for Holden: he had been non-partisan in appointing provisional officers to manage the state government and the courts; he was not a "leveller," a charge to which Holden was always subject because of his humble origins; as provisional governor he had been neither vindictive against old political opponents nor tyrannical in exercising his authority. Finally, the *Standard* called attention to the indisputable fact that Holden had labored diligently for the people of North Carolina as their interim governor. Twelve days after the convention met, fifty-three of the hundred and twenty delegates asked Holden to run for governor and he accepted their nomination. Some of the fifty-three felt obligated to Holden because he had secured pardons for them; others believed that Worth would not become a candidate; and several apparently supported Holden because they felt that Andrew Johnson preferred him to Worth.

The name of William Holden was anathema to many politicians in the state, and particularly to conservative Whigs and Unionists who had opposed him through twenty years of party warfare. It was primarily a group of Whig Unionists who searched for a suitable man to oppose Holden and finally decided upon Jonathan Worth; among those who began urging Worth to run against Holden, the most prominent names were Josiah Turner, Jr., Patrick H. Winston, Darius H

Starbuck, and, most of all, William A. Graham. The decision to run Worth against Holden was influenced by the fact that North Carolina was still outside the Union. What the state needed in its next governor was a consistent Unionist whose record could withstand a probing scrutiny by the people of the North and politicians in Congress. Jonathan Worth's record as a Unionist certainly was better than that of Holden, and nobody was more aware of this than William A. Graham, who exerted a strong influence among the conservative men of the state. In a letter to Dr. James G. Ramsey, one of Worth's closest political associates, Graham expressed his hope that all "our friends" would support Worth, and explained that he favored Worth over Holden because Worth had been the more consistent Unionist. He recalled that Worth had been an avowed nationalist in 1830 and 1831, when Holden was a mere boy and Worth was in the legislature denouncing the nullification doctrines of South Carolina. Holden had been a rabid secessionist in the 1850's while Worth "stood up for Fillmore and the Compromise of 1850." During the secession crisis Holden had become a Unionist and he had bitterly opposed the Confederacy, but these actions only gave to his vacillating course a strong tinge of inconsistency.[3] Holden's past course in politics provided Graham and other conservatives with a sufficient reason for bringing out a candidate against him. At a time when everything seemed uncertain, they sought a man whose principles could be relied upon—a "fixed star," as Graham called Worth—to oppose one whose position had changed as frequently as that of a "blazing comet."

When Graham, Patrick Winston, and other opponents of Holden first started searching for a suitable man to oppose Holden they approached Alfred Dockery, a Whig and Unionist who twenty years earlier had beaten Worth in a race for a seat in Congress. Dockery declined to run, expressed his intention to support Worth, and said that "he had always wanted to requite [Worth] for unjustly opposing [him] for Congress" in 1845.[4] After Dockery refused to become a candidate against Holden, those opposed to Holden began urging Worth to announce his entry into the race.

For several days Worth's mind was in a state of "most painful uncertitude" as to whether he would announce himself a candidate. Some of his political associates, notably John Pool, a devoted Unionist and former Whig candidate for governor, strongly urged him not to oppose Holden. They tried to convince Worth that a bitter political

campaign would damage the state's chances of a quick restoration to
the Union, and that Holden was the favorite of President Johnson,
but on October 17, Worth wrote Pool that he had decided to become
a candidate. He explained, even before he told anyone else he had
decided to run, that he considered the president "incapable of desiring
that his preferences should control the vote of the state."[5] Worth
firmly believed, and with justification, that his record of loyalty to the
Union was better than Holden's, and since he thought that "the real
interests of the State require that the name of a consistent opponent
of disunion ought to be run," he reluctantly yielded to the plea that
he become a candidate. Still another factor in Worth's decision was
Holden's refusal to recommend presidential pardons for Josiah Turner,
Jr., William A. Graham, and John A. Gilmer, all of whom had been
devout Unionists in 1861. Worth confided to Pool that "I am deeply
sensible to the expediency of harmony, but this harmony can be at-
tained only in one way, the withdrawal of Govr. Holden." He offered
to withdraw if Holden would also withdraw and allow Judge Edwin
G. Reade, the president of the convention, to run unopposed.[6]

Worth prepared a circular in which he announced his candidacy
and told of his reluctance to enter a race against Holden, a reluctance
based on a desire to avoid vituperation; "I love quiet," Worth said
simply. He said that he would not even consider running for governor
if he thought his candidacy would hinder the state's chances for a
quick re-entry into the Union. In a brief comment on his record as a
Unionist, Worth told the people that "I could not get the assent of my
mind or heart to take part in the beginning of what I was sure would
be one of the most terrible convulsions in history." The circular set
forth no program, but indicated strong approval of Andrew Johnson
and his plan of reconstruction. It denied that the president was opposed to Worth's candidacy; any assertion that he would compel the
people of North Carolina to consider his will would be unjust to
Johnson. Worth believed that the president was a just man, and
he referred to Johnson's magnanimity in allowing Mississippi to
organize its militia after the military commander of the state had
forbidden the militia to reorganize. Finally, the circular closed with
a promise, in words that read like a similar utterance by Abraham
Lincoln: "My past life and conduct are the best guaranty I can offer
as to what may be expected from me. . . . I should endeavor to soften
the animosities which have grown out of the horrible war now happily

ended. . . . I should endeavor to encourage a spirit of mutual forgiveness—a return to the habits of law and order and steadfast attachment to the Union, which made us so great and so prosperous a
people whilst we adhered to the counsels of Washington."[7] If the
North would concur in President Johnson's policy of reconstruction,
Worth hoped, a feeling of brotherhood would soon return.

After Worth wrote the circular announcing his candidacy, he
offered his resignation as provisional treasurer to Holden on October
18. The resignation was to take effect only if Holden appointed another treasurer, and Worth promised to perform his duties as long
as the governor desired him to continue. In the letter of resignation
he expressed to Holden a "desire that the personal rivalry between
us for a highly honorable position, may be generous, furnishing no
just occasion for marring the friendly, personal and official relations
which have hitherto existed between us."[8] The treasurer did not plan
to campaign actively, feeling that he could spend his time better by
remaining in office and selling the state property which he had been
collecting. Holden allowed Worth to act as treasurer throughout the
gubernatorial campaign, but six days after the election, on November 15, he directed him to step aside and turn the office over to Dr.
William Sloan. Piqued with Holden for removing him from a position he had hoped to keep until he was inaugurated, Worth wrote
Benjamin S. Hedrick: "Yesterday Holden exhibited his silly malice by
removing me from the office of Pub. Treas[r]—and appointing Dr. Sloan,
who had run for Congress in the Mecklenburgh district—and had got
almost no votes."[9]

The Raleigh *Standard* set the tone for the campaign and tried to
define the issues. It greeted the announcement of Worth's candidacy
with an insinuation that the treasurer was a traitor: "Well may Governor Holden exclaim, when thus stabbed by Mr. Worth—*et tu Brute!*"
"The Issue" was defined as "W. W. Holden and GO BACK to the
Union, or Jonathan Worth and STAY OUT of the Union." The
implication Holden and his supporters tried to create was that Worth
was not acceptable to the president or the people of the North, and
that if he were elected North Carolina would not be taken again into
the national councils: "The President and Northern people, on whose
grace and favor we are now dependent, would be offended if such a
person as Mr. Worth should be elected, who was in favor of the con
tinuance of the rebel State government, and who has lent himself as

an instrument to a faction composed of sore-headed Conservatives and original Secessionists. Mr. Worth and his friends are responsible for all the division and strife at present in Raleigh."[10]

Worth naturally was offended by the *Standard*'s half-truths, but he made no speeches in his own defense during the campaign. He did, however, write an open letter to the editor of the Raleigh *Sentinel* in which he vigorously denied that he was a candidate of the war party. He paid particular attention to the charge that he had "attempted to have the rebel State government continued" at the end of the war, by giving a detailed account of his role in the negotiations between Governor Vance and General Sherman. His motive had been to assure that the state would have some kind of government to maintain law and order.[11]

While the *Standard* damned Worth and his supporters, it filled its columns with praise of Holden. When it attempted to give the provisional governor credit for collecting and selling "nearly THREE HUNDRED THOUSAND DOLLARS" worth of state property, the editor of a paper which favored Worth recalled the dire financial straits of the state during the past summer and remarked: "In this extremity, his Excellency's beseeching eyes were turned towards that glorious old financier Jonathan Worth. Money must be had, and who but the aforesaid Jonathan knew where it was, or how to get it? So in process of time, he was invited to take his Excellency's empty money bag, and see if he could replenish it. This was his special duty and trust. How nobly and satisfactorily that trust has been executed, all the world knows."[12]

Worth's financial reputation was also dragged into a discussion of whether the state convention should repudiate the state's war debt. Holden's paper implied that Worth would be ruined if the debt were repudiated because Worth had sold some pre-war bonds from the Sinking Fund and replaced them with "war debt bonds."[13] This was one part of an effort to prove that "Mr. Worth and Friends are Plotting to have the People taxed to pay the War Debt."[14] In reply to this charge Worth felt compelled to review his stand on the question of repudiation, which was one of the few genuine issues of the campaign.

Before the state convention met, Worth was opposed to repudiation of the war debt, which was close to nineteen million dollars. "If you repudiate the whole war debt," he told one of his friends, "you break every Bank in the State, you destroy the University and common school, which own about ¼ of the stock in these Banks,—you beggar nearly a thousand widows and orphans whose all is invested in the Banks and State bonds . . . and you blot out of our constellation its brightest star—*Honesty*."[15] Personally, Worth would not lose anything if the war debt were repudiated, for he owned no stock in the banks which had loaned money to the state, and he did not have any state bonds. It rubbed his conservative grain the wrong way to see any individual or institution refuse to pay its honest debts, but he was willing that the debt should be scaled to its specie value.

In September, Worth had submitted to Holden a recommendation in his report as provisional treasurer that the convention should take no action on the war debt when it met in October. Holden and the *Standard* had apparently approved Worth's recommendation that the debt should be left for consideration at a later time, for Holden submitted the recommendation to the convention, and the *Standard* interpreted a plea it had made for "non-recognition" of the debt to mean that "the Convention should leave the war debt exactly as they found it. . . ."[16] At the time the convention met there seemed to be general agreement that consideration of the debt question should be postponed, at least until Worth completed his survey of the state's financial condition. From Washington, Holden's agent, Dr. R. J. Powell, reported that every member of the Cabinet, except Secretary of War Stanton, believed the convention should disregard the war debt.[17]

The convention discussed the debt question briefly and had tabled an ordinance of repudiation when Holden, for some unaccountable reason, asked President Johnson for an opinion as to what should be done about the war debt. Johnson replied in a telegram that "every dollar of the debt created to aid the rebellion against the United States should be repudiated finally and forever."[18] The president felt that the people of North Carolina should not be forced to pay for a war they did not want in the first place. Those who supported the Confederacy by loaning money to the state, Johnson said sarcastically, should call upon the Confederacy to pay them back—"They must meet their fate." Influenced by the telegram from the president, the members of the convention repudiated the war debt on the last day of the session.

When the *Standard* raised the charge that Worth still favored paying the war debt, Worth vigorously denied that there was a "cunning plot" among his supporters to repeal the ordinance of repudiation. He explained that the ordinance was passed because the members of the convention believed that North Carolina could not get back into the Union unless they bent their wills to the demand from Washington. Repeal of the ordinance would be a fraud against the United States and a disgrace to North Carolina, in Worth's view. "The assertion that I am a party to any such plot is a baseless untruth," Worth said; "the war debt of the state I now regard as a dead issue. . . . Let it sleep."[19]

Repudiation was not quite dead, but the real question upon which the voters of North Carolina would have to decide on November 9 was whether William Holden or Jonathan Worth would be the better governor for the state. Worth felt confident that he had a chance to win, but there was some feeling that many people would vote for Holden because they felt it was necessary to please the president and the people of the North. Unfortunately for Worth's chances, Holden had attracted attention as an opponent of the Confederacy and a leader of the peace movement, while Worth had no national reputation. Governor Vance summed up the feeling of some voters that it would be expedient to vote for Holden whether the state wanted him for governor or not: "A large majority of the voters in this region would go for Worth but for the general spirit of intimidation which pervades the whole community. They have no confidence in Holden, abuse him freely, but shake their heads and seem to think something terrible would happen if he were defeated."[20] Worth himself believed that this "spirit of intimidation" was the only obstacle to his election.

The election took place on November 9, 1865, only three weeks after Worth and Holden announced their candidacies. The returns came into Raleigh slowly. On the tenth, the *Standard* hoped for a large majority for Holden, but reported that Worth had won almost all the counties for which returns were available; the editors called these counties "Mr. Worth's strongest." As more counties reported, Holden's paper began to admit that "there is a good chance for Mr. Worth," but found great satisfaction in the fact that Worth's old home county, Randolph, had given Holden a majority. It was apparent by the fifteenth that Worth had won the election by a majority of about six thousand votes; in the final returns he captured fifty-four of the eighty-nine counties. When it became obvious that Worth had won, the *Standard* remarked that "our people have not advanced themselves at all in the eyes of Congress or the administration."[21] Afterwards the paper kept quiet about the election for a time. Then in December, it attempted to explain that Holden had lost because he had been too lenient towards "rebels" in his administration of the provisional government, and because he transmitted to the convention President Johnson's telegram demanding the repudiation of the war debt.[22] Holden later interpreted the results of the election in the same way the *Standard* explained them and added: "The returns of the election in the various counties," he said, "will show that I was supported mainly by the old Union men, and Worth for the most part by the Secessionists of the Democratic party."[23]

The allegation that Worth was the candidate of the former secessionists and that it was a disloyal element that elevated him into the gubernatorial chair was a serious charge, and it had some basis in the facts. Some of the strongest Union counties, among them Bertie, Wilkes, and Worth's own Randolph, cast their votes for Holden, and several prominent individual Unionists pitched their tents in Holden's camp. Yet, Worth could boast that "not one of the secession counties west of the mountains voted for me," and that "the most constant Union men of the State supported me generally."[24] Worth never quite understood why Randolph County failed to support him in 1865. With a little longer perspective behind him he could have seen that Holden had become the political darling of the strongly Unionist Randolph when he led the peace movement in 1863 and 1864. The citizens of Randolph, and of the other Union counties which preferred Holden, could justify their abandonment of Worth by remembering that Holden had been the peace candidate for governor in 1864, while Worth was the treasurer in an administration that insisted on carrying on the war.

Dr. James G. Ramsey, one of Worth's old Whig friends and an astute political observer, pointed out that many of the former secessionists had voted for Worth. He told Worth that "many of the secessionists voted for your opponent through policy; and [others] for you, to gratify their vindictive feelings towards him."[25] Ramsey noted that a number of conservative men who would normally have voted for Worth cast their ballots for Holden because of the uncertain relations with the national government. Still others refused to vote for Worth because they accepted the *Standard's* assertion that he headed a party of former secessionists. George W. Brooks, a Unionist Whig, best expressed the view of this group: "I would have sustained Gov. Worth at the last election if he could have been the candidate of the *Union men of the state* and could have been elected by them. But it was clear to my mind that if elected, he would have to be by the secessionists—and so it turned out."[26] Brooks also remarked that, because Worth had received the support of the secessionists, he would not be able to refuse them a share of the offices in the new state government.

Worth himself admitted that the secessionists and ardent supporters of the war had given him their votes, but he had a ready explanation for the fact that the strongest Union man in the state should be supported by the war party. He believed that *because* he had consistently supported the Unionist position the secessionists could at least admire him for his consistency, even though he had disagreed with them; but they could not forgive Holden for deserting their ranks in 1860 and 1861, when their doctrine was being subjected to its sternest test.[27] There cannot be any doubt that Holden's past record was one of the most important factors in the outcome of the election in November, 1865. One common man stated this in the simplest terms possible: "We are truly tired of thees men that has turned their cotes about so mutch they have worned booth sides out and cant mend or patch them to satisfactory."[28] That Holden received as much favor as he did from the voters is surprising, in view of the fact that his political coat *was* worn on both sides. The editor of the Fayetteville *Observer* felt assured "that but for the fear of many that it was *necessary* to elect Holden, he would not have rec[d] 10,000 votes."[29]

The campaign charge of the Holdenites that the election of Worth would damage North Carolina's chances of a quick restoration to the Union proved to be more than bombast. Holden's personal and unofficial agent in Washington, Dr. R. J. Powell, reported to the president shortly after the election that "the rebelious element aided by the aristocracy [were] much stronger and more bitter than I had supposed."[30] Powell encouraged Johnson to make his views about the election known and worded a telegram to be sent to Holden declaring that "the results of the recent election in North Carolina have greatly damaged the prospects of the state in the restoration of its Governmental relations"; the telegram also commended Holden for his work as provisional governor.[31] The president sent the telegram exactly as Powell had written it, and Holden used it to prove that he was the president's favorite.

Holden wrote to the president in much the same vein as Powell, claiming that Worth was elected by "original secessionists" and men who had backed Zeb Vance for governor in 1864. Holden spoke favorably of Worth himself, but contended that he had run for governor only because William A. Graham and Vance forced him into the race.[32] Like some other comments on Worth's election, Holden's report to the president simply was not true. Nobody "forced" Worth to become a candidate for governor against Holden, and those who did influence him to run were Whig Unionists, not original secessionists.

Other influential men in Washington besides the president received a wrong impression from Worth's election. A representative from central New York asked Dr. R. J. Powell why North Carolina had not elected a loyal governor, to which Powell retorted that Jonathan Worth was as "loyal" as Governor Fenton, of New York. Senator Wilson, of Massachusetts, told Powell he had heard that only two "loyal" men had been elected to the North Carolina legislature, and Secretary of State Seward made it perfectly plain that he was displeased with the election of Worth and with the legislature's selection of William A. Graham as a United States senator; "some things ought to have been different," Seward said.[33]

It was clear to Worth that the politicians in whose hands the fate of North Carolina rested were ignorant of his public record as a staunch advocate of Unionist principles, and he was deeply disturbed. He agreed with Benjamin S. Hedrick, who worked at the United States Patent Office and had been reporting to him the unfavorable reaction to the election in Washington, that the Northern mind should be "disabused" of the idea that his election was a sign of the disloyalty of North Carolina. Aware of the value of favorable publicity, Worth asked Hedrick to prepare an article for the northern newspapers explaining the outcome of the election; as a basis for the proposed article he forwarded to Hedrick the circular in which he announced his candidacy for governor and made public his views on the president's plan of reconstruction.[34] Hedrick got letters published in the New York *Evening Post* and the Springfield *Republican,* giving "the true state of affairs" in North Carolina.[35] He also provided information to correspondents of northern papers. One of these reporters wrote that "it is believed that the fact is not generally known at the North that Mr. Worth has at all times been a Union man, but this is strictly true."[36]

One result of the rancorous campaign, the election, and Worth's removal as provisional treasurer, was the final alienation of Worth and Holden. In the party battles of the ante-bellum period they had been on opposite sides, but in the politics of wartime they had frequently stood on common ground. The two men had worked together closely in the provisional government, but after the election of Worth as governor, they came to the parting of the ways. Holden himself had not joined in the attack on Worth during the gubernatorial campaign, but Worth held him responsible for the vile remarks in his newspaper. In 1864, when Holden was leading the peace movement, Worth had spoken favorably of him, but a month after the election of 1865, he referred to his late opponent privately as "this vile incubus," President Johnson's "satrap," "a bad man, whose standard of patriotism is devotion to himself. . . . He stinks in the nostrils of our people."[37] Worth was astonished "that the President does not understand and despise his malicious cunning and ignoble sycophancy."[38]

After the election there was some uncertainty as to how much longer the president would allow Holden to act as provisional governor, but on December 15, and again on December 22, Worth took the oaths of office as governor before Judge Daniel G. Fowle and the General Assembly; three oaths pledged Worth to true allegiance to North Carolina, support of the Constitution of the United States, and to the execution of his duties "without favor or affection."[39]

Secretary of State Seward notified Worth on December 23 that Holden had been relieved as provisional governor and directed to turn over the papers and property pertaining to that office. The directive to Holden stated that in the president's opinion "the time has arrived when . . . the care and conduct of the proper affairs of the State of North Carolina may be remitted to the constitutional authorities chosen by the people thereof. . . ."[40] This directive must have come as a shock to Holden, who had entertained hopes of prolonging his term in office, but he soon turned over the office to Worth, who assumed his new duties on December 28, 1865.

· XV ·

A Troubled Administration

WHEN JONATHAN WORTH became governor of North Carolina in December, 1865, the first major task that faced him was the restoration of the machinery of civil government. Even before he entered office Benjamin Hedrick had written from Washington that "it is absolutely necessary that a regular civil government be restored at the earliest possible moment."[1] There could be no hope of returning to the Union, or getting admission to the halls of Congress, until the state government began operating smoothly and the courts could maintain law and order.

During the previous summer General Schofield had arranged for the appointment of justices of the peace in each county and had organized county police forces. Holden, as provisional governor, continued the work of Schofield by appointing more justices, and municipal officers. The justices formed county courts, which then appointed the other county officers, including a sheriff and the necessary clerks.[2] These officers were intended to serve on a provisional basis only, and the convention declared in the fall that their terms should expire as soon as the provisional government ended. When Worth took office, the machinery of local government ceased to operate.

Complaints began to pour in on Worth almost immediately. A horse thief in Winston was about to be turned loose because there was no civil authority to investigate his case. An anonymous correspondent told Worth that "if [the horse thief were] handed over to the Military it would be equivalent to turning him upon the community to engage again in his villainy."[3] There was a highway robbery in Gaston County, but since the local magistrate had not been sworn in there was no one to apprehend the criminal. The superior court judge could not issue a bench warrant because he had not been sworn in either.[4] Worth replied to these complaints, and to others like them, by instructing the dissatisfied parties as to what justices still held power. If there were no justices in an area, new ones could be sworn in before any judge of the superior court elected by the legislature in November, 1865. Worth notified the judges immediately after his inauguration that they were to be sworn in as soon as they could report to Raleigh. Two had been sworn in by January 6, 1866, and the others were on their way to Raleigh. To those local officials who held criminals in their jails Worth said, "You should hold your rogue irregularly if you can't do it regularly."[5]

One incident in particular pointed to the need for a reopening of the civil courts. The convention had levied a tax to pay the expenses of operating the state government, but shortly after the sheriffs started collecting the tax, a rumor appeared in the newspapers that President Johnson had suspended collection. The military commandant at Wilmington forbade the sheriff of New Hanover County to collect any money from certain merchants "until the proper tribunal decides on the legality of the tax." Worth telegraphed the president to see if he had authorized the military authorities to interfere with the tax collection, and Johnson replied that "no orders in reference to the Sheriffs in North Carolina have been issued by me."[6] Seeing no reason why the military officials should intervene, Worth asked General Thomas Ruger, who was now in command of the state, to set aside the injunction of the commandant at Wilmington; he argued that the proper recourse to those who considered the collection of the tax illegal was an appeal to the civil courts.[7]

Ruger explained to Worth that he had authorized the commandant at Wilmington to stop the collection of the tax from the merchants there on the theory that they had been trading under a license from the War Department and were paying taxes to the United States government. The general insisted that it would not be fair to collect civil taxes when there was no civil court open to which the merchants could appeal for an injunction against the collection of the tax. Ruger promised that the order would be rescinded as soon as Worth informed him that the civil courts were open.[8]

Worth outlined a plan for the transition from provisional to regular government in a message to the people published two days after he took office. He congratulated the state upon the restoration of the government to its elected officials and asked forbearance until the machinery of government could be put into operation. He declared that local officials of the provisional government no longer had power to act, but clerks and sheriffs elected in November could begin to exercise their normal powers, and acts of provisional justices before they were replaced would be validated by the next legislature. Worth promised that the General Assembly would meet soon and correct the existing irregularities, and asked the people to maintain law and order and not to betray the confidence placed in them by the president.[9] After addressing his message to the people of the state, Worth also expressed to President Johnson his joy over the restoration of civil government. He asked the president to have confidence in him and promised to co-operate fully in carrying out Johnson's plans for the restoration of the Union "on terms compatible with the honor and prosperity of all its parts."[10]

Because of the pressing need for local magistrates and municipal officials, Worth convened the Council of State on January 3, 1866, and on the advice of the Council he summoned the legislature to meet on January 18. When the legislators assembled, Worth delivered a message in which he discussed at length the urgent need for a system of administering justice. He urged the assembly to appoint justices of the peace, but cautioned against appointing men whose qualifications were not known—a serious flaw in the ante-bellum judicial system. Another proposal was that municipal elections held since the end of the provisional government and acts of provisional officers during the period of transition should be validated. The convention had declared that state laws passed during the war period were still in force if they were not inconsistent with the state and national constitutions; Worth now asked that wartime laws be reviewed, and modified if necessary.

Worth also brought up the subject of justice for the recently freed Negroes. He told the members of the legislature that General Ruger had informed him there would be no military interference with the state courts if Negroes were allowed to testify and if they received the same punishment for a crime as a white man would receive. The Freedmen's Bureau was even more jealous of the rights of the Negroes than the military authorities, and its agents stood ready to try cases involving freedmen if they could not secure justice in the civil courts. The Bureau had been established before the end of the war as a temporary agency to help Negroes in areas controlled by the Union army and to manage abandoned or confiscated lands in the South. In 1866, Congress passed a bill over President Johnson's veto extending the life of the Bureau and expanding its functions. These included the distribution of rations; the establishment of schools for Negroes, in co-operation with charitable agencies; supervision of working agree- ments between whites and former slaves; and the establishment of jurisdiction in lawsuits involving Negroes.[11] Worth branded the Bureau as "at once anomalous and inconsistent with the ancient con- stitutional authority of the several states." It had jurisdiction over certain cases involving freedmen, and Worth pointed out that this split jurisdiction would put the civil judges in the awkward position of trying to serve two masters. He insisted that there was no disposition in North Carolina to mistreat or re-enslave the Negroes, and he ex- pressed the view that the freedmen should be allowed civil and religious freedom—but not social equality or the franchise.

The message to the legislature ended with a lament that North Carolina had not been admitted to the Union; its representatives to Congress had not been allowed to take their seats when they went to Washington in December, 1865. "It would seem," said Worth, that "we have reached that point of progress when distrust should yield to confidence; aversion to a spirit of harmony, if not cordiality." Worth was still hopeful for an early restoration to the Union, but he was aware that "the passions aroused in revolutions do not at once sub- side." Yet he could not help feeling that it was the politicians of the North, rather than the people of the North, who were fostering a spirit of jealousy, hatred, and distrust and keeping the South out of the Union.[12]

The legislature soon passed laws embodying Worth's recommenda- tions for the revival of the governmental machinery throughout the state. Provisional officers were given authority to swear in the regularly elected persons who were to succeed them, and power to continue in office until their successors were elected and qualified.[13] When the local officials were elected and qualified, the organization of the new government was complete: the state had a governor and other state officers, who had been elected in the fall of 1865; the state courts be- gan functioning when the judges were sworn in a few days after Worth took office, and the federal courts had been open since the summer of 1865. Ostensibly, North Carolina was ready to begin managing its own affairs.

After the state government was restored, Worth assumed the role of guardian of the state's institutions, and particularly of the courts, against the interference of the military authorities and agents of the Freedmen's Bureau. As the chief executive officer of the state he was ultimately responsible for seeing that the laws were fairly administered to both white and black, and he was ever conscious that the eyes of Congress and the North were upon him. Everything had to be done with the thought in mind that a step in the wrong direction might damage the state's chances of restoration to the Union by antagonizing the Radicals in Congress or the people of the North.

The most pressing problem facing North Carolina in early 1866, one which affected the state's relations with the national government more than any other, was the status of the former slaves. This was a question on which Worth had very definite views. He never expressed his feelings publicly, but he had to defend them to several of his Quaker friends who differed with him. The following selection from a letter to his Quaker brother-in-law, William Clark, who lived in Indiana, is representative of Worth's ideas about the Negro:

It is annoying to me that the Quakers generally—and especially you whom I know to be a sensible good man and acquainted with the negro, should believe under the circumstances that the African race is capable of attaining to a respectable degree of civilization. . . . If you really think they could be made good citizens, why do you not invite them to immigrate from the South and dwell among you? . . . I am no lover of slavery. I feel toward the negro not only no hatred but nothing but kindness and pity; but I know from observation of history that the African left to its own self-control, is so indolent and improvident, that he will not—indeed I think he cannot be made a good citizen. . . . I cannot give the Northern Radicals credit . . . for sincerity when they insist that the negroes can be made good citizens. . . . They are rapidly sinking into their natural position and by an irresistible law of nature, will soon perish out in contact with a superior race. . . .[14]

Worth's views probably differed little from those of the average Southerner in 1866. His whole experience seemed to prove that the Negro was inferior to his former masters, and it was obvious to him that the blacks were not yet ready to have full political privileges conferred upon them. His honest views and his conservative philosophy made it impossible for him to accept with a clear conscience or a sense of honor the policies of those who were trying to elevate the status of the Negro to a point near that of the whites.

Yet, Worth was a man who believed in fair play, and his sense of justice compelled him to defend, and even to champion, the rights of the Negroes. His main contribution to their welfare was to secure the introduction of Negro testimony into the courts of the state in cases to which Negroes were a party. He was quite aware of the expediency of giving black men the right to be heard in courts, for he had been reminded by his friends and relatives in the North that the Negroes must be given certain rights. William Clark encouraged the enactment of a liberal code of laws for the Negroes, but admitted that "I guess we want to compel you to do right by them while we are not willing ourselves to do so."[15] C. B. Dibble, a Northern merchant with whom Worth's brother Barzillai was going into business, informed Worth that there was no general disposition in the North to deal harshly or unjustly with the South, but that there was strong sentiment in favor of the freedmen.[16] With regard to Negro testimony, Dibble made the sensible comment that "the theory is to get all the evidence bearing on the case and then give such weight as circumstances seem to warrant and this might safely be done with the freedmen." Closer home, Worth's chief confidante and adviser, William A. Graham, favored Negro testimony "on the higher ground of right," and argued that it was necessary for the freedmen to protect themselves, now that they had no masters or overseers.[17] Worth himself thought "that the testimony of negroes ought to be heard in a case where a negro is a party," but he believed it would be necessary to give special instructions to jurors when the testimony of Negroes was introduced. He pointed out to Graham that the state would continue to be occupied by the military and the Freedmen's Bureau as long as the state law discriminated against the freedmen.[18]

The legislature Worth called into special session in January, 1866, enacted a "black code" before it adjourned. Based on a report of three distinguished lawyers appointed by Provisional Governor Holden late in 1865, North Carolina's code was probably the most liberal set of laws passed in the postwar South to deal with the far-reaching social problems created by emancipation.[19] The only section of the code to which Worth paid particular attention while the legislature was in session was the one dealing with Negro testimony. Many members of the Assembly insisted on adding to the section of the code permitting Negro testimony a proviso that the section should not go into effect "until jurisdiction in matters relating to freedmen shall be fully com-

mitted to the courts of this state"; this was obviously a protest against
the trial of Negroes by agents of the Freedmen's Bureau. Worth's best
informant in Washington reported that "the legislature of North
Carolina is doing the state vast injury in enacting a measure so just as
the allowing of every citizen to testify when called upon with pro-
visos."[20] Worth, fearing that the proviso might antagonize the wrong
persons in Washington—the Radicals—asked President Johnson for
his opinion of the wisdom of refusing to allow freedmen to testify
before the Freedmen's Bureau surrendered its jurisdiction over them.
Johnson replied candidly: "Policy at this time would suggest the passage of the bill without the proviso."[21]

After Worth secured the president's advice, he did everything he
could to have the proviso stricken from the bill, but his influence
failed. The legislators insisted on the proviso because they had
pledged to their constituents that they would vote against a law
permitting Negroes to testify. Most of them saw that it would be both
just and politically expedient to omit the proviso, but they considered
it "a necessary shield between them and their constituents."[22] Worth
then asked former governors Swain and Graham, who were in Washington, to have the effects of the proviso nullified and Negro testimony admitted to the state courts by asking President Johnson to order
that jurisdiction over freedmen be returned to the civil courts.[23] This
approach proved no more effective than the requests to the legislators.

The legislature's refusal to admit Negro testimony, even in cases
to which Negroes were a party, had repercussions which justified
Worth's fear that the Freedmen's Bureau would continue to interfere
with the courts. An agent of the Bureau, Captain R. A. Seely, notified
the sheriff of Craven County that the county court would not be
allowed to exercise jurisdiction over Sarah Richardson, a Negro who
had been caught selling liquor without a license. The reason Captain
Seely gave for his order to the sheriff was that Negro testimony was not
allowed in court.[24] The incident confirmed Worth's notion that it
would be expedient to admit Negro testimony. When the state convention met in May, 1866, for its second, and last, session,[25] he announced that General Ruger was reluctant to return jurisdiction over
the freedmen to the state courts before the testimony of Negroes was
admitted.[26] Acting on Worth's recommendation, the convention
struck out of the state law the proviso enacted by the legislature.

Negroes were now eligible to testify in cases involving their rights or the rights of other Negroes.

Even after the convention acted, Worth continued to hear complaints from the Freedmen's Bureau. An agent reported in December, 1866, that Negroes had been refused the right to testify in Cumberland County, in violation of the Civil Rights Act passed by Congress earlier in the year.[27] When the incident was reported to Colonel James V. Bomford, the chief officer of the Bureau in North Carolina, he called Worth's attention to the case, asked that he take whatever action was necessary to prevent a recurrence, and that Worth secure an explanation from the court of Cumberland County. Worth sent out an investigator, who reported that the county court had indeed refused to allow Negro witnesses to testify. The reasoning of the court was that, since the rights of no Negro were involved in the case, the state law forbade the admission of testimony by Negroes. Ironically, the testimony they were prepared to give would have been sufficient to secure an acquittal for the white defendants, who were working with the Negroes in the fields when the crime was committed; but the defendants were convicted.[28]

While the Freedmen's Bureau was still trying Negroes and interfering with the lower courts in cases involving freedmen, a more serious situation arose when white citizens in the state began sending petitions to President Johnson in which they maintained that Union men could not secure fair trials in the state courts. A group of citizens from Camden County who had fought on the Union side in the Civil War sent a statement to the president in which they alleged that the newly-instituted civil courts were discriminating against them because of their devotion to the Union. "They do not hesitate to show their hatred, by indicting us for the most trivial offences," the petitioners stated.[29] Soon after this plea for justice arrived in Washington, the acting Secretary of State admonished Worth to see "that no such unjust and merely vindictive prosecutions are caused or are instituted."[30]

When Worth received a copy of the Unionist petition from Camden County he requested that D. D. Ferrebee, the convention delegate from the county, and George W. Brooks, a United States district judge, investigate the charges made in the petition. Ferrebee and Brooks reported that only two of the men who signed the petition were under indictment—one for fornication and one for larceny—and that the courts did not discriminate against former Unionists. Ferrebee thought the petition evinced "a spirit to misrepresent and frustrate by exasperation and discontent the policy of [Worth] in restoring the state to its civil relations with the Federal Government."[31] Worth sent the facts reported to him by Ferrebee and Judge Brooks to Washington, and the president accepted them as the truth.

The charge that the state courts were guilty of discrimination against Union men was a constant source of anxiety to Worth. When such charges arrived in Washington they might supply more ammunition for the Radicals' arsenal of allegations about the condition of affairs in the South. The governor felt it was his duty, both official and political, to assure that justice was fairly administered in the state and to repudiate assertions that Union men were being mistreated in the courts. This duty consumed much of his time during the months between May and September, 1866.

The strife between former Unionists and secessionists was most intense in the mountain counties of the West, where the Civil War had indeed been a civil war, where families had been divided, and where hundreds of men had joined the Union army. There were many reports of discrimination from that area, the most interesting of which was a minor one involving two men named Ledford who had been arrested in Clay County for driving two "secessionists" from the county by force. After the Ledfords were tried and fined a hundred dollars they sent the president a petition stating that "we are called Tories and traitors for fighting for the United States." They explained that the man they had driven from the county had said that "Lincoln ought to have been shot long ago," and had denounced Colonel George W. Kirk, a Union partisan who had invaded the western part of the state late in the war, as a bushwhacker. The Ledfords insisted that a majority of the men on the jury which convicted them were former Confederates. The sheriff of Clay County sent along with the petition a statement that the Ledfords were loyal Union soldiers and that "there indictments was and is prosecuted against the Ledford boys through prejudis of the Rebel party. . . ." The clerk of court, three justices of the peace, the sheriff, and six other persons sent the president a petition certifying the facts submitted by the Ledfords.[32]

The first Worth heard of the Ledford case was when the petitions came down to him from Washington. He asked the delegate in the state convention from Clay County to give him information about the case, but he got very little; the informant did venture the opinion that the judge in the case, Augustus S. Merrimon, "held the scales of justice as a judge should do," but that the actions of the prosecuting attorney were "less satisfactory."[33] After talking to the delegate from Clay County, Worth wrote to Judge Merrimon asking for his viewpoint on the Ledford case. Merrimon, a Whig and former opponent of secession who was then active in Conservative circles and later became United States Senator and Chief Justice of the state Supreme Court, was well qualified to comment on the administration of justice in the mountainous west; he had been the solicitor of that district during the war.[34]

The judge's lengthy reply was a revelation of the conditions which prevailed in the western end of the state. Merrimon first described the facts in the case as he saw them. Needless to say, his rendering differed widely from the account sent to Washington by the Ledfords. He admitted that the case took on a political complexion when the defendants' attorney spoke favorably of the partisan activities of Colonel George Kirk and the prosecutor replied that Kirk was a "sorry fellow" who robbed hen roosts. Judge Merrimon at this point "took occasion to say to the Solicitor and gentlemen of the bar, that in future, nothing must be said . . . that might be offensive to the soldiery on either side of the late war, that the business of the court was to administer impartial justice and . . . to harmonize the discordant elements of society in this part of the state." Merrimon told Worth that most of the depredations being committed in that section of the state were the work of desperate and lawless men, many of whom had deserted the Confederate army and joined the Union forces. Those men who had been consistent throughout the war with either side were generally settled, law-abiding citizens. The desperadoes, once they were caught in some villainy, tended to "insist, that simply because they happened to join the Federal army, they have the right to commit those crimes with perfect impunity." Most of these wild characters, according to Merrimon, were Radicals, supporters of the Republican leaders Thaddeus Stevens and Charles Sumner, and enemies of President Johnson. The judge said he had done his best to be impartial, and he urged that Worth have President Johnson send an agent from Washington to observe the operations of the court system.[35]

The solicitor of the western judicial district was David Coleman, and it was against Coleman and the jury that the Ledfords' petition had been primarily directed. Judge Merrimon admitted that Coleman had been a strong secessionist and had commanded a North Carolina regiment during the war, but since the war the solicitor had indicted Confederates as well as Unionists. "I suspect the main ground . . . against him, is that he was a *Secessionist*," Merrimon concluded.[36] William Holden's newspaper, which had begun to adopt the Radical position, contributed to the attack on the courts and particularly on Coleman. Holden reported to his readers that, as solicitor, Coleman had brought a hundred and seventy-three indictments against Unionists and only three against secessionists at the spring term of superior court in Clay County; "such are the fruits of Governor Worth's administration," the editor added.[37] Coleman did not deign to defend himself, but he reported to Worth that "so far as concerns this Circuit, these charges against the juries have no foundation."[38]

Worth made many inquiries about the administration of justice in the state, and the answers he received convinced him that the courts were operating normally and fairly. He assured the Secretary of State, who took the side of the president in his fight with the Radicals, that "the law is ably and justly administered in this state."[39] This was true, in the sense that the courts were open and operating under able judges, but there can be little doubt that some North Carolinians were dragging the passionate animosities left over from the war period into their relationships with each other and were prosecuting each other in court for trivial reasons. Sam Jackson, who was still managing Worth's old law practice, told Worth that in Randolph County "the war and union men are trying each other—every *little scrape* that happened during the progress of the war is now being brought forward"; the grand jury of Randolph brought eighty indictments in one week during March, 1866.[40] In the northwest section of the state there were clashes in Allegheny and Surry counties between a secret Unionist organization called the Heroes of America and some cavalry troops which were being formed as a part of the state militia. The Unionists maintained that the cavalry troops were mostly former Confederate soldiers, and they feared attacks if the force were organized. Worth sent an agent into the northwest to investigate the disputes there, and the agent reported that "the extraordinary number of indictments for criminal offenses committed by both sides during the war . . . will necessarily serve to keep alive violent neighborhood hostilities."[41]

Some of the "violent neighborhood hostilities" in North Carolina manifested themselves in events that bordered on the ludicrous. A fight broke out in Salem on July 4, 1866, when "secessionists" attempted to keep the Unionists from celebrating Independence Day. The secessionists spiked the cannon which was to be fired as part of the proceedings, but the Unionists drilled another powder hole and went ahead with their celebration. The secessionists then "stormed" the celebration a second time and a general melee broke out; the Unionists claimed victory.[42] But all the bad feeling was not so amusing, as Worth found out when one of his former constituents wrote that he had exiled himself from the state because he feared retaliation for acts committed in the line of duty during the war; the exile had stayed away from home over a year "on account of the bitterness of some of the citizens of Randolph County."[43]

Worth began to believe that the petitions being sent to Washington and the complaints against the courts were part of a master plot to overthrow the state government. Late in July, 1866, he confided his fears to Benjamin S. Hedrick and reported a new development:

I am satisfied there is a concerted plan on foot, by imputing partiality to our Courts of Justice, to have martial law restored, if it be not already in force. We have a new military commandant, Genl. John C. Robinson. He professes to believe that a Union man cannot have justice in our Courts. To prove this he has had two officers, Col. Carr and Capt. Wolcott, traveling in several of the Western Counties and taking ex parte statements and affidavits to prove all sorts of iniquities against our Courts—a thing easily done in this way. Numerous petitions as he says, are sent to him asking for military protection. He has sent me copies of some of them. They show on their face, to an impartial mind, that they are got up for effect. . . . The combination is extensive. Master spirits for mischief are at the bottom of it and our poor old State is likely to suffer from the dirty birds willing to foul their own nests to reek vengeance on others.[44]

Worth never could prove that the attack on the courts by petitions, military investigators, and Radically-inclined newspapers was an organized conspiracy. Although it is easy to understand why he suspected that a plot existed, a number of facts weigh heavily against his suspicion: the petitions to Washington originated in widely separated areas; they were directed to the president instead of to Radical

Congressmen; and they came from areas in which Unionist sentiment had been and was still strong. Worth simply refused to acknowledge the existence of an unfortunate and unpleasant situation. Even Benjamin Hedrick, the best friend North Carolina had in Washington, was convinced that it was hard for a Union man to secure justice in some areas of the state. The Chief Justice of the state Supreme Court, Richmond M. Pearson, probably gave an accurate evaluation of the situation when he told Worth: "There can be no suggestion that Judges . . . have not acted with impartiality, but from what I have heard I fear there prevails a strong prejudice in the public mind against those who adhered to the U.S. Government, and that this feeling has to some extent influenced the action of jurors and grand jurors; but I can see no remedy for it except to let it wear away by time."[45]

Early in July, 1866, General John C. Robinson, who served the dual functions of commandant of the military force in the state and Assistant Commissioner of the Freedmen's Bureau, sent Worth a general order from the War Department charging the commandant to protect certain classes of citizens from prosecution in state and municipal courts; these classes included "loyal citizens" charged with acts against rebels during the war, and colored persons if the state law discriminated between races in the penalty it provided.[46] The general interpreted this order to mean that it was his duty to protect both Unionists and Negroes, but he hoped the state judicial officers would perform their duties in such a way that he would not have to relieve them. Robinson apparently assumed that the state was still under martial law.

Worth distributed Robinson's general order to the judges and solicitors throughout the state, at Robinson's request, and after consultation with William A. Graham. A week later he protested that he should not have been requested to distribute the order. Adhering to the doctrine of separation of powers in a republican government, Worth did not think that the executive should issue directives to the judiciary; it would be the judges' duty to disregard such directives, Worth believed. Furthermore, said the governor, the judges should obey the act of Congress under which the military order was issued, rather than the order itself. "The judges ought not to assume or refrain from jurisdiction . . . by virtue of a military order, while the country is in a state of peace," Worth insisted. He promised General Robinson he would make every effort to avoid a clash of civil and military jurisdiction, and expressed a hope that Robinson would not exercise the power he claimed to suspend a state judicial officer.[47]

A few days after General Robinson stated his intention to protect Unionists and freedmen, Worth sent him copies of the acts of the legislature and convention pertaining to freedmen. Since these acts provided no apparent discrimination against Negroes, Robinson directed the officers of the Freedmen's Bureau to turn over to the civil courts all cases involving freedmen, except suits involving the collection of wages under a contract witnessed by Bureau agents.[48]

Worth announced Robinson's concession in a circular to the people of the state in which he published his correspondence with the general and told of his defense of the state courts. He informed his constituents of the petitions which had been sent to Washington and of his investigations which proved the petitions to be false statements. The circular called for "peculiar diligence and circumspection" by justices of the peace and sheriffs at a time when the crime rate was uncommonly high, and pointed out that the only way to elevate the Negroes was for the white men to protect them in their lately acquired rights.[49]

The exchanges between Worth and General Robinson went on throughout the summer of 1866, with both protagonists maintaining their positions strongly.[50] Robinson was always polite in his dealings with Worth, and he made considerable efforts to see that his subordinates did not abuse their power. Occasionally he apologized to Worth for precipitate actions by agents of the Freedmen's Bureau or military officers and gave assurance that such actions would not occur again; but in spite of the general's good intentions, military officials and agents of the Bureau sometimes abused their authority.

Robinson had yielded a great deal when he deprived the Freedmen's Bureau of jurisdiction in most cases involving freedmen, but Worth was not satisfied with these concessions. Reports of discrimination against former Unionists and assaults upon Negroes continued to come to Robinson, and he invariably sent these on to Worth, urging the governor to take remedial action. Frustrated and exasperated, Worth insisted that Robinson should disregard the ex parte charges contained in the complaints of injustice; that solicitors and judges should be allowed to give their sides of the story, but that this was impossible because the only place where evidence could legally be gathered was in a trial. The governor felt that the only way Robinson's veiled threat to remove judges or solicitors could be enforced was in ex parte proceedings, and the very thought of such proceedings was intolerable to him. Yet when General Robinson offered him a chance to collect counter evidence, Worth did not perceive how this evidence could be gathered legally. He did, however, secure written statements from the judges and solicitors in the most troubled areas. These statements tended to confirm Worth's position, and his defense of the state from the threat of military interference was largely based upon them.

Worth wrote to the president in the summer of 1866, asking whether North Carolina was still under martial law, in an effort to find out the extent of General Robinson's power. On August 20, 1866, the president declared that civil authority had been restored throughout the United States, and Worth supposed that military orders resting on the assumption that martial law was still in force would be repealed.[51] The president never did answer the abstract question whether the state was still under martial law, but he promised through Edwin M. Stanton, the Secretary of War, to examine cases of military interference in North Carolina's affairs if specific facts were made available. Stanton, who was leaning far over towards the Radicals, said there would be no interference unless the president should order it.[52]

Because of the imputations that no justice could be had for Union men and Negroes in the state courts, Worth and the judges made special efforts to see that they received fair treatment. Every judge who sat on a bench in North Carolina during 1866 was conscious that any discrimination would be seized upon by the Radicals as a pretext for returning the state to military rule. Judge David Barnes expressed the judges' awareness of this fact to Governor Worth in a letter thanking Worth for refusing executive clemency to a band of white vigilantes in Craven County who had severely beaten a Negro man for petty thievery. The local citizens, greatly resenting Barnes' action in sentencing the vigilantes to imprisonment and fines, asked Worth to pardon the convicted criminals. He took advantage of the opportunity to lecture the petitioners on their obligations to obey the laws of the state: "Public justice and sound policy forbid that citizens should assume the province of judge and jury. . . . Having by constitutional ordinances emancipated our slaves, and enacted laws entitling them to trial by jury for alleged crimes, we owe it to ourselves, to the Negroes, and to enlightened public policy . . . to carry out legislation with fidelity."[53]

Thus Worth lectured prominent citizens of North Carolina, as well as the Assistant Commissioner of the Freedmen's Bureau, on the necessity of allowing the civil courts to secure justice for the freedmen. The one was willing to persecute, the other to protect, the freedmen. But Jonathan Worth was determined that there should be neither persecution by white citizens nor protection by the military or the Bureau if the laws of the state had to be overthrown. This insistence upon order and justice was deeply engrained in Worth's personality, and was an integral part of his conservative philosophy. He firmly believed that public order and justice, which were in his view the ends of any government, could best be maintained by the civil institutions of the state, and he stood ready at all times to defend those institutions from any encroachment. The central theme of his administration was a defense of his native state against the threat, and later the reality, of military rule.

· XVI ·

The Last Campaign

———•—•———

BECAUSE JONATHAN WORTH occupied the office of governor at such an unusual period in the state's history, his administration was in many respects peculiar. One of the unique aspects of it was that by the very nature of the situation he had to maintain what was then in existence rather than to move either forward or backward. Ordinarily a governor would be expected to have a positive program of some kind, perhaps some pet plan or project for the development of the state's economy or one of its social institutions, but Worth could have no such schemes. He could promote no grandiose program of economic progress, because the state was economically prostrate as a result of the war. His favorite social institution, the public school system, had to be closed down in 1865, and in spite of his efforts to raise money for the schools by selling some of the state's swamp lands, the schools did not reopen until after he left office. Worth's administration was necessarily one of protest, and it came at a time when material achievement was practically impossible. There could be no forward movement until the disjointed times became more normal and the state returned to its former position in the Union. He was an able and hard-working executive, but he never had a fair opportunity to work for the material advancement of the state as he had done in the golden years before the war.

Instead, he found himself permanently engaged in defending what had not been destroyed, and burdened with the tedious details of problems that never faced any other governor in the history of the state. Since the state had no Congressmen between 1865 and 1868, he had to assume the function ordinarily exercised by the Congressional delegation of recommending appointees to federal offices in the state. Another unusual service he rendered was supervising a program to provide artificial limbs to soldiers who had lost arms and legs in the war. He investigated the number needed, examined the types available, let the contract for the manufacture of the limbs, and even secured free transportation to Raleigh for the amputees and a bunk house in which they could live while their limbs were being fitted. The state paid only for legs; anyone who wanted an arm had to buy it himself.

Almost everything he did had its political overtones, even the humane effort to provide men with limbs. Before Worth ever got his "artificial limb establishment" into operation an unbelievably embittered citizen of North Carolina reported what he was doing to Thaddeus Stevens, the leader of the Radicals in the United States House of Representatives:

This legislature, on the recommendation of Governor Worth are, out of the State treasury, providing artificial limbs for maimed rebels. This sort of Compulsory Charity for treason may suit the palate of some, but the Union men of this State would rather be the dispensers of their own bounty—What! get legs and arms for wretches who when our poor fellows sick and helpless fell into their hands, buried them alive in pits—In the name of heaven if savage warfare, and its abettors are to be so respected let us unite in converting our Country into another Mexican Republic at once.[1]

Not everyone was as embittered as Stevens' informant, but Worth often had to cope with political animosities that reached the point of hatred. One way in which he attempted to salve wounded feelings was by securing pardons for those persons who had been excepted from President Johnson's amnesty proclamation of May 29, 1865. Provisional Governor Holden had processed over fifteen hundred applications for pardon during his short term, but he had allowed his political views to affect his recommendations as to what disposition should be made of applications when they reached Washington. He recommended pardons for several original secessionists, but feared that if he secured clemency for influential men of the party which had been in power during the war they would oppose the national administration.[2] An order of the convention of 1865 enabled those persons who had secured pardons to vote in the fall elections, and shortly before the election Holden published a list of five hundred names of persons who had presumably been pardoned, in order that they might vote in the election for governor and other officers.

When Worth took office as governor he found that "the five hundred" had not been pardoned, although Holden had forwarded their applications to Washington. There were also three hundred applications in the governor's office on which no action had been taken. For several months Worth was plagued with inquiries from men who wrote that they had sent their applications for pardon to Holden and had not heard of them since. When Worth found the untouched applications in his office he asked the president what to do with them, and Johnson asked him to forward them to Washington with recommendations as to whether each one should be accepted or rejected.[3] The governor then forwarded all the applications in his office to Washington, along with "a letter to the President stating that I favored universal amnesty, and that in view of the pardons already granted in this State I could perceive no principle which would warrant me in advising the rejection of any."[4]

Three weeks after Worth recommended that all those who had applied for executive clemency should be pardoned he asked Benjamin S. Hedrick to assist in securing the pardons. Hedrick, a former Professor of Chemistry at the University of North Carolina, had been driven out of North Carolina through the influence of William Holden, because he let it be known that he intended to vote for John C. Fremont in 1856. He naturally had no affection for Holden, but he still loved his native state. The exiled Hedrick worked diligently to secure the pardons, visited the president, and continually prodded the clerks in the State Department; his services were never paid for. Since he worked at the United States Patent Office he was not eligible to receive money from North Carolina. When Worth tried to pay him something he refused and said he offered his services gladly, in an effort "to supply as far as possible the want of any representation of the people here."[5]

Almost all the pardons Worth recommended had been granted by the end of May, 1866, but of the five hundred published in the newspapers by Holden before the election, almost none had been approved. Worth became tired of answering inquiries and complaints about the applications forwarded by Holden, and in June, he called the attention of the Secretary of State to the unprocessed applications and asked that they be approved and sent to him at once.[6] He made a special request to the president to pardon William A. Graham, Josiah Turner, Jr., and William T. Dortch, three of the most prominent men Holden had refused to pardon because of their past political activities. Worth told the president that "every body in this State (excepting a handful of Radicals) supports your policy. If you would pardon these three men it would give fervor to this support."[7] Most of the pardons for North Carolinians were granted by the last of July, 1866, but it was not until a year later that Josiah Turner, Jr.'s pardon reached Worth.[8]

Even after some individuals had received amnesty or pardon, local officials sometimes treated them as former rebels. This was the case in Rutherford County, where about forty citizens were denied the right to vote on the grounds that they had not taken the loyalty oath prescribed by the Amnesty Proclamation of May, 1865. Worth refused to intervene in these local disputes; instead, he advised the injured parties to appeal to the civil courts.[9]

Worth's course in helping to restore the state government, his defense of the state against the threat of interference by the military and the Freedmen's Bureau, and his efforts to secure universal amnesty met with general approval, and he decided, early in 1866, that he should run again for governor in that year. A number of motives brought about this decision. The fact that he firmly believed the people of North Carolina approved of his actions was in itself a stimulus, for Worth's personality was such that he thrived on approval. But the basic influences on his decision were political. Like other Conservatives, he felt that a man who was opposed to politicians of radical proclivities and to the Congressional plan of reconstruction should occupy the governor's office. Someone who would not tamely submit to the military authorities and the Freedmen's Bureau was needed as the chief executive of North Carolina, and Worth was such a man. In addition, he realized that he was the choice of those who were opposed to William Holden and the faction he led.

As in 1865, most of the conservative Unionist leaders approved Worth's decision and encouraged him to run, but John Pool made a strong attempt to keep him from announcing his candidacy, on the theory that an "excited contest" would damage the state's chance of an early return to the Union. Pool was a genuine Unionist, and a conservative too, but he still assumed that Worth was backed by a party of "war men." He insisted that Worth's election in 1865 over Holden was "considered a political success of the war men, as an organized party, running him for availability only"; a second election of Worth would be harmful to the state, in Pool's opinion.[10]

Worth had been reluctant to run for governor in the fall of 1865, but in April, 1866, he engineered his nomination for re-election.

When he began hearing rumors that he would be opposed by James M. Leach, a member of the Holden faction, Worth reasoned thus: Leach would be the candidate of Holden and he would need the support of those counties which had supported Holden in 1865. If these counties would nominate Worth at the May courts, and if those who had opposed him in 1865 could be induced to make a few speeches in his behalf, then Leach or any other potential opponent would not be able to "get up a tempest." Late in April, Worth asked one of his friends in Randolph, Alfred G. Foster, to put this strategy into effect by preparing a nominating resolution and introducing it at a political meeting in Randolph County.[11]

The meeting at which Worth was nominated was a stormy affair. The committee on resolutions brought out Foster's resolution nominating Worth, the Holdenites opposed it, and a three-hour debate followed in which the backers of Holden argued that they had not been notified of the meeting. One Holdenite suggested that all Union men walk out and a Worth man replied that "we all would have to leave."[12] Efforts to nominate Judge Robert P. Dick, a prominent judge from Greensboro whose sympathies were with Holden, failed, and the meeting nominated Worth for governor. Holden, who was again editing the *Standard*, reported the results of the meeting and announced that Judge Dick had made a speech, but he refused to believe that Dick had endorsed Worth's candidacy.[13]

After his nomination, Worth announced his candidacy in a circular to the people in which he gave as his reason for running the fact that his current administration seemed to be generally approved. He explained that he would not make a canvass because he could not take time from his duties. All the remarks in the circular pertained to national affairs, and, as in Worth's announcement of his candidacy in 1865, they expressed a patriotic and statesmanlike plea for the restoration of the Union:

As a part of my early education I was required to commit to memory and rehearse that portion of the farewell address of the father of his country, in which he so earnestly warns us to indignantly "frown upon the first dawning of any attempt to alienate any portion of our country from the rest." This became a fixed sentiment with me. The preservation of the Union has been the polar star of my political life.

· · · · · · · · · · · · · · · ·

The great object of all good men and wise statesmen should now be to mollify the passions which have grown out of the late conflict, and by all their influence to endeavor to restore *cordial reconciliation* between the lately alienated sections. The good of our whole nation requires *sincere* and *universal reconciliation*. This cannot be if proscription and mutual crimination be indulged. The sublime injunctions of holy writ which forbid the indulgence of malevolence, are universal in their application.

Both philosophy and religion rank forgiveness and charity among the chiefest of virtues, and as there are few of us who have not occasion to ask forgiveness for our own acts, let us be merciful to each other.[14]

Worth reviewed his record of Unionism again and denied that his previous election was a triumph for the disunionists. He asked his constituents to obey the laws of the state and nation, "however distasteful," to refrain from unwise denunciation of the victorious North, and to go on about their business, relying on Providence to bring the Radicals to "becoming magnanimity and . . . generous statesmanship."

The leader of the opposition to Worth was, as usual, William Holden. Worth was too popular for Holden to risk another candidacy so soon after Worth had beaten him in the fall of 1865, but the editor tried to find someone willing to run against his old opponent. Everyone approached by Holden or his followers refused to come out publicly against Worth, because "the position of a candidate against Governor Worth at this juncture was not one to be sought by anyone with political ambitions."[15] Holden then turned to the president and painted for him an unflattering picture of conditions in the state, apparently in an effort to encourage the president to help him put Worth and his followers out of office. Early in June, 1866, Holden went to Washington to lobby unsuccessfully for approval of his appointment by the president as minister to San Salvador. From his room at Ebbitt House he wrote the president:

Allow me to say that the cause of restoration is obstructed in our state by those in power; the truly loyal people are depressed and mortified; malcontents and rebels are exultant and defiant; ill feeling is engendered; injustice is perpetrated through the Courts by means of disloyal prosecuting officers, and Juries, and some magistrates, though our Judges are loyal, yet not always able to withstand the pressure of public opinion; treason and disloyalty are promoted and honored, while loyalty is evinced at the hazard of political, social, and pecuniary proscription.

All we ask is, that the truly loyal of our people shall govern until the State is restored to the Union.[16]

The political sky in North Carolina in 1866 was clouded by a campaign preceding an election held in August to determine whether the state should adopt a revised state constitution submitted for approval or disapproval by the convention of 1865-66; the election on the constitution was to be held two months before the regular state election, in order that the constitution, if it were approved, could go into effect before the regular election. The most basic change written into the constitution was one changing the basis of representation in the House of Commons from federal population to white population, a provision which would tend to give the western section of the state more political power. The campaign for and against the constitution was based not upon the merits of the constitution itself but upon the question whether the convention had power to revise the old instrument. If the acts of the convention were not valid, then the civil government of the state rested on no legal basis. Both Holden and Worth favored the adoption of the revised constitution, but Holden tried to create the impression that Worth and his supporters were trying to defeat the president's plan of reconstruction by rejecting it. On the eve of the election to determine whether the new constitution should be adopted, Holden reported to the president that the "rebellious leaders" of the state—the Worth men—were undermining the president's program of reconstruction by denying the validity of the acts of the convention. The ambitious editor admitted that Worth would vote for the constitution, but only "to hide appearances," and once again asked the president to assist him in throwing Worth and his followers from control of the state: "If you would aid us to the extent indicated by me, when in Washington, I am satisfied, we could wrest the State from the hands of these men." Holden encouraged the president to take over the state government again if the constitution were defeated.[17] The day after Holden made this plea, the constitution was defeated by a vote of 21,552 to 19,570, with most of the opposition votes coming from the East.[18] Worth commented on the election that "I voted and urged others to vote for the ratification of the proposed amendments to our Constitution and regret that the result of the election was for rejection."[19] The president turned a deaf ear to Holden's plea that he overthrow the state government if the constitution were rejected, and he refused to express approval of Holden and disapproval of Worth and his administration. This was enough to drive Holden into the camp of the Radicals, if he were not already there.

Worth was in constant communication with the president, and he made every effort to counteract Holden's adverse propaganda. He told Johnson plainly that it had been a serious, but forgivable, mistake to appoint Holden provisional governor in 1865 and reviewed the editor's record of vacillation to prove his point. He informed the president how Holden had flaunted before the people Johnson's telegram expressing disapproval of the results of the election of 1865, and reported the facts that Holden was advocating the adoption of the Fourteenth Amendment, which had been submitted to the state for approval in June, 1866; publishing Radical documents in the *Standard*; and trying to find a candidate to oppose Worth in the coming gubernatorial election. Worth could perceive nothing in his own background which might cause Johnson to be partial to Holden in preference to himself, and he told the president that Holden's constant assertions that the powers in Washington favored him "impairs the efficacy of my exertions to aid you in your noble efforts to restore a fraternal Union."[20]

Worth was confident of winning the election for governor in October, 1866, but for a time he feared that someone might come out against him on a platform demanding the repudiation of the debt created before the war. Although Worth himself believed the state should pay its honest debts, he felt that a majority of the people did not, and that if a candidate adopted a repudiation platform he would be very popular. Most of the debt was owed to northerners and many North Carolinians felt that it should not be paid because the North had destroyed much of the state's wealth by emancipating the slaves; "and they further insist," Worth told one of his sons-in-law, "that the National taxes will be as much as we can pay."[21] Soon after Worth became governor Josiah Turner, Jr., had written from Hillsboro that there was considerable sentiment for repudiation in his area, and that the political leaders there had not called a meeting "to endorse Worth or condemn Holden" because they feared that if a meeting were held a resolution requesting repudiation would be put forward.[22] Fortunately for Worth, no candidate chose to raise the issue of repudiation, probably because it would have been unwise to taunt the North with a threat of repudiation and because Worth's opponents were by no means united on the question. Milton Worth reported that he had seen "many of the Radicals . . . that are violently opposed to the repudiation movement."[23]

The hard fact the opponents of Worth had to face before the election was that there was no clear-cut issue on which they could hope to win. About all they could do was attempt to exploit prevailing discontents and discredit Worth and his followers. There were many ways by which this could be done. In March, 1866, for example, Holden reported that many Quakers were leaving the state because they were being persecuted for their Union sentiment; this was a rumor which had started in the North and had found its way into some northern newspapers. The *Standard* admitted that there were several possible causes for the emigration of Quakers: better lands in the Northwest, "poverty of our state generally," no schools, the presence of the military occupation force and the Freedmen's Bureau, and disappointment at the state's failure to get back into the Union; but Holden dismissed all these possible causes and attributed the emigration to "the predominance in the State government of the secession feeling."[24] His editorial opined that the Friends might have remained if North Carolina had not broken faith with President Johnson, and implied that Worth and William A. Graham were responsible for the conditions which were causing the Quakers to leave.

When Worth read Holden's editorial on Quaker emigration, he immediately wrote letters to his Quaker friends to find out if there was any real basis for the statements in it. Among those whom he asked for information was Nereus Mendenhall, who was perhaps the most influential Quaker in the state, the president of the school at New Garden which later became Guilford College, and one of Worth's appointees to the state's Literary Board. Mendenhall's reply was a flat refutation of Holden's editorial and at the same time a commentary on the propaganda techniques of Reconstruction politics:

. . . I had seen in the *New York Tribune* a statement that 75 members of the Society of Friends from Randolph passed through Washington on their way to Indiana driven away by the ex-soldiers of the rebel army. All this was news to me and subsequent inquiry has convinced me that not more than one-third of those 75 persons were Friends and that the departure of these was not requested by their neighbors—that they were in no sense driven off. I know of no such persecution or disposition to persecute either the Society of Friends or others, and were such persecutions to occur, thyself and Gov. Graham are among the very last men whom I should expect to find giving countenance thereto.[25]

A similar report came to Worth from Allen M. Tomlinson, one of his best friends in Randolph County, but it was not until 1868 that Worth finally discovered the source of Holden's rumor. Addison Coffin, who had led some of the Quakers from North Carolina to the West, informed him that a man named Halowell, from Carthage, Indiana, a clerk in the United States Patent Office, had started the story of persecuted Quakers "to make political capitol."[26] Coffin strongly denied that many Quakers were emigrating or had emigrated from North Carolina, and asserted that most of the migrants moved for economic, rather than political, reasons.

An incident of the national political campaign caused Worth to be sorely disappointed with his Quaker friends and brought painfully to his attention the leading "carpetbagger" in North Carolina politics, Albion W. Tourgée. Tourgée was a lawyer from Ohio, a former captain in the Union army, a handsome, one-eyed idealist who seemed to have an obsession for protecting the rights of Negroes.[27] He came to North Carolina shortly after the war and settled in Greensboro. In August, 1866, at a meeting in the Quaker meeting house on Deep River, among Worth's former constituents and best friends, Tourgée was selected to represent the Unionists of that section at a meeting of southern Unionists in Philadelphia.[28] At Philadelphia, Tourgée was one of the more prominent figures, advocating Negro suffrage and delivering a speech in which he told of the petitions to President Johnson from North Carolina and accused Worth of being "disloyal." Captain Tourgée also informed the convention that an unidentified Quaker had seen the bodies of fifteen dead Negroes pulled out of a mill pond.

Worth was furious when he read the account of Tourgée's speech in the New York *Herald*. He was by this time very sensitive to the repeated assaults upon himself and the civil authorities, and the righteous indignation of which he had always been capable reached the boiling point. He immediately wrote to Nereus Mendenhall, who had participated in the meeting which sent Tourgée to Philadelphia, and expressed disappointment that Mendenhall and other prominent Quakers had attended the meeting. He informed Mendenhall that Tourgée's statements about Unionist petitions to the president were a lie and said of the statement about the murdered Negroes in the pond that "he ought to be called upon to give the name of his informant, and the whereabouts of the pond."[29] Worth also prepared facts for an article in the Greensboro *Patriot* to expose what he considered Tourgée's "tissue of lies," but he decided not to publish his article after he concluded that it would be both unwise and unpleasant to open a controversy with such a man as "this contemptible Tourgée."[30] He was amazed and mortified that the Quakers had endorsed the Radical position by sending Tourgée and Jonathan Harris, an influential member of their own Society, to Philadelphia. His own endorsement went to a pro-Johnson convention which met in Philadelphia two weeks before the Unionist convention;[31] most of the delegates to the earlier convention were supporters of Worth, among them William A. Graham and John A. Gilmer.

Six weeks before the election for governor the Holdenites, who had begun to refer to themselves as the Union party, made one final effort to bring out a candidate against Worth and to define the issues involved in the election. Meeting in Holden's office at Raleigh on September 20, the leaders of the Union party nominated Worth's old opponent, Alfred Dockery, for governor and spelled out a platform in a series of resolutions. The resolutions, which clearly revealed the position of Worth's opponents and the difference between the adherents of Holden and those of Worth, were as follows: only loyal persons should hold office in North Carolina; the Fourteenth Amendment should be ratified; the people should demand that their representatives in the legislature approve the amendment; and, finally, the members of the Union party stood ready to co-operate "in any further action that in the wisdom of Congress and the Executive may be deemed necessary to guarantee to the state of North Carolina a Republican form of government. . . ." By these resolutions the men who made them virtually declared their acquiescence to whatever plan of Reconstruction would be handed down from Washington by an increasingly powerful Radical Congress—and therein lay the basic difference between the two parties which were now emerging in North Carolina. In addition to laying down a platform calling for the ratification of the Fourteenth Amendment, the Union party leaders meeting at Holden's office summed up all their grievances against Jonathan Worth:

. . We profoundly regret the defection of Governor Worth from the Union cause, his proscription for opinion's sake of Union men from office, and the injurious influence which the prominent instigators and actors in the rebellion are exerting over him in his official conduct.

We cannot hope that the State will be restored to the Union under his auspices; and, as we prefer principles to men, and believe the restoration of the Union to be more important . . . than everything else, we feel it to be our duty firmly to oppose his re-election.[32]

Holden had asked permission for the Union party "convention" to meet in the hall of the House of Commons and permission had been granted, but so few delegates appeared that they preferred to meet in the editor's office. Worth noted with great satisfaction that the meeting which had nominated Dockery was a "truly small affair," and Benjamin Hedrick called the gathering "an utter failure."[33] It must have been embarrassing to the Union party when General Dockery refused to become a candidate against Worth because the meeting which nominated him had been so small and because there was not enough time to canvass the state. Neither Worth nor Dockery did any campaigning, but Holden circulated tickets urging that Dockery be elected. On election day Worth won by far the largest majority of votes he ever received in his eight campaigns for public office; the official count was 34,250 for Worth and 10,759 for Dockery.[34] Dockery had majorities in only nine of the eighty-nine counties, six of them in the western part of the state where Union sentiment and loyalty to William Holden were strong; but even in the six western counties, Dockery's margin of victory was narrow—one vote in Polk and six in Gaston.

Worth was shocked again when his home county, Randolph, turned against him and gave his opponent a substantial majority. The defeat can be attributed to the staunchly Unionist Quakers, for in the Quaker stronghold at New Market, Dockery got twice as many votes as Worth. Sam Jackson sent Worth a copy of the returns from the county and said the result in Randolph could be explained by the fact that a "considerable majority" of the people in the county were members of the Union League, a secret organization which had been formed during the war to promote Union sentiment and was now being revived for political purposes.[35] Another informant attributed Worth's defeat in Randolph to the superior organization of the opposition, and reported that one candidate for the legislature "scared some of the timid into fits nearly he told them if they did not accept the Howard Amendment they would have the roape a round their necks and there property would be confiscated that word confiscate was delivered with much force and he raised to tip toe."[36] The adoption or rejection of the Fourteenth Amendment had become the central issue in state politics.

During the two months between Worth's second election as governor and his second inauguration, he fought and won another round in his never-ending battle with the Freedmen's Bureau. Notwithstanding the fact that General Robinson had discontinued the courts of the Bureau when Worth informed him that the laws and courts of North Carolina made no distinction between white men and Negroes, there were still cases in which the Bureau agents interfered with the courts of the state. The most notable example of this intervention resulted from a difference between the policy of the Bureau on apprenticeship and the laws of the state on the same subject. Worth and Robinson engaged in another exchange of views—an exchange in which Robinson expressed views bordering on Radicalism. The argument started in October, 1866, when Worth received a complaint from Daniel L. Russell, a planter in Brunswick County, that Bureau agents, on the order of Colonel Allen Rutherford, had nullified indentures from the county court by which Russell had secured some Negro girls as apprentices; one of the girls was sixteen years old. Worth asked General Robinson to explain on what grounds Colonel Rutherford had nullified the indenture bonds. "Do you claim for your officers," inquired Worth, "the right to decide when the court has transcended its jurisdiction?"[37]

The ordinarily calm Robinson was irritated at this inquiry from Worth. It had begun to annoy him to have so many of his actions protested and questioned by the governor, especially since he was only carrying out his orders as he interpreted them. The general pointed out to Worth that he had deprived the Bureau of most of its jurisdiction over the freedmen and that the agents had been warned repeatedly to avoid conflict with the civil authorities. But, said Robinson, "I feel myself called upon to continue to exercise a guardianship of the interest of the freed people, and therefore not only authorized, but in duty bound . . . to use all powers delegated to me to enforce the rights of these people."[38] It was on the grounds that the county court had discriminated against the Negro girls that the intervention by Colonel Rutherford took place, Robinson explained. According to Rutherford's instructions to his agents, "no child whose parents are able and willing to support it" could be apprenticed without the consent of the parents, and under no circumstances was a person over fourteen years old to be bound to service. This policy of the Bureau was in conflict with the state law, which allowed Negro boys to be bound out until they were twenty-one years old and girls until they were sixteen. The county court of Brunswick had violated the Bureau's rule by binding the children to Russell, whom General Robinson considered a "designing and unscrupulous man." To Robinson the whole proceeding in Brunswick looked like "a reestablishment of slavery under the mild name of apprenticeship."[39]

Robinson had Worth on the defensive, for Worth could not deny the facts in the Russell case. He attempted no vindication of Russell's conduct and admitted that civil justice had lapsed, but insisted that "the laws of the state furnish ample redress,"[40] and that, consequently, there was no cause for interference by the Freedmen's Bureau. The governor pointed out that Russell was subject to indictment by the children's parents, and that if the indentures had been illegally made they could be revoked by a civil court; furthermore, the children were entitled to release upon a writ of habeas corpus. Considering the condition of the Negroes at this period, and the attitudes of many whites toward them, Robinson must have considered Worth's argument a hollow one.

The controversy over apprenticeship dragged on for several weeks, until Worth reviewed the facts in a note to General O. O. Howard, the Commissioner of the Freedmen's Bureau at Washington. Howard then examined the correspondence between Worth and Robinson relative to the case of the Russell apprentices. Although the Commissioner admitted to Robinson that it was their duty to protect the rights of freedmen, he refused to rule that the Russell case showed clearly a disposition of the state courts to discriminate against Negroes in their application of the apprentice laws. Howard took the side of Worth because he felt that Robinson's order returning the administration of justice to the civil courts had abrogated the Bureau's earlier rules on apprenticeship.[41]

Worth won the argument with Robinson when General Howard supported his position, but Mr. Russell's indentures were nullified by the state Supreme Court on the ground that the Negro girls had not been present when the indenture bonds were signed. Unfortunately for the governor, there had been enough irregularity in the actions of the county court to validate Robinson's contention that the proceedings smacked of a reimposition of slavery. And late 1866 was a most unpropitious time for such a thing to happen.

· XVII ·

Opposing the Radicals

───◆───

THE MOST IMPORTANT QUESTION facing North Carolina and the South in the fall of 1866 was whether the Fourteenth Amendment should be ratified or rejected. When the North returned an overwhelming majority of the opponents of the presidential plan of Reconstruction to Congress in the election of 1866, it was apparent that the South would be compelled in one way or another to accept the amendment. But no one—not even the members of Congress—could be quite certain that if a state ratified the amendment it would be allowed to return to the Union. This element of uncertainty was enough in itself to cause southern opposition to the amendment, but the provisions of the proposed change in the Constitution were such that no conservative man devoted to southern principles could accept them. The amendment declared, in effect, that Negroes were citizens and that their rights could not be abridged; that states which denied Negroes the right to vote should have the basis of their representation in Congress reduced; and that no person who had taken an oath to support the Constitution of the United States and then participated in rebellion was eligible to public office, unless Congress removed his disabilities.[1]

Congress submitted the amendment to the states for approval in June, 1866. On July 4, Worth wrote to Benjamin Hedrick: "If three fourths of the States adopt the Howard amendment to the Constitution it may restore a worthless Union. It would be a reunion with mutual detestation and abhorrence between the lately alienated people. . . . I would submit to confiscation or any other calamity which brute force can impose before I would be guilty of the self-degradation of voting for this amendment."[2] Worth still saw public questions in terms of "Union or Disunion," as he had seen them in 1861, but now the disunionists were northern congressmen, not southern secessionists or doctrinaire abolitionists. He still cherished the concept of fraternal

Union, but neither his conscience nor his pride would permit him to approve the principles embodied in the Fourteenth Amendment. Through all his years as a lawyer and as a public servant he had tried to avoid controversy and recriminations and had put into practice the principle that it was never practical to settle a dispute by forcing either party to accept degrading terms. To him the amendment seemed designed to squeeze from the South its remaining self-esteem. He resented especially the provision which would make men like himself, Zebulon Vance, William A. Graham, and others ineligible to hold even the office of constable, while rabid secessionists and war men were not disqualified from office unless they had been public officers before the war.[3]

Worth's views on the Fourteenth Amendment and upon the problem of getting North Carolina back into the Union were more fully matured by the time the legislature met in November. His message was devoted almost entirely to federal affairs and to a lengthy discussion of why the legislature should not ratify the amendment. He defended the president's policy, pointing out that Johnson had been faced with the unprecedented position of having to deal with a situation in which the leaders of a rebellion were still in control of the rebelling states after they had been beaten. After reviewing the five sections of the amendment he stated his objections to it: the Congress proposing it was not properly constituted as long as the South had no representatives there; it was a piece of "omnibus legislation" dealing with too many subjects to be included in one amendment; it left secessionists and Confederate soldiers eligible for office and disqualified the ablest men in the state. "I can perceive in this proposed amendment nothing calculated to perpetuate the Union," Worth said, "but its tendency seems to me better suited to perpetuate sectional alienation and estrangement, and I have . . . no hesitation in recommending that it be not ratified."[4] The legislative committee appointed to examine the amendment submitted a report containing essentially the same objections Worth had stated in his message. On December 13, 1866, the legislature defeated the ratification of the amendment by majorities of forty-five to one in the Senate and ninety-three to ten in the House of Commons.[5]

In his message to the legislature, Worth also expressed the view that universal suffrage was "manifestly absurd" and proposed a "more equal diffusion" of the Negroes by shipping some of them to the North, using funds then appropriated to the Freedmen's Bureau. He suggested that the Assembly propose such a scheme to Congress, but if the legislators took Worth seriously they did not act on his suggestion. The editor of the Richmond *Examiner* did take the proposal seriously and commented favorably upon it, but he noted that the editor of the New York *Tribune*, Horace Greeley, looked at it in an entirely different light: "The New York Tribune is decided and indignant in his [sic] negative of it. It even goes so far as to allege that it is a disguised satire and not a business proposal which Governor Worth propounds. . . . Hence, Mr. Greeley regards Governor Worth as perpetrating an impudent joke."[6] But Jonathan Worth was not in the mood for jokes about a matter as serious as the Negro problem. He made the proposal to redistribute the Negroes in all seriousness, but of course nothing ever came of it.

While the legislature was in session Worth again came into conflict with the military authorities and the Freedmen's Bureau. This time the trouble was over the use of corporal punishment for crimes. In June, 1866, General Daniel E. Sickles had taken command of the military district including North and South Carolina. He had declared the federal and state courts open and discontinued military provost courts, but agents of the Freedmen's Bureau had continued to interfere with the state courts when they sentenced Negroes to corporal punishment.[7] One provision of Sickles' general order declaring the courts open was that "corporal punishment shall not be inflicted upon any person other than a minor. . . ."[8] Worth saw immediately that this provision was in direct conflict with the law of North Carolina, which authorized whipping as the punishment for bigamy, larceny, malicious maiming, and other crimes. Both white men and black had been whipped for many years in North Carolina for the simple reason that the state had no penitentiary. If the military order forbidding corporal punishment were enforced it would deprive the state courts of one of their customary methods of controlling crime.

Worth was not a strong advocate of corporal punishment, and he was not particularly concerned with the substance of the order forbidding it. What disturbed him was the implication that General Sickles should be able to suspend the execution of a state law; the exercise of such a power would assume that the state was under military rule, but the president had declared in August, 1866, that civil law was restored in the South. Worth asked Colonel James V. Bom-

ford, General Robinson's successor as Assistant Commissioner of the
Freedmen's Bureau and Commandant of the state,[9] not to enforce
Sickles' order in North Carolina until he could find out the presi-
dent's views on the matter in question. Bomford, who was almost al-
ways co-operative, promised to suspend the order temporarily and
Worth called upon President Johnson for advice.[10]

Before the president answered Worth's query about the whipping
order, a freedman named David Williams was sentenced in Salisbury
to receive "thirty-nine lashes on the bare back." When Colonel Bomford heard of this sentence he asked Worth to notify the judicial
officers of the state that whippings were no longer authorized. Bomford realized the predicament facing Worth and the judges and hoped
that Worth would use his influence to keep the judges from having
Negroes whipped; but Worth, preferring not to interfere in any way
with the judiciary, sent the home addresses of the judges to Colonel
Bomford and requested that he send copies of the military order directly to them. At the same time Worth confided his personal opinion
of the order forbidding corporal punishment to the Colonel: "General
Sickles had no right to issue these orders, and . . . the judiciary ought
not to obey them."[11]

The disagreement over corporal punishment would have remained
just another episode in Worth's running battle with the Freedmen's
Bureau had it not resulted in the appointment of a commission to
represent the state's interests at Washington when the fate of not only
the state but the entire South hung in the balance. Since the Assembly would have to change the laws of the state if Sickles' order on
corporal punishment were enforced, Worth sent to the legislators his
correspondence relative to the order. A few days earlier the Assembly
had passed a resolution authorizing Worth to send a commission to
Washington "to inquire into the alleged necessity for the order (lately
issued by Genl. Sickles) with a view to remove such necessity. . . ."[12]
The commission was also directed "to correct the misapprehension with
regard to the administration of justice in our state." Finally, the resolution asked Worth to serve as the leader of the commission and authorized him to select his associates.

Ostensibly, the commission was being sent to Washington to secure
the revocation of Sickles' order forbidding corporal punishment, but
its real purpose was to lobby against the overthrow of the state's civil
government. The activities of the commission were in direct response

to efforts by North Carolina Radicals to secure a further reconstruction of the state, and what the commissioners did must be considered against the background of the events transpiring in Washington as Congress met for its winter session of 1866-67.

There was a caucus at William Holden's house in Raleigh on November 28, at which the persons present decided to send a representative to Washington to lobby for abolition of the existing government of North Carolina.[13] Holden himself arrived in Washington on December 8, and took a room at the Ebbitt House with John Pool, D. A. Jenkins, C. L. Harriss, and James F. Taylor. After hearing an impressive performance by Madame Restori at the opera on Saturday night he and the other members of the delegation called on Thaddeus Stevens the next morning. Stevens listened to them for a while and asked them to put their ideas into the form of a restoration bill. It appeared certain to Holden after the conversation with Stevens that "the present State governments will be obliterated. It is only a matter of time."[14] On the day North Carolina refused to ratify the Fourteenth Amendment, Stevens introduced a bill providing for the call of a convention to organize a new government in North Carolina, but the bill died in committee before it reached the floor of the House; it was completely overshadowed and rendered unnecessary by the introduction of a sweeping measure calling for the reconstruction of the entire South.[15]

The best account of the activities of the North Carolina Radicals came from John Pool. Writing to Worth's secretary, William H. Bagley, from a very uncomfortable little steamboat in Currituck Sound, Pool, on his way back from Washington, reported that he had found three points "fully settled" among the Republican leaders in Congress: "1st, That the existing governments in the insurgent states should be superceded—2nd, That those who were engaged in the rebellion should not hold any place under the new governments . . . —and 3rd, That the negroes should vote."[16] There was not yet full agreement among the Republicans on the more radical notions of complete Negro suffrage, disfranchisement of southerners who had participated in the war, imposition of martial law and troops to enforce it, or continued exclusion from representation—to mention only the more prominent of the ideas of reconstruction which were floating in the political atmosphere of Washington as the Congressmen went home for their Christmas vacations.

John Pool was still basically a conservative man, in spite of his affiliation with those who were willing to adopt the position of the Radicals. He confessed that he found "many ultra measures in contemplation," and of these measures the one which frightened him most was the one which would cause the lands of rebels to be sold and distributed among the Negroes. Pool said it was he who had drawn up the special restoration bill for North Carolina and attempted to have the Radicals pass it "as an experiment." The bill was based on white suffrage and would have called a convention to meet in May, 1867, to reorganize the state government; its primary object, according to Pool, was the restoration of the state to its normal relations with the Union. In an effort to secure the introduction and passage of his measure, Pool visited not only Thaddeus Stevens, but Benjamin Wade, Zachariah Chandler, "and others like them." Although Holden and other North Carolinians had been in Washington crying for the overthrow of the existing Southern governments, Pool claimed to be the chief figure in the movement as it pertained to North Carolina. Both Pool and Holden knew that they were damning themselves in the sight of the conservative elements in their native state, but this did not seem to concern them greatly. "If they attack me," Pool threatened, "I intend to attack them with some of the boldest and most dangerous truths . . . that they have ever seen in print, North or South."[17]

The commission Worth appointed to counteract the schemes of Holden, Pool, and their associates included Judge A. S. Merrimon Lewis Hanes, who had been Holden's private secretary, Bedford Brown, Patrick H. Winston, Nathaniel Boyden, and James M. Leach; it was an able group, and the members were all conservative followers of Worth and advocates of the presidential plan of Reconstruction Worth also appointed John A. Gilmer, the former Unionist congressman, but Gilmer was unable to go because of ill health.[18] The commissioners did not go to Washington together, nor did they work as a unit when they arrived there.

Before the commission left North Carolina, Worth himself, accompanied by David L. Swain, the president of the university, and Thomas Ruffin, the former Chief Justice of the Supreme Court, went to Washington. He was certain that he had chosen the best possible men to go with him, for no man was better qualified than Judge Ruffin to achieve the immediate object of the visit, the withdrawal of Sickles general order on corporal punishment. The governor and his venerable associates arrived in Washington on the afternoon of December 15 and took rooms at the Ebbitt House. The town was swarming with public figures from the South who were on missions similar to that of the North Carolinians; there was a great deal of discussion about what was going on in Congress and what, if anything, the South could do about it. Before Worth had been in town twenty-four hours he had been called upon by the governor of Florida, a lobbyist from Texas, and a member of Congress from New Hampshire.[19] Judge Ruffin had conferred with Reverdy Johnson, a moderate member of the Joint Committee on Reconstruction and a former attorney general, and had secured an appointment with Attorney General Henry Stanbery.

Worth, Swain, and Ruffin talked with the president on December 17, about Sickles' order forbidding corporal punishment, and the president promised to consult his cabinet and decide what should be done about the order. The commissioners also gave Johnson a detailed account of the condition of affairs in North Carolina, "including the tone and disposition of the people which they represent, as peaceable and loyal."[20] When Worth and his two colleagues again saw the president two days later, he had decided that both Sickles' order on corporal punishment and interference by the Freedmen's Bureau in apprenticeship cases were not warranted.[21] On December 19, Johnson directed Sickles to issue orders suspending the operation of the sections of his earlier order conflicting with the state laws of North Carolina on apprenticeship and vagrancy.[22] The primary objective of the mission was accomplished.

Worth and Ruffin had a personal interview with General O. O. Howard, the Commissioner of the Freedmen's Bureau. From this interview and from the general tendency of Howard's administration of the Bureau, Worth came to the conclusion that Howard was a fair-minded man who was doing everything he could to allay sectional animosity by attempting to secure justice for all.[23] Judge Ruffin gave Howard a thorough explanation of North Carolina's laws on apprenticeship. Howard then promised Worth that orders would be delivered to agents of the Bureau in North Carolina instructing the agents not to interfere with the state courts when the laws treated whites and Negroes equally. After seeing the president and General Howard, Worth and his colleagues left Washington for home on the evening of December 19.[24]

The governor had to rush back to Raleigh for his second inauguration, on December 22. On the eve of his departure for Washington, he had ordered a new suit for the occasion. It was made of fine cotton cloth presented to Worth by a North Carolina manufacturer, and he hoped it might attract some attention to the quality of material that was being produced in North Carolina. After Worth took the inaugural oath in the House of Commons he excused himself for not preparing a formal address, explaining that he had been too busy in Washington. He told the legislature of the schemes put forward in Washington by Holden and his followers for the further reconstruction of the state, and suggested—as he had in 1861—that the differences between the North and South might best be settled by calling a national convention to amend the constitution. "I trust that I need not assure you," Worth continued, "that no act of mine, official or personal, under any circumstances, will give any countenance to the parricidal scheme of erasing North Carolina from the galaxy of States of the American Union."[25] The governor closed his brief address on a note of optimism: "We still have the Constitution . . . ,' and the state might still rely upon the Supreme Court to give a fair interpretation of it.

On the day after his inauguration, Worth went to Fayetteville to visit his youngest daughter, Mary, who was seriously ill. Early in October, she had taken a chill and a fever on a trip to Washington. Her father allowed her to go visiting in Fayetteville, and there her condition worsened. She died before he could reach her bedside. One of Worth's pages, Perrin Busbee, wrote that Mary was "the idol of the whole family." No one was quite sure what disease had taken her—Busbee thought she had consumption, but the family believed she had diptheria. "Almost the whole of Raleigh" mourned her death, for her cheery disposition had brightened many a gloomy day there. Busbee feared the effects of the death on the governor.[26]

Worth was profoundly grieved by his daughter's death, and he could hardly think of anything else. While he was in Washington with Swain and Ruffin, he had told them of his fears that Mary would never recover. When Swain sent a note of sympathy he replied:

Your kind letter of condolence was received. I cannot as yet recover from the afflicting shock. My lovely and beloved daughter whose life was so free from guile that I cannot remember even to have had occasion to rebuke her, is continually present to my mind, and so enervates me that I can scarcely perform my duties, now so numerous and diversified that I should scarcely be equal to their performance under other circumstances.[27]

While Worth was still suffering from the loss of Mary, he had to start facing another harsh reality, for reports began to come in from the commissioners he had appointed to follow him to Washington. Nathaniel Boyden had been the first to arrive. He and Benjamin Hedrick talked with Senator and Mrs. Henry Wilson of Massachusetts in the senator's room. The conversation was concerned mainly with freedmen, a subject in which Wilson was greatly interested. Boyden had just come off the fall judicial circuit in North Carolina, and he assured Senator Wilson that he could speak with authority on the treatment of Negroes, but Boyden said the wrong thing when he told Wilson that Negroes guilty of serious crimes had been whipped: "Mr. Wilson and lady seemed greatly shocked at the punishment of whipping and seemed wholly unaware of the fact, that we had no penitentiary."[28] The talk turned to Negro suffrage. Wilson was firmly convinced that "if the right of suffrage were given them, they would vote with their Northern friends." Nothing Boyden could say to the senator would convince him that the vote of the Negroes would be controlled by white men. Wilson only laughed at this view.

Before Boyden left Washington, he had a friendly chat with Representatives Dawes and Washburn of Massachusetts and with Senator Wade of Ohio, one of the more extreme of the Radical leaders. Wade had little to divulge of what was passing through the minds of the Radicals, but Boyden got the impression from him and others that the South was to be thoroughly reorganized. "Political power" would be the only object of such a procedure, thought Boyden. There was some prospect that some of the congressmen might "soften up" in their attitudes towards the South during the Christmas holidays— they and their wives had gone on a pleasure trip to hospitable old New Orleans, accompanied by the governor of Mississippi.[29]

The most optimistic report from the Washington commissioners came from J. M. Leach and Bedford Brown. They saw dissension among the Radical leaders as to the policy which should be followed towards the South. The respect with which Brown and Leach were received misled them into believing that the Radicals might become more moderate, but the commissioners informed Worth that even if

Thaddeus Stevens' extreme program were not adopted *in toto,* the South would still have to swallow that bitter pill, the Fourteenth Amendment.[30]

The success of the Radicals' efforts to place the South under military rule again depended to a large extent upon the assumption that law and order, and particularly justice for the freedmen, did not exist in the South. Worth was acutely conscious of this assumption, and he became worried, early in 1867, about several acts of violence and crime in the eastern part of the state. Colonel Allen Rutherford, who had been the central figure in the controversy over apprenticeship, and who was quite assiduous in his defense of the rights of freedmen, reported to Colonel Bomford in February, 1867, that bands of "regulators" were roaming about in Duplin, Sampson, and New Hanover counties, harassing the freedmen and stealing their stock. According to Rutherford, the civil authorities were "unable or unwilling" to stop these depredations by arrests and convictions in the courts.[31]

When Colonel Bomford received Rutherford's report of the conditions in the southeastern district, he brought it to Worth's attention, asking for any suggestion the governor might have to make. Surprisingly, Worth asked Bomford to send troops into the area. Complaints had been coming to him, as well as to the military authorities. In addition to the counties Rutherford had mentioned in his report, Worth indicated to Bomford that the "regulators" were also active in the counties of Onslow, Craven, Pitt, Johnston, and Greene. The difficulty was that neither the civil nor the military authorities could secure the names of the villains. The freedmen were too scared to mention names—and frequently they did not know any because the raiders came from other counties. Since there was no case in which an attempt to serve a warrant had been resisted, Worth was not empowered to use the state militia. In the previous fall, the governor had asked Judge David Barnes to call the outrages to the attention of grand juries so that inquiries could be made, but the grand juries had not taken action. Faced with all these circumstances, which tended to strengthen the contentions of the Radicals, Worth was willing to see federal troops sent into the area, in the hope that their presence would "embolden the parties wronged to expose the malefactors."[32] But the governor was not willing to admit any laxity on the part of the civil authorities in the troubled area.

When Congress reconvened after its Christmas recess, disgruntled persons in North Carolina were sending petitions and memorials to Washington which added color to earlier accounts of persecuted Unionists and mistreated Negroes. A letter in the Raleigh *Sentinel* told of one petition which had been circulated by three Negroes in Lexington and then sent on to Washington. It asked for the overthrow of the state government and the confiscation of the property of those who had fought for the Confederacy in the war.[33] Holden called the writer of the *Sentinel*'s letter a liar, but he admitted—with glaring inconsistency—that the petition, and numerous others like it, had been sent to Congress. The one in question, according to Holden, was signed by eighty-two persons. It did ask Congress "to reorganize the government of North Carolina, and to place it on such a basis as would make treason odious and loyalty respectable."[34] Holden further admitted that the memorialists called for confiscation of property, but he denied that confiscation would be applied to any except the leading rebels. He himself had given the petition from Lexington to Thaddeus Stevens for presentation to the House of Representatives. Throughout the Congressional debate on reconstruction Holden followed the Radical line. When Stevens' plan was being considered, the *Standard* commented that "the passage of this measure will open the way to a speedy settlement of our troubles, and will carry joy to the bosoms of thousands of persecuted Southern Unionists."[35]

Two of the commissioners Worth appointed to represent North Carolina in Washington, Nathaniel Boyden and Lewis Hanes, remained in the capital in consultation with other southern representatives, hoping they could decide upon a course of action. As a last desperate measure, they devised a compromise scheme to avert the passage of a reconstruction act by Congress. In the form of a constitutional amendment, to be substituted for the Congressional version of the Fourteenth Amendment, it omitted the punitive section of the Congressional version and granted limited Negro suffrage. The group also drew up a proposed amendment to the constitutions of the southern states embodying the provisions of the compromise plan.[36] The North Carolina legislature was supposed to lead the way in putting the plan into effect, and on February 21, 1867, Worth wrote to the governor of South Carolina that the "Genl. Assembly are trying to harmonise on the North Carolina plan of compromise. Will probably adopt it soon."[37] But, before the legislature could act, news arrived in Raleigh that Congress had finally agreed on an act to reconstruct the South; all hope of compromise was gone.

The Reconstruction Act of March 2, 1867, and two later acts passed to supplement it, declared that no legal state governments existed in the South and placed all the former Confederate states except Tennessee under military rule. Conventions were to be called in all the states to draw up new constitutions providing suffrage for all males over twenty-one years old who could meet a one-year residence requirement and who had not been disfranchised for participation in the rebellion. Negroes would be allowed to participate in the process of reconstruction, but those whites who had held public office before the war and then supported the Confederacy could neither serve as members of the constitutional conventions nor vote for members. When the new constitutions had been written and approved by Congress, and when the legislatures elected under the new constitutions had ratified the Fourteenth Amendment, the southern states would be admitted to the Union.[38]

When the First Reconstruction Act passed over the president's veto on March 2, Worth held a conference with former governors Graham and Vance, who urged him to go again to Washington. He believed that another trip was necessary "to ascertain as nearly as possible our present status and to decide after the best lights I can obtain, what North Carolina can do, if anything, to avert total ruin."[39] Since David Swain and Thomas Ruffin had been so helpful on the earlier mission to the capital, Worth asked them to go with him, but Ruffin had suffered a violent attack of some ailment and Swain's daughter was ill; neither could go.[40] When Worth arrived in Washington he found that the only inconvenience resulting from the failure of Ruffin and Swain to come with him was that their counsel was not available; he discovered that he could work more effectively alone. He visited the president, the attorney general, Senators Henry Wilson and Reverdy Johnson, and three southern governors. From these conversations he was able to determine what the various views on reconstruction were without committing himself to any definite policy. The idea which appealed to Worth most was to "fall into, and to guide the Revolution."[41] Since Congress had not specified *who* should call the conventions to reconstruct the southern states, Worth assumed that

North Carolina still had some room for political maneuvering, but it was soon made clear that the reconstruction process would be entirely under the control of the military authorities. Seeing that further discussion and inquiry was futile, Worth returned home. William Holden belittled his efforts to determine North Carolina's status, and sourly remarked that he should not have tried: "Our old Quaker ran off to Washington, without taking any action, to find out what he must do, with the act of Congress before his eyes. Dr. Fisher, [an officer of the Lunatic Asylum] ought to cage the whole concern until they become more quiet."[42]

The most immediate and difficult decision Worth had to make after the Reconstruction Act passed was whether he should join in an attempt to have the act declared unconstitutional by the United States Supreme Court. He realized that "the grave question whether we shall bend to the current and try thus to seek partial security—or stem it, and through the Supreme Court, run the hazards of going down with the Court, and suffering confiscation and all the calamities of unbridled democracy, is a fearful responsibility."[43]

In January, he had informed the Council of State that a plan to overthrow the government of North Carolina was before Congress and had expressed his purpose to appeal to the Supreme Court. The council agreed that the Congressional plan would be unconstitutional and advised the governor to bring a test case before the court.[44] Before the First Reconstruction Act passed, Worth had discussed the possibility of a court action with representatives of Alabama and Mississippi.

On March 4, 1867, the Senate of Louisiana met informally and requested that Lieutenant Governor Albert Voorhies communicate with the governors of the other southern states about the possibility of a joint suit to prevent the execution of the First Reconstruction Act. The feeling of the Louisiana senators was that the only chance to head off the Radicals was by a direct plea to the Supreme Court. If a suit were started in an inferior court, the Congressional plan would be in operation before a decision could be reached. Thinking that joint action would be more effective than individual state action, the senators asked Worth for his views on the possibility of joint action.[45]

Worth did not answer immediately, preferring to wait until after a meeting of the Council of State he had called to meet late in March.

Before the Council met, the governor, acting on the suggestion of his most trusted adviser, William A. Graham, asked Benjamin R. Curtis, the former justice of the Supreme Court who had rendered the dissenting opinion in the famous Dred Scott case, for an opinion on two questions. As Curtis phrased them, the questions were: "Whether the First Reconstruction Act is a constitutional law"; and "whether the State of North Carolina can obtain a judicial decree in the Supreme Court of the United States to arrest and restrain the execution of that law." Curtis perceived that the second question was the one which really mattered, for all practical purposes, and he confined his remarks to answering it. Justice Curtis' considered opinion was that the Supreme Court would refuse to entertain a suit by a state seeking to restrain the president from executing a law of Congress.[46] Judge Thomas Ruffin also gave Worth an opinion on the two questions which was basically the same as that of Curtis.

Several persons, including Josiah Turner, Jr., and former governor Thomas Bragg, advised Worth to participate in the joint action before the Supreme Court. Turner advised his friend Worth to face the policy of Congress with "sullen silence" and "masterly inactivity," but said that "I am for *judicial resistance* to the *last*. With the Executive, the Court, God and justice on our side, how could they put this Bill upon us. . . ."[47]

Finally, Worth decided to follow his own inclination and the advice of Graham, Ruffin, and Curtis. When the Council of State met on March 26, he expressed his firm belief that the Reconstruction Acts were unconstitutional, but recommended "that we had better yield obedience to these Acts, and make no attempt to seek the protection of the Supreme Court of the United States."[48] The governor wrote to the lieutenant governor of Louisiana, declining to act jointly with Louisiana and other states in the proposed test case. He reasoned that even if the Supreme Court should uphold an injunction it would take so long to put it into effect that Congress would have time to institute military control, and that if the court should rule adversely, the South's efforts might further antagonize the Radicals and push them to even more extreme measures.[49]

The Reconstruction Act declared the state government provisional, and Worth was uncertain whether he would be allowed to act as governor. The question whether he *should* continue in his position with the state under military rule apparently did not bother him until his brother Milton said, "I cannot see how you are to reconcile it to your feelings to hold your place under the military unless it be to keep Holden or some other dog out of the place. I feel as though republican government had gone up."[50] A few days after Congress declared the state government provisional, Worth ordered enough phosphate and guano to plant sixteen acres of cotton, in order that he might have something to keep himself busy if he were thrown out of office. Patrick Winston urged him strongly that it was important for him to hold his office, and Benjamin Hedrick counseled acquiescence to the act of Congress.[51] With little hesitation, Worth concluded that it would probably be the best thing for the state if he remained in office. "If I say I will not execute the law," he told his son, "it must result in putting the executive power in hands likely to use it more oppressively than I would, without any tendency to avert the evils."[52]

Worth and General Sickles

THE PERIOD OF MILITARY RULE in North Carolina extended from March 21, 1867 to July 2, 1868, and Worth held on to the office of civil governor throughout the entire period. The state government continued to operate as it had before, with the governor and the courts exercising their normal functions; the legislature of 1866-67 adjourned on March 4, and did not meet again. Power lay in the hands of a military ruler, and Worth was in the delicate position of having to represent what he considered to be the interests of the state without antagonizing whatever general happened to be in command of the Second Military District. His moderately conservative mind, his devotion to the principle that a people should be allowed to govern themselves, and his viewpoints as a southerner all made it very painful for him to observe the ideas of the victorious North being imposed by force on his own state and the entire South. A southern governor and a northern general could look at a particular situation and arrive at entirely different conclusions as to what caused it and what should be done about it. Worth could inform the generals of his own opinions, give them advice, and explain North Carolina's laws and institutions to them, but, in the final analysis, that was all he could do to avert the "revolution" which was taking place as the state went through its second reconstruction.

Two generals, Daniel E. Sickles and Edwin R. S. Canby, commanded the Second Military District until North Carolina resumed its normal relations with the federal government. Sickles, who had been in command of the federal troops in North and South Carolina before the Reconstruction Acts were passed, assumed command of the district on March 21, 1867. He issued an order declaring that the civil governments were provisional, but that they would be allowed to exercise their former jurisdiction except in cases where he saw fit to order investigations and trials by military commissions. Local and state laws were to remain in effect unless they conflicted with the Constitution and laws of the United States, proclamations of the president, or orders of the commanding general. Military officials were to report dereliction of duties by the civil authorities, and post commanders could make arrests if state and local officials failed to act promptly when action was needed. The order by which Sickles assumed command of the state and laid down the outlines of his policy included a plea for obedience, co-operation, and zealous execution of the laws in force.[1]

Soon after Sickles assumed control, he invited Worth to come to Charleston for a conference on conditions in North Carolina. Worth made the visit, sharing the hospitality of Sickles' home, and from the time of his visit he remained in the good graces of the general. In the meeting, Sickles agreed that Worth and Governor Orr, of South Carolina, should continue to make appointments to which they were entitled, and that Sickles would appoint officers who were normally elected by the people.[2] A specific case arose and the policy on appointments became clearer when the office of sheriff in Randolph County became vacant because the sheriff had failed to renew his bonds at the February term of the county court. There was some uncertainty as to whether the office should be filled by an appointee of General Sickles. According to Worth's interpretation of the Reconstruction Acts, they did not deny civil authorities the power to fill vacancies, but he consulted Sickles before informing his friends in Randolph what they should do.[3] In this matter, as in most others, Sickles proved to be lenient. He allowed the civil authorities the power of appointment to which they were normally entitled, but his ruling was subject to this limitation: no person should be appointed to civil office who was disqualified under the third article of the Fourteenth Amendment; consequently, new appointees had to be able to swear that they had never held a public office and afterwards participated in the rebellion.[4] In a sense, Worth had more power than he had exercised before the state went under military rule, for Sickles asked him to recommend appointees to almost all the offices which became vacant, and his nominees were usually appointed. One interesting exception came when the Bank of Lexington went into receivership. Worth recommended the Clerk and Master in Equity of Davidson County as the receiver, but Sickles, acting on the advice of the commanding officer in Greensboro, appointed someone else.[5] The case of the receivership also gives some idea of the extent to which military authority was exercised.

Sickles governed his district by issuing what amounted to a code of laws in the form of military orders. An order would be sent out to the post commanders, and within a few days after it appeared in the newspapers, Worth would start receiving inquiries about what the order meant. General Order Number Ten is a case in point. Designed to relieve the people of the district from a serious economic situation, it was admittedly an extraordinary measure, but the circumstances seemed to demand it. The conditions which the general order was designed to remedy were listed in the preamble: there was an unusually large number of debtors; grain and produce crops had failed in the summer of 1866; many families were without adequate shelter and clothing; and the inability of some persons to pay their taxes made it impossible for the counties to raise relief funds. General Order Number Ten was a sincere attempt to mitigate the severity of these circumstances. Basically, it was a stay law which suspended the execution of judgments in cases involving contracts made between December 19, 1860 and May 15, 1865. The order also provided a homestead exemption for families and crop liens for laborers; reaffirmed the earlier order against corporal punishment; substituted hard labor for death as the penalty for burglary and larceny; and declared that Worth and Governor Orr still possessed their normal pardoning power.[6]

Sickles "legislated" on a variety of subjects. When a military order on distilling went out one citizen plaintively wrote to Worth: "Does Genl Sickels order prohibit the distilling [of] fruit and a beverage made from soaking honeycomb after it has been squeased."[7]

Such fundamental and sweeping decrees as General Order Number Ten inevitably caused consternation and confusion in North Carolina, particularly among those who were responsible for the execution of the laws. The solicitor of Granville County told Worth that the homestead exemption made it virtually impossible to collect fines and forfeitures; property up to five hundred dollars was exempt from seizure by the courts, and most offenders were poor whites or Negroes who did not have enough property to make them subject to a fine or forfeiture.[8] Two attorneys in Raleigh sent Worth a long set of legal questions about General Order Number Ten. The following samples are typical:

> In North Carolina, highway robbery, which is Larceny from the person committed on the highway . . . is punished with death. Is such punishment prohibited by Section 14?
> Does Section 5 apply to actions for the recovery of money upon contracts the consideration for which was the hire of negroes for one or more years?
> Does Section 2 apply to the action of ejectment?[9]

Worth had neither the time nor the authority to interpret the law in answer to the many queries he received. He sent the inquiries on to General Sickles, who never gave detailed explanations of his orders, but left it to the civil courts to interpret them and to impose sentences when they had been violated.

There was considerable doubt in Worth's mind as to whether he could pardon a man convicted under the provisions of a military order by a state court. This doubt was resolved in the case of Ruffin Hatch, a seventeen-year-old Negro who had been convicted under General Order Number Ten and sentenced to two years in prison for stealing forty-two dollars. Two months after Hatch's conviction, his attorney petitioned Worth for a pardon. Worth then asked Sickles whether he would be permitted to pardon Hatch. The general's answer referred Worth to the paragraph of General Order Number Ten which specified that the governor could pardon anyone convicted in a civil court, but did not mention whether this included convictions under a military order. Sickles ruled that the order contemplated the application of the pardoning power "in cases where sentences are imposed by the ordinary criminal courts in conformity with the directions of military orders."[10] The effect of this ruling was that Worth could nullify Sickles' orders by the application of his pardoning power, if the orders were enforced in the state courts.

One section of General Order Number Ten forbade the carrying of arms by anyone except military personnel. The mayor of Raleigh protested to Worth that it was impossible to enforce the civil law if policemen, night watchmen, and persons in similar positions could not arm themselves. Farmers also needed guns to drive away squirrels from their corn; the rice bird was still another problem. Worth asked Sickles to modify the order banning firearms, in view of the obvious need for exceptions to its provisions, but the general did not respond favorably.[11]

The order forbidding civilians to carry firearms represented an effort to reduce the high crime rate in North and South Carolina. Conditions were so bad in Lenoir County that Worth had to order a special court of oyer and terminer to deal with the situation there.[12] Twelve or fifteen of the worst desperadoes in the county were rounded up and placed in the county jail. Worth, fearing that their accomplices might break the jail and release them, and unable to place an armed guard around the jail because Sickles forbade the carrying of arms, asked the commander at Raleigh to have the jail guarded by military personnel.[13] This type of situation made it necessary for Sickles to take firm control over the peace officers of North Carolina and the system of controlling lawlessness.

The First Reconstruction Act, in addition to outlining a plan of restoration to the Union, declared that "it shall be the duty of each officer . . . to protect all persons in their rights of persons and property . . . and to punish, or cause to be punished, all disturbers of the public peace and criminals." Sickles chose to allow the civil authorities the opportunity to secure law and order, but he also created provost courts throughout his district. One of these courts was particularly distasteful to Worth, who lamented its existence on several occasions. It was established in May, 1867, to try cases arising in the post of Fayetteville, which embraced Cumberland, Harnett, Moore, Montgomery, and Richmond counties. The jurisdiction of the court included cases not covered by the articles of war, excluding murder, manslaughter, rape, and arson; these more serious offenses were to be tried in the regular civil courts, unless the post commander at Fayetteville saw fit to employ a military commission.[14] Worth's main objection to the court, aside from the fact that it had no basis in the state law, was that it consisted of three judges "having no pretension to legal learning." He told one friend that "I regard this Court as more of a burlesque on justice, than the celebrated Court held by Sancho Panza."[15] Worth asked Sickles to abolish the court, but his plea was unsuccessful.

The problem of corporal punishment cropped up again during the summer of 1867 and resulted in an effort to establish a penitentiary for the state. Worth had proposed in his message to the legislature of 1866-67 that a penitentiary be established; a joint committee reported favorably, but no action was taken to implement Worth's suggestion.[16] The legislature adopted the alternative solution of having convicts sentenced to hard labor on chain gangs instead of being whipped or pilloried. The penitentiary question appeared again when Sickles reaffirmed in General Order Number Ten that corporal punishment should not be used and state judges refused to sentence vagrants to hard labor with ball and chain because they felt that shackling with a ball and chain amounted to corporal punishment. What could a sheriff do with a man sentenced to hard labor? Worth thought the judges' interpretation that ball and chain labor was corporal punishment was farfetched, and he told General Sickles as much: "The confinement by ball and chain is not the 'punishment' but the means necessary to compel the convict to submit to the 'punishment,' which is *hard labor.*" [17]

On August 1, 1867, Sickles ordered the formation of a board "to consider and report upon the expediency, practicability, and cost of providing a suitable temporary place of confinement for prisoners undergoing sentence for felony."[18] The board, consisting of Worth, the state treasurer, and four members of the legislature, met in Worth's office and took steps to find out from the county court clerks how many felons were confined throughout the state and how many were to be tried at the next court term. The group had trouble settling on how much a temporary central prison would cost. There was also the problem of finding a suitable location. Worth strongly favored a site on Deep River near the coal and iron mines there, but this place was so inaccessible that it was not suitable for a temporary prison.[19] The board had made a start towards the establishment of a penitentiary when Sickles was relieved of command and the project had to be dropped.

Worth and Sickles worked closely together in their efforts to guard the interests of the people of North Carolina, and the two men found it easy to keep their personal relations on an amicable basis, but by June, 1867, Worth was firmly convinced that Sickles was exercising more authority than he possessed. In an effort to prove to President Johnson that the general had exceeded his authority, Worth made a detailed analysis of the Reconstruction Act of March 2, 1867. "What then is the power of the military under the Sherman Bill," he asked.[20] "Is it absolute, as is generally supposed, over the civil government in the states or is it restricted, as I think it is, to the preservation of 'peace and order,' and *to that end,* to the investigation of crime and the punishment of criminals?" Worth employed a simple analogy to illustrate his view of the nature of the power of the military commanders: if someone stole a horse, Sickles could investigate the matter, but if the same person claimed a horse, the general should have nothing to do with the case. Neither should he concern himself with civil rights nor tamper with purely civil courts.

Worth's views were based on a close reading of the First Reconstruction Act, a law to which he probably devoted more thought than he did to any other piece of legislation he encountered in his political career. He perceived that the preamble did not declare the state government nonexistent, but merely stated that no "*legal* state government" existed. This hairsplitting distinction in Worth's mind was the central feature of his thinking about the great legal problem that was Reconstruction, for his argument rested on the theory that the act had legalized the state government by making it, in effect, an agency of the United States government: ". . . our government is not the government of North Carolina, but the government of the United States in North Carolina;—and the Executive is a United States officer and the courts in the state are United States courts. . . ." How then could the military power, personified by General Sickles, interfere with the state government, except in those particulars specified by Congress? One section of the Reconstruction Act seemed to Worth to forbid any interference with the existing government except by the "paramount authority of the United States"; and, in the thinking of Jonathan Worth, the military was not the paramount authority.

Having finished his somewhat abstruse, but very clever—and probably unsound—analysis of the Reconstruction Act, Worth summarized both his views and the actions of Sickles which had brought them into being:

> I do not think that Congress intended to invest General Sickles with power to provide who shall be jurors in our civil courts, or who shall not ride together, or how rent shall be paid, or to compel crops to be impounded and kept until they rot or are stolen, or that a debt contracted in North Carolina on the 19th December, 1860 shall not be paid because South Carolina seceded on the 18th. . . .[21]

Worth's opinion on the extent of Sickles' power was perhaps a bit strained, but it was not much different from a similar one of a more official character written by the Attorney General of the United States, Henry Stanbery. Stanbery opined that Sickles had "no authority to enact or declare a new code of laws for the people within his district under any idea that he can make a better code than the people have made for themselves."[22] The attorney general believed that Sickles had placed himself in a position equal to that of Congress when he issued his General Order Number Ten. When Stanbery's opinion appeared, Sickles requested that he be relieved from command and demanded that a court of inquiry be convened to investigate his actions,[23] but the president turned down his requests. A few days after Stanbery delivered his opinion on the first two Reconstruction Acts, Congress removed all doubt about the power of the military commanders by declaring that the state governments "were to be continued subject in all respects to the military commanders . . ." and by making it perfectly clear that the commanders had power to appoint and remove civil officers in their respective districts.[24]

Worth was not the only North Carolinian in a high public office who resented Sickles' application of his broad authority. A serious situation arose in July, 1867, when Judge Augustus S. Merrimon resigned because he believed it would be inconsistent with his official oath to enforce military orders which conflicted with the state law. Worth at first refused to accept the resignation, fearing that other judges might follow Merrimon's lead, and hoping he could induce Merrimon to reconsider his decision. He informed Sickles of the resignation and asked the general to come to Raleigh for a conference with all the judges, in an effort to reconcile the differences between the civil and military law and to prevent further resignations. Sickles could not come to the proposed meeting, but he advised Worth to call the Council of State and choose a successor for Merrimon if the judge did not withdraw his resignation; the new judge would have to be eligible under the Reconstruction Acts. Upon receipt of Sickles' telegram declining to come to Raleigh, Worth called a special meeting of the Council of State and asked all the superior and Supreme Court judges to meet in Raleigh. After the Council and the judges met with Worth, he accepted Merrimon's resignation and appointed a new judge. Sickles approved both the resignation and the new appointment.[25]

Sickles interfered with the courts in many ways, but the act which aroused more of Worth's conservative ire than any other was General Order Number Thirty-Two, requiring that all persons, including Negroes, who had been assessed for taxes and had paid taxes during the current year should be placed on the jury lists. The state law, which had been drawn in the days when the propertied interests still dominated the state, allowed the county justices to place only the names of freeholders on the jury lists. Worth was convinced that the amount of property a man had accumulated was one of the best indices to his fitness for public service of any kind, and he was horrified at Sickles' jury order, but he probably spoke more for himself than for the people when he told President Johnson that "I need not describe the horror of our people at the idea of having their character, lives, and property in the keeping of juries thus constituted."[26]

Shortly before the September terms of court were scheduled to begin, two judges on the way to their circuits informed Worth that the commandant at Raleigh had instructed them that courts could not be held unless the juries were selected according to General Order Number Thirty-Two. Worth immediately notified Sickles that the fall terms would not be able to meet because the new jury lists had not been made. According to the general order, all who had paid taxes in the current year were supposed to be included on the jury list. But since the fiscal year did not end until September 30, and the sheriffs did not submit tax returns until after October 1, it had been impossible to revise the jury lists.[27] Sickles accepted this explanation and immediately suspended the relevant section of his jury order. The juries for the fall terms of court in 1867 were to be selected as they formerly had been.[28]

The governor would not leave well enough alone. After Sickles suspended the jury order, Worth asked if he had intended to abrogate the state law providing that only freeholders could serve on juries. He expressed his contempt for the idea that all men who paid a poll tax should be eligible to serve on juries: "If your order is intended to let into the jury box all who shall have paid a poll tax, vast numbers of white men will be made eligible [who are] by no means fit to serve as jurors."[29] The governor said he had no objection if Sickles meant to make Negroes eligible who were "otherwise qualified." In short, Worth wanted jurors to be property owners, not the lowest classes on men without land. His objection to the jury order was clearly based on the anti-democratic attitude he had held ever since the days of Andrew Jackson, the attitude which caused him to oppose "unbridled democracy" in the form of Negro suffrage or any other innovation which threatened to place men of radical proclivities in control of the state government.

When General Sickles began putting into operation the plan of reconstruction outlined by Congress in March, 1867, Worth worked closely with him, particularly during the time when the voters were being registered. Both Worth and General Nelson A. Miles, the Assistant Commissioner of the Freedmen's Bureau, had their ideas as to how the registrars were to be selected. Worth suggested that the prominent men in each county be allowed to recommend the registrars, who would in turn recommend election officials.[30] Miles's plan was for agents of the Freedmen's Bureau to suggest three persons "in each election district of their respective sub-districts" to serve as registrars. One of the three was to be a Negro, one could be an agent of the Bureau or a former officer in the Union army, and one should be a native who could take the test oath required by the Reconstruction Acts.[31] Worth naturally was opposed to Miles's plan. He pointed out to General Sickles that there was "no such thing in this state as election districts of defined boundaries," as Miles apparently assumed there were. Persons could vote in any place designated as a poll within their own counties. The governor frowned also upon the use of Negroes for registrars, on the ground that most of them were illiterate. Sickles had not intimated to Worth that Negro registrars would be used, and Worth suspected, correctly, that Miles had taken the initiative in requiring their use.[32]

Sickles chose to follow Worth's plan of selecting registrars, and he asked Worth to recommend three men from each county. On April 20, Worth sent a circular to each county asking the names of suitable persons for him to recommend as registrars. Most respondents said they would make recommendations as soon as they could find suitable persons. The election officials had to be able to take the test oath, and in some cases it was hard to find three persons who could take it. From Enfield came word that "I do not know a single man of character in the county who could accept the position of register," but two weeks later three persons were suggested.[33] One of Worth's conservative friends, B. S. Gaither, preferred that the soldiers in the occupation force act as registrars. He supposed that if "Southern Loyalists" got control of the registration they would exclude what he considered true southern men.[34] Daniel L. Russell, the central figure in the apprenticeship controversy, asked Worth to recommend a carpetbagger from his county as a registrar "if being a register would prevent his being a candidate" for the constitutional convention.[35] Former governor Henry T. Clark recommended as registrars for Edgecombe County the local agent of the Freedmen's Bureau, a former lieutenant colonel in the Union army, and a local merchant.

When General Miles issued his circular to his agents directing them to recommend registrars, several of the men appointed by Worth to recommend qualified persons declined to nominate anyone until they could secure an explanation. Worth could give none. He asked Sickles if Miles's circular had been authorized and insisted that the plan to put a Negro on every registration board would be most unsatisfactory.[36] Sickles replied that Miles's actions did not have his official sanction, and he sustained Worth in his view that the best men should be appointed to the registration boards, whether they were Negroes or not. At the same time, Sickles suggested that the appointment of "such colored men as may be found competent and worthy would tend to promote confidence and good feeling among the freed people. . . ."[37] No Negroes applied to Worth to be put on the registration boards, but a few were nominated by Worth's agents in the counties; these he included among the names he sent to Sickles. By the first week in June, he had sent his nominations for all but three counties to Charleston. Sickles appointed them and they became the official registrars for the election. The recommendation of registrars gave Worth his only opportunity to participate in the process of reconstruction; he was not eligible to vote because he had been a public officer before the war.

Before the registration began in North Carolina, Attorney General Stanbery delivered an opinion in which he discussed the power of the registrars and placed very narrow limits on the extent to which persons could be disfranchised by the provisions of the Reconstruction Acts.[38] The opinion stirred up so many questions about the details of the reconstruction process that Sickles reported to the Adjutant General that it was "not expedient to commence registration in this district until it shall be finally determined who may be registered."[39] Congress soon cleared up the questions about the power of the election officials and the test oath when it passed the Third Reconstruction Act, but Sickles postponed the date for the completion of registration because the dire economic conditions in North and South Carolina made it necessary for the people to "lay by" their crops before they became involved in the registration and election process.

Early in August Worth issued another circular, this one explaining the Third Reconstruction Act and strongly urging everyone who was eligible to register and vote for delegates to the constitutional convention. He warned both whites and blacks not to consolidate against each other, reminded the people of the crucial issues to be voted upon, and emphasized that registration was essential; no one could vote on the new constitution unless he registered for the election to determine whether a convention should be called. Neglect or refusal to register Worth called "a voluntary surrender of the right to take part in governmental affairs."[40]

Worth's relations with General Sickles came to a rather abrupt end before the registration was completed. President Johnson removed Sickles on August 27, 1867, for refusing to obey a writ of habeas corpus issued by a federal judge to four civilians who had been convicted for murdering three of Sickles' soldiers.[41] Sickles had also sustained the commandant of the post at Wilmington when the commandant refused to allow a United States marshal to enforce a judicial decree issued by Judge Salmon P. Chase in a case heard before the United States Circuit Court at Raleigh in June, 1867.[42] When Sickles departed, Worth was left to face General Edwin R. S. Canby, a stolid professional soldier whom the governor soon came to regard "as an unostentatious and candid Radical."[43]

· XIX ·

Worth and General Canby

WHEN GENERAL CANBY replaced Sickles, Worth offered to assist the new commander in any way he could and expressed the hope that their official relations would be mutually agreeable. Canby thanked him for the offer and expressed a similar desire: "I hope also to make our intercourse as agreeable to you as it will certainly be useful to me."[1] Canby left Washington for his new assignment, planning to visit the capitals of the states composing his district for conferences with Worth and Governor Orr, but when he discovered that the pressure of his duties would confine him at first to Charleston he asked Worth to make "any suggestions in relation to matters of interest in your state which you may think it proper to make."[2] This polite exchange marked the beginning of a relationship which was conducted with mutual courtesy, candor, and respect. Worth never understood nor liked Canby as well as he did Sickles, for Canby neither sought nor followed his advice as frequently as Sickles had. Then there was the fact that Canby had a long background as a professional soldier, while Sickles had been a politician at heart. Yet, in spite of a certain lack of rapport between the governor and the general, they stayed on relatively good terms, and Worth still wielded considerable influence in the affairs of the state he had been elected to govern.

Soon after Canby took command, Worth asked him to consider "a few suggestions touching the orders of Genl. Sickles, several of which I think ought to be revoked or essentially modified." He then criticized Sickles' jury order, especially calling attention to the fact that it conflicted with North Carolina's traditional freehold provision. The provost court in Fayetteville, consisting entirely of civilians untrained in the law, Worth branded "the most extraordinary tribunal ever established in this country for the administration of justice." He asked that the court be abolished, or that he be allowed to submit evidence showing that it was useless. Finally, Worth criticized Sickles' stay law, on the grounds that North Carolina had one of its own; he admitted, however, that many people in the state approved the sections of General Order Number Ten which embodied the stay law.[3]

Canby refused to abolish the provost court, and he did not modify the jury order until later, but he apparently devoted a great deal of time and thought to Worth's criticism of the stay law. He prepared and sent to Worth an extremely able defense of the stay order, and he refused to revoke it. Many arguments, both for and against the stay law, had poured into the headquarters at Charleston. From these letters Canby summarized for Worth the main objections to the law: it was unnecessary because state legislation had been passed; it was unequal and worked imperfectly in particular cases; and it was unconstitutional, impairing the obligation of contracts. Canby pointed out that there was some question as to the validity of the act passed by North Carolina and that there would probably have been a disastrous number of court cases under it if Sickles had not provided relief for debtors. With regard to the second major objection—that the stay order operated unequally—Canby admitted the validity of the argument, but noted that inequalities "would naturally follow the application of any rules to a great extent of territory and a great diversity of interests," whether they were under civil or military control.[4] He promised to modify General Order Number Ten in such a way as to remove the inequalities against North Carolina which stemmed from the fact that the order was based primarily on conditions in South Carolina. As to the question of the constitutionality of the military stay law, that was left for the civil courts to decide. While admitting that the order had been misapplied in some instances, Canby declined to revoke it, on the ground that it had been issued only in the face of "exceptional circumstances and a controlling necessity."[5] It became apparent to Worth from his early exchanges of views with Canby that his policies would differ very little from those of Sickles, and there was, in fact, no basic change.[6]

A revealing episode in Worth's relations with General Canby occurred during the last three months of 1867 after the sheriff of Caswell County, Jessie Griffith, was arrested by the military authorities and taken to Charleston to be tried before a military commission.

This was by no means an isolated case of arrest and trial by the military, but it was the one which placed the most severe strains on Worth's efforts to control his indignation towards the existence of a military government. It resulted in the longest and most impassioned plea against what he considered "military despotism," and, more important, it was a clear example of the tragic misunderstanding and divergence of viewpoint between civil and military authorities in the Reconstruction period, and between a conservative and one who was inclined to support the Congressional position. For these reasons, "The Case of the Caswell County Sheriff" is an excellent case study in the details of military government and in Worth's attitude towards it.

The case originated in 1864, when one William Johnson, a Union scout, and two others, held up a farmer and took enough provisions to enable them to reach the Union lines. After the war a civil court in Caswell County convicted Johnson of constructive burglary and sentenced him to death. The Johnson trial first came to the attention of the military authorities in April, 1867, when Albion W. Tourgée gave General Sickles a carpetbagger's version of the facts in the case.[7] A month later Worth pardoned Johnson, and Sickles paid no more attention to the case, but in October, 1867, Canby's judge advocate took up the matter where Tourgée had left off. He investigated the circumstances surrounding the arrest and trial of William Johnson and wrote a report which outlined the basic facts and gave the military version of why the sheriff of Caswell County was eventually arrested: "So soon as Johnson was convicted, in the Superior Court, he was thrust into jail, chained down in an iron cage, nine feet square by six feet high, without fire or sufficient clothing, or any means of warmth, during the winter season, in which condition he was forced to remain until about the sixth day of May 1867, when he was released upon an absolute pardon, granted by Gov. Worth. . . ."[8] According to the judge advocate, the judge had admitted as evidence in the trial Johnson's activities in guiding General Stoneman's raid into North Carolina, and his remarks against secessionists, including his desire that all secessionists should be dead and in Hell. The solicitor who prosecuted Johnson and secured his conviction had been the commanding officer of the North Carolina regiment which the defendant had deserted before he became a Union scout. The judge advocate concluded his report with a recommendation that the sheriff

who had incarcerated Johnson in jail should be arrested and tried by
a military commission for cruel treatment of a prisoner,[9] and the
sheriff soon found himself awaiting trial in Charleston.

Worth wrote a long letter to the president concerning the arrest
in which he discussed the case and made the generalizations that military arrests had been frequent;[10] that these arrests were made without
confronting the accused persons with their accusers; that defendants
were taken far from home for trial and incarcerated for months in military prisons. Often, according to Worth's somewhat exaggerated account, arrests had been made on the basis of affidavits from persons
"of bad character."[11] Some of Worth's generalizations were based
upon a case which had arisen in the summer of 1867, when his friend
Duncan G. McRae, a magistrate from Fayetteville, had been tried and
acquitted before a military commission at Raleigh. McRae had been
taken to Fort Macon and held for two months without bail or information of the charge against him, but at his trial the evidence against
him proved so flimsy that the charge was dropped.

The president handed Worth's complaint to General Grant, who
was Canby's superior, and Grant passed it on to Canby. Canby then
gave Grant the military authorities' side of the Caswell County case
in a heavily documented report. He explained that he had arrested
the sheriff upon the complaint of Albion W. Tourgée, whose statements seemed entitled to some consideration because he had once been
the judge advocate of the Fourteenth Army Corps; upon the report
of the lieutenant who investigated Tourgée's complaint; upon the
reports of Canby's provost marshal and judge advocate; and, finally,
upon transcripts of the record of William Johnson's trial in the superior court of Caswell County. With all this evidence before him,
Canby ordered the arrest of the sheriff, "as one of the agents of the
injustice and oppression that has [sic] been practiced upon Johnson"
because he was a former Union scout.[12]

Having explained to General Grant why he arrested the sheriff of
Caswell County, Canby then made a defense of the manner in which
the military trial was conducted. The prisoner was carried to
Charleston—"not thirty-six hours from his home"—because he could
secure a quicker trial there than anywhere else, a commission being
convened there at the time of the arrest. He was released once and
allowed to return home, and once the trial was postponed until a wit-

ness for the defense could get time off from his work. While on the subject of trials, Canby pointed out the legal errors in the trial of William
Johnson, the proceeding which had resulted in the arrest of the sheriff.
In the first place, Johnson was tried for an offense committed during
the war under an indictment drawn by a grand jury "of a court whose
process ran in the name of a hostile government"; consequently, the
indictment was invalid.[13] Furthermore, the two men with Johnson
when he committed his crime had been convicted for larceny during
the war and pardoned on the condition that they join the Confederate
army, whereas Johnson was tried after the war for constructive burglary and sentenced to death. Canby's explanation to Grant was a
severe indictment of the civil courts of North Carolina, and Worth
was never able to deny the specific facts on which it was based.

Canby felt that the whole trouble in this business of persecuting
Union men was that the general amnesty act passed by the North
Carolina legislature in December, 1866, was not well drawn. According to the general's interpretation, the act offered adequate protection for persons who had been in the regular Union forces, but it did
not extend similar protection to guides, spies, and guerillas. Canby
now accused the legislature of "ingenious omissions" in writing the
law and the North Carolina courts of "ingenious constructions" in
executing it.[14] The implication was that William Johnson, whose arrest and conviction had resulted in the proceedings against the Caswell County sheriff, had been the victim of a defective amnesty act.
Canby closed his long explanation to General Grant with a denial of
Worth's imputations against military justice as it was practiced in the
Second Military District:

Charges of military despotism are easily made, and if they are accompanied by specific allegations are as easily disproved, but to a
charge so vague and indefinite as that now made by the Governor I can
only state that military arrests are not made without previous investigation or without strong evidence of guilt; that prisoners are not
"transported to distant places of confinement and detained for months
without preliminary trial. . . ." If a speedy trial has not always been
secured, it has been delayed in the interests of the accused, and that
when trials have been protracted it has resulted from the unusual
latitude allowed the prisoners in conducting their defense.

After his report had gone in to Washington, Canby furnished Worth
with a copy of it. Naturally, Worth had to make a reply, and he was

able to answer Canby fairly effectively. He had to start with an apology for making insinuations against Canby in his letter to the president on the matter of the Caswell County sheriff. It was essential that Worth stay on good terms with the general, and his apology was necessary— it was also sincere—but the ground of apology was not the solidest footing for a legal argument. Worth denied that he had meant to accuse Canby of using his authority "oppressively or unjustly," realizing that he had acted according to the practices of regular military justice. But Jonathan Worth could never quite understand what "justice" meant to a military man: "It is natural that each of us should have his partiality for the rules of administering justice to which we have been accustomed—your practice having been in the *military*—mine in the *civil* courts of the country."[15] Even so, there were certain personal safeguards which should be observed "by every tribunal administering criminal justice," whether civil or military. These safeguards had not been used in the proceedings against the sheriff of Caswell County. As to the character of the witnesses against the sheriff—and here Worth had in mind Albion W. Tourgée —Worth made no effort to prove them "bad" men, but said he had never heard anything good about them. The governor knew nothing to warrant Canby's allegation that William Johnson had been prosecuted because he was a Union man. Neither had he received any complaints from any citizen that North Carolina's amnesty act was drawn in such a way as to discriminate against Union men; if anyone had been victimized by the act, Worth would have pardoned him, as he had pardoned William Johnson. In reply to Canby's statement that if Johnson had been executed under a conviction by an "illegal" grand jury it would have been murder, Worth proved that the jury was not illegal. He cited an ordinance of the state convention of 1865 which validated the judicial proceedings of the war years. Worth admitted that if Johnson was in reality tried for leading General Stoneman's army into North Carolina, the judge, the jury, and the prosecutor should have been punished; but why the sheriff—a "mere ministerial officer"? Canby never answered this question, which struck at the heart of the case. All the general ever said was that the sheriff was arrested for political persecution of a former Union soldier. To Jonathan Worth such an explanation could never suffice, but he did realize that Canby was acting from a "conscientious conviction of duty," and he continued to respect the general, even while disagreeing wholeheartedly with him.[16]

Throughout the period of military rule Worth continued to defend North Carolina and its institutions against what he thought were unwarranted interventions, but he never openly opposed the process of reconstruction outlined by Congress in the Reconstruction Acts. One section of the acts made it the duty of the district commanders "to remove from office . . . all persons . . . who use their official influence in any manner to hinder, delay, prevent, or obstruct" the reconstruction process.[17] When Worth saw this provision, he realized he would have to maintain a political silence if he were to keep the office of governor. He was of course intensely interested in what the outcome of North Carolina's reconstruction would be, and in private correspondence he frequently stated his objections to a program which he knew would culminate in Negro suffrage, Republican rule, and his removal from office.

Most of the eligible voters in the state had been registered by the middle of October, 1867. On the eighteenth, Canby issued an order declaring that an election would be held on November 19 and 20, at which the voters would decide whether a constitutional convention should be called; a majority of those registered had to vote before the election would be valid. One hundred and twenty delegates to the convention were to be chosen at the election.[18] The total number of registered voters was 174,717;[19] 103,060 of these were white men, and 71,657 were Negroes.[20]

Six months before the election, North Carolina had become a two-party state. The Republican party was organized at a meeting in Raleigh on March 27, 1867,[21] and by November, it had developed into a highly efficient organization consisting of almost all the Negroes in the state and those whites who were willing to follow the Congressional plan of reconstruction. William Holden was the acknowledged leader and chief spokesman of the Republican party, but the best statement of the kind of thinking which caused white North Carolinians to join the Republican ranks came from Thomas Settle, a former Democrat who realized that the Civil War had wrought great changes. Speaking to a crowd of both whites and Negroes in Rockingham County shortly after the formation of the new party, Settle discussed most of the basic issues which separated a Republican from

Conservatives like Jonathan Worth, William A. Graham, and other old Whigs. Some Conservatives professed to fear that their property would be confiscated if the Republicans came into power. Settle vigorously denied that the Republicans, as a party, favored confiscation, but he admitted that individual party members such as Thaddeus Stevens had given the impression that they did. He realized that "there has been a general breaking up of the old ideas and we are now taking a new start in the world"; the South should acknowledge the existence of a changed situation and make the best of it. "Yankees and Yankee notions are just what we want in this country," continued Settle. "We want their capital to build factories, and work shops, and railroads, and develop our magnificent water powers." The Republican spokesman counseled friendship between the races, and commented on the Congressional plan of reconstruction: "It seems to me to be madness and folly to oppose it."[22] Advocating ideas similar to those expounded by Thomas Settle, the Republicans were determined to elect their candidates to the constitutional convention. The Union League managed to organize most of the Negroes for the Republicans, and Holden called upon the white working men to throw out the aristocrats and slaveholders who had dominated the state as far back as men could remember.[23] Three weeks before the election a highly confident Republican carpetbagger, John T. Deweese, predicted that "we will carry two thirds of the Convention and Cary all the state by twenty or thirty thousand Majority."[24]

Worth naturally was opposed to the Republicans, and his views were typical of the attitude of most Conservatives. He did not believe a state should be forced to alter its fundamental laws in obedience to a Congressional fiat that conflicted with the Constitution of the United States. Believing that a government based upon universal Negro suffrage would be founded "upon ignorance instead of intelligence—even if there were no disfranchisement of white men," he felt that all men who were opposed to Negro suffrage and the punitive feature of the Fourteenth Amendment should vote against the call of a constitutional convention.[25] His only hope was that the Conservatives could defeat the call of the convention by refusing to vote for or against it. Since a majority of the registered voters had to vote in order for the election to be valid, Worth advised his family and friends not to vote on the question whether a convention should be held, but to vote for Conservative delegates. This was the strategy adopted by the leaders of the Conservatives, but many among the rank and file of the party apparently did not understand how they could defeat the convention by refusing to vote. Worth's son-in-law, J. J. Jackson, said to his wife Lucy shortly before the election, ". . . you may say to the Govr. that we can't quite see how *not voting at all* on the convention question will be more certain to kill off the convention than voting against it."[26] David Worth wrote his father from Wilmington that the Conservatives there seemed "cowed," and were so hopeless of victory that they were making no efforts to defeat the call of the convention and the election of Republican delegates.[27]

On election day over fifty thousand voters, mostly Conservatives, stayed at home, and the Republicans won an overwhelming victory. The calling of a convention was approved by a majority of almost three to one; of the hundred and twenty delegates chosen, all but thirteen were Republicans.[28] After the election General Canby announced that the constitutional convention would meet in January, 1868.

Early in December, 1867, Worth started to Newburgh, New York, to represent the heirs of a man named Henry E. Lutterloh in a lawsuit involving the Lutterloh estate, but at Washington he became sick and was not able to go on to New York.[29] Before he left Washington to return home, he visited President Johnson and gave him a long recital of the various types of injustice practiced by the military authorities in North Carolina—trial of civilians by military commissions and provost courts, setting aside judgments of civil courts, and the removal of the sheriff and seventeen magistrates of Jones County. The president strongly encouraged Worth to publish the facts about military rule in the newspapers, but Worth explained that he feared removal from office if he offended General Canby. Johnson then proposed that the governor draw up a full report of the condition of affairs in North Carolina and send it to him at Washington.[30] When Worth returned to Raleigh, his doctor confined him to his home for a month and began treating him for chronic diarrhea. During the Christmas holidays he compiled a thirty-page narrative of military intervention in the affairs of North Carolina and sent it to the president. Johnson wanted such information to "show to the nation the absurdity of military government."[31] But the time had long since passed when he could vindicate the position he had taken against the Congressional plan of reconstruction. Compiling the narrative was in itself an exhausting task; Worth informed his brother Milton: "I do not think my mental machinery has been disordered or weakened —or had any rest—during my late bodily infirmity."[32]

The most troublesome situation Worth had to deal with during the interval between the convention election of 1867 and the constitutional convention of 1868 was another vacant judgeship. Soon after General Canby took command of the Second Military District and Worth began asking him questions about Sickles' jury orders, Canby declared that the freehold qualification for jurors was abolished in North Carolina. Late in November, 1867, Judge Daniel G. Fowle resigned. He explained to Worth that he considered Canby's jury order 'the first order requiring the courts to be participators in overriding the laws of the state."[33] Fowle stated in his letter of resignation that he had submitted to military orders restraining him from performing certain acts expected of judges; this might be called a "sin of omission." But he could not conscientiously allow himself to be compelled into an overt act contrary to the law of the state.

Worth accepted Fowle's resignation and, with Canby's approval, called the Council of State to appoint a successor. When the Council met he recommended John F. Poindexter and the Council approved,[34] but Poindexter refused to accept the appointment. He gave no lengthy explanation of his refusal but remarked "that under *existing circumstances* I could not accept the office—and even if I desired it I should be unwilling to take the iron-clad oath, indeed I could not take it conscientiously."[35] One potential successor to Judge Fowle was R. H. Bromfield, the Register in Bankruptcy at Salisbury, but he also declined the office. His friends advised him not to accept the judgeship, but the main reason he declined was that his position as Register in Bankruptcy promised to become quite lucrative.[36] Worth also asked D. B. Baker, of Wilmington, to take the vacant judgeship, but he refused, fearing that he would end up in prison at Fort Macon for refusing to comply with military orders.[37]

The large number of civil and criminal cases in the courts and the resulting need for special terms made it necessary that the vacant judgeship be filled as soon as possible. Worth failed to notify General Canby of the steps being taken to find a suitable successor for Judge

Fowle, and Canby began making inquiries of his own. Indeed, Canby got the impression that Worth and his council were being obstructive by their long delay—until he heard about Worth's illness. Early in January, 1868, Canby informed Worth that he was considering the appointment of Albion W. Tourgée, the carpetbagger Worth detested more than any other, to fill a vacancy in North Carolina. The only reason he had not appointed Tourgée earlier was that Worth had made complaints about his character in the course of the controversy over the arrest of the Caswell County sheriff—which had been made on Tourgée's complaint. Now Canby gave Worth a chance to substantiate his allegations against Tourgée. He asked the governor to give him the names and addresses of those persons from whom he had received information about the Ohio lawyer and carpetbagger. Canby considered it "of great interest to the public that men of unblemished character should fill the public offices; and of no less importance to the nominee that an opportunity should be afforded him to vindicate his character from public charges. . . ."[38]

Worth immediately began securing information about Tourgée. He wrote to his friends in Greensboro and in Caswell County asking for a list of names of men who would sustain him in his allegation that Tourgée was not fit to be a judge. Worth's mind had been set against Tourgée ever since the latter appeared before the Southern Unionist Convention at Philadelphia in 1866 and told the delegates that fifteen dead Negroes had been dragged from a mill pond in North Carolina. On the very day that Canby indicated he might make Tourgée a judge, the ex-sheriff of Caswell County wrote that "Turgee was chairman of the board of registration in one of the districts in this county and shewed him self to be a lowdown dog in human shap."[39] Most of Worth's informants in Greensboro, where Tourgée had settled after the war, sent unfavorable comments in reply to the governor's request for information. Ralph Gorrell mentioned that Tourgée was not licensed to practice law in North Carolina, and David F. Caldwell charged that "he has certainly done much to inflame the minds of the *freedman* against the whites."[40] Much of the information Worth received was based on hearsay, as Caldwell admitted. One informant professed to have a letter giving an unfavorable account of some speeches Tourgée had made—but he could not find the letter. Benjamin S. Hedrick accused the prospective judge of fraud in an attempt to have the United States Commissioner at Greensboro removed and himself appointed, but Hedrick did not know the details of this "gross fraud."[41] In reality, Tourgée was by no means the "vile wretch" Worth thought he was, but he was an outspoken Republican and champion of the rights of the Negroes; this in itself was sufficient to make him despicable to Worth and his conservative friends.

When the leading Conservative newspaper, the Raleigh *Sentinel*, joined in the attack on Tourgée, calling him a man of doubtful reputation whose appointment would be offensive to the people of North Carolina, Holden retorted through the *Standard* that no one could satisfy the *Sentinel*, regardless of his good qualities; that Tourgée's political associates had not denounced him; that he was "as much a 'gentleman' as Jonathan Worth"; and that he was a sober man who had studied law at Harvard.[42] Benjamin Hedrick, who had once attended school at Harvard, had a friend in Cambridge search the records of the Harvard Law School to see if Tourgée had attended there. "No such person had been there within the last 25 years," Hedrick reported.[43]

Fortified in his convictions that Tourgée would not be an acceptable judge, Worth sent Canby a long list of "character references" —men who would confirm what he had said about the carpetbagger. He did not mention the charges his informants had made against Tourgée, but he quoted from Tourgée's speech before the Philadelphia convention and stated that "the respectable people of the State believe every statement in the foregoing quotation was a malicious falsehood. . . ."[44] Canby finally decided not to appoint Tourgée and to give Worth and his council one more chance to find a judge satisfactory to them, but he made it clear to the governor that no one who mourned the defeated Confederacy would be acceptable to him; apparently the general was thinking about a case in South Carolina in which he had removed a judge from office for praising "our holy and lost cause" and criticizing the Reconstruction Acts in an address to a jury.[45] Worth searched vainly for a judge whose background would be acceptable to General Canby until he thought of the new name of Colonel Clinton A. Cilley, a former officer of the Union army and the Freedmen's Bureau, who had married a girl from North Carolina and was practicing law in Lenoir. Over two months after Judge Fowle's resignation, the Council of State approved a recommendation by Worth and appointed Colonel Cilley;[46] Canby approved the appointment three weeks later. North Carolina got a carpetbagger for its Superior Court bench, but he was at least much more acceptable to Worth than Albion W. Tourgée, who, at the time of Cilley's appointment, was busy in Raleigh helping to rewrite the state constitution.

The Constitutional Convention of 1868 was in session at Raleigh from January 14 to March 17. Worth had nothing to do with the convention itself, but before it met he went through some mental turmoil trying to decide whether he should risk removal from office by refusing to sign a warrant to pay its expenses. The treasurer, Kemp Battle, could not pay the expenses unless Worth authorized payment. As usual, the governor, and in this instance the treasurer too, relied upon William A. Graham for advice. Graham advised Battle that he would not be justified in paying the convention expenses, even if Worth drew the warrants and the comptroller ordered him to pay. The elder statesman of the Whigs even went so far as to say that the treasurer should take the state's money and deposit it in Baltimore or New York, where it could not be used by the convention. In this matter Battle differed with Graham, but said he would "stand by the Governor." He reasoned that the Reconstruction Acts were unconstitutional, but, according to Whig theories of government, it was the duty of executive officers to obey laws until they were declared unconstitutional by the courts. Had not Andrew Johnson and Jonathan Worth been obeying laws which they considered repugnant to the constitution? The treasurer, who had a scholarly bent, paraphrased for Graham the idea of the great English conservative, Edmund Burke, that "it is wise statesmanship to do the best *practicable*, rather than make fruitless efforts to attain the best theoretical."[47] He then applied this Burkean maxim to a defense of Worth's obedience to the Reconstruction Acts: Worth was the agent of the people of North Carolina for two years; if he disobeyed a military order—i.e., an order to pay the expenses of the convention—he would be removed from office and could not live up to his obligation to serve the people during the term for which he had been elected. "Is it not 'wise statesmanship' to say 'I submit to the duress because thereby I may be able to do much good to the people?'" Battle pointed out that Worth had not committed positive violations of the state law in obeying the Reconstruction Acts but had "in effect refrained from doing what the law commanded." The governor's actions in filling the vacant judgeships might be cited as an example; in other circumstances Worth would probably have appointed different men, but the requirement that new appointees be able to take a test oath necessarily affected the selection of new judges.[48] Having established his argument that it would be expedient to pay the convention, Battle stated that it would be illegal for him to remove the state's funds to Baltimore or New York, and that the people would ultimately have to pay the expenses of the convention.

When the showdown came, Worth had decided that he would not risk being removed for refusing to authorize payment of the expenses of the convention. Josiah Turner, Jr., asked the question, "Why act so as to put a radical in your place?"[49] Worth then wrote to the treasurer:

Since learning that Gov. Graham is of opinion that it will be inexpedient for you or me, in case of my removal from office by military authority, to resort to any legal steps for restoration, I am clearly of opinion that we owe it to North Carolina to hold on to our positions, if we can do so without positive dishonor.

.   .   .   .

I think, therefore, that it should be managed, without its appearing to be done by your request, that Canby super-add his order to that of the Convention, and that you yield obedience.[50]

When the convention ordered Battle to pay the delegates their per diem expenses, he refused until a tax was levied to provide the necessary money to replace what he would have to take from the treasury. After the convention levied the tax, Battle paid the members their per diem and mileage.[51]

The Constitutional Convention of 1868, dominated by seventy-eight native white Republicans, sixteen carpetbaggers, and thirteen Negroes, designed an instrument of government different in many respects from the old constitution. It abolished the courts of equity—and Worth's old office of Clerk and Master—made the office of judge elective, and abolished the system of county courts; the administrative functions of the county courts were turned over to county commissioners. The new constitution abolished property qualifications for the governor and members of the legislature, and lengthened the governor's term of office from two to four years. A state board of education was to replace the old Literary Board; it was to administer a system of public schools for both whites and Negroes. The most radical departure from the previous system, and the one which offended Worth more than any other, was the adoption of universal suffrage.[52]

The proposed changes in the existing system were far too extensive for Jonathan Worth to accept. For sixty-five years he had lived happily under a constitution written in the year his father was born, 1776. Democratic changes had crept into the old constitution in 1835 and in 1857, but many outdated features still existed until 1868. Worth was not a die-hard conservative unwilling to permit any change at all, but he could not make himself believe that universal suffrage and certain other features of the new constitution would not be an abomination to the state. He summarized his objections in a letter to one of his sons-in-law who asked him to make a public address against the adoption of the constitution.

I entertain no doubt that if I were to go to New Salem and make a speech against the new Constitution, I would be *immediately removed from office*. . . . I look upon the Constitution as a virtual confiscation of the lands of the State. Most of it must soon change hands under the taxation required by this proposed Constitution. The Fountains of Justice will be corrupted by the Judiciary system proposed, and the universal suffrage feature . . . would leave property and character and virtue unprotected. Every impulse of my nature impels me to use all the influence I possess to defeat a scheme I deem so utterly ruinous—but I feel that I owe it to those who elected me and that I can best contribute to preserve our liberties by holding on to my position as long as I can without dishonor. In this view I decided long ago to make no speech and publish no address against the reconstruction acts as they are falsely called.[53]

Thus Worth came to the conclusion that he would not openly campaign against the new constitution. Neither would he oppose the Republican candidates who would inevitably run for office at the election to vote on the constitution and to choose new state officers and congressmen. But behind the scenes he communicated to William A. Graham and Zebulon B. Vance what he thought the policy of the Conservatives should be: oppose the constitution and nominate a man with a record similar to his own who could win the vote of "equivocal Radicals."[54] The Republicans nominated William Holden for governor, but there was a moderate faction in the party strongly opposed to him; this was the group Worth called equivocal Radicals. When the Conservatives nominated Vance late in February, Worth strongly

urged him not to run, on the grounds that his war record would alienate those Republicans who might vote for a Conservative candidate in
preference to the radical Holden. Vance withdrew from the race, and
the Conservatives chose as their candidate Thomas S. Ashe, a pre-war
Democratic legislator who had served in the Confederate Congress.
The Democrats and Whigs had long opposed each other, but now they
entered into an unnatural coalition in a last ditch effort to defeat the
Constitution of 1868 and keep Holden and his followers out of office.
Worth never quite felt comfortable working with the Democrats, and
neither did his secretary, William H. Bagley, who wrote to Benjamin
Hedrick, a Republican: "It is a matter of *disgust* with me to be forced
into a support of the Democracy. But how, in the Devil, can I vote
to *disfranchise* Bartholomew F. Moore, and *enfranchise* "Boots," the
Barber?—the one, a life-long Union man, and one of the ablest lawyers
in the whole Union; and the other a dirty barber as *dishonest* as he is
dirty, and as *ignorant* as he is *dishonest?*"[55]

Worth foresaw that there would be intense feeling preceding and
during the election, and he asked General Canby to take "all reasonable precautions" to avoid aspersions against the fairness of the election. He reminded Canby that all the officials of the election for delegates to the convention had not been men who commanded the honor
and respect of their communities. It would be well, Worth suggested,
to have one poll keeper at each ballot box from the faction opposed to
the constitution;[56] such an arrangement "would tend to silence imputations against the fairness of the election." Worth had heard it
rumored—truthfully—that only one ticket would be used at the election. On this ticket would appear the blocks for approval or rejection
of the constitution, the names of candidates for county and state officers, and candidates for Congress. Worth suggested to Canby that the
election procedure would be improved if separate boxes and tickets
were used for the constitutional question and for each set of officers.
The adoption of this suggestion would have meant that each voter
would face four ballot boxes with four tickets. The only reason Worth
could give for wanting multiple ballots and boxes was that if only one
ticket were used "it would require a monster box to hold the tickets."[57]

Before Canby received Worth's suggestions about how the election
should be conducted, he had already issued an order that the election
be held and a circular giving instructions to the election officials. The

difficulty facing the general when he organized the election machinery was finding election officials who could meet the requirements specified in the Reconstruction Acts. The Second Reconstruction Act specified "that the commanding general of each district shall appoint as many boards of registration as may be necessary, consisting of three loyal officers or persons, to make and complete the registration, superintend the election, and make return to him of the votes. . . ." A "loyal" person was considered to be one who had never held any public office and afterwards participated in rebellion. The shortage of eligible personnel made it necessary to consolidate polling places in some counties, a practice which was condemned at the time. It also rendered impracticable Worth's suggestion that the election machinery be expanded by increasing the number of ballot boxes and tickets; such an expansion would have increased the opportunities for fraud, in Canby's opinion. The general considered his election order carefully before issuing it. Although no complaints had come to him about the last election conducted under his order, he realized that there had been certain defects in the procedure, and he now tried to remedy them.[58]

When the voters went to the polls on April 21, 22, and 23, 1868, they signified their eagerness to complete the process of reconstruction and return to the Union by approving the constitution, electing William Holden as governor, and choosing a Congressional delegation that included only one Conservative. The Republicans also won control of the state legislature, making it certain that North Carolina would ratify the Fourteenth Amendment. To Worth's utter disgust, Albion W. Tourgée, who had been the most prominent figure in the constitutional convention, won a seat on the superior court bench.

Soon after the election the Charlotte *Democrat* made the following editorial comment: "It is a little remarkable that the name of Gov. Worth has scarcely been mentioned in the late campaign in this State. We never voted for Gov. Worth, but it is due to him to say that he has discharged his duties so faithfully and fairly, that neither party could find good cause for complaint." The Raleigh *Sentinel* reprinted the *Democrat*'s remarks, said that there was no "nobler Roman" in the state than Jonathan Worth, and added: "He is one of the few left among us, whose integrity and virtues connect us with the better days of the past, and such constitute the jewels of the State."[59] Worth naturally was pleased by the favorable comments of a Democratic paper, and after the *Democrat*'s article appeared in several other papers, he wrote the editor a note of thanks:

Your late editorial . . . expressing your conviction that my administration has been faithful and patriotic, considering your political stand point, has been very gratifying to me. I have no future aspirations —and my past career, whether good or evil, has never looked to office. I have felt gratified by your article because I know that all my actions have sprung from the honorable purpose to discharge my duties properly, and next to the approval of my own conscience I derive satisfaction from the approval of my fellow man. Accept my thanks for the approving article which I know sprung from as honorable and noble motives as I claim to have always controlled my own conduct.[60]

When Worth saw the results of the election, he knew that his days as governor of North Carolina were numbered. As soon as Congress approved the Constitution of 1868, when General Canby saw fit to remove the existing state officers and install the recently elected ones, and when the Republican legislature ratified the Fourteenth Amendment, it was highly probable that Congress would admit the delegates from North Carolina. The process of reconstruction would then be complete. During the transition period Worth had more free time than usual, and he spent several hours of it in a vain effort to invalidate the recent election of state officers. He begged Senator James R. Doolittle, a moderate Republican from Wisconsin, "to make an effort to set aside the election held under military auspices and congressional enactment, and allow us an election as provided for under our Constitution."[61] Similar pleas were addressed to Senator Reverdy Johnson and William Pitt Fessenden, the chairman of the Joint Committee on Reconstruction, who apparently had repented of his Radicalism by refusing to vote for the impeachment of President Johnson. The governor's main argument against the election was that, while the new constitution did not provide for any disfranchisement, the officers elected to serve under the government it established had been chosen by an election at which several thousand white voters were disfranchised. He also protested against the use of a single ballot, insisting that there were so many names on the ticket for so many offices that not one voter in a hundred could tell the names of the candidates for whom he voted. In his pleas to the congressmen, Worth portrayed Holden as an original secessionist and an insincere champion of the Negroes, and he roundly scored three of the judges elected in

April: "A. W. Tourgée," Worth moaned to Fessenden, "is elected a
Judge of the Superior Court of law. *He has never practised law in this
State nor had a license to practice.* . . . He has not listed or paid one
red cent of County or State tax in the County, Guilford, in which
he claims citizenship."[62] Worth's efforts to nullify the election proved
to be in vain; he never received replies from the congressmen to whom
he wrote, and Congress ultimately approved the election of state
officers and the Constitution of 1868.

One great embarrassment to General Canby in directing the tran
sition from Conservative government under Worth to Republican
government under Holden was that several of the officers elected in
April—among them the governor, the lieutenant governor, and a few
members of the legislature—were still disqualified from office by the
Fourteenth Amendment; an even greater number were ineligible be
cause they could not take the test oath required in the Third Recon
struction Act. Worth's fate now depended on how long it would take
Congress to remove these disabilities. After the election, Canby told
General Grant that "in my judgment, some action by Congress will be
needful in order to remove this embarrassment." He also informed
Grant that there were no personal objections to the officers who were
concerned; that Congressional relief would secure men "devoted in
good faith to the interests of reconstruction"; and that relief by Con
gress would meet the approval of most of the people of North and
South Carolina, while disarming those who might be inclined to oppose
the new Republican governments.[63] Grant had already given an inter
pretation of the Reconstruction Acts which meant, in effect, that the
disabilities provided in them did not apply to the recently elected state
officers of the southern governments. Anyone disqualified under the
Fourteenth Amendment could hold office after securing relief from
Congress.[64] This type of relief was what Canby now sought. On June
25, 1868, Congress removed the disabilities of seven hundred North
Carolinians, mostly Republicans, and passed a law declaring that the
Congressional delegations of North Carolina and five other southern
states would be admitted when the legislatures met and ratified the
Fourteenth Amendment. Under the provisions of this law Holden
called the legislature to meet on July 1, 1868.[65]

Worth worked closely with Holden to insure that the normal
operations of the state government were not disturbed by the transition

from one set of officers to another. To avoid confusion he refused to issue bonds authorized by the convention, and when Halifax County needed a court of oyer and terminer, he secured a promise from Holden that the appointment of Judge Anderson Mitchell would be confirmed.[66] It was peculiarly fitting that Worth's last official act was the appointment of the state's directors for the railroads in which the state had an interest, for he had always been vitally interested in internal improvements and transportation facilities. Canby had issued an order that "officers" should not be appointed until the new administration was installed, but Worth concluded that railroad directors were not officers and appointed them on June 30. The next day he explained to General Canby that he would not have appointed the directors if he had anticipated his sudden removal.[67]

Canby, following the procedure outlined by Congress, removed Worth and appointed Holden governor on June 30. The legislature met on July 1 and ratified the Fourteenth Amendment on the second Military rule came to an end as soon as the legislature ratified the amendment.[68] Four days later North Carolina returned to the Union when Congress admitted three members of the Congressional delegation.

Holden delivered his inaugural address on July 4, 1868. After he completed his speech, he went to the Executive Office to get the keys to the office from Worth. There he found Worth, his secretary, Bagley, and one of the pages. When Holden came in, Worth was polite to him, although a little curt. He asked Holden to record in the governor's letter book a remonstrance against his removal in which he denied the validity of Holden's election and said: "I do not deem it necessary to offer a futile opposition, but vacate the office without the ceremony of actual eviction, offering no further opposition than this my protest."[69] When the departing governor questioned his successor's title to the office, Holden refused to argue with him, "because it was settled already by the action of Congress and the federal government." After a further exchange in which each man denied being the first to call the other a liar, Worth offered to confer with Holden on any problems concerning his new office. When Worth finally got up to leave he looked about the grounds of the capitol and said pathetically: "They have taken my pony too." Holden pointed out the pony and shook hands with ex-governor Worth, who then mounted and rode for home. His public career was at an end.[70]

· XX ·

Resting on the Oars

———◆———

WHEN WORTH SURRENDERED the keys of the Executive Office to Holden on July 4, 1868, he rode directly to his own house on Lenoir Street, for he had never lived in the governor's mansion. General Sherman occupied the mansion in April, 1865, and from that date to May, 1867, various military officials, including the commandant of the federal troops in the state and the Assistant Commissioner of the Freedmen's Bureau, lived there. Most of the furniture disappeared, the wallpaper was in tatters, and the fences around the grounds were used for firewood. The legislature of 1866-67, hoping that Worth might be able to move into the house to which he was entitled by the laws of the state, appropriated five thousand dollars for repairs to the mansion and authorized Worth to apply to the United States Quartermaster Department for rent on the mansion to compensate him for having to use his own estate, Sharon, as the executive mansion.

After the legislature made the appropriation for repairs to the mansion, Worth notified General Sickles, who, in his usual obliging manner, ordered the commandant of North Carolina to restore the premises to the governor.[1] Worth hired a superintendent to manage the repairs, but the work had to be suspended because the repairs were costing so much that he feared the appropriation would not be adequate to pay for them. When he applied to the quartermaster department of the force stationed at Raleigh to collect rent, his request went through Charleston to the Quartermaster General at Washington, who decided that the state was not entitled to the rent. The governor, calculating that the United States government owed him over eighteen hundred dollars, appealed to the Secretary of War, but he never received an answer. Soon after Holden replaced Worth as governor, Worth informed him of his futile efforts to collect the rent and submitted an account of the repair work. A year later, Worth asked John Pool, who had been elected to the United States Senate, to see what he could do about the rent. Pool visited the Quartermaster General and soon informed Worth that "he is not at all favorably disposed."[2] This was the last thing Worth ever heard about the rent. The futile effort to collect what was justly due to him increased his already strong distaste for military rule and everything it signified.

Worth's routine duties as governor and his defense of North Carolina's laws and institutions consumed almost all his waking hours, leaving him little time to attend to the things he loved most, his family, his business enterprises, and his law practice. Many of his public duties were tiresome, and prospects for the state were often dreary, but in his personal affairs there was much to sustain a spirit which, in normal times, was buoyant and optimistic. One event which gave him great personal satisfaction was the marriage of his next-to-youngest daughter, Adelaide, to his private secretary, William Henry Bagley, in March, 1866. Bagley was a bright young lawyer and newspaper editor before the war. After serving in the army during the early part of the war, he resigned to become a state senator in 1864. He began courting "Addie" Worth in 1864 when he came to Raleigh to serve in the Senate. Worth hired his future son-in-law to serve as his secretary after he had to refuse a position as superintendent of the United States Mint at Charlotte because he could not take the oath required of federal office-holders.[3] His work as private secretary was thorough and efficient, and in his role of son-in-law he easily won the approval and affection of the governor and Mrs. Worth.

No matter how busy Worth was, he somehow managed to keep a close watch on his brothers, sisters, children, and even on his former slaves, and to assist them in any material way he possibly could. The only really dark spots in an otherwise bright family picture were the deaths, in 1866, of his mother, who was eighty-five years old, and his youngest daughter, Mary. Brother Addison almost went bankrupt after Sherman's army destroyed most of his property in 1865, but by 1868, he was beginning to recover what he had lost. Brother Milton was doing a prosperous business in merchandise at Asheboro, and Barzillai was in the shipping and commission business with C. B. Dibble on Pearl Street in New York City. Jonathan undoubtedly would have been better satisfied if he himself had been in some business, but he chose instead to serve the public. He never could see any hope for real prosperity in either the South or the North as long as the political affairs of the country were deranged by the anomalous situation which prevailed in the postwar years. Throughout his life his devotion to a peaceful federal union was, to some extent at least, based on the belief that the Union created in 1789 was the best possible environment for the development of commerce and industry.

When Worth became governor, all his children but two, Adelaide and Mary, had married and established their own homes. When Adelaide married she and her husband remained in Raleigh with her parents. David Worth, after serving as salt commissioner during the war, resumed his business operations in Wilmington and became very prosperous, one of the leading businessmen of the state. Worth was always proud of David and was equally pleased that all his daughters had married well—Roxana to a wealthy planter, Lucy, Elvira, and Adelaide to lawyers, and Corinna to a druggist. He treated his sons-in-law as if they were his own sons, generously distributing his favors equally among them. All the children except Roxana were able to take care of themselves, but Worth and David devoted considerable time to helping Roxana manage the three plantations she inherited after her husband, John McNeill, died and left her with three young daughters. Ten years after McNeill died, Worth was still clearing up the details of settling his estate. He advised Roxana on her business affairs, found supervisors for her farms, and helped her in any other way he could. The governor was usually patient and calm—even in his disputes with political opponents and military commanders—but in one case involving his daughter's interests he manifested a rare loss of patience. The president of North Carolina's first statewide dental society, Dr. W. F. Bason, made Roxana a set of false teeth, set in gutta-percha, "which, from unsuccessful manufacture, were worthless."[4] Roxana gave Dr. Bason a note to pay for her teeth, but when she sent money to pay off the note, the dentist insisted he could not find her note. Worth then intervened in his daughter's behalf, asked that the note be cancelled, and threatened "to leave it to a judicial tribunal to decide whether you are entitled to any pay [at all] for such a job." After a heated exchange in which Bason offered to settle for twenty dollars in gold, Worth sent the twenty dollars and the dentist returned the note. It was one of the rare occasions when he talked hatefully to anyone. He browbeat the dentist into a settlement, admitting "I have lost all patience with the contemptible scoundrel";[5] but this admission came only after repeated efforts to settle the matter. It was the type of unpleasantness Worth had always tried to avoid in both his private and his public life.

After the war Worth managed to keep in touch with some of his former slaves who had been in a sense members of his family. When Stephen married the widow of one of Barzillai Worth's slaves, Jonathan gave them a house, rent-free, and served as security for Stephen when he bought a horse and dray with which he made his living working for wages. Lyle went to Indiana to live with Worth's brother-in-law, William Clerk. Mack migrated to Florida, where he worked as a wagoner. Don and Jo "each married a young wife and at last accounts were doing no good." Don grew "very lean" because he could no longer eat the large helpings of "fatback" he had eaten while he was a slave. Zylpha and her three children remained with the Worths, and in spite of the fact that she was well cared for, she once induced the local agent of the Freedmen's Bureau to issue her two overcoats.[6] When Worth considered sending Zylpha and her children to live with his old friend, A. M. Tomlinson, they did not wish to leave, and at Mrs. Worth's request, they continued to live at Sharon. Worth confessed to Tomlinson that it was Zylpha's two boys he wanted to get rid of. They were a bit troublesome, he said, but an occasional thrashing would cure them: "I think that Moses, who prescribed stripes for certain offenses, was wiser than modern philanthropists who regard whipping as a relic of barbarism."[7]

While Worth was governor he could not devote as much time or attention to business ventures as he had given before, but he continued to rely upon investments in his favorite projects as a source of personal income. His salary, four thousand dollars a year, was inadequate to maintain himself and his family in the style to which they had been accustomed, or in the manner that was expected of the highest officer in the state. Fortunately for him, he had invested his money wisely, and not much of the property in which he had an interest happened to be in the path of General Sherman's army. The Cape Fear Steam Boat Company, in which Worth and all his brothers had shares, continued to thrive after the war, and paid the largest dividend it had ever paid in January, 1866; Worth's part of the dividend was almost nine hundred dollars.[8] Early in 1866, the company bought a new boat, and, to Worth's delight, named it "The Governor Worth."

The governor also continued to receive money from his investment in the Cedar Falls Manufacturing Company, the factory in Randolph County which he had promoted since 1830.

During the war Worth and Sam Jackson had bought twenty-five thousand pounds of cotton and paid for it with Confederate bonds. When it became apparent to the original owner of the cotton, an eccentric Anson County planter named Ingram, that Confederate securities would become worthless, he had refused to deliver the cotton. Soon after the war Worth wrote to Ingram and asked that the cotton be delivered, pointing out that when the trade was made in 1863 there was a possibility that both parties might lose by the transaction, "There was mutual hazard. The cotton was liable to confiscation, seizure by the enemy, destruction by fire, etc. The money, as in all cases of paper currency, was liable to become worthless. . . . We took our risks—fortune favored me."[9] Even after Worth offered to compromise by paying Ingram additional money the old man balked, but after the civil courts opened in 1866, Worth threatened a lawsuit, and Ingram agreed to deliver the cotton. Most of it was sold in New York through Swepson, Mendenhall, and Company and through the firm in which Barzillai Worth was a partner, Dibble, Worth and Company.

With the proceeds from the sale of his cotton Worth planned to establish his daughter Corinna's husband, Dr. William C. Roberts, in a drug store—Worth always called it an apothecary shop. In 1865, he spent three thousand dollars setting up Roberts and Roxana Mc-Neill in a general merchandise business, but they soon failed. Worth then borrowed three thousand dollars and used it to help Roberts open a drug store at Salisbury with Worth's nephew, W. C. Porter. The governor's effort to help his son-in-law proved to be an unfortunate venture from beginning to end, and resulted in his owning a drug store which he did not want. Porter sold his interest to Roberts in November, 1866, because Roberts felt that Porter did not trust him, did not treat him as an equal partner, and "had forced on him a disagreeable and offensive clerk to watch over him."[10] Two months later the business was failing and it had become apparent that Roberts was ill with consumption. Worth did everything he could to keep Roberts from blaming himself for the failure; the beneficent father-in-law, who stood to lose a considerable amount if the venture failed, laid the blame on the men from whom the stock of the shop had been purchased, and upon Providence for making Roberts ill. He tried to cheer Roberts, and advised him to come to Raleigh for a period of rest and recuperation.[11]

When Dr. Roberts became too ill to continue at the apothecary shop Worth decided that, in order to save his investment, he would become a partner in the business. A druggist named G. B. Poulson had been helping Roberts manage the store. Instead of selling out the stock on hand, Worth chose to let Poulson manage the store, and he raised another thousand dollars to invest in additional stock. Poulson knew the drug business well. He was to carry on the actual operations of the store; Worth would supply the capital and share equally in the profits. This arrangement proved to be mutually satisfactory, and by February, 1868, the apothecary shop was doing well; in that month Worth received three hundred dollars as his share of the recent earnings. The only misfortune that affected the store occurred in April, 1868, when a fire destroyed several hundred dollars worth of the stock in a warehouse, but fortunately the loss was covered by insurance. In October, Worth sold out his interest in the apothecary shop to Poulson, and wrote to his son David, "I am glad to get out of it."[12]

The apothecary shop was the only new business in which Worth was deeply involved after the Civil War, but after he was removed as governor, he had to think seriously about how he was to maintain himself and his family. Shortly before the election of new state officers in April, 1868, he was so uncertain about his future that he considered buying a house in Randolph County, "with the view, when I get clear of politics, of selling merchandise from it."[13] Three weeks after he went out of office, he was already growing restless and becoming eager to get back into some business or legal venture. "I have laid on my oars, having no enterprise or business on foot, about long enough," he said.[14] Having about three thousands dollars on hand which he did not like to see idle when it could be invested in something, he proposed to a man who had recently surveyed some of the state's swampland, that they buy one of the timbered swamps and set up a mill for making shingles and shakes. Another venture Worth considered briefly was the establishment of a mill somewhere between Raleigh and Goldsboro to make "superior" meal for distribution to nearby towns. In all these proposed plans Worth's role would have been that of capitalist, with the partner managing the business. It was the way he had used his idle money ever since he began investing in various small businesses in the 1830's.

Looking for something to keep himself, as well as his money, occupied, Worth proposed to Judge Augustus S. Merrimon that they open a law office together in Raleigh, but Merrimon's children, who had grown up in the pleasant mountain atmosphere of Asheville, longed to return to the mountains, and Merrimon told Worth that if the children left Raleigh he could not remain there.[15]

One alternative Worth never seriously considered after he left office was going back into politics as a candidate for public office. Several of his friends, including Josiah Turner, Jr., and Judge Merrimon, urged him to accept a nomination as the Conservative candidate for Congress against the carpetbagger, John T. Deweese, in the fall elections of 1868, but Worth realized that "The democrats deemed themselves strong enough to have no further use for me."[16] He lamented the bygone glories of the only party to which he had been enthusiastically devoted, and said to his brother-in-law, "since the old Whig party went under, there has been no party to which an honest, good man could cordially attach himself."[17] In August, 1868, he received several invitations to speak at public rallies for the Conservative party and its candidates, and he accepted four of the invitations. Completely disillusioned with the policies of the Republicans in North Carolina, and with the election of Grant for President, which he considered an endorsement of Congressional reconstruction, he gloomily confided his thoughts to his brother Milton:

> I continually think it is better for all of us to sell out at *any sacrifice*, and move to Minnesota or California where the States are out of debt and common schools and universities paid for out of the National Treasury, and railroads built every where out of the public lands. Here, it seems to me, negro drones and their baser allies, will eat out all the honey in the hive. I see no hopes for an honest man.
>
> I am out of money or employment, old, and in bad health, and I view things through a distorted eye.[18]

Worth was not exactly out of money, but he was old—in terms of the life expectancy for his time—and his health was growing increasingly worse. He had never been very strong physically, but before he accepted the confining and sedentary duties of public treasurer and governor he had kept himself fit by staying out in the open air much of the time—supervising his farms and riding the court circuits on horseback from county to county. Early in September, 1867, he had contracted an illness from which he never completely recovered. On the way to Asheboro for a short visit he had a severe chill and had to stop at a house along the way. A fever followed the chill, but he decided to go on to the home place at Asheboro. For several hours after he arrived there he was delirious, and diarrhea set in. Brother Milton treated him and his symptoms soon disappeared, but eleven days passed before he felt strong enough to return to Raleigh. When he told his son David about the attack he explained: "I contracted my chills by a buggy ride from Edenton to Elizabeth City between 5 P.M. and 2½ A.M. of the next when the whole region was full of malaria—a very imprudent ride."[19] As a result of this attack Worth swore off whiskey for a while, believing that it caused his diarrhea; to replace the whiskey he asked David to get him some good brandy.

Worth soon realized that he might not have long to live, and, in a manner that was entirely characteristic of his lifelong practice of paying close attention to details, he began straightening out his personal affairs. "Deeming it almost criminal to leave any personal business in condition to be troublesome to those who may be my administrators," he began compromising some minor lawsuits in which he was involved. Finally, only two suits remained against him, both arising from his administration of the estate Roxana McNeill's husband had left to her in 1857. In March, 1868, he wrote his last will and testament, in which he left to Mrs. Worth the residence at Raleigh, five hundred dollars in cash, the dividends from his stock in the Cedar Falls Company, and his household furniture, "including my piano, my best carriage and harness and carriages horses—and all my corn, bacon, and other provisions on hand at my death."[20] The will named David Worth and William H. Bagley as the administrators of the estate, and declared that all the property which was not left to Mrs. Worth should be divided equally among Worth's "dutiful and affectionate" children.

Two months after Worth left the governor's office he decided to take a trip to New England and the Midwest, hoping to improve his health by taking a leisurely vacation and visiting relatives and friends in New York and Indiana. Late in August, 1868, he went "by easy stages" through Washington to New York City, where he visited his brother Barzillai. He made a side visit by boat to Hartford, Connecticut, spent part of a day there, and rested at the country house of

Barzillai's business partner. After returning to New York, he and Barzillai set out by way of Niagara Falls and Cleveland to visit their three sisters who had moved to Indiana before the Civil War. After two pleasant weeks in Indiana, Jonathan came back to Raleigh and Barzillai returned to New York. During the early part of the trip, Worth reported that he could not observe "either benefit or injury from my travels," but soon after he returned—seven pounds heavier and feeling much better than when he left, he said to a friend: "I was out about a month and for the past two weeks have been perfectly well. . . . The trip . . . not only restored my health but afforded me constant pleasure with no alloy save the depletion of a purse not well filled and constantly sinking without any accretion."[21]

Worth's hopes for returning health would rise as his condition seemed to improve; then they would fall in another siege of weakness, chills, and diarrhea. At least one of his attacks resulted from over-exertion and exposure. A mill dam on Roxana McNeill's plantation had broken and her business affairs were in a "deplorable" condition by the end of 1868. Worth spent most of the month of December supervising repairs on the mill dam and applying his financial skill to his daughter's tangled business arrangements. "It was a terrible effort for me," he told his brother Barzillai. "My mental condition and personal anxiety were injurious to me in my feeble condition." Brother Milton, who still practiced medicine occasionally, scolded Jonathan for working on the mill dam: "I [advise] you to give all your time and attention to the improvement of your health. I do not think building mill dams in the winter exactly the thing, but hope when you get through that job that you will find time to try more gentle exercise."[22]

Through the early months of 1869, Worth remained at Sharon in a state bordering between health and sickness. Not ill enough to be confined to his bed, he was not well enough to engage actively in business or to resume his law practice.

Perhaps he spent some time reading. He preferred the Bible, Milton, and the poems of Robert Burns, and had a great fondness for Scott's Waverley novels, especially his often reread favorite, *Rob Roy*. He did spend some time corresponding with the editors of the Raleigh *Sentinel* and the Wilmington *Journal* when they published a series of extracts from his letters to General Canby in which he had protested so strongly against military rule. These letters, he thought, "furnish in the most reliable shape, a historical record of the devilish despotism under which we lived during my administration and I confess that I felt a strong personal wish that the public should know that I did not meanly cringe for the mere purpose of retaining office."[23] Thankful that his mentality had not been affected by his long illness, he pointed out to brother Milton that the letters being published in the papers had been written during one of his worst attacks of diarrhea.

During the third week in May, 1869, Worth went to Asheboro, planning to go from there to Fayetteville with Sam Jackson to attend to some business for Roxana. He arrived in Asheboro with his usual strength, but when diarrhea began to bother him again, his daughter Elvira convinced him that he should remain to be treated by Milton. His brother prescribed quinine, held him to a strict diet, and made him rest, "trusting in the recuperative powers of a good constitution." The sparse diet annoyed Worth greatly, for his appetite was still strong. By the end of the first week in June he was strong enough to go fishing, but he caught "more ticks than minnows" and exhausted himself by tramping through thick holly and bamboo bushes along the creek and walking almost two miles back home without resting. Craving a glass of cool buttermilk, but daring not to drink it against the doctor's orders, he complained to Mrs. Worth that Milton was starving him to death: "He is still confident my health will be restored by persevering adherence to the non-eating treatment."[24]

When it became obvious to Worth that neither his brother nor his doctor in Raleigh would be able to cure him, he made one last desperate effort to regain his health and strength by undergoing treatment at Rockbridge Alum Springs, a spa in the Virginia mountains thirty miles southwest of Staunton on the Calf Pasture River. The trip to the springs was more harmful than helpful, for he was in poor condition to travel, and it was three hundred long miles from Raleigh to Rockbridge. The lap of the journey beyond Richmond was particularly tiresome. Leaving Richmond at eight o'clock in the morning, the Worths did not arrive at Staunton until late in the afternoon. There had been no stop for lunch and the roads were hot and dusty all day. At Staunton, Worth quenched his thirst by drinking iced milk and eating "too freely" of tomatoes and mutton. Immediately after lunch he left Staunton and arrived in Goshen at six o'clock. The remaining ten miles to the springs had to be covered by stagecoach over a rough road. "This ride was horrible. It gave me headache—almost concussion of the brain. . . ." Worth had to lie down on one of the seats of the stage, and as soon as he lay down his stomach became upset. Two miles from the springs he had to stop the stage and get out, but when he stepped out the door, he fell face downward in the dust "from extreme exhaustion."[25]

Thus began the futile sojourn at Rockbridge Alum Springs. The doctors there merely continued the same type of treatment he had been receiving at home, but added to his diet the mineral water from the spring. After two weeks at Rockbridge, Worth informed his son-in-law, William H. Bagley: "I am not gaining strength and flesh, or appetite—Otherwise I feel well." He found no one at the resort whose company was congenial and, afflicted with ennui, he found himself reading the newspapers "down to every advertisement." As it became clear to him that the doctors were doing him no good, he longed to be back in Raleigh with the simple, common-sense advice of his doctor there. When he began to get uneasy and irascible he considered it a favorable symptom, a spark of life. With plenty of time to write, he wrote to Bagley frequently, describing his condition and discussing the most down-to-earth matters: "Is my corn crop worthless? . . . Are my rutabagas coming up well?" He scarcely mentioned politics, but expressed dismay when he read in the papers that the prominent North Carolina Whig, George Badger, was beginning to act like a Republican.

Worth soon began to fear that he might get too weak to come home before he died, and decided to return to Sharon. About all he got out of his twenty-six-day stay at the spa was a board bill for $156, a bar check for fifteen more dollars, and a bill from Dr. H. R. Noel for seventy dollars.[26] These expenses he paid on August 12 and returned to Raleigh.

After Worth and Mrs. Worth arrived at Sharon, he weakened steadily, and on September 5, 1869, at eleven o'clock in the evening, he died quietly in his bed. When his funeral was held two days later, all the state offices and business houses in Raleigh closed their doors in respect, and the state officers joined in his funeral procession. From Sharon the solemn procession moved to the Presbyterian church,[27] where the pastor, Drewry Lacy, preached the funeral sermon, using as his text St. Paul's remarks in the fourth chapter of First Thessalonians: "I would not have you to be ignorant brethren, concerning them which are asleep. . . ."[28] After the funeral service Worth was buried on the top of the hill in Oakwood Cemetery. He lies there still, in the shade of a slender magnolia tree. At the head of his grave is a plain spire of marble engraved with his name and the simple epitaph, "Faithful in all."

No epitaph could be more fitting, for Jonathan Worth was indeed faithful, and the very simplicity of the inscription is perfect for a man who was almost plain in appearance, speech, and manner. Holding firmly to the virtues of personal integrity, moderation, and above all honesty to himself and his convictions, he was loved by many and respected even by those who disagreed with him and opposed him on matters of policy affecting his state and the nation. In a public career that included six terms in the legislature, two as state treasurer, and two as governor, he inevitably made political enemies, but even in the bitterness of campaign strife no one could seriously question the strength of his character or the sincerity of his devotion to the moderate conservative principles which served as the guide to his actions as a private citizen and a public officer. Kemp Battle said this better than anyone else when he wrote that "Governor Jonathan Worth . . . was a model of the true, sensible, and steadfast gentlemen of the old school. His only oath was 'ding.' His principles were like the eternal rock."[29]

This man of principle had his flaws, to be sure. Sometimes his devotion to principle resulted in a stern inflexibility. Even when the tide of history was flowing against him he remained at heart the lover of Union, the devoted Whig, the conservative anti-democrat in a time of great social change. Because he usually acted on the assumption that he was right and his opponents wrong, he was over-sensitive to criticism. Finally, he was so involved with his worldly affairs that he tended to place material things at the top of his scale of values.

At the end of Worth's last letter book is a black-bordered page with these words on it: "Sacred to the Memory of Our Father, Jonathan Worth; Who died September 5th A. D. 1869, aged 67 years, 9 months, and 13 days.[30] A Kind Husband, The Best of Fathers, A True Friend, A Patriotic Citizen, An Honest Man. . . ." This tribute is all he would have wanted.

Notes

Chapter I

1. Genealogical chart in possession of writer. Based on the original public records of Nantucket, it was compiled in 1854. A notation on the chart indicates that it was "Approved by B. Franklin Folger, June 14, 1854." The Southern Historical Collection possesses copies among its Worth Papers. See also Samuel A. Ashe (ed.) *Biographical History of North Carolina from Colonial Times to the Present* (Greensboro, 1905-17), III, 466.

2. Guion G. Johnson, *Ante-Bellum North Carolina: A Social History* (Chapel Hill, 1937), p. 355; see also Ethel S. Arnett [and W. C. Jackson], *Greensboro, North Carolina: The County Seat of Guilford* (Chapel Hill, 1955), p. 12.

3. William W. Hinshaw, *Encyclopedia of American Quaker Genealogy* (Ann Arbor, 1936), I, 583.

4. The Minutes are in the Guilford County Library.

5. Women's Minutes, Deep River Monthly Meeting, Nov. 5, 1798.

6. Minutes of New Garden Monthly Meeting, Aug. 27, 1773.

7. Hinshaw, *Quaker Genealogy*, I, 645; Stephen B. Weeks, *Southern Quakers and Slavery* (Baltimore, 1896), p. 109.

8. May McAlister, "A Biographical Sketch of David and Eunice Worth," (unpublished MS in possession of Jonathan Daniels of Raleigh), p. 1. The writer is indebted to Mr. Daniels, who is Worth's great-grandson, for permission to use this sketch and other family materials, including the family Bible, pictures of Worth and his wife, and correspondence concerning the genealogy of the Worths.

9. Ashe, *Biographical History*, III, 466-67.

10. McAlister, "Biographical Sketch," p. 2.

11. Johnson, *Ante-Bellum North Carolina*, pp. 356-57.

12. Zora Klain, *Quaker Contributions to Education in North Carolina* (Philadelphia, 1924), *passim*.

13. The brief sketch, incomplete, is printed in J. G. de Roulhac Hamilton (ed.), *The Correspondence of Jonathan Worth* (Raleigh, 1909), I, p. vi. This collection consists almost entirely of letters written after 1848.

14. It is impossible, for lack of specific information, to date Worth's entry into the Academy any closer than late 1820 or early 1821; he matriculated probably in January, 1821.

15. Raleigh *Register*, Dec. 17, 1819.

16. Raleigh *Register*, Feb. 9, 1821.

17. Fannie M. Farmer, "Legal Education in North Carolina, 1820-1860," *North*

Carolina Historical Review, XXVIII (1951), 276. The state's historical journal will be cited as *NCHR*.

18. *Ibid.*, pp. 285-86.

19. Hugh T. Lefler (ed.), *North Carolina History Told by Contemporaries* (Chapel Hill, 1934), p. 199.

20. This vignette of conditions in the state during Worth's early years is partially based on Hugh T. Lefler and Albert Ray Newsome's chapter entitled "The 'Rip Van Winkle State'" in their *North Carolina: The History of a Southern State* (Chapel Hill, 1954), pp. 298-311.

21. Statistical table attached to Murphey's "View of the Internal Improvements Contemplated by the Legislature of North Carolina" (Raleigh, 1819).

22. "Report on Education," (Raleigh, 1817), in William H. Hoyt (ed.), *The Papers of Archibald D. Murphey* (Raleigh, 1914), II, 52.

23. "Mr. Murphey's Report to the Legislature of North Carolina on Inland Navigation," (December, 1816), in *Murphey Papers*, II, 35-48.

24. "Report on Education Submitted to the Legislature of North Carolina," (1817), in *Murphey Papers*, II, 63-83.

25. "A View of the Internal Improvements Contemplated by the Legislature of North Carolina," in Murphey's *Memoir on the Internal Improvements Contemplated by the Legislature of North Carolina and On the Resources and Finances of that State* (Raleigh, 1819).

26. Hillsboro *Recorder*, April 28, 1824.

27. Charles Whedbee, "William H. Bagley," (printed MS in possession of Jonathan Daniels, Raleigh), p. 10.

28. *Ibid.* Unfortunately, the men's minutes for this period have been lost.

29. Hillsboro *Recorder*, April 30 and Oct. 29, 1828.

30. Murphey to Ruffin, Haw River, July 26, 1829, in *Murphey Papers*, I, 382-83.

31. Murphey to William D. Murphey, Jan. 2, 1830, in *Murphey Papers*, I, 385.

32. Murphey to Thomas Ruffin, Greensboro, Aug. 31, 1830, in J. G. de Roulhac Hamilton (ed.), *The Papers of Thomas Ruffin* (Raleigh, 1918), I, 539.

33. Randolph County Deed Book, No. 14, p. 524.

34. *The Seventh Census of the United States* (Washington, 1853), p. 308; J. A. Blair, *Reminiscences of Randolph County* (Greensboro, 1890), p. 44.

35. Record of Appointments of Overseers, in court minutes for May, 1825.

36. Fannie M. Farmer, "The Bar Examination and Beginning Years of Legal Practice in North Carolina, 1820-1860," *NCHR*, XXIX (1952), 170.

37. *Worth Correspondence*, I, p. v.

38. Randolph County Deed Book, No. 16, pp. 48-49.

39. *Ibid.*, No. 17, p. 440.

40. Copy of Hoover's bond, dated Jan. 26, 1826, Jonathan Worth Papers, Southern Historical Collection. The bulk of Worth's personal papers is in the North Carolina Department of Archives and History at Raleigh; there are small collections in the Duke University Library and in the Southern Historical Collection at Chapel Hill. All of these will be cited as Worth Papers, but the location of the materials in the small collections will be noted.

Chapter II

1. J. G. de Roulhac Hamilton (ed.), *The Correspondence of Jonathan Worth* (Raleigh, 1909), I, p. v.

2. Raleigh *Star*, Aug. 19, 1830.

3. Charles M. Wiltse, *John C. Calhoun* (Indianapolis, 1944-51), II, 90.

4. Quoted in Greensboro *Patriot*, May 19, 1830.

5. Henry M. Wagstaff, *State Rights and Political Parties in North Carolina, 1776-1861* (Baltimore, 1906), p. 50.

6. Issue of Nov. 30, 1831.

7. *Journal of the House of Commons of North Carolina*, 1830-31, p. 161.

8. *Ibid.*, p. 175.

9. *Ibid.*, p. 187.

10. *Ibid.*, pp. 256-57.

11. *Ibid.*, pp. 283-84.

12. Jan. 6, 1831.

13. Jan. 18, 1831.

14. Greensboro *Patriot*, Jan. 12, 1831.

15. Raleigh *Star*, Aug. 18, 1831.

16. Wagstaff, *State Rights*, pp. 52-54.

17. *House Journal*, p. 175.

18. *Ibid.*, p. 275.

19. *Ibid.*, p. 196.

20. *Ibid.*, pp. 253-54.

21. Letter quoted in Arthur C. Cole, *The Whig Party in the South* (Washington, 1913), p. 6.

22. *House Journal*, p. 214.

23. *Ibid.*, p. 248.

24. *Ibid.*, p. 278.

25. Minutes of the Society, *passim*, in Southern Historical Collection.

26. Ruth K. Nuermberger, *The Free Produce Movement: A Quaker Protest Against Slavery* (Durham, 1942), pp. 9-10.

27. Dec. 28, 1830.

28. Issue of Jan. 12, 1831.

29. *House Journal*, p. 147.

30. *Ibid.*, pp. 194, 211, 249.

31. *Ibid.*, p. 217.

32. *Ibid.*, p. 228.

33. Hugh T. Lefler and Albert Ray Newsome, *North Carolina: The History of a Southern State* (Chapel Hill, 1954), pp. 332-41.

Chapter III

1. J. G. de Roulhac Hamilton (ed.), *The Correspondence of Jonathan Worth* (Raleigh, 1909), I, p. v.

2. Worth Letters, State Archives of North Carolina.

3. Deed of trust in Randolph County Deed Books, No. 19, pp. 71-73. The deed lists Worth's debts in detail.

4. Worth to John M. Morehead, Jr., Raleigh, Feb. 25, 1868, *Worth Correspondence*, II, 1163.

5. William H. Hoyt (ed.), *The Papers of Archibald D. Murphey* (Raleigh, 1914), I, p. xxiv.

6. Minutes of the Court of Equity of Randolph County, March 26, 1833.

7. Edward Cantwell, *The Practice of Law in North Carolina* (Raleigh, 1860), I, 138-39.

8. Minutes of the Court, *passim.*

9. Index to Real Estate Conveyances, Randolph County; Deed Books, *passim.* The figures do not include sales made by Worth as Clerk and Master, trustee, or attorney.

10. Randolph County Deed Book, No. 26, pp. 308-9.

11. *Ibid.*, No. 27, pp. 11-12.

12. Minutes, Court of Pleas and Quarter Sessions, August Term, 1835.

13. A typical advertisement—for Gray's Ointment—appears in the Asheboro *Southern Citizen* of Feb. 8, 1839.

14. John H. Wheeler, *Historical Sketches of North Carolina from 1584 to 1851* (Philadelphia, 1851), p. 350.

15. Minutes of Court of Pleas and Quarter Sessions, August Term, 1838.

16. J. A. Blair, *Reminiscences of Randolph County* (Greensboro, 1890), p. 12.

17. Wallace B. Goebel, "A History of Manufactures in North Carolina Before 1860" (Master's thesis, Duke University, 1926), p. 129.

18. *Public Laws of North Carolina*, 1828-29, Ch. 73. The official name of the company was The Manufacturing Company of the County of Randolph. Worth later became its president.

19. Blair, *Reminiscences*, p. 60.

20. *Ibid.*, p. 61; Goebel, "History of Manufactures," pp. 129-31.

21. Braxton Craven, "Address by Dr. Braxton Craven Delivered in Year 1880 on Occasion of Naomi Falls Mill Dedication," in *History of Randleman, N.C.* (Randleman, 1944), p. 86.

22. *Ibid.*, pp. 86-87.

23. Goebel, "History of Manufactures," p. 133.

24. These sketches of Worth's brothers are based on those in Samuel A. Ashe (ed.), *Biographical History of North Carolina from Colonial Times to the Present* (Greensboro, 1905-17), III, 454-65, and on many letters throughout the Worth Papers in the State Archives.

25. Goebel, "History of Manufactures," p. 136.

26. Wheeler, *Historical Sketches*, p. 348.

27. Asheboro *Southern Citizen*, July 6, 1838, gives an account of the meeting and a copy of the resolutions.

28. *Ibid.*, July 20, 1838.

29. *Ibid.*, Feb. 7, 1840.

30. *Worth Correspondence*, I, p. vi.

31. Nov. 18, 1839, quoted in E. M. Carroll, *Origins of the Whig Party* (Durham, 1925), p. 211.

32. See above, pp. 24-28.

33. Hugh T. Lefler and Albert Ray Newsome, *North Carolina: The History of a Southern State* (Chapel Hill, 1954), p. 329.

Chapter IV

1. Asheboro *Southern Citizen*, Oct. 2, 1840.

2. Raleigh *Register*, Nov. 13, 1840.

3. Asheboro *Southern Citizen*, Aug. 21, 1840.

4. *Ibid.*

5. J. G. de Roulhac Hamilton (ed.), *The Correspondence of Jonathan Worth* (Raleigh, 1909), I, p. vi.

6. Asheboro, *Southern Citizen*, Feb. 8, 1839.

7. *Ibid.*, June 14, 1839.

8. Letter from "A Visitor," *Southern Citizen*, Nov. 1, 1839.

9. *Southern Citizen*, June 14, 1839.

10. Asheboro, March, 1853, Worth Papers, Southern Historical Collection.

11. Charles L. Coon (ed.), *The Beginnings of Public Education in North Carolina: A Documentary History, 1790-1840* (Raleigh, 1908) contains all the documentary evidence needed for a study of the educational movement in North Carolina prior to 1840.

12. *Public Laws of North Carolina*, 1825-26, Ch. 1.

13. The letters are published in Coon, *Documentary History*, II, 545-613.

14. *Southern Citizen*, Feb. 4, 1837; June 1, 1838.

15. *Ibid.*, Aug. 3, 1838.

16. The law is printed in Coon, *Documentary History*, II, 886-90.

17. *Southern Citizen*, Feb. 22, 1839.

18. For samples of newspaper comment and speeches on the law see Coon, *Documentary History*, II, 893-912.

19. *Southern Citizen*, Aug. 30, 1839.

20. Minutes, 1840-61, *passim.*

21. M. C. S. Noble, *A History of the Public Schools of North Carolina* (Chapel Hill, 1930), p. 61.

22. Worth's figure on the population does not quite agree with that given in the 1840 census. "Abstract of the Census of North Carolina, for the Year 1840," *Legislative Documents*, 1840-41, No. 23, p. 2. His calculation also omits from the income of the Fund thirty-six thousand dollars in dividends from the Raleigh and Wilmington Railroad Company, the collection of which was very uncertain.

23. "Report of the Joint Committee on Education, on the Subject of the Common Schools," *Legislative Documents*, 1840-41, No. 20.

24. *Journal of the Senate of North Carolina*, 1840-41, pp. 198-200.

25. *Ibid.*, p. 225.

26. *Public Laws of North Carolina*, 1836-37, Ch. 23.

27. Moore's speech, one of the few published during the debates on the school law, is printed in the Raleigh *Register*, Feb. 5, 1841.

28. This summary of the school law is based on a copy in the Fayetteville *Observer*, July 14, 1841.

29. *Senate Journal*, 1840-41, pp. 78, 255-56, 125.

30. Issue of Jan. 12, 1841.

31. March 23, 1841.

32. Raleigh *Star*, quoted in Greensboro *Patriot*, April 6, 1841.

33. *Southern Citizen*, Feb. 7, 1840.

34. Worth's notation on a report to the state Board of Literature, Dec. 6, 1846.

35. Reports of the Superintendent of Common Schools, Randolph County, 1840-64, Feb. 13, 1841; Nov. 7, 1846; Oct. 28, 1848; Feb. 14, 1852; and April 15, 1861.

36. Superintendent's Report, March 26, 1842; July 4, 1842.

37. Worth to Wiley, Asheboro, Sept. 21, 1855, *Worth Correspondence*, I, 47.

38. Common School Teachers Certificate, issued by Worth and Hale, in T. L. L. Cox Papers, Duke University Library.

39. Message to the Legislature of 1850-51, *Legislative Documents,* 1850-51, No. 1, p. 22.

40. *Ibid.,* pp. 21-22.

41. Notation on Worth's annual report for 1846, Dec. 6, 1846.

Chapter V

1. Fisher to Worth, Salisbury, April 8, 1841, in J. G. de Roulhac Hamilton (ed.), *The Correspondence of Jonathan Worth* (Raleigh, 1909), I, 35-36.

2. Samuel Silliman to Worth, Salisbury, April 17, 1841, *Worth Correspondence,* I, 36-37.

3. Rencher to Worth, Salisbury, April 22, 1841, Worth Papers.

4. Greensboro *Patriot,* April 6, 1841.

5. "To the Freedmen of the Tenth Congressional District," Salisbury, April 28, 1841, *Worth Correspondence,* I, 37-40.

6. *Ibid.,* p. 43.

7. Worth to Fisher, Lexington, May 8, 1841, Fisher Papers, Southern Historical Collection.

8. Returns in Raleigh *Register,* May 25, 1841.

9. H. C. Jones to Worth, Salisbury, May 13, 1841, Worth Papers, Southern Historical Collection.

10. *Worth Correspondence,* I, p. vi.

11. *Whig Clarion* (Raleigh), Nov. 29, 1843.

12. Worth to Mangum, Asheboro, July 8, 1844, in Henry T. Shanks (ed.) *The Papers of Willie Person Mangum* (Raleigh, 1955), IV, 153.

13. Greensboro *Patriot,* April 19, 1845.

14. *Ibid.,* April 5, 1845.

15. *Ibid.,* May 3, 1845.

16. Proceedings in Greensboro *Patriot,* May 10, 1845.

17. Greensboro *Patriot,* July 12, 1845.

18. *Ibid.,* July 26, 1845.

19. Report of the meeting, *Ibid.,* May 24, 1845.

20. David F. Caldwell to John Sherwood, Greensboro, undated, Caldwell Papers, Southern Historical Collection.

21. Certificate in Caldwell Papers, dated Aug. 5, 1845.

22. John Sherwood to Caldwell, Asheboro, Aug. 5, 1845, Caldwell Papers.

23. *Patriot,* Aug. 9, 1845. Complete returns are in the issue of Aug. 30.

24. John H. Wheeler to Polk, Beatysford, Aug. 12, 1845, printed from Polk's papers in *North Carolina Historical Review,* XVI (1939), 446.

Chapter VI

1. Unsigned letter to the Greensboro *Patriot,* dated Asheboro, May 4, 1841, in *Patriot* of May 25.

2. Worth to W. Starbuck, Asheboro, Mar. 20, 1852, Worth Papers.

3. Worth to T. C. and B. G. Worth, Asheboro, Aug. 23, 1859, Worth Papers.

4. Worth to F. Cooper, Asheboro, Jan. 8, 1858, Worth Papers.

5. Worth to Lucy Baldwin, Asheboro, Oct. 14, 1852, Worth Papers.

6. Worth to G. J. Thomas, Asheboro, Jan. 20, and Feb. 2, 1853, Worth Papers.

7. Worth to Thomas McKenzie and Sons, Asheboro, Nov. 18, 1853, Worth Papers.

8. Worth to H. A. London, Asheboro, Nov. 8, 1858, William Lord London Papers, Southern Historical Collection.

9. Worth to Troy, Asheboro, Oct. 8, 1850, Worth Papers.

10. Worth to Coffin, Asheboro, Mar. 13, 1853, Worth Papers.

11. Worth to Sackett, Belcher, and Co., Asheboro, Oct. 7, 1859, Worth Papers.

12. Record of the births and marriages in Worth's family Bible, in possession of Jonathan Daniels.

13. Asheboro, March 16, 1846, Worth Papers.

14. Worth to David Worth, Asheboro, June 3, 1858, Worth Papers.

15. Worth to Friend Uriah Hunt, Asheboro, Dec. 30, 1851, Worth Papers.

16. Worth to Dr. ——— Whitehead, undated, Worth Papers.

17. Worth to W. J. Long, Asheboro, Nov. 6, 1852, Worth Papers.

18. Worth to Ralston, Asheboro, Sept. 20, 1858, Worth Papers.

19. Worth to S. S. (or J. J.) Jackson, Asheboro, Jan. 28, 1858, Worth Papers.

20. Asheboro, Mar., 1853, Worth Papers, Southern Historical Collection.

21. Joseph Carlyle Sitterson, "Economic Sectionalism in North Carolina," *North Carolina Historical Review*, XVI (1939), 139.

22. U. S. Census (Slaves), Southern Division, Randolph County, original tabulation on microfilm in State Archives.

23. *Ibid.*, 1860.

24. Stephen B. Weeks, *Southern Quakers and Slavery* (Baltimore, 1896), pp. 225-27.

25. Stephen Worth to Worth, Lassiters Mills, Nov. 29, 1868, Worth Papers.

26. Worth to R. Sterling, Asheboro, Feb. 15, 1860, Worth Papers.

27. Worth to Robert M. Sloan, Asheboro, Mar. 13, 1860, Worth Papers.

28. Worth to Dr. ——— Blucher, Asheboro, Jan. 25, 1853, Worth Papers.

29. Worth to Ann Alston, Asheboro, June 28, 1853, Worth Papers.

30. Worth to S. S. Jackson, Asheboro, Jan. 24, 1854, Worth Papers.

31. Worth to II. Marley, Asheboro, April 14, 1860, Worth Papers.

Chapter VII

1. Asheboro, Feb. 24, 1860, Worth Papers.

2. Asheboro, Mar. 16, 1846, Worth Papers.

3. Worth to John M. Ford, Asheboro, Feb. 18, 1850, Worth Papers.

4. *Raleigh News and Observer*, July 2, 1905.

5. Worth to Craven, Asheboro, April 29, 1861, Worth Papers.

6. Worth to Patrick H. Winston, Asheboro, Mar. 10, 1858; Worth to John Lyon, Asheboro, May 3, 1858, Worth Papers.

7. Worth to Charles Hamlin, Asheboro, Aug. 9, 1858, Worth Papers.

8. Worth to Gorrell, Asheboro, Jan. 8, 1855, Ralph Gorrell Papers, Southern Historical Collection.

9. Worth to Yelverton and Walker (the New York merchants), Asheboro, Sept. 21, 1858, Worth Papers.

10. Worth to Bonnell, Brown, Hull, and Co., Asheboro, Feb. 17, 1858, Worth Papers.

11. Worth to Sackett, Belcher, and Co., Asheboro, Jan. 19, 1856, Worth Papers.

12. "Income For Salaries and Fees Commencing July 1st, 1859," in account book of Samuel S. Jackson (Southern Historical Collection), p. 8.

13. Worth to Hennys, Smith, and Townsend, Asheboro, Feb. 15, 1860, in J. G. de Roulhac Hamilton (ed.), *The Correspondence of Jonathan Worth* (Raleigh, 1909), I, 99.

14. Ad in issue of April 21, 1846, and subsequent issues.

15. *Randolph Herald*, June 9, 1846.

16. Worth to Addison Worth, undated, Worth Papers.

17. Copy of agreement in Worth Papers.

18. Worth to D. A. Davis, Asheboro, May 14, 1850, Worth Papers.

19. Worth to ——— McConnell, Asheboro, April 2, 1853, Worth Papers.

20. The name of the firm changed by 1858 to Springs, Oak, and Company, and later to Aumont and Oak.

21. Worth to David Springs, Asheboro, June 30, and Dec. 20, 1850, Worth Papers.

22. Worth to Springs, Asheboro, May 27, 1851, Worth Papers.

23. Worth to Springs, Asheboro, April 18, 1852, Worth Papers.

24. Worth to Springs, Asheboro, Sept. 24, 1853, Worth Papers.

25. Asheboro, Mar. 31, 1858, Worth Papers.

26. Order dated Sept. 24, 1853, Worth Papers.

27. Worth to David Springs, Asheboro, April 6, 1851, Worth Papers.

28. Worth to an unnamed brother, Asheboro, Mar. 3, 1850, Worth Papers.

29. The note and record of payments is in Worth Papers for 1867.

30. Coffin to Worth, Salisbury, Nov. 3, 1867, Worth Papers.

31. Worth to Alfred Brown, Asheboro, July 19, 1853, Worth Papers.

32. Worth to Mendenhall, Asheboro, Dec. 8, 1855, Worth Papers.

33. Worth to Rayner and Gilmer, Asheboro, May 28 and Aug. 5, 1853, Worth Papers.

34. *Ibid.*

35. Worth to T. C. and B. G. Worth, Asheboro, Dec. 2, 1855, Worth Papers.

36. Worth to John M. Rose, Asheboro, Nov. 3, 1855, Worth Papers.

37. *Randolph Herald*, June 16, 1846.

38. J. P. Mabry to Worth, Lexington, Jan. 8, 1866, Governor's Papers, 1866; Worth to W. T. Howell and Company, Asheboro, Feb. 7, 1850, Worth Papers.

39. Worth to George Page and Company, Asheboro, Mar. 13, 1860; Worth to William Virden, Asheboro, Mar. 13, 1860, Worth Papers.

40. Worth to Sackett, Belcher, and Company, May 7, 1853, Worth Papers.

41. Randolph County Deed Books, No. 32, pp. 102-3.

42. Worth to William R. Holt, Asheboro, Apr. 18, 1860; Worth to T. C. and B. G. Worth, Asheboro, Aug. 12, 1855, Worth Papers.

43. Worth Papers, *passim*.

Chapter VIII

1. Worth to Gilmer, Asheboro, May 26, 1858, in J. G. de Roulhac Hamilton (ed.), *The Correspondence of Jonathan Worth* (Raleigh, 1909), I, 55-56.

2. Worth to Michael Cox, Asheboro, Sept. 23, 1858, Worth Papers.

3. *Worth Correspondence*, I, p. ix.

4. Cecil K. Brown, *A State Movement in Railroad Development* (Chapel Hill, 1928), p. 69. This monograph is a thorough study of the North Carolina Railroad.

The discussion of the background of the railroad controversy is based largely on this work and the primary sources used by Brown.

5. *Proceedings of the General Meeting of the Stockholders of the North Carolina Railroad Company* (Greensboro, 1851), p. 4.

6. Brown, *State Movement*, p. 77.

7. *Report of Stockholders*, Mar., 1855, p. 3, copy of "An Act for the Completion of the North Carolina Railroad."

8. *Report of Stockholders*, July, 1856, p. 10.

9. *North Carolina Standard* (Raleigh), July 29, 1854.

10. *Journal of the Senate of the General Assembly of the State of North Carolina, At Its Session of 1858-'9* (Raleigh, 1859), p. 50.

11. *Ibid.*

12. *Report of the Joint Select Committee on the North Carolina Railroad, Legislative Documents*, 1858-59, No. 71, p. 3.

13. *Report of the President of the North Carolina Railroad to the Governor of the State, January 20, 1859* (Salisbury, 1859).

14. *Ibid.*, p. 9.

15. *Committee Report*, p. 30.

16. Charles F. Fisher, *Communication From the President of the North Carolina Railroad in Reply to the Report of the Chairman of the Joint Committee on the North Carolina Railroad* (Raleigh, 1859).

17. *Ibid.*, p. 16.

18. *Ibid.*, p. 19.

19. *Ibid.*, p. 27.

20. Brown, *State Movement*, p. 87.

21. "Appendix" to Fisher's *Reply*.

22. Raleigh *Standard*, Feb. 23, 1859.

23. *Ibid.*

24. *Senate Journal*, 1858-59, pp. 430-31.

25. *Worth Correspondence*, I, 68.

26. Raleigh *Register*, Mar. 16, 1859.

27. *Ibid.*

28. Worth to Holden, Asheboro, Mar. 21, 1859, *Worth Correspondence*, I, 67-68.

29. Raleigh *Standard*, Mar. 2, 1859.

30. *Ibid.*, Mar. 9, 1859.

31. Worth to John W. Syme, Asheboro, Mar. 2, 1859, *Worth Correspondence*, I, 62.

32. Worth to Peter D. Swain, Asheboro, Mar. 3, 1859, *Worth Correspondence*, I, 64.

33. *Worth Correspondence*, I, 61.

34. Worth to Syme, Asheboro, Mar. 3, 1859, *Worth Correspondence*, I, 62.

35. The member was William F. Green, who failed to sign the final report. In Green's minority report he indicated that he did not sign the majority report because the committee had not had time enough to make a thorough investigation.

36. Quoted in Raleigh *Standard*, Mar. 23, 1859.

37. *Ibid.*

38. Worth to Isaac H. Foust, Asheboro, April 18, 1859, *Worth Correspondence*, I, 74.

39. Brown, *State Movement*, pp. 133-34.

40. Greensboro *Patriot*, Feb. 10, 1860.

41. *Ibid.*

42. Worth to Tod R. Caldwell, Asheboro, Nov. 4, 1859, *Worth Correspondence,* I, 80.

43. Letter from Worth to the editors of the Greensboro *Patriot,* Asheboro, Dec. 9, 1859, in *Worth Correspondence,* I, 85-88.

44. Worth to E. J. Hale and Sons, Asheboro, Feb. 14, 1860, *Worth Correspondence,* I, 95-97.

45. Worth to Barringer, Asheboro, Feb. 15, 1860, *Worth Correspondence,* I, 98.

46. Worth to L. Blackmer, Asheboro, June 9, 1860, *Worth Correspondence,* I, 119.

47. Worth to Chesley Faucett, Asheboro, May 4, 1860, *Worth Correspondence,* I, 115.

48. The only good account of the road is included in Robert B. Starling, "The Plank Road Movement in North Carolina," *North Carolina Historical Review,* XVI (1939), 1-23, 147-74.

49. Undated letter in Worth Papers.

50. Worth to W. T. Howell and Co., Asheboro, 1852, Worth Papers.

51. Worth to John Rose, Asheboro, Nov. 3, 1855, Worth Papers.

52. Worth to Nathan Stedman, Asheboro, March 7, 1856, Worth Papers.

53. President's Report to the Stockholders, April, 1857.

54. Worth to John Rose, Asheboro, Jan. 29, 1858, Worth Papers.

55. Worth to Morehead, Asheboro, Oct. 20, 1860, Worth Papers.

Chapter IX

1. Worth to Jess (?) Thornburgh, Asheboro, Dec. 20, 1850, Worth Papers.

2. Worth to J. L. Morehead, Asheboro, May 1, 1852, Worth Papers.

3. Worth to William A. Graham, Asheboro, July 12, 1852, Graham Papers, Southern Historical Collection.

4. Worth to John A. Gilmer, Asheboro, Mar. 9, 1858, in J. G. de Roulhac Hamilton (ed.), *The Correspondence of Jonathan Worth* (Raleigh, 1909), I, 55.

5. *Journal of the Senate of North Carolina,* 1858-59, p. 382.

6. Ethel Arnett [and W. C. Jackson], *Greensboro, North Carolina: The County Seat of Guilford* (Chapel Hill, 1955), pp. 63-64; Clement Eaton, *Freedom of Thought in the Old South* (Durham, 1940), pp. 139-41.

7. Worth to McNeill, Asheboro, Mar. 10, 1860, *Worth Correspondence,* I, 110-13.

8. McNeill to Ruffin, Fayetteville, Mar. 12, 1860, in J. G. de Roulhac Hamilton (ed.), *The Papers of Thomas Ruffin* (Raleigh, 1918), III, 73.

9. Worth to the Rev. G. W. Bainum, Asheboro, Mar. 31 and May 2, 1860, *Worth Correspondence,* I, 113, 115.

10. Worth to Chesley Faucett, Asheboro, May 4, 1860, *Worth Correspondence,* I, 116.

11. Worth to Alexander Kelly, Asheboro, June 3, 1860, Worth Papers.

12. William K. Boyd, "Ad Valorem Slave Taxation," *Trinity College Historical Society Papers,* Ser. 5, pp. 32-36.

13. *Senate Journal,* 1858-59, pp. 28, 73-74, 224.

14. Raleigh *Standard,* Aug. 15, 1860

15. William A. Graham, "The North Carolina Union Men of Eighteen Hundred Sixty-One," *North Carolina Booklet,* XI (July, 1911), 3-4.

16. Fragment of a letter in *Worth Correspondence,* I, 125-26.

17. *Senate Journal,* 1860-61, p. 99.

18. Raleigh *Standard,* Dec. 11, 1860.

19. *Senate Journal,* 1860-61, pp. 120-21.

20. Raleigh *Standard,* Dec. 20, 1860.

21. *Senate Journal,* 1860-61, p. 122.

22. *Ibid.,* p. 126.

23. Worth to C. B. Mallett, Senate Chamber, Dec. 19, 1860, C. B. Mallett Papers, Southern Historical Collection.

24. Raleigh *Standard,* Jan. 12, 1861.

25. J. Caryle Sitterson, *The Secession Movement in North Carolina* ("The James Sprunt Studies in History and Political Science," Vol. XXIII, No. 2 [Chapel Hill: 1939]), p. 203.

26. *Senate Journal,* 1860-61, p. 147.

27. *Ibid.,* p. 232.

28. *Ibid.,* pp. 213-44.

29. Remarks are in Worth Papers and in *Worth Correspondence,* I, 128-29.

30. *Public Laws of North Carolina,* 1860-61, pp. 27-31.

31. *Senate Journal,* 1860-61, p. 235.

32. These arguments are well summarized in Graham, "North Carolina Union Men," pp. 6-7; excellent coverage of the convention campaign is in Sitterson, *Secession Movement,* pp. 211-29.

33. Printed in *Worth Correspondence,* I, 129-33; original copy is in Worth Papers.

34. Raleigh *Standard,* Mar. 6, 1861. Returns for the state are in the same paper on Mar. 20.

35. Worth to Dr. C. W. Woolen, Asheboro, May 17, 1861, *Worth Correspondence,* I, 147.

36. Worth to T. C. and B. G. Worth, Asheboro, April 26, 1861, Worth Papers.

37. The proclamation and Ellis's message to the legislature are in *Senate Journal,* First Extra Session, 1860-61, pp. 3-13.

38. *Ibid.,* p. 19.

39. *Ibid.,* p. 28.

40. *Worth Correspondence,* I, 140.

41. The extant portion of this circular is in *Worth Correspondence,* I, 135-37.

42. Asheboro, May 15, 1861, *Worth Correspondence,* I, 144.

43. *Journal of the Convention of the People of North Carolina* (Raleigh, 1862), pp. 1-16.

Chapter X

1. Worth to T. C. and B. G. Worth, Asheboro, May 13, 1861, in J. G. de Roulhac Hamilton (ed.), *The Correspondence of Jonathan Worth* (Raleigh, 1909), I, 141.

2. *Ibid.*

3. *Ibid.*

4. Worth to John B. Troy, Asheboro, May 21, 1861, *Worth Correspondence,* I, 150.

5. Worth to Gray, Asheboro, June 5, 1861, *Worth Correspondence,* I, 154.

6. Worth to Gilmer, Asheboro, July 31, 1861, Worth Papers.

7. Asheboro, Dec. 13, 1861, Worth Papers.

8. Worth to Captain B. F. Carr, Asheboro, Mar. 30, 1862, Worth Papers.

9. The convention, since it was a constituent body, was in theory superior to the legislature, but both the convention and the legislature could make laws.

10. Worth to William L. Scott, Raleigh, Sept. 14, 1861, William L. Scott Papers, Duke University Library.

11. *Journal of the Senate of North Carolina*, 1860-61, Second Extra Session, pp. 74, 77.

12. *Ibid.*, pp. 169, 174.

13. *Ibid.*, p. 80.

14. *Ibid.*, pp. 202, 214.

15. Worth to William L. Scott, Raleigh, Sept. 14, 1861, William L. Scott Papers, Duke University Library.

16. "Stay laws" are designed to prohibit the collection of debts. They are anathema to conservative men, especially of the creditor class, and to persons who believe that contracts should not be impaired, even in unusual circumstances.

17. Raleigh *Standard*, Feb. 12, 1861.

18. *Senate Journal*, 1860-61, 2nd Ex. Sess., pp. 231-32.

19. Worth to H. L. Myrover and Worth to Addison Worth, Asheboro, Oct. 5, 1861, Worth Papers.

20. Worth to Capt. Thomas D. Hogg, Asheboro, Dec. 13, 1861, Worth Papers.

21. Worth to Addison Worth, Asheboro, April 9, 1862, Worth Papers.

22. Worth to Worth and Daniel, Asheboro, Feb. 1, 1862, Worth Papers.

23. Worth to Jesse H. Lindsay, Asheboro, April 12, 1862, Worth Papers.

24. Worth to Hogg, Asheboro, Mar. 2, 1862, Worth Papers.

25. E. Merton Coulter, *The Confederate States of America, 1861-1865* (Baton Rouge, 1950), p. 247.

26. Worth to Milton Worth, Asheboro, Dec. 30, 1861, *Worth Correspondence*, I, 161.

27. Worth to Worth and Daniel, Asheboro, Feb. 1, 1862, Worth Papers.

28. Worth to Ebenezer Emmons, Asheboro, April 5, 1862, *Worth Correspondence*, I, 166.

29. J. M. Worth to Worth, Wilmington, Dec. 16, 1862, *Worth Correspondence*, I, 215; Worth to W. Woodfin, Asheboro, Oct. 6, 1862, Worth Papers.

30. S. G. Worth to Worth, Wilmington, Dec. 25, 1862, *Worth Correspondence*, I, 216-17.

31. *Ordinances of the Convention of 1861-62* (Raleigh, 1862), Fourth Session, No. 34.

32. Worth to Tomlinson, Asheboro, April 4, 1862, *Worth Correspondence*, I, 165.

33. Worth to Martin, Asheboro, April 3, 1862, Worth Papers.

34. Asheboro, May 1, 1862, *Worth Correspondence*, I, 167-68.

35. The statement, dated July 9, 1862, is in the Marmaduke Robbins Papers, Southern Historical Collection.

36. Worth to Mendenhall, Asheboro, April 1, 1862, Worth Papers.

37. Worth to Jordan, Asheboro, April 9, 1862, Worth Papers.

38. Worth to Jordan, Asheboro, Nov. 1, 1862, Worth Papers.

39. *Ibid.*

40. Worth to Col. J. O. McDaniel, Asheboro, Oct. 22, 1862, Worth Papers.

41. Asheboro, May 15, 1862, *Worth Correspondence*, I, 169-70.

42. Worth to A. G. Foster, Asheboro, June 27, 1862, *Worth Correspondence*, I, 174.

43. *Ibid.*

44. Letters to the commanding officers are in *Worth Correspondence*, I, 177-87.

45. Manuscript returns in Marmaduke Robbins Papers, Southern Historical Collection.

Chapter XI

1. Asheboro, Sept. 28, 1862, in J. G. de Roulhac Hamilton (ed.), *The Correspondence of Jonathan Worth* (Raleigh, 1909), I, 190.

2. Worth's opponent in the railroad controversy had been killed at Manassas in 1861.

3. Dec. 2, 1862.

4. Kenneth Rayner to Thomas Ruffin, Raleigh, Nov. 23, 1862, in J. G. de Roulhac Hamilton (ed.), *The Papers of Thomas Ruffin* (Raleigh, 1918), III, 271.

5. Courts to Ruffin, Raleigh, Nov. 24, 1862, *Ruffin Papers*, III, 272.

6. *Journal of the House of Commons of North Carolina*, 1862-63, pp. 66-67; *Journal of the Senate of North Carolina*, 1862-63, p. 73.

7. Martitia and Mary Worth to Worth, Asheboro, Dec. 8, 1862, Worth Papers.

8. Martitia and Adelaide Worth to Worth, Asheboro, Dec. 14, 1862, Worth Papers.

9. *House Journal*, 1862-63, p. 77.

10. Treasurer's Report, Nov. 19, 1860. The reports of the Public Treasurer may be found in the *Legislative Documents* for the year in which they were submitted to the governor and legislature.

11. See above, pp. 115-16.

12. *Public Laws of North Carolina*, 1860-61, First Extra Session, Ch. 4. Cited hereafter as *Public Laws*.

13. *Ordinances*, No. 34.

14. *Public Laws*, 2nd Ex. Sess., 1860-61, Chs. 14 and 18.

15. *Ordinances*, No. 16. Seven weeks later the convention declared that this issue should no longer bear interest. *Ordinances*, No. 2.

16. *Ordinances*, 3rd Sess., No. 35.

17. *Public Laws*, 1862-63, Ch. 29.

18. *Public Laws*, Adj. Sess., 1862-63, Ch. 71.

19. *Public Laws*, Adj. Sess., 1863, Chs. 26 and 35; Adj. Sess., 1864, Ch. 18; Regular Sess., 1864-65, Chs. 23 and 26.

20. Treasurer's Report, Jan., 1866; Treasurer's Report, Sept., 1865; Benjamin U. Ratchford, "A History of the North Carolina Debt, 1712-1900 (Ph.D. Thesis, Duke University, 1932), pp. 135, 140.

21. Worth to Zebulon D. Vance, Raleigh, June 29, 1863, *Legislative Documents*, 1863-64, No. 1.

22. Lancaster and Company to Thomas Ruffin, Richmond, Feb. 18 and Mar. 6, 1863, *Ruffin Papers*, III, 293, 301.

23. Worth to B. A. Sellars, Raleigh, June 18, 1863, Worth Papers.

24. Treasurer's Report, May, 1864.

25. Treasurer's Report, Nov., 1862.

26. Worth to R. Y. McAden, Raleigh, June 13, 1863, Worth Papers.

27. North Carolina Comptroller's Reports, 1861-64, *passim*.

28. Treasurer's Report, May 17, 1864.

29. *Ordinances*, 1st Sess., No. 22.

30. See p. 127.

31. "Report of the Public Treasurer on the Revenue Bill," *Legislative Documents,* 1866-67, No. 8.

32. *Public Laws,* 1862-63, Ch. 53.

33. Ratchford, "North Carolina Debt," p. 151.

34. Comptroller's Report, 1863.

35. *Public Laws,* Extra Sess., 1863, Ch. 13.

36. *Ordinances,* 4th Sess., No. 35.

37. Resolution of Feb. 1, 1865, *Public Laws,* 1864-65.

38. Worth to W. J. Yates, Raleigh, Dec. 25, 1863, *Worth Correspondence,* I, 275-80; Governor Vance's message to the legislature, Nov. 17, 1862.

39. *Public Laws,* 1862-63, Ch. 29.

40. Worth to Dortch, Raleigh, Jan. 19, 1863, in *The War of The Rebellion: A Compilation of the Official Records of the Union and Confederate Armies* (Washington, 1880-1901), Series 4, II, 364.

41. Endorsement on *Ibid.,* Jan. 29, 1863.

42. *Public Laws,* 1862-63, Ch. 32.

43. *Ibid.,* Ch. 71.

44. Treasurer's Report, May, 1864.

45. Worth to Governor Vance, Raleigh, June 29, 1863, *Legislative Documents,* 1863-64, No. 1.

46. Treasurer's Report, May 17, 1864.

47. Letter in *Worth Correspondence,* I, 275-80.

48. Worth to Ruffin, Raleigh, Feb 21, 1864, *Ruffin Papers,* III, 371.

49. Report to the legislature, Adj. Sess., 1864, in *Legislative Documents,* 1864-66.

50. *Public Laws,* Adj. Sess., 1864, Ch. 23.

51. Resolution of December 22, 1864, *Public Laws,* 1864-65.

52. Samuel A. Ashe, *History of North Carolina* (Raleigh, 1908) II, 923.

53. Richard C. Todd, *Confederate Finance* (Athens, 1954), pp. 70-71.

54. Worth to Governor Vance, Raleigh, June 29, 1863, *Legislative Documents,* 1863-64, No. 1.

55. *Ordinances,* 3rd Sess., No. 35.

56. Message to special session of the Legislature, June 30, 1863, in *Legislative Documents,* 1863-64.

57. Worth to Graham, Raleigh, April 24, May 1, May 5, 1863, Graham Papers, Southern Historical Collection.

58. Worth to Vance, Raleigh, April 20, 1863, Governors' Letter Books (Vance), I, 229-30.

59. Worth to Vance, Raleigh, June 29, 1863, *Legislative Documents,* 1863-64, No. 1.

60. Richmond M. Pearson to Vance, Raleigh, June 1, 1863, Zebulon Vance Papers, State Archives.

61. Memminger to Worth, Richmond, May 18, 1863, *Legislative Documents,* 1863-64.

62. Jones to Worth, Milledgeville, Georgia, May 28, 1863, *Legislative Documents,* 1863-64.

63. Message to called session, in *Legislative Documents,* 1863-64.

64. Worth to Vance, Raleigh, June 29, 1863, *Legislative Documents,* 1863-64.

65. "Report of the Joint Select Committee on the Currency," *Legislative Documents,* 1863-64, No. 2.

66. *Public Laws,* 1862-63, Ch. 12; Treasurer's Report, Nov., 1863.

67. *Public Laws*, 1862-63, Ch. 12.

68. Order of Jones County Court, June Term, 1863, submitted to the legislature by Worth and printed in *Legislative Documents*, 1863-64, No. 1.

69. Worth to Governor Vance, Raleigh, June 29, 1863, *Legislative Documents*, 1863-64, No. 1.

70. Resolution of Dec. 14, 1863, *Public Laws*, 1863-64.

71. Treasurer's Report, May, 1864.

72. *Public Laws*, 1864, Ch. 15.

73. Ratchford, "North Carolina Debt," p. 146.

74. Treasurer's Report, Nov., 1864.

75. Treasurer's Report, Nov., 1863.

76. Worth to J. J. Jackson, Asheboro, May 19, 1862, *Worth Correspondence*, I, 171.

77. Fragment of a letter in *Worth Correspondence*, I, 233, *ca.* April 19, 1863.

78. Treasurer's Report, Nov. 1863.

79. Todd, *Confederate Finance*, p. 74.

80. Treasurer's Report, May, 1864.

81. Worth to Thomas Ruffin, Raleigh, Feb. 21, 1864, *Ruffin Papers*, III, 371.

82. Worth to Jackson, Raleigh, Nov. 30, 1863, Worth Papers.

83. *Ibid.*

84. Treasurer's Report, May, 1864.

85. Resolution of May 25, 1864, *Public Laws*, 1864.

86. Governors' Letter Books (Vance), II, 136-37.

87. Worth to J. B. Hare, Raleigh, Aug. 3, 1864, Worth Papers.

88. Treasurer's Report, May, 1864.

89. Congress changed the law in June, 1864, when it allowed the states to swap all old treasury notes for 4 per cent bonds payable in twenty years. As an alternative the states could take for their old notes one-half in new notes or one-half in 6 per cent bonds. Todd, *Confederate Finance*, p. 77.

90. *Public Laws*, 1864, Ch. 15.

91. Resolution of May 28, 1864, *Public Laws*, 1864.

92. Treasurer's Report, Nov., 1864.

93. For accounts of Worth's negotiations with the Confederate treasury, see letters from Worth to Thomas Ruffin of July 18, July 21, and July 25, 1864 in *Ruffin Papers*, III, 403, 405, 407.

94. Worth to William C. Smith, Raleigh, Sept. 22, 1864, Worth Papers.

95. Worth to George Makepeace, Raleigh, Dec. 2, 1864, Worth Papers.

96. Worth's calculation of the debt for the fiscal year ending in September did not include debts in Europe or profits from the blockade account.

97. Treasurer's Report, Nov., 1864.

98. Worth to Thomas Ruffin, Jan. 7, 1865, *Ruffin Papers*, III, 438; *Public Laws*, 1864-65, Chs. 23 and 26.

99. Worth to Judge —— Sheppard, Raleigh, Jan. 12, 1865, Worth Papers.

100. Worth to Graham, Raleigh, Feb. 15, 1865, Graham Papers, Southern Historical Collection.

101. Ratchford, "North Carolina Debt," pp. 157, 158, 158-59.

Chapter XII

1. Wake County Deed Books, No. 24, p. 52; No. 23, p. 594. The price of Sharon had risen rapidly during the war. Two years earlier Worth could have bought it for less than half of what he paid for it.

2. Adelaide Worth to William H. Bagley, Raleigh, Mar. 29, 1864, Bagley Papers, Southern Historical Collection.

3. Raleigh, April 12, 1864, Bagley Papers.

4. Worth to Worth and Company, Raleigh, Oct. 9, 1864, Worth Papers.

5. Wilmington, Jan. 24, 1864, in J. G. de Roulhac Hamilton (ed.), *The Correspondence of Jonathan Worth* (Raleigh, 1909), I, 227.

6. Affidavit in Worth Papers.

7. Isaac M. Broyles and William E. Piercy to Vance, Burnsville, Apr. 19, 1863, Worth Papers.

8. For an account of other difficulties Worth faced in administering the relief act see above, p. 155.

9. Worth to A. H. Welch, Asheboro, May 1, 1862, Worth Papers.

10. Worth to Thomas D. Hogg, Asheboro, May 10, 1862; Worth to Thomas J. Sumner, Raleigh, June 2, 1864, Worth Papers.

11. Worth to Colton, Raleigh, June 13, 1864, Worth Papers.

12. Raleigh, June 23, 1864, Worth Papers.

13. Worth to I. Jarrett, Raleigh, July 16, 1864, *Worth Correspondence*, I, 325.

14. Worth to Jackson, Raleigh, Aug. 28, 1864, Worth Papers.

15. Worth to James Russell, Raleigh, Apr. 25, 1864, Worth Papers.

16. Worth to J. J. Jackson, Raleigh, July 7, 1864, Worth Papers.

17. Worth to S. S. Jackson, Raleigh, Jan. 5, 1864, Worth Papers.

18. This was five hundred dollars more than the judges of the Supreme Court received and half of what the governor was paid. No state official except the governor drew a higher salary than the treasurer. Vance's notation of "Warrants Issued, March 28, 1865," in Vance Papers, State Archives.

19. Worth to —— Sheppard, Raleigh, Jan. 12, 1865, Worth Papers.

20. Worth to "My Dear Nephew" (either Shubal or Albert Worth), Raleigh, Feb. 14, 1865, Worth Papers.

21. This was the company which Worth had helped to establish in 1830; he had kept stock in it since that date and had been active in the stockholders' meetings. In 1858, while he was in the legislature, he personally secured a new charter for the company. *Public Laws*, 1858-59, Ch. 245. It has not been possible to determine when Worth was elected president or how many times he served in that position.

22. Worth to Makepeace, Raleigh, Apr. 23, 1863, Worth Papers.

23. Receipts in Worth Papers, Southern Historical Collection.

24. Ingram to Jackson, undated letter, Worth Papers, Southern Historical Collection.

25. Jackson to Worth, Asheboro, Oct. 3, 1863, Worth Papers.

26. Worth to Battle, Raleigh, Apr. 1, 1863, Battle Papers, Southern Historical Collection.

27. Worth to Starbuck, Raleigh, Jan. 9, 1865, Worth Papers.

28. Worth to Mrs. M. M. Andrews, Raleigh, Sept. 19, 1864, Worth Papers.

29. Worth to William C. Smith, Raleigh, Oct. 4, 1864, Worth Papers.

30. Worth to David Worth, Raleigh, Apr. 25, 1863, Worth Letters, State Archives. The collection in which this letter is contained is kept separate from the Jonathan Worth Papers. It consists largely of letters to Jonathan's son, David.

31. Worth to Jackson, Asheboro, May 19, 1862, *Worth Correspondence*, I, 171.

32. Worth to Isaac Jackson, Raleigh, Jan. 11, 1864; Worth to John Pool, Raleigh, Feb. 6, 1864; Worth to ——— Branch, Raleigh, Jan. 13, 1865, Worth Papers.

33. Worth to Daniel Worth, Raleigh, Apr. 16, 1864; Worth to B. G. Worth, Raleigh, May 18, 1867, Worth Papers; Inventory of Worth's Estate, Wake County Records, State Archives.

34. Worth to Jackson, Raleigh, Aug. 19, 1864, Worth Papers.

35. Worth to Jackson, Raleigh, Aug. 4, 1864, Worth Papers.

36. Worth to Dr. J. J. Hamlin, Raleigh, July 5, 1864, Worth Papers.

37. Worth to Daniel Worth, Raleigh, July 7, 1863, Worth Papers.

38. Worth to Dr. J. J. Hamlin, Raleigh, July 5, 1864, Worth Papers.

39. Worth to S. S. Jackson, Raleigh, July 11, 1864, Worth Papers.

40. Worth to Russell, Raleigh, July 11, 1864, Worth Papers.

41. Worth to J. M. Worth, Raleigh, Sept. 16, 1864, Worth Papers.

42. Raleigh, Sept. 9, 1864, Worth Papers.

43. Worth to J. A. Worth, Raleigh, July 7, 1864, *Worth Correspondence*, I, 317.

44. Worth to Mallett, Raleigh, June 18, 1863, Worth Papers.

45. Worth to Col. Peter Mallett, Raleigh, June 2 and Sept. 3, 1864, Worth Papers.

46. Worth to Vance, Raleigh, Apr. 3, 1863, *Worth Correspondence*, I, 229.

47. Worth to David Worth, Asheboro, Nov. 1, 1863, *Worth Correspondence*, I, 191.

48. David Worth to Worth, Wilmington, Jan. 24, 1863, Worth Papers.

49. J. M. Worth to Worth, Wilmington, Jan. 27, 1863, *Worth Correspondence*, I, 228.

50. See above, pp. 131-32.

51. Ella Lonn, *Salt as a Factor in the Confederacy* (New York, 1933), p. 100.

52. Worth to J. M. Worth, Raleigh, May 30, 1863, Worth Papers.

53. Raleigh, July 26, 1863, *Worth Correspondence*, I, 247.

54. Worth to William A. Graham, Raleigh, June 8, 1864, *Worth Correspondence*, I, 309.

55. Raleigh *Standard*, July 1, 1864.

56. Worth to Graham, Raleigh, June 8, 1864, *Worth Correspondence*, I, 311.

57. Worth to Vance, Raleigh, July 19, 1864, Worth Letters; see also letters to Vance of June 30 and July 8, 1864 in *Worth Correspondence*, I, 315, 319.

58. Lonn, *Salt*, p. 103.

59. Message in *Legislative Documents*, 1864-65.

60. The best detailed discussions of the peace movement may be found in two articles in the *North Carolina Historical Review:* Richard E. Yates, "Governor Vance and the Peace Movement," XVII (1940), 1-26, 89-114; Horace W. Raper, "William W. Holden and the Peace Movement in North Carolina," XXXI (1954), 493-517.

61. Worth to Henshaw, Raleigh, July 23, 1863, *Worth Correspondence*, I, 245.

62. Worth to Henshaw, Raleigh, Aug. 24, 1863, *Worth Correspondence*, I, 257.

63. Raleigh, Feb. 8, 1864, *Worth Correspondence*, I, 291-92.

64. Worth to Jackson, Raleigh, Jan. 5, 1864, *Worth Correspondence*, I, 220-21.

65. Worth to S. S. Jackson, Raleigh, Jan. 5, 1864, Worth Papers.

66. Worth to Tomlinson, Raleigh, Jan. 7, 1864, Worth Papers.

67. This petition and the letter to Starbuck in which it was included are printed in *Worth Correspondence*, I, 286-88.

68. There was a special session of the legislature in May, 1864, but it was

occupied with questions pertaining to state finance, instead of to the peace movement.

69. Tyson's correspondence with the prisoners and many interesting sidelights on the peace movement may be found in the Bryan Tyson Papers, Duke University Library.

70. Copy of petition in Worth Papers.

71. Worth to J. M. Worth, Raleigh, June 28, 1864, Worth Papers.

72. Worth to Holden, Raleigh, Apr. 23, 1864, *Worth Correspondence*, I, 307.

73. "Destructives" was a term of opprobrium which the Conservatives applied to the extreme members of the Confederate faction. Worth frequently used it.

74. Holden to Calvin J. Cowles, Raleigh, Mar. 18, 1864, William W. Holden Papers, State Archives.

75. Worth to J. M. Worth, Raleigh, June 28, 1864, Worth Papers.

76. Worth to Vance, Raleigh, May 1, 1864, Vance Papers, State Archives.

77. Samuel A. Ashe, *History of North Carolina* (Greensboro, 1925), II, 922.

78. Worth to J. J. Jackson, Raleigh, Jan. 24, 1865, Worth Papers.

79. Worth to J. M. Worth, Raleigh, Feb. 9, 1865, *Worth Correspondence*, I, 346

80. Worth and Company to Worth, Wilmington, Feb. 4, 1865; Worth to David Worth, Raleigh, Feb. 9, 1865, Worth Papers.

81. Worth to J. J. Jackson, Raleigh, Feb. 19, 1865, Worth Papers; *Worth Correspondence*, I, 352.

82. Worth to William A. Graham, Raleigh, Mar. 7, 1865, Graham Papers, Southern Historical Collection.

Chapter XIII

1. Resolution of July 7, 1863, in *Public Laws of North Carolina*, 1864-65.

2. Worth Papers.

3. Worth to Ruffin, Raleigh, Feb. 20, 1865, in J. G. de Roulhac Hamilton (ed.) *The Papers of Thomas Ruffin* (Raleigh, 1918), III, 445.

4. *Ibid.*

5. Worth to S. S. Jackson, Raleigh, Mar. 14, 1865, in J. G. de Roulhac Hamilton (ed.), *The Correspondence of Jonathan Worth* (Raleigh, 1909), I, 367.

6. Asheboro, Mar. 16, 1865, *Worth Correspondence*, I, 368-69.

7. Raleigh, Apr. 9, 1865, *Worth Correspondence*, I, 380.

8. Worth to Lewis Johnson, Raleigh, June 30, 1868, Worth Papers.

9. See p. 292.

10. Raleigh, Mar. 23, 1865, William H. Bagley Papers, Southern Historical Collection.

11. Worth to Martitia Worth, Greensboro, Mar. 25, 1865, Worth Papers.

12. Worth to J. J. Jackson, Greensboro, Apr. 8, 1865, *Worth Correspondence*, I 378.

13. Worth to J. A. Worth, Company Shops, Apr. 22, 1865, *Worth Correspondence* II, 1288-89.

14. A firsthand account by Governor Vance of the end of the government and the flight from Raleigh is in the David L. Swain Papers, Southern Historical Collection A good contemporary account in published form is Cornelia Phillips Spencer, *The Last Ninety Days of the War in North Carolina* (New York, 1866).

15. Telegram in Field Files, Bureau of War Risk Litigation, Nos. 10875-79, Duke University Library. The writer has found no response from Beauregard.

16. Marmaduke S. Robbins, in Raleigh *News and Observer,* July 2, 1905. Robbins, as Treasurer of the Literary Fund, was a member of the party in charge of the valuables.

17. Vance to Johnston and Johnston to Vance, Greensboro, Apr. 24, 1865, Vance Papers.

18. Johnston to Vance, Greensboro, Apr. 24, 1865, Vance Papers.

19. Johnston to Vance, Greensboro, Apr. 26, 1865, Vance Papers.

20. *The War of the Rebellion: A Compilation of the Official Records of the Union and Confederate Armies* (Washington, 1880-1901), Series 1, XLVII, 848.

21. Vance to Johnston, Greensboro, Apr. 19, 1865, Vance Papers.

22. Worth described his mission to Raleigh and the return of the records in a letter to the editor of the Raleigh *Sentinel* which was printed in the issue of Oct. 30, 1865.

23. Dr. J. G. de Roulhac Hamilton speculates, in his *Reconstruction in North Carolina,* that if Lincoln had lived he would have appointed someone besides Holden, and adds in a footnote (p. 108): "The late D. F. Caldwell, of Guilford, stated that he had authoritative information that President Lincoln had considered his name and that of Jonathan Worth, and had finally decided upon the latter for the position. The author has been unable to find any other evidence substantiating this or, in fact, any contradicting it." Neither has the present writer found any evidence confirming Caldwell's "authoritative information." Certainly Worth himself never suspected that Lincoln was considering him for provisional governor, and if the president thought of it he never committed his thoughts to paper.

24. Jonathan T. Dorris, "Pardoning North Carolinians," *North Carolina Historical Review,* XXIII (1946), 370-71.

25. Worth signed the oath on July 24, 1865, but it was not filed in the Department of State until June, 1866. Certificate signed by William H. Seward, June 6, 1866, Worth Papers.

26. Photostatic copy of Petition for Pardon, No. 964A, State Archives.

27. The order was issued from Headquarters, Department of North Carolina, Army of the Ohio. A copy is in the Worth Papers.

28. "Property Agent" was not the title of a regular officer of the state government, but it was used to describe the duties Worth was to perform.

29. The article announcing the appointment is reprinted in William K. Boyd (ed.), *The Memoirs of W. W. Holden* (Durham, 1911), II, 49.

30. Cox to Worth, undated letter, printed in Raleigh *Standard,* Oct. 6, 1865.

31. Worth to Holden, Raleigh, Oct. 2, 1865, in Raleigh *Standard,* Oct. 6, 1865.

32. *Ibid.*

33. Raleigh, June 13, 1865, Governors' Letter Books (Holden), p. 1.

34. McCulloch to Heaton, Washington, June 17, 1865, Governors' Letter Books (Holden), p. 3.

35. Worth to W. B. Stephens, Raleigh, Aug. 21, 1865, *Worth Correspondence,* I, 398.

36. Holden to Hugh McCulloch, Raleigh, Oct. 19, 1865, Governors' Letter Books (Holden), p. 84.

37. Seward to Holden, Washington, July 8, 1865, in Raleigh *Standard,* Oct. 6, 1865.

38. Worth to Holden, Raleigh, Oct. 2, 1865, Raleigh *Standard,* Oct. 6, 1865.

39. White to Worth, London, Aug. 5, 1865, printed with Treasurer's Report, Sept. 4, 1865.

40. B. G. Worth to Worth, Wilmington, July 29, 1865, Worth Papers.

41. Kemp P. Battle, *Memories of an Old-Time Tar Heel*, ed. William J. Battle (Chapel Hill, 1945), p. 209.

42. Worth to Addison Worth, Raleigh, July 30, 1865, *Worth Correspondence*, I, 386; Worth to Holden, Raleigh, Oct. 2, 1865, in Raleigh *Standard*, Oct. 6, 1865; David Worth to Worth, Wilmington, Dec. 25, 1865, Worth Papers.

43. Holden to Hugh McCulloch, Raleigh, Oct. 19, 1865, Governors' Letter Books (Holden), p. 84.

44. J. G. de Roulhac Hamilton, *Reconstruction in North Carolina* (New York, 1914), p. 193.

45. Worth to George W. Swepson, Raleigh, Feb. 6, 1866, *Worth Correspondence*, I, 496.

46. Mendenhall to Worth, New York City, Feb. 2, 1866, Governors' Letter Books, I, 58-59.

47. Sloan to Worth, Raleigh, Feb. 17, 1866; Jones to Worth, Raleigh, Feb. 12, 1866, in *Legislative Documents*, 1865-66, No. 13.

48. It is impossible to determine exactly how much the state earned by collecting and selling its surplus property, for many of the records have been lost. Holden in his *Memoirs* (II, 56), places the figure at $150,000, and Hamilton accepted Holden's estimate, which is, however, too low. D. H. Hill concluded that the sales of cotton alone amounted to $176,806.40 (*North Carolina in the War Between the States: Bethel to Sharpsburg* [Raleigh, 1926], I, 364), but there is no way to determine how much it cost to collect and transport the cotton. The total receipts for both rosin and cotton after January 1, 1866, were $61,234.97, according to the Comptroller's Report for 1866.

Chapter XIV

1. Holden's proclamation was printed in the Raleigh *Standard* for several weeks beginning June 12.

2. Worth to Dr. W. P. Pugh, Raleigh, July 23, 1865, in J. G. de Roulhac Hamilton (ed.), *The Correspondence of Jonathan Worth* (Raleigh, 1909), I, 383.

3. Graham to Ramsay, Hillsboro, Oct. 13, 1865, James G. Ramsay Papers, Southern Historical Collection.

4. Winston to Worth, Windsor, Mar. 4, 1866, Governors' Papers.

5. Worth to Pool and Lewis Thompson, Raleigh, Oct. 16, 1865, *Worth Correspondence*, I, 430.

6. Worth to Pool, Raleigh, Oct. 17, 1865, *Worth Correspondence*, I, 432.

7. "To the People of North Carolina," circular dated Oct. 17, 1865, in North Carolina Room, UNC Library.

8. Worth to Holden, Raleigh, Oct. 18, 1865, *Worth Correspondence*, I, 434.

9. Raleigh, Nov. 17, 1865, Hedrick Papers, Duke University Library.

10. *Standard*, Oct. 19, 1865.

11. The letter was published in the *Sentinel* on Oct. 30.

12. Raleigh *Sentinel*, Nov. 6, 1865.

13. *Standard*, Nov. 1, 1865.

14. Caption of an article in the *Standard*, Oct. 26.

15. Worth to Jesse Walker, Raleigh, Sept. 14, 1865, *Worth Correspondence*, I, 420.
16. Issues of Aug. 4 and Aug. 31, 1865.
17. Worth's letter to the editor in *Sentinel* of Oct. 30, 1865.
18. Washington, Oct. 18, 1865, Governors' Letter Books (Holden), p. 83.
19. Worth to Editor of the Raleigh *Sentinel*, Raleigh, Oct. 28, 1865, in *Sentinel* of Oct. 30.
20. Vance to D. L. Swain, Statesville, Nov. 3, 1865, Vance Papers, State Archives.
21. Nov. 15.
22. Dec. 15, 1865.
23. *Memoirs*, II, 68.
24. Worth to John Pool, Raleigh, Apr. 23, 1866, *Worth Correspondence*, I, 558.
25. Ramsay to Worth, Palermo, May 10, 1866, Worth Papers.
26. Brooks to William H. Bagley, Elizabeth City, June 28, 1866, Worth Papers.
27. Worth to B. S. Hedrick, Raleigh, Nov. 17, 1865, Hedrick Papers.
28. T. L. Russell to Worth, New Hope Academy, Feb. 2, 1866, Worth Papers.
29. E. J. Hale to Worth, Fayetteville, Mar. 6, 1866, Governors' Papers.
30. Powell to Johnson, Raleigh, Nov. 26, 1865, reprinted from Johnson Papers in *North Carolina Historical Review*, XXVII (1951), 68.
31. The telegram is in the body of *Ibid.* Dr. Hamilton printed it in his *Reconstruction in North Carolina* (p. 141). He apparently was not aware of its origin.
32. Raleigh, Dec. 6, 1865, reprinted from Johnson Papers in *NCHR*, XXVII (1951), 76-78.
33. Powell to Worth, Washington, Dec. 15, 1865, Governors' Papers.
34. Worth to Hedrick, Raleigh, Nov. 17, 1865, Hedrick Papers.
35. Hedrick to Worth, Washington, Dec. 19, 1865, Governors' Papers.
36. Clipping from an unidentifiable New York paper containing a dispatch from Washington.
37. Worth to B. S. Hedrick, Raleigh, Dec. 16, 1865, Hedrick Papers.
38. Worth to Hedrick, Raleigh, July 4, 1866, *Worth Correspondence*, II, 666.
39. Oath Book, Jonathan Worth, State Archives.
40. Seward to Holden, Washington, Dec. 23, 1865, Governors' Letter Books (Worth), I, 3.

Chapter XV

1. Hedrick to Worth, Washington, Dec. 15, 1865, Governors' Papers.
2. Kenneth E. St. Clair, "Judicial Machinery in North Carolina in 1865," *North Carolina Historical Review*, XXX (1953), 418, 427, 431.
3. Winston, Jan. 3, 1866, Worth Papers.
4. Worth to B. S. Guion, Raleigh, Jan. 4, 1866, Worth Papers.
5. Worth to G. J. Wilson, Raleigh, Jan. 6, 1866, Worth Papers.
6. Telegram, Johnson to Worth, Washington, Jan. 2, 1866, Governors' Papers.
7. Worth to Ruger, Raleigh, Jan. 4, 1866, Governors' Letter Books, I, 7.
8. Ruger to Worth, Raleigh, Jan. 4, 1866, Governors' Letter Books, I, 22.
9. The message, dated Executive Office, Dec. 30, 1865, is in the Raleigh *Standard*, Jan. 1, 1866.
10. Worth to Johnson, Raleigh, Jan. 10, 1866, Governors' Letter Books, I, 266.
11. Walter L. Fleming, *Documentary History of Reconstruction* (Cleveland, 1906), I, 315-26.

12. Message in *Legislative Documents*, 1865-66, No. 7, pp. 1-22.

13. *Public Laws*, 1865-66, Chs. 4 and 26.

14. Raleigh, Dec. 28, 1867, in J. G. de Roulhac Hamilton (ed.), *The Correspondence of Jonathan Worth* (Raleigh, 1909), II, 1095.

15. Clark to Worth, Economy, Indiana, Dec. 17, 1865, Worth Papers.

16. Dibble to Worth, New York City, Jan. 1, 1866, Worth Papers.

17. Graham to J. W. Burton and J. Holderby, Hillsboro, Feb. 6, 1866, in Raleigh *Standard*, Feb. 14, 1866.

18. Worth to Graham, Raleigh, Jan. 12, 1866, *Worth Correspondence*, I, 467.

19. James Blackwell Browning, "North Carolina Black Code," *Journal of Negro History*, XV (1930), 472.

20. B. S. Hedrick to Worth, Washington, Feb. 24, 1866, Governors' Papers.

21. Worth to Johnson, Raleigh, Mar. 4, 1866; Johnson to Worth, Washington, Mar. 6, 1866, Governors' Letter Books, I, 56.

22. Worth to D. L. Swain, Raleigh, Mar. 16, 1866, Governors' Papers.

23. *Ibid.*

24. Seely to Sheriff of Craven County, Newbern, Mar. 30, 1866 Worth Papers.

25. This was the adjourned session of the convention which met in the fall of 1865 to ratify the Thirteenth Amendment, abolish slavery, and reorganize the state government. It met from May to June, 1866, for the principal purpose of revising the state constitution. J. G. de Roulhac Hamilton, "The North Carolina Convention of 1865-66," in *Publications of the North Carolina Historical Commission*, Bulletin No. 15 (1913), pp. 56-68.

26. Message to convention in Raleigh *Standard*, May 30, 1866.

27. Justin Hodge to General Allen Rutherford, Fayetteville, Dec. 10, 1866, Governors' Letter Books, I, 320.

28. J. G. Shepherd to Worth, Fayetteville, Dec. 31, 1866; Worth to Bomford, Raleigh, Jan. 1, 1867, Governors' Letter Books, I, 321.

29. Copy of petition in Governors' Letter Books, I, 92-93.

30. F. W. Seward to Worth, Washington, May 15, 1866, Governors' Letter Books, I, 92. The State Department was not officially responsible for the administration of justice, but it was the agency through which the president frequently corresponded with Worth.

31. Ferrebee to Worth, South Hill, May 24, 1866, Governors' Letter Books.

32. Petitions dated Apr. 22, 1866, Governors' Letter Books, I, 124-25.

33. Worth to Merrimon, Raleigh, June 2, 1866, *Worth Correspondence*, I, 600.

34. Samuel A. Ashe, *Biographical History of North Carolina from Colonial Times to the Present* (Greensboro, 1905-17), VIII, 334-42.

35. Merrimon to Worth, Asheville, June 7, 1866, Governors' Letter Books, I, 125-28.

36. *Ibid.*

37. Raleigh *Standard*, June 13, 1866.

38. Coleman to Worth, Asheville, June 8, 1866, *Worth Correspondence*, I, 603.

39. Worth to William H. Seward, Raleigh, June 18, 1866, Governors' Letter Books, I, 129.

40. Jackson to Worth, Asheboro, April 2, 1866, Worth Papers, Southern Historical Collection.

41. William S. Mason to Worth, Raleigh, Aug. 17, 1866, Governors' Papers.

42. J. L. Johnson to B. S. Hedrick, Abbott's Creek, July 16, 1866, Hedrick Papers.

43. J. M. Little to Worth, Charleston, S.C., Feb. 16, 1867, Worth Papers.

44. Worth to Hedrick, Raleigh, July 25, 1866, *Worth Correspondence,* I, 693-94.
45. Pearson to Worth, Richmond Hill, July 31, 1866, Governors' Letter Books, I, 340.
46. Robinson to Worth, Raleigh, July 3, 1866, Governors' Letter Books, I, 140.
47. Worth to Robinson, Raleigh, July 11, 1866, Governors' Letter Books, I, 141.
48. Order to agents of the Bureau, Governors' Letter Books, I, 143.
49. "To the People of North Carolina," July 23, 1866, in Raleigh *Sentinel,* July 25, 1866.
50. For the correspondence, charges, and counter charges see Governors' Letter Books, I, 146-73.
51. Worth to Johnson, Raleigh, Aug. 27, 1866, Governors' Letter Books, I, 184.
52. Stanton to Worth, Washington, Aug. 7, 1866, Governors' Letter Books, I, 191.
53. Worth to M. E. Manly *et al.,* Raleigh, Nov. 2, 1866, Governors' Letter Books, I, 240.

Chapter XVI

1. John Robinson to Stevens, Goldsboro, Feb. 22, 1866, printed from Thaddeus Stevens Papers in *North Carolina Historical Review,* XVIII (1941), 181-82.
2. Horace W. Raper, "William Woods Holden: A Political Biography" (Ph.D. thesis, The University of North Carolina, 1951), pp. 115-16.
3. Worth to Johnson, Raleigh, Dec. 28, 1865, Worth Papers; Johnson to Worth, Washington, Dec. 30, 1865, Governors' Letter Books, I, 264.
4. Worth to Asa Biggs, Raleigh, May 21, 1866, in J. G. de Roulhac Hamilton (ed.), *The Correspondence of Jonathan Worth* (Raleigh, 1909), I, 593-94.
5. Hedrick to Worth, Washington, April 24, 1866, Worth Papers.
6. Worth to William H. Seward, Raleigh, June 18, 1866, *Worth Correspondence,* I, 631.
7. Worth to Johnson, Raleigh, July 10, 1866, *Worth Correspondence,* I, 678.
8. Hedrick to Worth, Washington, July 26, 1866, Worth Papers; R. S. Morrow to Worth, Washington, June 19, 1867, Governors' Papers.
9. V. J. Palmer to Worth, Rutherford County, May 5, 1866; William H. Bagley to V. J. Palmer, Raleigh, May 21, 1866, Governors' Letter Books, I, 96-97.
10. Pool to William H. Bagley, Windsor, Apr. 13, 1866, Worth Papers.
11. Worth to Foster, Raleigh, Apr. 28, 1866, Marmaduke Robbins Papers, Southern Historical Collection.
12. H. J. Harris to Worth, Trinity College, May 9, 1866, Worth Papers, Southern Historical Collection.
13. Raleigh *Standard,* May 23, 1866.
14. "To the People of North Carolina," circular dated June 11, 1866, in North Carolina Room, University of North Carolina Library.
15. J. G. de Roulhac Hamilton, *Reconstruction in North Carolina* (New York, 1914), p. 178.
16. Holden to Johnson, July 11, 1866, printed from Johnson Papers in *NCHR,* XXVIII (1951), 227.
17. Holden to Johnson, Raleigh, Aug. 1, 1866, printed from Johnson Papers in *NCHR,* XXVIII (1951), 367.
18. Returns from the counties are in Governors' Papers for Aug., 1866.
19. Worth to William J. Wilson, Raleigh, Sept. 18, 1866, *Worth Correspondence,* II, 787.

20. Worth to Johnson, Raleigh, Sept. 15, 1866, printed from Johnson Papers in *NCHR*, XXVIII (1951), 368-69.

21. Worth to J. J. Jackson, Raleigh, Apr. 15, 1866, *Worth Correspondence*, I, 539.

22. Turner to Worth, Jan. 1, 1866, Worth Papers.

23. Milton Worth to Worth, Asheboro, June 7, 1866, Worth Papers, Southern Historical Collection.

24. Raleigh *Standard*, Mar. 21, 1866.

25. Mendenhall to Worth, New Garden, Mar. 31, 1866, *Worth Correspondence*, I, 523.

26. Coffin to Worth, Amo, Indiana, June 8, 1868, Worth Papers.

27. Roy F. Dibble, *Albion W. Tourgee* (New York, 1921), p. 26.

28. This meeting was held during the first week in September. Its resolutions severely criticized the reconstruction policy of President Johnson and insisted that the South should ratify the Fourteenth Amendment before being readmitted to the Union. Hamilton, *Reconstruction in North Carolina*, p. 180.

29. Worth to Mendenhall, Raleigh, Sept. 10, 1866, *Worth Correspondence*, II, 773.

30. Worth to Editor of the *Patriot*, Raleigh, Sept. 10, 1866; Worth to John A. Gilmer, Raleigh, Sept. 11, 1866, *Worth Correspondence*, II, 774-77.

31. Worth to D. F. Caldwell, Raleigh, Sept. 6, 1866, *Worth Correspondence*, II, 769.

32. A printed copy of the proceedings of the meeting which drew up these resolutions is in the B. S. Hedrick Papers at Duke University Library.

33. Worth to C. C. Clark, Raleigh, Sept. 21, 1866, *Worth Correspondence*, II, 789; Hedrick to Worth, Washington, Sept. 24, 1866, Worth Papers.

34. R. D. W. Connor (ed.), *North Carolina Manual, 1913* (Raleigh, 1914), p. 1002.

35. Jackson to Worth, Asheboro, Oct. 18, 1866, Worth Papers.

36. Jesse Walker to Worth, New Market, Oct. 29, 1866, Worth Papers, Southern Historical Collection.

37. Worth to Robinson, Raleigh, Oct. 29, 1866, Governors' Letter Books, I, 234.

38. Robinson to Worth, Raleigh, Oct. 30, 1866, Governors' Letter Books, I, 235, 239.

39. *Ibid.*

40. Worth to Robinson, Raleigh, Nov. 1, 1866, Governors' Letter Books, I, 237-39.

41. Howard to Robinson, Washington, Dec. 19, 1866, Governors' Letter Books, I, 326.

Chapter XVII

1. Two other sections forbade payment of the South's war debt and gave Congress power to enforce the first four sections "by appropriate legislation."

2. J. G. de Roulhac Hamilton (ed.), *The Correspondence of Jonathan Worth* (Raleigh, 1909), II, 666-67.

3. *Ibid.*; Worth to Jesse Wheeler, Raleigh, Sept. 7, 1866; Worth to D. H. Starbuck, Raleigh, Sept. 29, 1866, *Worth Correspondence*, II, 770, 796.

4. Message in *Legislative Documents*, 1866-67, No. 1, pp. 1-30.

5. *Journal of the Senate of North Carolina*, 1866-67, p. 138; *Journal of the House of Commons of North Carolina*, 1866-67, pp. 183-84.

6. Article quoted in Raleigh *Sentinel*, Dec. 15, 1866.

7. J. G. de Roulhac Hamilton, *Reconstruction in North Carolina* (New York, 1914), p. 169.

8. A copy of the order is in Governors' Letter Books, I, 251-53.

9. When the Freedmen's Bureau was first established it had its own officers, but in 1866 and afterwards, the officer in command of the federal troops in the state served as Assistant Commissioner.

10. Bomford to Worth, Raleigh, Nov. 29, 1866, Worth to Johnson, Raleigh, Nov. 30, 1866, Governors' Letter Books, I, 254.

11. Bomford to Worth, Raleigh, Dec. 7, 1866; Worth to Bomford, Raleigh, Dec. 13, 1866, Governors' Letter Books, I, 309, 310.

12. The resolution is in Governors' Letter Books, I, 325.

13. Worth to Benjamin Hedrick, Raleigh, Nov. 29, 1866, Hedrick Papers.

14. Holden to Mrs. Holden, Washington, Dec. 9, 1866, Holden Papers, State Archives.

15. Hamilton, *Reconstruction*, p. 188.

16. Pool to Bagley, Currituck Sound, Dec. 15, 1866, Worth Papers.

17. *Ibid.*

18. Gilmer to Worth, Greensboro, Jan. 2, 1867, Worth Papers.

19. Worth to William H. Bagley, Washington, Dec. 16, 1866, Worth Papers.

20. New York *World*, Dec. 18, 1866.

21. On December 18, Johnson did consult the cabinet about Sickles' whipping order. All members agreed that the general had exceeded his authority. Gideon Welles, *Diary of Gideon Welles* (New York, 1911), II, 644.

22. E. D. Townsend to Sickles, Washington, Dec. 19, 1866, Governors' Papers.

23. Worth to Howard, Raleigh, Jan. 7, 1867, Governors' Letter Books, I, 349.

24. New York *World*, Dec. 20, 1866.

25. "Inaugural," in *Legislative Documents*, 1866-67, No. 25.

26. Perrin Busbee to B. S. Hedrick, Raleigh, Dec. 26, 1866, Hedrick Papers.

27. Worth to Swain, Raleigh, Jan. 5, 1867, *Worth Correspondence*, II, 858.

28. Boyden to Worth, Salisbury, Dec. 29, 1866, Worth Papers.

29. *Ibid.*

30. Brown and Leach to Worth, Washington, Jan. 13, 1867, Worth Papers.

31. Rutherford to Col. Jacob F. Cheer, Wilmington, Feb. 12, 1867, Governors' Letter Books, I, 378.

32. Worth to Bomford, Raleigh, Feb. 18, 1867, Governors' Letter Books, I, 379-80.

33. "J. H." to Editor of the *Sentinel*, Lexington, Jan. 2, 1867.

34. Raleigh *Standard*, Jan. 16, 1867.

35. Jan. 30, 1867.

36. Raleigh, *Sentinel*, Feb. 6, 1867.

37. Worth to James L. Orr, Raleigh, *Worth Correspondence*, II, 894.

38. *United States Statutes at Large*, 1866-67, Ch. 153.

39. Worth to David L. Swain, Raleigh, Mar. 3, 1867, *Worth Correspondence*, II, 908.

40. Ruffin to Worth, Hillsboro, Mar. 5, 1867; Swain to Worth, Chapel Hill, Mar. 6, 1867, Worth Papers.

41. Worth to William A. Graham, Washington, Mar. 12, 1867, Graham Papers, Southern Historical Collection.

42. Clipping from Raleigh *Standard* in Governors' Papers.

43. Worth to William A. Graham, Washington, Mar. 12, 1867, Graham Papers.

44. Journal, Council of State, 1855-89, pp. 194-95.

45. Voorhies to Worth, New Orleans, Mar. 6, 1867, Governors' Letter Books, I, 399-400.
46. Worth to Curtis, Washington, Mar. 18, 1867; Curtis to Worth, Boston, Mar. 20, 1867, Governors' Letter Books, I, 397-99.
47. Turner to Worth, Hillsboro, Mar. 24, 1867, Worth Papers.
48. Journal, Council of State, 1855-89, pp. 202-3.
49. Worth to Albert Voorhies, Raleigh, Mar. 29, 1867, Governors' Letter Books, I, 400-1.
50. Milton Worth to Worth, Asheboro, Mar. 1, 1867, Worth Papers.
51. Winston to Worth, Windsor, Mar. 1, 1867, Hedrick to Worth, Washington, Mar. 3, 1867, Worth Papers.
52. Worth to Worth and Daniel, Raleigh, Mar. 7, 1867, *Worth Correspondence*, II, 915.

Chapter XVIII

1. General Order No. 1, Second Military District, Mar. 21, 1867. Sickles' orders may be found in *Senate Executive Documents*, 40th Cong., 1st Sess., No. 14.
2. Orr to Worth, Columbia, S.C., July 29, 1867, Governors' Papers.
3. Worth to Sickles, Raleigh, May 10, 1867, Governors' Letter Books, I, 458-59.
4. J. W. Clous to Worth, Charleston, May 19, 1867, Governors' Letter Books, I, 476.
5. Worth to Major W. L. Worth, Raleigh, May 7, 1867; Major W. L. Worth to Worth, Greensboro, May 25, 1867, Worth Papers.
6. General Order No. 10, Second Military District, Charleston, April 11, 1867.
7. J. M. Wooten to Worth, Catharine Lake, June 24, 1867, Worth Papers.
8. J. S. Amis to Worth, Oxford, June 13, 1867, Governors' Papers.
9. R. C. Badger and Ed. Graham Haywood, Apr. 20, 1867, Governors' Letter Books, I, 455-57.
10. E. W. Dennis to Worth, Charleston, July 11, 1867, Governors' Letter Books, I, 515.
11. Worth to Sickles, Raleigh, April 19, 1867, Governors' Letter Books, I, 415-16.
12. Petition to Worth and commission to Judge Edward J. Warren, Governors' Letter Books, I, 467-68.
13. Worth to Col. J. V. Bomford, Raleigh, May 18, 1867, Governors' Letter Books, I, 468-69.
14. Special Order No. 55, Charleston, May 27, 1867, in *Senate Executive Documents*, 40th Cong., 1st Sess., No. 14, pp. 84-85.
15. Worth to Henry T. Clark, Raleigh, Sept. 23, 1867, in J. G. de Roulhac Hamilton (ed.), *The Correspondence of Jonathan Worth* (Raleigh, 1909), II, 1049-50.
16. "Report of Committee on a Penitentiary," in Raleigh *Sentinel*, Dec. 15, 1866.
17. Worth to Sickles, Raleigh, Aug. 2, 1867, Governors' Letter Books, I, 541-42.
18. Special Orders No. 114, Charleston, Aug. 1, 1867, copy in Governors' Papers.
19. Worth to Sickles, Raleigh, Aug. 14, 1867, Governors' Letter Books, I, 560-61.
20. The following discussion is based on a lengthy letter from Worth to the president dated June 8, 1867, in Governors' Letter Books, I, 489-94.
21. Letter to Johnson cited in previous note.
22. Stanbery to Andrew Johnson, Washington, June 12, 1867, in Raleigh *Sentinel*, June 19, 1867.

23. Sickles to The Adjutant General, Charleston, June 19, 1867, in *House Executive Documents,* 40th Cong., 1st Sess., No. 20, p. 35.

24. *United States Statutes at Large,* 1867-69, Ch. 30.

25. Worth to The Judges, Raleigh, Aug. 6, 1867, Governors' Letter Books, I, 547-48; Special Orders No. 131, Charleston, Aug. 21, 1867.

26. Worth to Johnson, Raleigh, June 8, 1867, Governors' Letter Books, I, 489-91.

27. Worth to Sickles, Raleigh, Aug. 10, 1867, Governors' Papers.

28. Sickles to Worth, Charleston, Aug. 10, 1867, Governors' Letter Books, I, 552.

29. Worth to Sickles, Raleigh, Aug. 15, 1867, Governors' Letter Books, I, 561.

30. Worth to Sickles, Raleigh, Apr. 29, 1867, Governors' Letter Books, I, 441.

31. Miles's circular to Freedmen's Bureau Agents, Raleigh, Apr. 26, 1867.

32. Worth to Sickles, Raleigh, Apr. 29, 1867, Governors' Letter Books, I, 440-42.

33. H. Joyner to Worth, Enfield, Apr. 23 and May 10, Governors' Papers.

34. Gaither to Worth, Morganton, Apr. 24, 1867, Governors' Papers.

35. Russell to Worth, Robeson County, Apr. 25, 1867, Governors' Papers.

36. Worth to Sickles, Raleigh, May 15, 1867, Governors' Letter Books, I, 465-66.

37. Endorsement on *Ibid.,* dated Charleston, May 26, 1867.

38. Henry Stanbery to Andrew Johnson, Washington, June 12, 1867, in *Raleigh Sentinel,* June 19, 1867. Stanbery's opinion contended that participation in the rebellion, per se, did not disqualify a person from registering. Military officers of the state in the prewar period, municipal officers, and state agents should be allowed to register. Furthermore, "disloyal sentiments, opinions, or sympathies would not disqualify," and involuntary conscripts into the Confederate armies or forced contributors to the South's war effort were not disqualified. Congress could not tolerate Stanbery's opinion and invalidated it by writing into the Third Reconstruction Act that "no district commander or member of the board of registration . . . shall be bound in his action by any opinion of any civil officer of the United States."

39. Sickles to Adjutant General, Charleston, July 6, 1867, *Senate Executive Documents,* 40th Cong., 1st Sess., No. 14, p. 60.

40. "To the People of North Carolina," Aug. 3, 1867, in *Raleigh Sentinel,* Aug. 7, 1867.

41. W. A. Swanberg, *Sickles the Incredible* (New York, 1956), p. 291.

42. J. G. de Roulhac Hamilton, *Reconstruction in North Carolina* (New York, 1914), p. 232.

43. Worth to B. G. Worth, Raleigh, Oct. 25, 1867, *Worth Correspondence,* II, 1061.

Chapter XIX

1. Canby to Worth, Charleston, Sept. 12, 1867, Governors' Letter Books, I, 583-84.

2. *Ibid.*

3. Worth to Canby, Raleigh, Sept. 10, 1867, Governors' Letter Books, I, 576-78.

4. Canby to Worth, Charleston, Oct. 12, 1867, Governors' Letter Books, I, 620-24.

5. *Ibid.*

6. The only complete discussion of Canby's role as enforcer of the Reconstruction Acts is Max L. Heyman, "The Great Reconstructor: General E. R. S. Canby and the Second Military District," *North Carolina Historical Review,* XXXII (1955), 52-80. The article has since been published in Heyman's *Prudent Soldier: A Biography of Major General E. R. S. Canby, 1817-1873* (Glendale, Calif., 1959).

7. Tourgee to Sickles, Greensboro, Apr. 11, 1867, in *NCHR*, XXVIII (1951), 486-87.

8. Edgar W. Dennis to Louis V. Caziarc, Charleston, Oct. 4, 1867, in *NCHR*, XXIX (1952), 258-59.

9. *Ibid.*

10. This charge had a solid basis in facts. Between March 2, 1867, the date of the First Reconstruction Act, and July 24, 1868, when North Carolina returned to the Union, 1,137 persons were arrested by the military authorities in the Second Military District. Of these, 435 were released after preliminary hearings. Between January 1, 1867, and June 30, 1868, 550 cases were tried before military commissions, and in 450 of these, the defendants were judged guilty. There were only six convictions for murder; in these cases, the sentence was remitted wholly (1) or partially (5). North and South Carolina were lumped together in the military reports, and it is impossible to separate them. It seems safe to say that there were far more arrests and trials in South Carolina than in North Carolina. *House Executive Documents,* 40 Cong., 3rd Sess., No. 1, pp. 352-53.

11. Letter to Andrew Johnson in Governors' Letter Books, I, 635-36.

12. Canby to Grant, Charleston, Nov. 14, 1867, in Governors' Letter Books, I, 682-87.

13. This was a reference to Johnson's first trial. Before the war ended he had been convicted, but he escaped from the civil authorities and was retried after the war.

14. During the course of the discussion with Worth over the Caswell County case and military justice in general, Canby issued an order interpreting the legislature's amnesty act and extending protection to all persons who had been excluded by omission. General Order No. 134, Charleston, Nov. 27, 1867, in *House Executive Documents,* 40 Cong., 2nd Sess., No. 342, pp. 75-76.

15. Worth to Canby, Raleigh, Nov. 30, 1867, Governors' Letter Books, I, 688-92.

16. *Ibid.*

17. *United States Statutes at Large,* 1867-69, Ch. 30, Sec. 4.

18. General Order No. 101, Charleston, Oct. 18, 1867.

19. Canby to Worth, Charleston, Oct. 24, 1867, Governors' Letter Books, I, 641-42.

20. Raleigh *Standard,* Nov. 27, 1867. About five thousand additional voters registered during a five day period when Canby allowed the registration books to be opened and revised.

21. Raleigh *Standard,* Apr. 3, 1867.

22. Notes of a speech delivered at Spring Garden, Rockingham County, Settle Papers, Southern Historical Collection.

23. Raleigh *Standard,* Oct. 30 and Nov. 6, 1867.

24. Deweese to Elihu M. Washburne, Raleigh, Oct. 30, 1867, in *NCHR*, XVIII (1941), 394.

25. Worth to David Worth, Raleigh, Oct. 24, 1867, in J. G. de Roulhac Hamilton (ed.), *The Correspondence of Jonathan Worth* (Raleigh, 1909), II, 1058.

26. Jackson to Lucy Worth Jackson, Pittsboro, Oct. 16, 1867, Worth Papers.

27. David Worth to Worth, Oct. 28, 1867, Worth Papers.

28. J. G. de Roulhac Hamilton, *Reconstruction in North Carolina* (New York, 1914), pp. 251, 253.

29. Worth to Louis Lutterloh, Raleigh, Dec. 20, 1867, Worth Papers.

30. Worth to William H. Bagley, Washington, Dec. 9, 1867, Worth Papers.

31. *Ibid.*

32. Worth to Milton Worth, Raleigh, Feb. 7, 1868, Worth Papers.
33. Fowle to Worth, Raleigh, Nov. 28, 1867, Governors' Letter Books, I, 681.
34. Journal, Council of State, 1855-89, pp. 210-11.
35. Poindexter to Worth, Germantown, Jan. 2, 1868, Governors' Letter Books, II, 22.
36. Luke Blackmer to Worth, Salisbury, Jan. 31, 1868, Worth Papers.
37. William F. Wright to Worth, Wilmington, Jan. 13, 1868, Worth Papers.
38. Canby to Worth, Charleston, Jan. 4, 1868, Governors' Letter Books, II, 23.
39. J. C. Griffith to Worth, Yanceyville, Jan. 4, 1868, Worth Papers.
40. Gorrell to Worth, Greensboro, Jan. 8, 1868; Caldwell to Worth, Greensboro, Jan. 9, 1868, Worth Papers.
41. Hedrick to Worth, Washington, Jan. 12, 1868, Worth Papers.
42. Raleigh *Standard,* Jan. 15, 1868.
43. Hedrick to William H. Bagley, Washington, Jan. 16, 1868, Worth Papers.
44. Worth to Canby, Raleigh, Jan. 9, 1868, *Worth Correspondence,* II, 1124-27.
45. Canby to Worth, Charleston, Jan. 19, 1868, Governors' Letter Books, II, 45-47.
46. Journal, Council of State, 1855-89, pp. 214-15.
47. Battle to Graham, Raleigh, Jan. 24, 1868, Battle Papers, Southern Historical Collection.
48. *Ibid.*
49. Turner to Worth, Company Shops, Battle Papers.
50. Worth to Battle, Raleigh, Jan. 26, 1868, *Worth Correspondence,* II, 1140-41.
51. Hamilton, *Reconstruction,* p. 260.
52. For a thorough, but highly critical, discussion of the convention and the new constitution see *Ibid.,* pp. 253-78.
53. Worth to S. S. Jackson, Raleigh, Apr. 9, 1868, *Worth Correspondence,* II, 1184-85.
54. Worth to Graham, Raleigh, Feb. 27, 1868, *Worth Correspondence,* II, 1166.
55. Raleigh, June 2, 1868, Hedrick Papers.
56. This suggestion came originally from Zeb Vance. Vance to Worth, Charlotte, Mar. 22, 1868, Worth Papers.
57. Worth to Canby, Raleigh, Mar. 25, 1868, Governors' Letter Books, II, 101. Worth complained after the election that there had been too many names on the single ballot. His proposal to have several boxes and ballots sounds much like the schemes later used in the South to disfranchise ignorant Negroes by confusing them and causing them to drop their ballots in the wrong box; but there is no evidence that Worth had such devious intentions in 1868.
58. Canby to Worth, Charleston, Apr. 11, 1868, Governors' Letter Books, II, 117.
59. May 2, 1868.
60. Worth to W. J. Yates, Raleigh, May 5, 1868, *Worth Correspondence,* II, 1194.
61. Worth to Doolittle, Raleigh, May 11, 1868, *Worth Correspondence,* II, 1197-98.
62. Worth to Fessenden, Raleigh, May 26, 1868, *Worth Correspondence,* II, 1210-14.
63. Canby to Grant, Charleston, May 4, 1868, in *House Executive Documents,* 40 Cong., 2nd Sess., No. 276, pp. 2-4.
64. Grant to George G. Meade, Washington, Apr. 29, 1868, in *House Executive Documents,* 40 Cong., 2nd Sess., No. 276, p. 14.

65. The act is reproduced in Edward McPherson, *Political History of the United States During the Period of Reconstruction* (Washington, 1871), pp. 337-38.

66. Worth to C. B. Mallett, Raleigh, May 6, 1868, *Worth Correspondence*, II, 1196; Worth to Holden, Raleigh, Governors' Letter Books, II, 165.

67. Worth to Canby, Raleigh, July 1, 1868, Governors' Letter Books, II, 171. Canby annulled the appointments on July 3. Raleigh *Standard*, July 8, 1868.

68. Canby to Holden, Charleston, July 3, 1868, in Raleigh *Standard*, July 8, 1868.

69. Governors' Letter Books, II, 17.

70. William K. Boyd (ed.), *The Memoirs of W. W. Holden* (Durham, 1911), pp. 108-10.

Chapter XX

1. Sickles to Worth, Charleston, May 31, 1867, Governors' Letter Books, I, 497.

2. Pool to Worth, Washington, May 3, 1869, in J. G. de Roulhac Hamilton (ed.), *The Correspondence of Jonathan Worth* (Raleigh, 1909), II, 1283.

3. Charles Whedbee, "Major William Henry Bagley" (an address given in 1929 when Bagley's children presented his portrait to the Supreme Court of North Carolina), pp. 5-6.

4. Worth to Bason, Raleigh, July 25, 1867, Worth Papers.

5. Worth to Daniel Worth, Raleigh, Aug. 13, 1867, Worth Papers.

6. Worth to William Clark, Raleigh, Jan. 14, 1869, Worth Papers.

7. Worth to Tomlinson, Raleigh, Jan. 9, 1869, Worth Papers.

8. Account sheet from Worth and Daniel, Jan., 1866, Worth Papers.

9. Worth to Ingram, Raleigh, Aug. 24, 1865, *Worth Correspondence*, I, 402.

10. Porter to Worth, Greensboro, Nov. 8, 1866, Worth Papers, Southern Historical Collection.

11. Worth to Roberts, Raleigh, Jan. 1, 1867, Worth Papers.

12. Worth to David Worth, Raleigh, Oct. 15, 1868, Worth Papers.

13. Worth to Sewell Farlow, Raleigh, Mar. 22, 1868, Worth Papers.

14. Worth to W. G. Lewis, Raleigh, July 23, 1868, Worth Papers.

15. Worth to Merrimon, Raleigh, Aug. 21, 1868, *Worth Correspondence*, II, 1241-42; Merrimon to Worth, Raleigh, Sept. 11, 1868, Worth Papers.

16. Worth to William H. Bagley, New York City, Sept. 9, 1868, Worth Papers.

17. Worth to William Clark, Raleigh, Jan. 14, 1869, *Worth Correspondence*, II, 1261.

18. *Worth Correspondence*, II, 1256.

19. Worth to David Worth, Asheboro, Sept. 18, 1867, Worth Papers.

20. A copy of the will is in the Worth Papers at the State Archives.

21. Worth to William H. Bagley, New York City, Sept. 7, 9, and 10, 1868, Worth Papers; Worth to A. C. Cowles, Raleigh, Oct. 7, 1868, *Worth Correspondence*, II, 1251.

22. Milton Worth to Worth, Asheboro, Dec. 22, 1868, Worth Papers.

23. Worth to Editors of the Wilmington *Journal*, Raleigh, Jan. 21, 1869, *Worth Correspondence*, II, 1267.

24. Worth to Martitia Worth, Asheboro, June 8, 1869, Worth Papers.

25. Worth to William H. Bagley, Rockbridge Alum Springs, July 18, 1869, Worth Papers.

26. Receipts in Worth Papers.

27. After Worth was "disowned" by the Quakers for marrying Martitia, he never joined another church, and in his available writings he never directly expressed any religious views. It is apparent, however, from remarks he made when his daughter Mary died, that he believed in the immortality of the soul and the operation of "Divine Providence" in human affairs. (Worth to William Clark, Raleigh, Apr. 5, 1867, Worth Papers.) In another rare revelation of his attitude towards religion, he once told a Jewish rabbi that he looked favorably upon all religious groups "which encourage the observance of the requirements of the Decalogue . . ." (Worth to Rabbi Nathaniel Jacobi, Raleigh, Oct. 3, 1867, Worth Papers).

28. Raleigh *Sentinel*, Sept. 8, 1869.

29. Battle, *Memories of an Old-Time Tar Heel* (Chapel Hill, 1945), p. 204.

30. This calculation is incorrect. It should have been "66 years, 9 months, 18 days."

Selected Bibliography

―――――•―――――

MATERIALS IN MANUSCRIPT FORM

Repositories

DU—Manuscript Division, Duke University Library, Durham, North Carolina

GC—Guilford College Library, Guilford College, North Carolina

NCA—North Carolina Archives, Raleigh, North Carolina

RC—Randolph County Court House, Asheboro, North Carolina

SHC—Southern Historical Collection, The University of North Carolina at Chapel Hill

Applications for Pardon. NCA.

Appointments of Overseers, Randolph County, 1816-31. Microfilm in NCA.

William H. Bagley Papers. SHC.

Battle Family Papers. SHC.

James F. Boyd Papers. DU.

David F. Caldwell Papers. SHC.

Census Rolls, Randolph County, 1830, 1840, 1850, 1860. Microfilm in NCA.

Walter Clark Papers. NCA.

Common School Reports, Randolph County, 1843-64. NCA.

T. L. L. Cox Papers. DU.

Deed Books, Randolph County, 1824-60. RC.

Charles Fisher Papers. SHC.

Genealogical Chart of Worth Family. SHC.

Ralph Gorrell Papers. SHC.

Governors' Letter Books, Jonathan Worth. NCA.

Governors' Letter Books, Provisional Governor William W. Holden. NCA.

Governors' Letter Books, Zebulon B. Vance. NCA.

Governors' Papers, Jonathan Worth. NCA.

William A. Graham Papers. SHC.
Edward J. Hale Papers. NCA.
Benjamin S. Hedrick Papers. DU.
Benjamin S. Hedrick Papers. SHC.
William W. Holden Papers. DU.
William W. Holden Papers. NCA.
Estates Papers of Jonathan Worth, Wake County Records. NCA.
C. C. Jones, Jr., Papers. DU.
Journal of the Council of State, 1855-89. NCA.
William Lord London Papers. SHC.
Hugh McRae Papers. DU.
Charles Beatty Mallett Papers. SHC.
Minutes of the Court of Equity, Randolph County, 1825-46. Microfilm
    in NCA.
Minutes of Court of Pleas and Quarter Sessions, Randolph County,
    1825-52. RC.
Minutes of New Garden Monthly Meeting, Society of Friends, 1773.
    GC.
Minutes of the North Carolina Manumission Society. Typed copies in
    SHC.
Oath Books of Jonathan Worth. NCA.
James G. Ramsey Papers. SHC.
Report of the Superintendent of Common Schools for Randolph
    County, 1850-64. Microfilm in NCA.
Marmaduke Robbins Papers. SHC.
William L. Scott Papers. DU.
Thomas Settle Papers. SHC.
Lyndon Swaim Papers. DU.
David L. Swain Papers. SHC.
George W. Swepson Papers. NCA.
Tax Lists, Randolph County, 1835-40. RC.
Tax Lists, Wake County, 1866. NCA.
Bryan Tyson Papers. DU.
Zebulon B. Vance Papers. NCA.
Calvin H. Wiley Papers. NCA.
Women's Minutes, Deep River Monthly Meeting, Society of Friends,
    1798. GC.
Worth Letters. NCA.
Jonathan Worth Papers. DU.
Jonathan Worth Papers. NCA.
Jonathan Worth Papers. SHC.

PUBLISHED CORRESPONDENCE AND DOCUMENTS

Coon, Charles L. (ed.). *The Beginnings of Public Education in North Carolina: A Documentary History, 1790-1840.* Raleigh: Edwards and Broughton, 1908.

Hamilton, Joseph G. de Roulhac (ed.). *The Correspondence of Jonathan Worth.* Raleigh: Edwards and Broughton, 1909.

—— (ed.). *The Papers of Thomas Ruffin.* Raleigh: Edwards and Broughton, 1918.

Hoyt, William H. (ed.). *The Papers of Archibald D. Murphey.* Raleigh: North Carolina Historical Commission, 1914.

McPherson, Elizabeth Gregory (ed.). "Letters from North Carolina to Andrew Johnson," *North Carolina Historical Review,* XXVIII (1951), 63-88, 219-38, 362-76, 486-517; XXIX (1952), 104-20, 259-69, 400-32, 569-79.

Newsome, Albert R. (ed.). "The A. S. Merrimon Journal, 1853-54," *North Carolina Historical Review,* VIII (1931), 300-30.

Padgett, James A. (ed.). "Reconstruction Letters from North Carolina," *North Carolina Historical Review,* XVIII (1941), 171-96, 278-301, 373-98.

Shanks, Henry T. (ed.). *The Papers of Willie Person Mangum.* Raleigh: State Department of Archives and History, 1955.

NORTH CAROLINA PUBLIC DOCUMENTS

Claims Against the State. Raleigh: M. S. Littlefield, 1870.

Journal of the Convention of the People of North Carolina. Raleigh: John W. Syme, 1862.

Journal of the House of Commons of North Carolina, 1830-31, 1831-32, 1862-63. Raleigh: State Printer, 1831, 1832, 1863.

Journal of the Senate of North Carolina, 1840-41, 1858-59, 1860-61. Raleigh: State Printer, 1841, 1859, 1861.

Ordinances of the Convention of 1861-62. Raleigh: John W. Syme, 1862.

Ordinances Passed By The North Carolina State Convention at the Sessions of 1865-'66. Raleigh: William E. Pell, 1867.

Public Laws of North Carolina, 1830-31, 1840-41, 1858-67. Raleigh: State Printer, 1831, 1841, 1859-67.

Public Laws of the State of North Carolina Passed By the General Assembly at the Sessions of 1861-'62-'63-'64, and One in 1859. Raleigh: William E. Pell, 1866.

Report of Board of Claims, On the Finances of the State, to 30th September 1862. Raleigh: W. W. Holden, 1863.

Report of the Joint Select Committee Appointed Under a Joint Resolution to Enquire Into the Causes Why Soldiers Were Paid in Confederate Treasury Notes Instead of North Carolina Treasury Notes. Raleigh: W. W. Holden, 1863.

Reports of the Public Treasurer of North Carolina, 1860-66, North Carolina *Legislative Documents,* 1860-66.

Response of [the] Public Treasurer to Resolutions of the House of Commons. Raleigh: W. W. Holden, 1863.

UNITED STATES GOVERNMENT DOCUMENTS

"Correspondence Relative to Reconstruction," *Senate Executive Documents,* 40th Cong., 1st Sess., No. 1.

"General Orders—Reconstruction," *House Executive Documents,* 40th Cong., 2nd Sess., No. 342.

"Murder of Union Soldiers in North Carolina," *House Executive Documents,* 39th Cong., 1st Sess., No. 98.

"Report of Brevet Major General E. R. S. Canby, Commanding Late Second Military District," *House Executive Documents,* 40th Cong., 3rd. Sess., No. 1.

"Report of the Commissioner of the Bureau of Refugees, Freedmen, and Abandoned Lands," *House Executive Documents,* 39th Cong., 2nd Sess., No. 1.

Report of the Joint Committee on Reconstruction. Washington: Government Printing Office, 1866.

"Reports on the Second Military District," *House Executive Documents,* 40th Cong., 2nd Sess., No. 276.

The War of the Rebellion: A Compilation of the Official Records of the Union and Confederate Armies. Washington: Government Printing Office, 1880-1901.

NEWSPAPERS

Fayetteville *Observer,* 1845, 1858-61.
Greensboro *Patriot,* 1830-31, 1841, 1845, 1859-60.
Hillsboro *Recorder,* April 30 and October 29, 1828.
Holden Record (Raleigh), March and April, 1868.
New York *World,* December, 1867.
Raleigh *Register,* 1840-41.

Raleigh *Sentinel*, 1865-68.
Raleigh *Standard*, 1840-41, 1858-68.
Raleigh *Star*, 1830-31, 1840-41.
Randolph Herald (Asheboro), 1846-47.
Southern Citizen (Asheboro), 1837-40, 1844.
Western Carolinian (Salisbury), 1830-31.
Whig Clarion (Raleigh), 1843-44.

MEMOIRS AND DIARIES

Battle, Kemp P. *Memories of an Old-Time Tar Heel*, ed. William J.
    Battle. Chapel Hill: The University of North Carolina Press, 1945.
Blair, J. A. *Reminiscences of Randolph County*. Greensboro: Reece
    and Elam, 1890.
Boyd, William K. (ed.). *The Memoirs of W. W. Holden*. Durham:
    The Seeman Printery, 1911.
———. "Reverend Brantley York on Early Days in Randolph County
    and Union Institute," *Trinity College Historical Society Papers*,
    Series VIII (1908), 15-34.
McCulloch, Hugh. *Men and Measures of Half a Century*. New York:
    Charles Scribner's Sons, 1889.
Welles, Gideon. *Diary of Gideon Welles*. New York: Houghton
    Mifflin Company, 1911.

BOOKS BY WORTH'S CONTEMPORARIES

Cantwell, Edward. *The Practice of Law in North Carolina*. Raleigh:
    Strother and Marcom, 1860.
Caruthers, Eli W. *Interesting Revolutionary Incidents: And Sketches
    of Character, Chiefly in the "Old North State."* Philadelphia:
    Hayes and Zell, 1856.
Foote, William Henry. *Sketches of North Carolina*. New York: Robert
    Carter, 1846.
Spencer, Cornelia Phillips. *The Last Ninety Days of the War in North
    Carolina*. New York: Watchman Publishing Company, 1866.
Tyson, Bryan. *A Ray of Light; or, A Treatise on the Sectional
    Troubles, Religiously and Morally Considered*. Brower's Mills,
    N.C.: Published by author, 1862.
Wheeler, John H. *Historical Sketches of North Carolina, from 1584 to
    1851*. Philadelphia: Lippincott, Grambo and Company, 1851.

PERIODICAL ARTICLES

Battle, Kemp P. "The Secession Convention of 1861," *North Carolina Booklet*, XV (April, 1916), No. 4, 177-202.

Boyd, William K. "Ad Valorem Slave Taxation," *Trinity College Historical Society Papers*, Series V (1905), 31-38.

——. "Fiscal and Economic Conditions in North Carolina During the Civil War," *North Carolina Booklet*, XIV (April, 1915), No. 4, 195-219.

——. "William W. Holden," *Trinity College Historical Society Papers*, Series III (1899), 39-78, 90-130.

Brooks, Aubrey Lee. "David Caldwell and His Log College," *North Carolina Historical Review*, XXVIII (1951), 399-408.

Browning, James Blackwell. "North Carolina Black Code," *The Journal of Negro History*, XV (1930), 461-73.

Davis, J. R. "Reconstruction in Cleveland County," *Trinity College Historical Society Papers*, Series X (1914), 5-31.

Dorris, Jonathan T. "Pardoning North Carolinians," *North Carolina Historical Review*, XXIII (1946), 360-402.

Farmer, Fannie M. "The Bar Examination and Beginning Years of Legal Practice in North Carolina, 1820-1860," *North Carolina Historical Review*, XXIX (1952), 159-71.

——. "Legal Education in North Carolina, 1820-1860," *North Carolina Historical Review*, XXVIII (1951), 271-98.

Graham, William A. "The North Carolina Union Men of Eighteen Hundred Sixty-One," *North Carolina Booklet*, XI (July, 1911), 3-16.

Green, Fletcher M. "Gold Mining in North Carolina," *North Carolina Historical Review*, XIV (1937), 1-19, 135-55.

Hamilton, Joseph G. de Roulhac. "The North Carolina Convention of 1865-66," *Publications of the North Carolina Historical Commission*, Bulletin No. 15 (1913), 56-68.

——. "The N. C. Courts and the Confederacy," *North Carolina Historical Review*, IV (1927), 366-403.

Heyman, Max L. "The Great Reconstructor: General E. R. S. Canby and the Second Military District," *North Carolina Historical Review*, XXXII (1955), 52-80.

Johnson, Guion G. "Social Characteristics of Ante-Bellum North Carolina," *North Carolina Historical Review*, VI (1929), 140-57.

Jones, Houston G. "Bedford Brown: State Rights Unionist," *North Carolina Historical Review*, XXXII (1955), 321-46, 483-512.

Raper, Horace W. "William W. Holden and the Peace Movement in

North Carolina," *North Carolina Historical Review*, XXXI (1954), 493-517.

Ruark, Bryant Whitlock. "Some Phases of Reconstruction in Wilmington and the County of New Hanover," *Trinity College Historical Society Papers*, Series XI (1915) 79-111.

Russ, William A., Jr. "Radical Disfranchisement in North Carolina, 1867-1868," *North Carolina Historical Review*, XI (1934), 271-83.

St. Clair, Kenneth E. "Debtor Relief in North Carolina During Reconstruction," *North Carolina Historical Review*, XVIII (1941), 215-36.

———. "Judicial Machinery in North Carolina in 1865," *North Carolina Historical Review*, XXX (1953), 415-39.

Schell, Herbert S. "Hugh McCulloch and the Treasury Department, 1865-1869," *Mississippi Valley Historical Review*, XVII (1930), 404-21.

Sellers, Charles G., Jr. "Who Were the Southern Whigs?" *American Historical Review*, LIX (1954), 335-42.

Sherill, P. M. "Quakers and the North Carolina Manumission Society," *Trinity College Historical Society Papers*, Series X (1914), 32-51.

Starling, Robert G. "The Plank Road Movement in N. C.," *North Carolina Historical Review*, XVI (1939), 1-23, 147-74.

Todd, Richard C. "The Produce Loans: A Means of Financing the Confederacy," *North Carolina Historical Review*, XXVII (1950), 46-75.

Webb, Elizabeth Yates. "Cotton Manufacturing and State Regulation in North Carolina, 1861-'65," *North Carolina Historical Review*, IX (1932), 117-37.

Worth, Laura Stimson. "The History of Education in Randolph County," *North Carolina Education*, XII (September, 1945), No. 1, 51-61.

Yates, Richard E. "Governor Vance and the End of the War in North Carolina," *North Carolina Historical Review*, XVIII (1941), 315-39.

———. "Governor Vance and the Peace Movement," *North Carolina Historical Review*, XVII (1940), 1-26, 89-114.

BIOGRAPHIES, MONOGRAPHS, AND GENERAL STUDIES

Albright, James W. *Greensboro, 1808-1904.* Greensboro: Joseph J. Stone and Company, 1904.

Arnett, Ethel S. *Greensboro, North Carolina: The County Seat of Guilford.* Written under the direction of Walter Clinton Jackson. Chapel Hill: The University of North Carolina Press, 1955.

Bassett, John S. *Anti-Slavery Leaders of North Carolina.* Baltimore: Johns Hopkins Press, 1898.

Brown, Cecil K. *A State Movement in Railroad Development: The Story of North Carolina's First Effort to Establish an East and West Trunk Line Railroad.* Chapel Hill: The University of North Carolina Press, 1928.

Burgess, Fred. *Randolph County: Economic and Social.* Chapel Hill: University of North Carolina Department of Rural Social Economics, 1924.

Caldwell, Bettie D., compiler. *Founders and Builders of Greensboro.* Greensboro: Joseph J. Stone and Company, 1925.

Carroll, Eber M. *Origins of the Whig Party.* Durham: Duke University Press, 1925.

Cole, Arthur C. *The Whig Party in the South.* Washington: American Historical Association, 1913.

Connor, Robert D. W. *Ante-Bellum Builders of North Carolina.* Greensboro: The College (?), 1914.

Coon, Charles L. (ed.). *North Carolina Schools and Academies, 1790-1840.* Raleigh: Edwards and Broughton, 1915.

Crawford, Robert B. "North Carolina Politics During the Civil War." Unpublished M. A. thesis, Duke University, 1940.

Dibble, Roy F. *Albion W. Tourgée.* New York: Lemcke and Buechner, 1921.

Goebel, Wallace B. "A History of Manufactures in North Carolina Before 1860." Unpublished M. S. thesis, Duke University, 1926.

Hamilton, Joseph G. de Roulhac. *Party Politics in North Carolina, 1835-1860.* ("The James Sprunt Studies in History and Political Science," Vol. XV, Nos. 1 and 2) Chapel Hill: The University of North Carolina Press, 1916.

———. *Reconstruction in North Carolina.* New York: Columbia University Press, 1914.

Hill, Daniel Harvey. *North Carolina in the War Between the States: Bethel to Sharpsburg.* Raleigh: Edwards and Broughton, 1926.

Johnson, Guion G. *Ante-Bellum North Carolina: A Social History.* Chapel Hill: The University of North Carolina Press, 1937.

Klain, Zora. *Quaker Contributions to Education in North Carolina.* Philadelphia: Westbrook, 1924.

Konkle, Burton A. *John Motley Morehead and the Development of North Carolina, 1796-1866.* Philadelphia: William J. Campbell, 1922.

Lefler, Hugh T. and Albert Ray Newsome. *North Carolina: The*

History of a Southern State. Chapel Hill: The University of North Carolina Press, 1954.

McFayden, Henry C. "The Administration of Governor Jonathan Worth, 1865 to 1868." Unpublished M. S. thesis, The University of North Carolina, 1943.

Noble, M. C. S. *A History of the Public Schools of North Carolina.* Chapel Hill: The University of North Carolina Press, 1930.

Norton, Clarence Clifford. *The Democratic Party in Ante-Bellum North Carolina, 1835-1861.* ("The James Sprunt Studies in History and Political Science," Vol. XXI, Nos. 1 and 2) Chapel Hill: The University of North Carolina Press, 1930.

Nuermberger, Ruth K. *The Free Produce Movement, A Quaker Protest Against Slavery.* Durham: Duke University Press, 1942.

Pegg, Herbert Dale. "The Whig Party in Ante-Bellum North Carolina." Unpublished Ph.D. thesis, The University of North Carolina, 1932.

Raper, Horace W. "William Woods Holden: A Political Biography." Unpublished Ph.D. thesis, The University of North Carolina, 1951.

Ratchford, Benjamin U. "A History of the North Carolina Debt, 1712-1900." Unpublished Ph.D. thesis, Duke University, 1932.

Sitterson, Joseph Carlyle. *The Secession Movement in North Carolina* ("The James Sprunt Studies in History and Political Science," Vol. XXIII, No. 2) Chapel Hill: The University of North Carolina Press, 1939.

Todd, Richard C. *Confederate Finance.* Athens: University of Georgia Press, 1954.

Wagstaff, Henry. *State Rights and Political Parties in North Carolina, 1776-1861.* Baltimore: John Hopkins Press, 1906.

Weaver, C. C. *History of Internal Improvements in North Carolina.* Baltimore: Johns Hopkins Press, 1903.

Weeks, Stephen B. *The Beginning of the Common School System in the South, or Calvin Henderson Wiley and the Organization of the Common Schools of North Carolina.* Washington: Government Printing Office, 1898.

———. *Southern Quakers and Slavery.* Baltimore: Johns Hopkins Press, 1896.

REFERENCE SOURCES

Ashe, Samuel A. (ed.). *Biographical History of North Carolina from Colonial Times to the Present.* Greensboro: C. L. Van Noppen, 1905-17.

Connor, Robert D. W. (ed.). *A Manual of North Carolina*. Raleigh: Edwards and Broughton, 1913.

Hinshaw, William Wade. *Encyclopedia of American Quaker Genealogy*. Ann Arbor: Edwards Brothers, Inc., 1936.

Johnson, Allen and Dumas Malone (eds.). *Dictionary of American Biography*. New York: Charles Scribner's Sons, 1928-36.

National Cyclopaedia of American Biography. New York: James T. White and Company, 1892——.

MISCELLANEOUS ITEMS

Annual Reports of the Fayetteville and Western Plank Road Company, 1850-60, North Carolina *Legislative Documents*, 1850-60.

McAlister, May. "A Biographical Sketch of David and Eunice Worth." Unpublished MS in possession of Jonathan Daniels, Raleigh.

Report of Colonel Walter Gwynn, Chief Engineer North Carolina Railroad Company, to the Board of Directors at Meeting in Salisbury, January 10, 1856. Salisbury: J. J. Bruner, 1856.

Report of the President of the North Carolina Railroad to the Governor of the State, January 20, 1859. Salisbury: S. W. James, 1859.

Smith, Mary Shannon. "Union Sentiment in North Carolina During the Civil War," *Proceedings of the State Literary and Historical Association of North Carolina*. Raleigh: Edwards and Broughton, 1916.

"To the People of North Carolina," circular, North Carolina Room, The University of North Carolina.

Whitener, Daniel J. "Public Education in North Carolina During Reconstruction 1865-1876," *Essays in Southern History Presented to J. G. de R. Hamilton*. Chapel Hill: The University of North Carolina Press, 1949.

Index